Predicament of the University

HENRY DAVID AIKEN

Predicament of the University

INDIANA UNIVERSITY PRESS

BLOOMINGTON / LONDON

Published in Canada by Fitzhenry & Whiteside Limited, Don Mills, Ontario

Library of Congress catalog card number: 79-143618

ISBN: 253-12970-2

Manufactured in the United States of America

FOR

William Frankena

Philip Rahv

Robert Silvers

Contents

Part I / ON GOING TO BRANDEIS

Part II / THE UNIVERSITY IN CRISIS: Some Commentaries

Contents

Acknowledgments

LET ME FIRST EXPRESS MY GRATITUDE TO THE FOLLOWING friends for help in clarifying my ideas about the higher learning and the predicaments of the American university: Daniel Bell, Peter Diamondopoulos, William Frankena, Arnold Kaufman, Stephen Toulmin, Philip Rahv, Israel Scheffler, Harold Weisberg, Joseph Weisenbaum, and Morris Weitz. Their conversations and writings have provided an indispensable counterpoint to my own thinking, all the more so when they have disagreed with me. My debt to many students at Harvard, the University of Michigan, and Brandeis is even greater, for it is they who have made me conscious of aspects of university life in America about which I might otherwise have remained unaware. As always, my debt to my beloved teacher, preceptor, and friend, the late Ralph Barton Perry, continues to be beyond telling.

I thank the following institutions for various forms of assistance, financial and otherwise, for the continuing work in progress of which large portions of this volume are a part: to the Harvard Graduate School of Education which appointed me Alfred North Whitehead Fellow for the academic year of 1968–69; to the National Foundation for the Humanities for a generous grant-in-aid (1968–69) which made possible foreign travel that gave me essential new perspectives upon the problems of higher education in other countries; to the Danforth Foundation for the privilege of serving as seminar leader at its Workshop in Liberal Education in the summers of 1968 and 1969; to the Nobel Foundation for inviting me to participate in its symposium on "The Place of Value in a World of Fact," which was held at Stockholm in the summer of 1969; and, most recently, to the Commission on M.I.T. Education for the privilege of participating in a number of its enlightening sessions at Endicott House in the spring of 1970.

To the intellectual stimulation, editorial assistance, and abiding loyalty to my aspirations as a teacher and writer, of my wife Helen Rowland Aiken let me simply say: *sine qua non.*

I also thank the following editors and publishers by whose permission various earlier versions of essays included in this volume are reprinted:

The Center for Research and Development in Higher Education, University of California, Berkeley, and Western Interstate Commission for Higher Education for permission to republish "How Late Is It?" from *Value Change and Power Conflict*, edited by W. J. Minter and P. O. Snyder, October 1969.

Harper's Magazine Inc. for permission to republish "The New Morals," *Harper's Magazine*, Vol. 236, No. 1413, February 1968.

Houghton Mifflin, for permission to republish "Analytical Philosophy and Educational Development," from *Philosophy and Educational Development*, edited by George Barnett, 1966.

The Journal of Aesthetic Education for permission to republish "Art and Anti-Art," Vol. 2, No. 3, July 1968.

The National Art Education Association for permission to republish "Learning and Teaching in the Arts," the Lowenfeld Lecture for 1969.

The New York Review of Books for permission to republish "The American University, Part I: The Sick University," October 1966; "The American University, Part II: What is Liberal Education?" November 3, 1966; "The Revolting Academy," June 1969, and "Guardians of Law and Order" (originally "Yes Men"), February 12, 1970.

The State University of New York Press for permission to republish "Reason, The Higher Learning, and The Good Society," from *Perspectives in Education, Religion, and the Arts*, Vol. III of *Contemporary Philosophical Thought*, The International Philosophy Year Conferences at Brockport, 1970.

The University of Georgia Press for permission to republish "Rights of Youth" from *Education and Ethics*, edited by W.T. Blackstone and George L. Newsome, 1969.

Introduction

HAD ANYONE ASKED EVEN A DECADE AGO WHETHER THE university had a future, the reply would surely have been, "Don't ask silly questions." Did not every youth passionately desire to go, not to college only, but to the university? Hadn't government support of higher education, both at the state and at the national level, increased phenomenally since the Second World War? Hadn't older private universities such as Harvard made amazingly successful endowment drives involving sums that would have sufficed to found two or three well-to-do institutions before the war? A whole new state university system had recently been established in New York; in California new campuses were mushrooming all over the state, and even in Massachusetts, despite its plethora of private universities and colleges, a flourishing state university now existed. In 1948, the Jewish people established in Waltham, Massachusetts, a new private university which only twelve or so years later had already assembled a brilliant faculty while at the same time building classrooms, libraries, research laboratories, museums, and dormitories. And if, somewhat ominously, Brandeis continued to be financed largely with soft money, one might have asked, "Who needs hard money when the supply of soft money is virtually infinite?"

In the affluent society (to employ the catch phrase coined by Professor Galbraith) such a question did not seem at all ridiculous. And when a few of us raised doubts about the ability of even the affluent society to perform such educational miracles while conducting large-scale "defensive" wars abroad, we were laughed out of court. Indeed some realists argued that war, being as it is a mother of invention, the university, which had now become the indispensable feeder institution to the emerging national society with its voracious "military-industrial establishment" (the phrase, still new, had been introduced in his farewell address by President Dwight Eisenhower), was bound to prosper even more than it had done during the preceding decade.

In short, never had the outlook for the American academy seemed brighter. For the first time faculty salaries, at least in the better universities, had increased to the point where ordinary academicians could do more than pretend to belong to the leisure class. Since the war there had been for the young Ph.D. a sellers' market. Accordingly, many of our ablest young men, who in an earlier period would have been attracted to business and industry or to the so-called learned professions, were delighted at the prospect of an academic career which promised sufficient pecuniary as well as social rewards. Despite sharply increasing tuition rates, students continued to come to the university in ever larger droves. And for those whose parents could not afford to pay their way, scholarships and fellowships were provided for all who could profit from a higher education in utopia.

How, then, can it be that scarcely a decade later the whole situation has so radically reversed itself? How, indeed, is it possible that in so short a time steady conservative academicians, not given to alarm, are now asking all seriously, not what sort of future is in store for the American university, but whether it has a future at all?

Many obvious reasons come to mind: student revolt, which some (I think mistakenly) now believe to have passed the point of no return; the discovery that even the world's most affluent nation cannot fight an endless war and continue to do all the other things that are necessary to the internal development of what John Stuart Mill called a "progressive society;" the sudden awareness that most of the urban universities are now encysted in appalling slums whose hostile inhabitants see the academy, not as a symbol of enlightenment but of repression, invidious class distinction, and elitism; the reemergence of anti-intellectualism, not only in reactionary state houses but also in the now conservative federal government.

However, none of these explanations goes to the heart of the matter. Perhaps the point may best be seen by rephrasing the question about the future of the university: what would happen to the higher learning in America if the university, as it now stands, should disappear as its primary institutional home? I have asked many colleagues this question and, (to me at least) not so surprisingly, I have frequently received the answer: "Nothing." What would happen, so the argument goes, is simply that the higher learning, whose continuing importance both to national security and industrial productivity no one disputes, would be conducted under different, probably more efficient, auspices. Bright young high school graduates would be recruited both by industry and government for the forms of technological and scientific training necessary to those institutions. "Think tanks," now maintained under the auspices of such institutions, would of course have to be expanded. But that could easily be done in part by renting (at a reasonable price) the facilities of the university to industry and government. In short, if the academy disappeared, then so much the better. Existing problems created by malcontents within the student body and (more occasionally) within the faculty would automatically disappear, having been proscribed both by law and by the conditions of entrance and preferment within the new agencies of higher learning. Inefficient academic administrators, whose loyalties are now divided and whose educational and public relations activities now combine to make their jobs untenable, would be replaced by experts able to organize a national business and make it prosper and who would be empowered to enforce their policies.

To sentimental humanists who worry about the decline of culture and the debasement of taste the hard answer is ready: the universities have not prevented the decline of cultural and aesthetic values in America; on the contrary they are themselves conspicuous manifestations and victims of that decline. By common agreement, general education has not been a success. At best it provides the undergraduate with a thin patina of ethical and aesthetic culture which contributes as little to his virtue as a citizen as it does to his capacity to use his leisure time in self-improving ways. What, then, about the young man's (or woman's) need for moving visions of a better life for all, which are the tests of a truly progressive society? To this the answer is also ready: as everyone knows, the end of the age of ideology is at hand. Who needs prolonged instruction about the millenarian dreams of the Platos, the Benthams and Marxes, or, coming down to our own time, the Lenins, the Marcuses, or Bertrand Russells? And to the fatuous admirers of Castro and Mao, the reply, quite simply, is that the world is sick unto death of revolutions which merely lead men from one form of slavery into another. The existing problems of mankind—war, overpopulation, reclamation and use for everyone of the world's resources, the advancement of underdeveloped regions, and, above all, the introduction of the attitudes and methods of scientific and technological inquiry (the true higher learning)—are themselves scientific and technological problems with which the followers of Lenin and Marcuse, not to say Castro and Mao, are incompetent to deal.

To be sure, as more reflective members of our ruling elites once again begin to perceive, the end of ideology does not automatically attend its own announcement. In the Soviet Union members of the ruling elite are doubtless as thoroughly committed to the anti-ideology of pragmatic realism as their opposite numbers in this country. But just as the young people of Russia must still be dosed with the opiates of Marxist ideology, so our own young must be properly indoctrinated into the accommodative principles of Christian philanthropy and liberal democracy. "Indoctrinated?" The word is unattractive? Then substitute "enculturated." Every cohesive society must enculturate its young. But this is a task for the family, the church, and, where they fail, the school and the media. It should not encumber institutions of higher and hence specialized and professional learning.

I for one am radically dissatisfied with such answers. I am also dissatisfied with an educational system that now produces minds of high calibre for whom such answers come all too naturally. The present volume is in part a manifest of that discontent.

Part One, which I have entitled "On Going to Brandeis," is the record of one academician's effort, in an unphilosophical age, to come to terms with his own vocation as philosopher and teacher and his belief that such a vocation has an indispensable place in a healthy university. In it I explain how it happened that in mid-career I was impelled to give up a professorship in the oldest, wealthiest, and, in some respects, most distinguished of American universities, in order to participate in the life of an immensely promising young university that, as I hoped, embodied new conceptions of the higher learning. As will be seen, that hope has not been entirely fulfilled. Despite its bright promise, Brandeis is now caught up in all the problems which now confront its older and wealthier sister universities. It also faces a number of distinctive problems which have caused some of its most loyal supporters to wonder about its chances of survival. All private universities, including Harvard, are now battening down the hatches. How much more difficult is the situation of a new, private, minority-group university in a time when government support has been radically curtailed, the great foundations are diverting their funds to other causes, and the minority group in question has international commitments of such urgency that the cause of Brandeis seems miniscule by comparison.

But such pressing external problems are interlocked with others both external and internal. Among the external problems is the question whether our emerging national society still cherishes the values of educational pluralism which the private universities and colleges represent. At the primary and secondary school levels, this question has already become one of greatest urgency for our large and increasingly well-to-do Roman Catholic population. How much more urgent is it for an institution of higher learning, supported largely by a much smaller minority group, whose orientation is by intention nondenominational and nonsectarian? In another way, it may well be asked, what distinctive educational values does Brandeis represent which cannot as well be served either by existing secular private universities, such as Harvard, or by the public state or city universities? As matters stand, the answer is uncertain.

These problems are not unrelated to others which, at this juncture, are internal not to Brandeis only but also to other essentially liberal arts colleges now in the process of becoming or trying to become graduate universities of high quality. If Brandeis makes it,

[5

can it do so on terms other than those which will oblige it either to reduce its aspiration to become a normal graduate university or else to give up its hope to create a university whose college is still committed for all its students to an education in the liberal arts? If some have their way, Brandeis, following the lead of Harvard and Berkeley, will become a knowledge factory, a small complex of think tanks for precocious apprentices in particular advanced scientific and professional disciplines. In short, was there any point to my going to Brandeis? The answer is not a purely personal one.

In *Part Two*, I examine a number of influential commentaries upon the university in its time of crisis. The prime mover of those discussions has proved to be Clark Kerr, the ex-president of that extraordinary educational complex called "the University of California," which now serves as a model for similar institutions in other states and regions.

I conclude that all of these analyses and the recommendations attending them are essentially eclectic and unavailing. They all accept existing academic realities as given, and all meaningful reforms as pragmatic and piecemeal. Most of them cling, however marginally, to the ideal of the university as an institution of liberal, as well as professional, education. None is fully content with the concept of the multiversity or knowledge factory or with the students which are its ordinary product. Yet all seem to leave us with two main alternatives: either (a) the university must become an institution of truly "higher" learning, where faculty members and their student apprentices conduct their own advanced studies with a view to a purely professional competence, or (b) it must become a collegiate extension of the high school or *Gymnasium* which leaves the higher learning to postgraduate institutes for advanced study.

Here and there efforts are made to refurbish existing amalgams of (a) and (b). In particular, Professor Daniel Bell has attempted to revive the dying movement of general education. Yet even he confines general education to the college; were his proposals adopted, the graduate university would remain unaffected. In fact, it remains unclear whether his proposals would do much more than increase the sophistication of bright preprofessional college students so that they might proceed to their graduate studies with a clearer understanding of the methods of inquiry proper to their respective subjects. By his own confession, Professor Bell's reforms of general education are not based upon a new philosophy of the higher learning. The result is that the prevailing educational purposes of the university, not to mention its existing structures, continue to go unchallenged. The much-discussed work, *The Academic Revolution*, by Professors Christopher Jencks and David Riesman, is no exception. On the contrary, the "revolution" which they describe and in which they largely acquiesce is simply the one instituted three-quarters of a century ago when the better liberal arts colleges were converted into graduate-universities. Like Professor Bell, they genuflect dutifully before the ideal of liberal education. Yet they have no thought of updating that ideal in such a way that it could be justifiably extended from the university college to graduate and professional schools.

Nowhere is there a sustained effort to reconceive the university *and* its college so that a continuous and meaningful interaction would take place *at all levels* between professional and liberal education. And nowhere is there an effort to break through the present college–graduate school bifurcation.[1]

In *Part Three*, a variety of suggestions are presented which are intended to show in particular how the humanities might be overhauled. Of all the areas now comprehended under the higher learning, the humanities remain in the profoundest disarray. In principle one might think it is to the humanists that we must turn for ideas for the reform of higher education. This is far from being true. On the whole, our academic humanists, as I have found, show a more perfunctory interest in the restoration, not to say renovation, of liberal learning in the university than their colleagues in the natural and social sciences and in administration (the most articulate of whom, let it be noted, have come to administration not from the humanities but from the sciences). There are quite natural, if not good, reasons for this. Of all the domains within the university, the humanities, whose professors are rarely active contributors to humane letters, art, and philosophical inquiry, are the most unstable and insecure. Especially in the graduate schools, humanists acquire respectability not by cultivating their own gardens but by playing apes to science and scientific history. Of all victims of the cults of scientism, special-

[7

ism, and professionalism, they are perhaps the most deracinated. And while imaginative scientists are at long last trying to cope with the place and problems of value in a world of fact, the humanists are still busy proving their own credentials simply as masters of myopic facts about the world of values.

The situation in philosophy is the most curious of all. Since the Second World War, the movement of linguistic philosophy, owing in large part to the stimulus of the writings and teachings of Ludwig Wittgenstein, has contributed much to our understanding of the diversity of symbolic forms and at least in principle to the corresponding forms of life which they at once serve and govern. As I try to show, the linguistic philosophers have placed at our disposal powerful intellectual tools which can be put to use in clarifying the leading concepts of the educational vocabulary itself. It is now possible, accordingly, to remove some of the more vicious conceptual confusions which now prevail in academic circles and hence remove the disorders in practice that attend such confusions. Yet, with few exceptions, the very philosophers who might contribute most to the removal of these confusions have avoided the philosophy of education and of human culture like the plague. Were one to judge by professional journals of philosophy, the same philosophers seem scarcely to notice that, for want of enlightened ideas of all the ranges of higher learning, the contemporary university is literally in danger of its life.

In the essays under *Part Three* I offer an outline of what a liberated analytical philosophy might contribute to the reformation of existing notions of educational practice and development, especially on their higher levels. In a long chapter entitled "Learning and Teaching in the Arts," I present a rather complex case study of what is involved in enabling the serious student to better understand a work of art. In so doing, however, I am simply reapplying such conceptual instruments as I have acquired in consequence of my own analytical studies in the philosophy of art. Finally, the chapter entitled "Art and Anti-Art" is an attempt to apply such tools historically with a view to understanding what can be made in our own time of the movement of anti-art which scandalizes so many orthodox academicians.

I do not mean in this section to join those who bemoan the "threat" of science within the academy. It is not science but its trivialization by misguided "empiricists" within the humanities and social sciences which should worry serious philosophers of higher education. Theoretical science (it should go without saying) is one of the great achievements of the human imagination, and we desperately need men who will search out, serenely and in good faith, the wisdom in and about science, about its history, its fruits, its promise. Before we make a scapegoat of science, let us remind ourselves that we are science, just as we are also art, and government, and religion. And the *arts* of scientific analysis and explanation are among the crown jewels of any academy worthy of the name. There is no reason to fear the technological applications of science within the university as long as they are employed in the service of significant learning and the amelioration of the human lot. The bane of liberal education is not technology as such, but a subservient technology too closely and uncritically tied to the self-serving or war-like interests of industry and the nation state.

Part Four contains two essays which attempt a philosophical approach to the aspects of the situations of young people in our time which have a profound bearing upon their roles both in society and in the university. These essays may also be seen, in part, as an application of the methods of analytical philosophy within the domain of ethics. As such they have close ties to the essays in *Part Three*.

Part Five provides an outline of the basic educational philosophy which underlies the entire book. It speaks for itself. However, one warning must be made. When an earlier version of it was read in 1968 at the opening session of the International Philosophical Year at the College of the State University of New York at Brockport, some critics mistook my intention. In the sense of the term described in the paper, I am an opponent of the rationalist philosophy which has prevailed in the West since the time of Plato and I regard the philosophy or ideology of higher education based upon it as misguided. As will be explained, I also consider its social implications both illiberal and elitist. In no sense, however, am I an opponent either of reason or of the ideal of reasonableness. Just the contrary. It is, in my view, the misguided and repressive theory of rationality, of which Plato's *Republic* is in some respects the great source book, that so many thoughtful students and teachers alike are rebelling against today. They refuse, as I think rightly, to assume that the advancement of learning is to be measured solely by the progress of the mathematical sciences. They refuse, I also think rightly, to suppose that the higher learning should, as if by definition, be devoted exclusively, or even primarily, to studies to which the quantificational methods of mathematical logic can be applied. But behind this they object to a conception of intelligence in which the human mind is a glorified computer and man himself is a machine for making ever more refined computations. Perhaps without realizing it, they are exponents of Pascal's distinction between modes of cognition which embody the *esprit de géometrie* and those which embody the *esprit de finesse*. More saliently, they begin to understand the inner meaning of Pascal's famous dictum, "The heart has its reasons which reason does not know." This does not imply, as their critics contend, that they are irrationalists, but rather that they begin to understand that the wisdom of life cannot be reduced to knowledge of the world.

Of course Pascal's conception of intelligence, and hence of the higher learning, won't do either. For his *esprit de finesse* can easily be accommodated by the rationalists who, since the time of Plato, have contended that the foundational conceptions of any science whatever are known through a form of intellectual intuition. From my point of view, intuition in any sphere represents only a point of departure, not a method of verification. Knowledge is an achievement, not a natural endowment, and it is achieved through action and work alone. My complaint against contemporary versions of rationalism is that the only forms of intelligent work that they are prepared to acknowledge are those which culminate in the achievements of the formal and natural sciences and their simulations by the "sciences of man."

What is wanted, of course, if the university as the central institution of higher learning is to survive, is a more subtly and complexly inflected philosophy of human nature and culture that will do better justice to all the ranges of human intelligence, achievement, and perplexity. The world is too much with us, and as Pascal, and more emphatically Kierkegaard, knew, man has an immense need of solitude. But he is also a social and, more particularly, a communal animal. Just as his educational ideals, for worse or better, reflect his conceptions of himself, so his conceptions of himself are largely reflexes of the practices of the societies and communities to which he belongs. Hence there can be no serious reformation of the higher learning apart from a more general reformation of our social institutions and the modes of communal participation which, too often, are improverished by the conventional roles our institutions thrust upon us.

Inklings of these trends are at present more evident to some of our radical youths than to their elders, too many of whom have long since made their own sad truce with social and institutional necessity. But instead of learning from these youths the lessons which, in that regard at least, they might teach us, we treat them as outcasts, ungrateful "cop-outs," or, more simply, spoiled brats whom in meaningless alternation we harshly discipline and weakly placate.

Our inconsistencies go even deeper. In this regard we still have something to learn from the reading of Plato. Just as in the ancient world, Athens regarded itself as the school of Greece, so Plato conceived his Academy as the school of Athens. And because, in his view, knowledge of the good is the highest, most difficult of all forms of human knowledge, he accordingly reserved its study by young academicians for their last years in the Academy. But once they had acquired knowledge of the good, Plato considered them fit to join the guardian class and to participate without ado in the governance of society and its essential educational institution. Our eccentric practice is just the opposite of Plato's. We regard knowledge of the good as the easiest of all educational achievements and so have consigned the task of normative education to the primary and secondary schools and, more grudgingly, to general education programs for underbred freshmen and sophomores. In this same spirit, we have instituted the practice of "advanced standing" for clever incomers to the university who, being presumed to have already all the knowledge of the good they will ever need, are encouraged to get on as rapidly as possible with their preprofessional careers. One would suppose from this that by the time they are seniors, not to say graduate students, already more advanced in their mathematical and scientific prowess than many faculty members, they would be encouraged to devise and teach courses of their own and to participate fully in the governance of the graduate university. They have not been and still are not encouraged to do any of these things. Just the contrary, they have been obliged to fight their way into the company of their seniors where they are at once resented and condescended to by the old guard. The situation is worse in the wider society. Even our brightest, most inventive youngsters are viewed as mature human beings and citizens not in act but in potency. We assign them duties to the state of the most arduous and dangerous sort. We confront them with moral choices which we ourselves are not equipped to make. Yet we systematically deny them the right to share in the decisions that determine what their stately and citizenly duties shall be. And when they protest, in their disorderly ways, we set the unruly police and the state militias upon them, knowing in advance that the counterviolence we inflict upon them will further divide them from ourselves.

It would be a mistake to conclude from these remarks that I am an uncritical victim of the cult of youth which, superficially at least, afflicts our whole society. Plato is right: knowledge of the good life and the good society comes slowly. In many respects our students remain immature. But if we are consistent we must also acknowledge how immature we, their teachers and would-be preceptors, also are. The system of higher education which produces them is little different from that which produced us. If they are shallow, then it is because we are shallow. If they lack a sense of history, then in justice we must admit our own sense of history to be as faltering as their own. If they lack the power to relate their "major" to the other main forms of human culture it is because we, who lack the same power, do not even try to provide them with an education which will continuously envelope their special studies in the larger contexts of human understanding. They live, culturally and humanly, from hand to mouth. But so do we. Unless we are prepared to reeducate ourselves, we scholars and experts, cannot fault them for their failures in trying to do so.

The fact is that the overwhelming weakness of our system of higher education is that it makes no provision for educating and reeducating its own graduates and only grudgingly admits to the university educatable adults who for economic and other reasons have been unable to proceed at once from the high school. For twenty years at Harvard, and now again at Brandeis, I have taught course after course in "adult education," sometimes with more lasting effect than I get from my undergraduate and graduate students. Throughout this book I endlessly complain about general programs for the young which have no follow-through and which accordingly are educationally disfunctional. But I still more bitterly condemn peripheral adult education programs taught mainly by moonlighters under the condescending auspices of something called university extension. High school teachers in considerable numbers take such courses, but most university professors would consider themselves declassed were they to take a course in "extension."

What, then, is to be done? For a beginning we must reform the whole ideology of the higher learning so that no scholar, however precocious he may be in the field of his professional work, will assume that he is a savant. Secondly, we must open the doors of the university to any person, regardless of his age, who seeks to enlarge his mind. And if we continue to make an issue of degrees, we must be ready to grant him a degree, not merely as an "adjunct in arts and sciences," but in the degrees we regularly accord young undergraduate and graduate students. In a truly democratic society the distinctions and accolades which the university bestows must be available to all. Nor should anyone enjoy power within the university unless he is willing from time to time to *attend* it. For power exercised by men who no longer participate in the work of those whom they presume to govern is an alienative and predatory power, as ruinous to the self as it is destructive to the institution and the society. Thus the philanthropic trustee who attends meetings of the board but to whom it never occurs to attend the university is alienated from it whether he realizes it or not. And so too is the donor whose self-congratulatory gifts sink the university ever more deeply in debts for which others will have to pay the educational price.

Unless the trustee and the donor, including the long-departed alumnus, are prepared and enabled to go back to the university as learners, they are not contributors to the higher learning but its unconscious enemies. But the same holds, in even greater degree, of the professor, secure in his tenure and grants-in-aid. Teaching

[*1 3*

and learning, as our students know, go together. He who has nothing to learn has nothing to teach. And he who has no sustained readiness to learn—and there is no learning without participation—has nothing any longer to offer but school exercises which have no place within the university.

Already the university has moved far down the road toward its own demise. But institutions, as I shall have occasion to argue in a later chapter, are human creations, not things. They can survive, but only if we care enough to make them survive and if we are ready to make the changes necessary to make them worthy of survival.

Admittedly the prospect is not bright. How many of us believe any longer that the university should be a place where every member, young and old, apprentice and master, professor, administrator, and trustee, is engaged, not merely in pursuing a career but in the endless pursuit of what Matthew Arnold once called "our total perfection"? Not very many. But more, I am convinced, than was true even two or three years ago. And for this we have to thank, not the old pros, but our fractious students and their friends on the faculties and in the administrations.

The critical as well as the constructive ideas developed in the present volume are the result of innumerable discussions, many of them heated, not only with students and colleagues but also with troubled friends outside the academy. These ideas do not add up to a comprehensive philosophy of higher education. I shall be content if they contribute something toward the preparation for such a philosophy which, Plato (and Marx) to the contrary, must be the work of many hands. It is easy enough to say, but immensely difficult to believe, that what we most need in the university, as in the society, are new sons of Socrates, conscious of what they do not know, yet not overwhelmed by that fact. But the name of Socrates has more than one connotation. It connotes discourse, dialectic, and intellectual conflict. And, despite Nietzsche, it also connotes action, determined and, when it has to be, abrasive.

In my view, admittedly heterodox, it is not conflict and action that will destroy the university but domination. And domination in our time has become an obsession of the American people.

Many complain, and with justice, that some of our students on the far left desire not to contest the existing order in the academy but to dominate or else destroy it. But these same students are merely inverted images of their elders, both inside and outside the university. All of us confuse leadership with domination, just as we confuse authority with power. It is not conflict which is turning the campus into an armed camp and which is making a shambles of the educational process; it is the will to domination. And this, once more, is why I invoke the name of Socrates rather than Plato or Marx or, coming down a number of steps, Marcuse, as the presiding spirit of these discourses. It is also why, even at this late date, I am not ashamed to call myself, in education as in other matters, a liberal and a devotee of the liberal arts and liberal education. For the liberal, while he demands change and thrives on conflict, refuses any form of domination over the mind and soul of man. The university, as far as I am concerned, has only one final end: the continuing education, throughout its ranks, of self-governing, self-fulfilling, and generous men. Such an end is one to which few pay more than lip service. And that is why, I am bound to say, the university remains in peril of its life.

Part I

ON GOING TO BRANDEIS

I

Preface:

ON THE IDEA OF THE UNIVERSITY

THE NOTION OF WRITING A BOOK ON THE IDEA OF THE
university has been in my mind since the earliest sixties. In part
this is owing to the reading I had been doing in preparation for
a course, "The American Pragmatists and Education," which I
gave for a number of years at Harvard under the joint auspices of
the Philosophy Department and the Graduate School of Education.

The three greatest American pragmatists, C. S. Peirce, William
James, and John Dewey, with each of whom I discovered a deep
if qualified affinity, were all concerned with educational problems;
indeed it is not too much to say that pragmatism, in its classical
sense, is essentially a philosophy of education. The pragmatists'
theories of meaning and knowledge, the central topics of modern
philosophy, are in essence theories of the learning and the achievements that are a consequence of learning. For all of them, whatever their differences in other respects, knowledge is not a God-
given intuition of immaculate truth but an achievement which is
the product of "experience." But in their view experience is *experience*, not the ghostly attenuation of it which, beginning with
Locke, has been the preoccupation of most philosophers who call
themselves "empiricists." For the latter, experience meant, by a
strange irony, not the actual forms of experience, memorable and
useful, by which men guide their lives, but untutored intuitions of
ideas and their correspondences with the "objects" with which
they presumably agree. For the pragmatist, ideas, their meaning

as well as their truth, are acquired through the experiences of men involved in solving and learning to solve human problems. As Peirce contended, and as I also believe, we come to understand the meaning of an idea only by learning its use in its own contexts of inquiry. Peirce himself was preoccupied with scientific ideas and the forms of inquiry which result in scientific knowledge. The great contribution of William James to the philosophy of pragmatism was to extend Peirce's *dicta* for clarifying our ideas beyond the contexts of scientific learning and inquiry to all the various situations—scientific, moral, religious, and metaphysical—in which men desire to know whereof they speak and why. And it was James who developed a richer pragmatic theory of truth and of knowledge in which what we assert as true or profess to know, in any sphere of human activity, is a consequence of what we have done and achieved (or fancy ourselves to have done and achieved) in coping with the problems arising in that distinctive type of situation. For James, it meant nothing to say that a human utterance is true if and only if it corresponds to the facts. For the problem still remains in any domain: what are the "facts" and how we are to tell when our ideas correspond to them? A man who has an inadequate experience of moral and religious problems will have no notion of what may relevantly count as religious or moral facts and, accordingly, of what truly corresponds to them. It remained for Dewey to extend and to apply James' liberated and pluralistic conceptions of human understanding and truth to our appreciations of literature and the arts and to the complex learning and knowing situations over which the school and the academy presumably preside. For those who have eyes to see, the primary contentions of the most influential linguistic philosophers in England, Ludwig Wittgenstein and (in his very different way) John Austin, are closely related to the pragmatists' theories of meaning and knowledge. For them, a word or a form of words is understood only in the circumstances in which we learn its uses, and knowledge of its uses is testable by one's ability to show how its uses may be learned. In the case of Wittgenstein as in that of the pragmatists, however, understanding and knowledge of any symbolic form is ancillary to the conduct of life. In his view, also, really to learn and to understand something is thereby to change one's life.

For me such convictions remained largely academic as long as I continued at Harvard. In a vague way which I did not fully comprehend at the time, I began to wonder whether, in the existing academic setting, I really had a vocation as a teacher of philosophy. I believed, but could apply only schematically, the pragmatic thesis that understanding is a function of learning. For the ranges of learning which America's most distinguished university afforded were for the ordinary professor curiously limited and truncated. Like that of my colleagues, my life remained bookish, and even my academic experience was tied to the daily rounds of a philosophy professor in Emerson Hall. How, then, could I write a book on the idea of the university, knowing as I did so little about it, even after a decade and a half of teaching in one of its more remote provinces?

In short, as will be explained in the pages that follow, I came to feel that America's most ancient and, in may ways still, most illustrious university, was less a great open house of human learning than a cloister whose classrooms and studies were so many beautifully appointed cells, each sequestered from the rest. To be sure, as I knew, Harvard had its close ties to the national government and industry, to which many of my colleagues in other fields had ready access. Such ties, in fact, seemed to me increasingly all too close. Thus, to vary the figure, I began to worry whether the university, like an established church, did not in many ways too closely identify the good society with the society presided over by the American nation-state and the good life with the life of decent citizens and servants of that state.

At all events it became clear that, for me, new perspectives upon the academy were in order, and when the opportunity came to go to Brandeis I took it, albeit with many hesitations and misgivings. To many of my colleagues and students, such a decision appeared perverse: what in the world could Brandeis offer that Harvard did not already supply in greater range and depth? It was not easy to give a plausible answer. On the day I resigned from Harvard, a reporter from the *Crimson* called to inquire why I was leaving. The tone of his voice implied that I had done something unthinkable, like renouncing my citizenship or abandoning a baby on someone's doorstep. I replied, somewhat evasively, that I wasn't leaving Harvard but going to Brandeis. By stages, however, this statement came to appear to me as the deliverance of an oracle, whose meaning would have to be unravelled before I could write a book about the idea of the university in America. Like all proper oracular utterances, this one was superficially false, for certainly I was leaving Harvard, and Brandeis, as yet, was scarcely more than a name. Moreover, as I eventually saw, its meaning not only concerned me, an obscure professor of philosophy; it also had something to do with what was, and is, happening to the American university itself. Only much later did I realize that, on its positive side, it had to do with possibilities for change throughout the higher learning in America represented by a new, volatile, unavoidably experimental institution, founded by an important minority group, and pervaded by a sense of its own minority group status and its special commitment to the education of the members of all such groups, whatever their ethnic or religious origins.

Brandeis's own future, as will be seen, is still uncertain. Many forces pull it into the establishment which Harvard so majesterially represents. In any case, the idea of "going to Brandeis" is now indissolubly intermixed with my own developing ideas of the contemporary university, not only as it is but as it should be. But these ideas are connected also with my developing conception of the philosopher's vocation. At last, it has dawned on me, to vary a theme of Socrates in Plato's *Republic*, that I can gain a clearer idea of the contemporary philosopher's vocation only by acquiring a better understanding of the university's own vocation within our own troubled and perplexed republic. However, lacking Plato's speculative genius, I had actually to go to Brandeis in order to achieve some part of this understanding. The following chapters are a record of how, by slow stages, I learned how and what a true university might be. As the "coda" will make clear, however, "going to Brandeis" and being there are not the same thing: the "idea," although necessarily embedded in actualities, is no more to be equated with realities which I discovered at Brandeis than they are with those I found at Harvard. I am still "going to Brandeis." What the end will be remains to be seen.

2

On Leaving Harvard

DURING MY YEARS AS A GRADUATE STUDENT AT HARVARD, I was kept so busy in the department of philosophy taking the courses and seminars necessary to pass the preliminary examinations for the Ph.D., writing a dissertation, and doing my stint as a teaching fellow, that I had little time to ask myself about either the quality of the department or the philosophical significance of what I was learning. For the time being, there could be no doubt, our business was not the pursuit of wisdom but the acquisition of a professional competence in a particular academic subject. For that reason, but also because we were not encouraged to stray from Emerson Hall, none of us had time to attend more than an occasional lecture by famous professors in other fields. Our wider impressions of Harvard were therefore few and it was impossible to tell whether such samplings as we made were at all typical.

Having come from the Far West, I for my part was greatly pleased by the old Georgian buildings and the great spreading elm trees in Harvard Yard. The general atmosphere of tradition, assurance, and unostentatious wealth of the university had its effect on me as it has on so many others. Harvard Square was rather drab in those days, but the university gained then, as it gains now, from its location across the Charles River from Boston, with all its reminders, not only of nineteenth century gentility and cultivation, but also of the steady nurturing of strong and independent minds that did not burke at civil disobedience or even revolution when human rights were infringed and governments

[23

behaved tyrannically, of leaders in the Abolitionist movement, of philosopher-poets who preached gospels of self-reliance, simplicity, and the primacy of the spiritual life. But however stirred I might be by these associations, my conception of the existing university as an educational institution remained nebulous.

One thing, however, was plain to all of us: if for sentimental, social, and financial reasons the College was still frequently referred to as "the heart" of the University, its vital intellectual centers were now the graduate and professional schools. This was apparent in the attitudes as well as in the training of the abler undergraduates themselves. Because the so-called "middle group" courses at Harvard are attended both by undergraduates and graduates, I soon discovered that many seniors majoring in philosophy were better drilled as well as more sophisticated in certain ways than I was, even after a year of graduate work. But except in a few instances the range of their interests and the independence of their minds compared unfavorably with those of my old classmates at Reed College in Oregon.

Graduate students in other subjects, like ourselves, were locked in their own specialized studies, and our general conversation, when we met them, was likely to consist of commonplaces. They knew and cared little about what was being taught in the department of philosophy. Whether this might imply anything except that people at Harvard tend to stick to their own lasts, few of us paused to consider. All the same it was difficult to avoid the conclusion that, despite the lustre of its so-called "golden age" of philosophy in the time of James and Santayana, to which references were constantly being made in pronouncements of one sort or another about Harvard Traditions, Harvard was not a philosophically saturated institution. On this score, despite the fact that Harvard had ten or so full-time teachers of philosophy, not to mention numbers of hard-worked teaching fellows, whereas my own alma mater, Reed, possessed only one professor of philosophy and education and an historian who gave a remarkable two-year course in intellectual history, there was a spread and intensity of philosophical reflection among both students and faculty at Reed such as I have encountered only once since then—at Brandeis. Most of our teachers at Harvard candidly presented themselves as "pros" who when the day's quantum of teaching and research was done, did not care to "talk philosophy" at all.

When I returned to Harvard on permanent tenure in 1946, I soon became aware that, to say the least of it, the university's attitude toward philosophy generally and the department in particular was, and for some time had been, decidedly ambivalent. One evidence was the factor of size. By comparison with even Stanford in the thirties, where I did my first graduate work, Harvard's department had then seemed both large and prosperous. Yet after the war and into the fifties, when the university as a whole was expanding rapidly, the department grew little, if at all. At first one was disposed to attribute this to the greater concern of President Conant, himself a research chemist, about the preeminence of Harvard's brilliant departments of natural and biological science and its somewhat "harder" social sciences than with the progress of the humanities. But even after the advent of Mr. Pusey, a classicist by training, reputedly much concerned about the spiritual life, the department tended, if anything, to shrink a bit in both size and importance within the university.

Size, of course, isn't everything. Unhappily, compensating factors were not many. Like other colleagues, I acquired friends in other parts of the university, but it was as a tutor in one of the undergraduate houses (Kirkland) that I met those I came to know best, most of whom, like Thomas Kuhn and Richard Ellman, in the end slipped away to other universities and colleges. In passing it is well to say that the house system with its senior and junior common rooms remains the one effective countervailing force at Harvard against tendencies toward specialism, professionalism, and cultural isolation that pervade the university. Kirkland House remains one of the green places in the Harvard of my memory, and I owe a good deal to it and to its civilizing common rooms. In general, however, we in the philosophy department were made to feel that our subject was peripheral to the main intellectual, social, and political enterprises to which the university's resources were committed. A certain amount of philosophizing had always been done in the physics department by people like Percy Bridgman and Phillip Frank, but such philosophical physicists paid even less attention to the official departmental epistemologists than the latter did to them. This was all the more ironical, since the theory of knowledge, as our epistemologists conceived it, did not culminate in platonic visions of the Good or even in an attempt to clarify forms of human understanding that might lie beyond the range of positive science. On the contrary, they took it virtually for granted that knowledge of the sort achieved in the more exact natural sciences is precisely that to which all minds concerned with truth aspire, and they defined rationality itself by means of it. But what insider cares to be told in other terms by outsiders what he already knows or believes? In fact most of the scientists I knew found more profit, or at any rate amusement, in talking to philosophers who might have something to say about music or politics than to those who proposed to enlighten them about the logic of science.

The intellectual relations between philosophy and the social and psychological sciences were only slightly different. On our side, W. V. Quine, for example, found something congenial to his own way of thinking in B. F. Skinner's intransigent behaviorism. Morton White, who was interested in problems about the nature of historical knowledge, found companionship among the Harvard historians. In my own way I was variously stimulated, for example, by Harry Murray's explorations of human personality and by Talcott Parsons' laborious ruminations on such great European sociologists as Weber, Durkheim, and Pareto. But these were exceptions, and most of the passages were one-way.

The attitudes of people in the humanities toward philosophy were more curious. On the one side, men like Douglas Bush complained bitterly at the rampant and egregious "positivism" of the department, which he assumed to be hostile on principle to imaginative literature even though in his own scholarly writings he himself appeared to treat works of literary art mainly as "objects" of historical inquiry. Little did he know, or care, that there might be found at Harvard a contemporary philosophy of art which sought systematically to explain the relevance of historical and other contexual analyses to a richer and more controlled experience of works of imaginative literature. On the other side, brilliant polymaths like Renato Poggoli and Perry Miller, writing as scientific investigators of literature who, in Harry Levin's phrase, supply at most "contexts of criticism," were not amused when the same philosophy of art with perfect consistency treated their work as a prologomena to the fundamental study of any serious work of art: that is to say, the effort to discover in a poem, a novel, a picture, or a sonata, a compelling being which exists as art only in our own direct encounters with it. Not unnaturally, the polymath, for whom the common reader is a mere ignoramus and experience a form of indulgence, resents being asked to play a quiet second fiddle. Unmollified by the philosopher's recognition of the need for first-rate second fiddles, he reciprocates by brushing aside the former's "esthetics" as an exercise in, as well as an excuse for, dilettantism.

Either way, philosophers were generally viewed by people in other departments within the humanities as pariahs, damned if they didn't and damned if they did. To my colleagues in the philosophy department such a situation was not particularly frustrating either philosophically or personally. Why should it be, since they too were specialized scholars, well-satisfied to be installed in secure professorships in America's oldest and most distinguished institution of higher learning? A few of them enjoyed well enough a night at the theatre or an afternoon at the Boston Museum of Fine Arts, but those were things completely dissociated from their work as professional philosophers. For them "the humanities" was merely an administrative rubric, and philosophy's place within it a matter of academic convenience. But to myself, who have found that notions of convenience generally reflect a way of life and that administrative rubrics often correspond to deep-lying preconceptions and attitudes of which neither the administrator nor the administrated is aware, the classification of philosophy as one of the humanities meant much more. Even academic philosophy is not a science, and it deludes itself when it pretends to be such. When other branches of the humanities play the ape to science, it is for the philosopher to show them what they may have forsaken or betrayed in the process. The fact is that the spirit of positivism had penetrated all the humanities at Harvard. Professors of English literature themselves were not interested in the great critical issues raised by Hume's essay, "On the Standard of Taste," because their work did not involve questions of taste. Professors of German had no stake in the effort of the idealists to distinguish between *Geisteswissenschaft* and *Natur-*

wissenschaft, since for them that very distinction is merely an item in the objective record of German intellectual history. To my mind, however, the distinction is fundamentally important to the work of all genuine humanists.

Now and then impatient colleagues intimated that I seemed to want something no respectable institution of higher learning was equipped to provide, since forms of insight and responsibility of the sort I had in view were the vocations, not of proper scholars concerned with knowledge about the objective world of fact, but of poets, prophets, intellectuals, and "wisdom-philosophers." So little did they realize how deeply they themselves had begged the fundamental questions about the scope and functions of higher learning, that one was obliged to ask whether the university in our time has a place for philosophers who suppose there may be an issue about the aims of higher education in a "knowledge factory" such as Harvard, no less than California, had become?

My own frustrations deepened as I pondered the history of my illustrious department—and it is worth emphasizing in passing that a number of my own teachers or colleagues, including Ralph Barton Perry, C. I. Lewis, and, more recently, Quine, have been generally recognized as among the distinguished thinkers of their own generations in American philosophy. There was in fact ample precedent for the situation in which I found myself, particularly during the "golden age" itself. Significantly, that age had been an era of great changes in the fortunes of both the university and the nation; it lasted from C. W. Eliot's ascendency as president of Harvard, when the liberal arts tradition still remained strong enough to provide a meaningful dialectical response to the nascent graduate university, until the entrance of the United States into the First World War, when Harvard, like its sister institutions, joined in the jubilee which symbolized the nation's emergence as a world power. Before then, the private university—or rather, college—provided a sanctuary, a place of repose where young men might acquire, if not a philosophy of their own, then at least a veneer of cultivation. Henceforth, both private as well as public universities, no longer isolated from the main currents of our social and political life, increasingly committed their moral energies as well as their newly extended intellectual resources to the service of the American system. From that time to this, although individual professors and presidents have frequently sounded alarms, sometimes in the name of academic detachment, at other times in the name of a higher service to humanity, the basic movement of the university as an institution has been toward ever closer ties to the worlds of business, industry, and government. For true philosophers, plainly, it could not be an age of complacency.

Santayana was perhaps the first member of the department to perceive clearly the sea changes that occurred when Harvard, following Johns Hopkins, went German, i.e., became entangled in the arms of what William James called "the Ph.D. octopus." In his *A General Confession* he remarks, "The liberal age in which I was born and the liberal circles in which I was educated flowed contentedly toward intellectual dissolution and anarchy." Santayana referred, of course, not to political liberalism, variant forms of which were becoming at this very time the prevailing political ideology at Harvard, but to liberalism as a unifying educational and cultural principle. Characteristically, he himself made little effort to resist the drift of things at Harvard; rather, in the middle of the winter of 1912, upon receiving a legacy that made him independent, did he simply resign, cease teaching, and go abroad to live. Was Santayana a special case? By the standards of my own teachers and colleagues, who rarely mentioned either him or his works, it would seem so. In the widest sense, Santayana was always a moral philosopher, concerned with the wisdom of life, whose meaning as he understood it was conveyed as much through the inflexions of his marvellous prose as through any explicit articulations of attitude or belief. To be sure, his books abound in still unnoticed insights into the forms of expression that variously serve to guide the life of reason. Indeed, he perceived with a clarity unmatched by that of any of his contemporaries that rationality, as it manifests itself in common sense, science, the primary institutions of social life, art, and religion, is not all of a piece, and that if one identifies reason with logic, then logic itself has many forms unknown to formal logicians and mathematicians. His tolerant discriminations of role and function among the symbolic forms which mainly concerned him—that is, in the "humanistic" domains of poetry, the arts, ethics, religion, and philosophy itself—might have saved a half century of twentieth-century philosophy from the debacle of scientism into which it was led by Bertrand Russell and his successors. Though he sometimes twitted the pragmatists for keeping their own noses too close to the grindstone of America's manifest destiny in the late nineteenth and early twentieth centuries, Santayana's approach to any form of conceptual analysis was in its own way profoundly pragmatic: that is to say, he sought always to clarify the meanings of ideas by determining their actual workings within the familiar contexts in which they are normally employed by serious men. In this respect he anticipated in many striking ways both the approaches and the results of the "philosophers of ordinary language," who derive from the later teachings and writings of Wittgenstein. But also, like the pragmatists and unlike the followers of Wittgenstein (though not Wittgenstein himself), Santayana's governing interest in such "analytical" investigations always remained philosophical: that is, he sought clarity not simply for the sake of "knowledge," at least as the scientist conceives it, but for the sake of self-understanding and self-control.

This did not mean that Santayana was ever contemptuous either of science as such or of its rightfully large and central place within the university curriculum—just the reverse; entirely free from misology he regarded romantic obscurantism and irrationalism as the bane of modern life. It meant, rather, that a German-style university, bent exclusively on the advancement of science, is no home for a philosopher-poet, concerned in his own reasonable way with the whole being of the human spirit.

Superficially the case of William James seems entirely different from that of Santayana, whose philosophy he once referred to disparagingly as a "perfection of rottenness." James was an immense success at Harvard, as a teacher, as an influence, and as a personality. No Harvard building is likely to bear Santayana's name, but that of James has now been immortalized by a great white high-rise block near Harvard Yard, inhabited by well-funded psychologists and social scientists. I am not sure what James would have thought either of the building or of a good deal of what goes on there. He loathed German-style graduate schools and once proposed to Santayana, with whom his relations were always ambivalent, that they join forces in an attack on the "desiccating and pedantifying" process of the American Ph.D. Browbeaten by his older friend, the founder of the pragmatic school in American philosophy, C. S. Peirce, James acquired a phobic distaste for formal logic and mathematics. But when he remarked in a letter that "Technicality seems to me to spell 'failure' in philosophy," he was generally misunderstood. Like Santayana, however much he might disagree with *him* over just such "technical issues," he contended that philosophy is, or ought to be, an activity that concerns the full human being and not just the scientific researcher attempting to make his own ideas clear. His significant disagreements with Peirce turned on the question of what ideas most need clarifying and how they are to be made clearer. A more consistent contextualist than Peirce, James, like Santayana, believed that the meanings of all ideas, and not merely scientific ones, are to be looked for in the distinctive circumstances of their own common uses and according to the characteristic operations of the mind which they govern. He sought recognition for all varieties of religious experience, abnormal as well as normal, and he talked, paradoxically, about "the will to believe." In more anxious moments James, unlike Santayana, sometimes appeared to be an irrationalist; at his best, however, he was, or meant to be, an antirationalist, opposed only to any sort of institutional domination in the world of the mind. He both loved and believed in cranks like his friend Peirce, whom President Eliot denied the right to lecture in Harvard Yard, and he fought a gallant retreating battle to keep the academic environment from which he could not escape open to varieties of authentic human learning not recognized by respectable institutions for advanced study.

The truth is that James himself was a freak. In the era of the burgeoning graduate university he prospered at Harvard almost against his will. Conventional academic and social life in Cambridge stifled him. Again and again he offered his resignation only to be cajoled by the president into remaining. Success of any sort in this country is never easily renounced, and James knew whereof he spoke when he said that "success is a bitch-goddess." In his diary for 1905–1906, which sounds at times like T. S. Eliot's "Difficulties of a Statesman," the word "resign" recurs endlessly like a sort of litany. Once more he sent in his resignation and then managed to make it stick. On doing so, as Ralph Barton Perry remarks in his incomparable *Thought and Character of William*

James, James experienced a profound sense of relief. At last he was "alone with God" and "truth," free like Santayana to devote his energies, now greatly depleted, entirely to their service.

For me, as for Perry, the most impressive person among my own teachers, it did not come to that—nor did we wish it so. Being alone with the alone is well enough for a season but it does not make a life, and the truth to which I, like Perry, have aspired requires dialogue as well as solitude. The companionship and criticism of students—and the great joy of teaching at Harvard has always been its bountiful supply of gifted young minds—was indispensable to the philosopher's own educational development. Teaching them, one is forever being taught: forced by their unbelief to review assumptions one can no longer take for granted, obliged to confront attitudes and forms of sensibility from which the middle-aged in other spheres of work are too often immunized, made to face directly into freshening winds of doctrine from which the contemporary scholar in his air-conditioned study is as effectively insulated as any executive in his high-rise suite. A wise teacher does not forget the differential roles that he and his students must inevitably play, any more than he ignores the fact that his own stage in the human life cycle presents problems of individual and social identity unlike theirs. But if one knows how to keep one's place, learning from one's students, although abrasive and sometimes humiliating, can be a source of endless self-renewal. In fact both the direct and indirect rewards of teaching—as long as numerous and leisurely coffee breaks are provided—are among the greatest goods which academic life can confer upon any intellectual. Rather is it the grading of meaningless examinations, the rounds of meetings, and conferences with their perfunctory amiability and desultory shoptalk, and above all, the ritual "functions," which make academic life all too often a grind and a bore.

Within limits, let me add, any sensible man must bow to the principle of the division of labor in the academy as elsewhere. What must be insisted, rather, is that presidents and deans, if they are to concern themselves with educational issues, take frequent sabbatical leaves of their own during which they give and take courses like any ordinary faculty member or student, that they queue up for their daily pabulum and learn by living there what is being said and done in the shadow university. At Harvard, as elsewhere, it is not the division of labor as such that should be called into question, but the remoteness of those in the high administrative echelons from the common life of the university and their inaccessibility to all but those just below them in the chain of command. When, on state occasions, ordinary members of the faculty meet President Pusey, they feel themselves to be in the presence, not of a colleague, but of a man from Mars whose "Harvard" and theirs merely go by the same name. Unhappily most members of the faculty simply chalk it up to "the system" which the President of Harvard is as powerless to change as any professor. It seems never to occur to them that if this be true, then the system is in need of radical changes. But where is one to make a beginning?

For myself it could only be made by playing out an adversary role within philosophy itself. It was essential, however, to be discriminating, for unlike certain philosophical insurgents in other universities, I had no wish either to junk logic or to oppose linguistic philosophy. That way lies both educational intolerance and philosophical obscurantism. It is true of course that mathematical logic is now an independent formal discipline with closer ties to the rest of mathematics than to philosophy, including the more analytical sort where application of its rigid quantification schemas frequently obscures rather than clarifies ordinary ways of thinking, especially in the spheres that most interest the humanist: the problem of knowledge and the arts, criticism, ethics, political and social thought, and religion. On this point the younger logicians, more interested in the internal progress of logic than in its imagined virtues as an all-purpose tool for conceptual analysis, themselves emphatically agreed with my position. Therefore, as long as, at Harvard, logic and philosophy were obliged to go on living together under one leaky departmental roof, there was nothing for it, on this score, but to live and let live. But we were in a minority. And we protested vainly against a lockstep system of qualifying examinations that required all graduate students in the department, regardless of their interests, to pass an exam in mathematical logic.

Conceptual analysis is another matter. Most great philosophers, from Socrates to Hume and from Kant to the pragmatists, have found it indispensable to their own purposes to distinguish the primary intentions and functions of the human mind. Indeed, from the beginnings of Western culture, lovers of knowledge have invariably been led to ponder what they mean by knowledge; moralists have been obliged to consider what they are doing in saying that something is good or right or just; worshippers, in the midst of their prayers, have wondered what in God's name they may be praying to. At Harvard, the proper complaint could not be that we had too much linguistic analysis but that we had too little else. Or, rather, it is that our contemporary analysts, unlike the greatest philosophers of the tradition, seem no longer concerned about the philosophical and educational relevance of their investigations. They remain, in effect, scholars' scholars who, even when they acknowledge in principle the immense diversity of symbolic forms, confine their own attention mainly to those employed by their academic colleagues in sorting out matters of material fact. In practice, the languages of morals and art, not to mention religion and politics, have been made to appear as of secondary philosophical importance, and the main weight of the departmental curriculum, during my tenure, continued to rest on forms of understanding presumed uncritically to reach their apotheosis in the technical researches of scientific scholars.

How should it be otherwise? Academic philosophers are academicians first and philosophers second—in this respect they are precisely like academic sociologists, political scientists, and theologians. They want respectability, and respectability nowadays is conferred by the graduate university whose presiding deity is scientific research. Nor, in our contemporary secularist and materialist culture with its insatiable appetite for the products made possible by the scientific technology, are analytical philosophers quick to achieve distinction from their efforts, however subtle or profound, to explain the meaning of God in authentically religious discourse or the senses in which a work of art or a moral principle may be said to be true. And when, as philosophers of science, with their attendant accomplishments as mathematical logicians, they become resentful upon finding their departments so far removed from the corridors of academic power, they, like other scientists, have little trouble finding more adequately rewarding jobs outside the academy. What reason then have they, already indoctrinated since their student days by the prevailing ideology of the higher learning in America, to turn in midcareer to the study of symbolic forms whose primary meaning belongs to the subjective life of the human person? No wonder that, when reminded that a Socrates, a Maimonides, a Kierkegaard, or, not least, a Wittgenstein, would have replied that there are very good reasons, at least for anyone who pretends to be a philosopher, they are apt to be impatient or simply uncomprehending.

Not all of my colleagues were so, but in such matters, comprehension without a comradely will to action and hence to share the corresponding risks of alienation and disrepute, is almost as dispiriting as none at all. Thus by stages, I came to realize that the role of departmental adversary was without effect: either, therefore, one would retreat by stages into the role of a compliant court jester permitted to mock but never threaten, or, more likely in the end, into a foot-dragging accomplice of a corporate destiny one can no longer disown.

But philosophy is not the whole of things, nor can it ever be so for the true philosopher. Human life has other reaches and other fulfillments to which at his own best, the philosopher is content to serve as midwife. Furthermore, he has had to realize that it is unreasonable to define man even for educational purposes as merely the rational animal. Rational, man undoubtedly must be; but, save for rationalists, he is not *the* rational animal; he is also, like the mole, the underground animal, the self-searching and self-transcending animal, the destructive and creative animal. And an education has its indispensable role to play in enabling him to fulfill himself properly in all these forms of human being. As a philosopher, as a teacher, and therefore as a man, I necessarily had many stakes outside my department. Nor was I prepared to accept the fact, despite all appearances, that in this connection "outside" must forever mean "outside the university." As matters stood academic philosophy might be a place for "good soldiers," but only in Ford Maddox Ford's ironic sense. There had been all too many good soldiers among my professional colleagues, both at Harvard and elsewhere, and I was not about to resign myself to their company. Was it still not possible somehow that within the humanities and, beyond the humanities, within the wider faculty of arts and sciences, one might find fellow citizens of the "republic of the spirit" who, respecting the indispensable place of the study of all varieties of symbolic forms, including language, in any self-critical liberal education, perceive that such an education requires also the cultivation of every active power of the liberal mind? Indeed, might one not perhaps better fulfill one's own vocation by searching out such comrades everywhere in the university and making common cause with them in creating, if necessary, a "shadow university" where free spirits, among faculty and students alike, might share skills and insights derived from ranges of human experience which the university establishment no longer acknowledges as part of the higher learning?

So it seemed. As it happened, however, the university committed itself in the middle forties to a substantial program of general education which almost by definition seemed bent on making good the very deficiencies about which I have here complained. Indeed, it is arguable that in this instance it was not the faculty, jealous of its own vested professional interests, that was quickest to recognize and to attempt to rectify the immense educational limitations of the graduate university, but an enlightened administration which perceived that Harvard had fallen far behind some of its distinguished sister universities and colleges.

How had this happened? In part, it was owing to the still powerful thrust of the sacred elective system, adopted in President Eliot's time, which had proved so useful during the period in which Harvard passed from a four-year liberal arts college to a professionalized graduate university. The elective system had long been accepted uncritically as an evidence of Harvard's vaunted liberalism at least at the undergraduate level, though the liberality it represented was miscellaneous and political rather than educational; in fact it left the student free to study what he pleased in a haphazard, unstructured way which, in the new university context, all too often precluded any opportunity to acquire in depth a genuinely liberal education. Yet it was generally accepted as an adequate educational balance within the College to the increasing stress upon the "major," itself a practice which suited all too well departments with large vested interests in preparing undergraduates for their careers in the learned professions, in business, industry, and government, and a bit later, in the graduate university itself. This emphasis was in turn underscored by the tutorial system, which in bringing students into closer contact with members of the faculty, too often had the effect of tying the student ever more closely, especially in his junior and senior years, to his major subject.[1]

At any rate, during the early years of World War II, the Conant administration, whose loyalty to the prevailing American system and Harvard's own prosperous connections with it was even deeper than its dedication to the advancement of scientific learning, came in its own way to recognize that, so far as liberal education was concerned, the elective and tutorial systems had proved inadequate. And so belatedly, but with much fanfare, Harvard established a "G.E." program that would prepare undergraduates for the demands of citizenship in an imperiled "free society."

The program, as explicated in the famous "Red Book" (its formal title was *General Education in a Free Society*) has been described many times, so I shall mention here only those aspects of it that most concerned me as a philosopher and exponent of liberal education. The Red Book talked grandly and vaguely of the "supreme need of American education . . . for a unifying purpose and idea." But unlike President Hutchins with his highly controversial plan at Chicago, its authors seemed to have only the vaguest notion of what such an idea might be. It seemed that the great cure-alls, which would make university students whole, were democracy and the "Great Tradition of Western Civilization." In the humanities this meant in particular, "Great Texts of Literature": e.g., "Homer, one or two Greek tragedies, Plato, the *Bible*, Virgil, Dante, Shakespeare, Milton, Tolstoy"; in the social sciences, "Western Thought and Institutions," as exemplified in the writings of "Aquinas, Machiavelli, Luther, Bodin, Locke, Montesquieu, Rousseau, Adam Smith, Bentham, and Mill, to mention no others . . ."; in the physical sciences (where general education has always had its most recalcitrant problems—and faculty), the emphasis was to be on methods and concepts as exemplified in the historical development of the sciences. Of course, it didn't work out precisely that way. The best teachers, once they got into the G.E. program, went their own ways as best they could under the cover of catalogue entries that would satisfy the conscience of the Committee on General Education.

At first, let me say, the philosophy department had great difficulty getting accredited by the Committee. The humiliating fact was that we were not considered fit to teach even the philosophical classics, which both in the humanities and in the social science programs comprised a large part of the writings which the student would be asked to read. We were regarded as "analysts," "logicians," and therefore, as far as general education was concerned, horrible examples of specialized irrelevance. Eventually, however, Morton White and I managed to confect a course that brought us within the pale. We were forbidden to use the word "philosophy" in our title, and Humanities 5 was tardily launched under the sumptuous title: "Ideas of Man and the World in Western Civilization." It was also insisted that we include nonphilosophical as well as philosophical texts in our reading lists. This was fine with me, for I, who was to do the first half of the course from the Greeks up through the Renaissance, could at least satisfy a long-standing urge to lecture on the Greek tragedies and Shakespeare, the *Book of Job* and St. Augustine, as well as philosophers like Plato, the Stoics and the Epicureans, who were well off my "professional" beat. And in his part of the course, Morton White, for a time at least, lectured on some modern "literary" authors including, as I remember, Dostoievsky, Stendhal, and Kierkegaard. To the great satisfaction of the philosophy department, the course somehow prospered. Our enrollments swelled and swelled until we could provide teaching fellowships for nearly any philosophy graduate student who needed the money and could stand the gaff. We had some brilliant section leaders including among others, Susan Sontag, Marshall Cohen, and Stanley Cavell, all of whom have gone on to higher things, not all of them, thank God, confined to academic philosophy.

For a time I enjoyed teaching the course, for reasons that were discreditable as well as creditable. I tried at least to convey to my classes some awareness of the many levels of significance in the plays of Aeschylus, Euripides, and Shakespeare, and without denigrating the value of scholarly research, I also made it plain that the fundamental interest of such works of dramatic and poetic art belongs to the domain which Kierkegaard calls "the subjective." And the same was true in my discussions of the philosophical and religious works dealt with in my part of the course.

The feedback on this score was satisfactory, and I honestly believed that I was really doing something to combat the prevailing and spiritually desiccating rationalism at Harvard. But I also took too much pleasure in disporting myself in front of five hundred or so undergraduates, and the numbers game became for me, as for virtually everyone else in the program, an obsession.

Gradually, however, it became clear to me how ridiculous, if also economical, is such a way of performing the tasks of teaching in the humanities, where everything turns on the opportunity for conversation between teacher and student. At Harvard, as elsewhere, size, on very many levels, has been a mania as well as at times a necessity. In this respect, at least, the famous Humanities Course at Columbia, which is divided into sections of twenty-five or so, is much superior. Unfortunately, the list of books read in that course is wholly prescribed and there are far too many books to read. In that way the Harvard program, or the part I had to do with, was superior. But though one was free, say, to stress Euripides or omit Don Quixote, one was nonetheless tied to the "Great Books" principle, and there was evident disapproval on the part of the G.E. committee when I suggested reading *in extenso* some of the wonderful lyric poetry of our own language in place of certain cardboard monuments which many classics become when read in translation.

In the end, therefore, I found myself fighting rather than teaching "Hum. 5" and so I opted out of general education at Harvard, to the disgruntlement of some of my departmental colleagues. Of course they wouldn't have dreamed of teaching such a course themselves, but they saw it as a useful recruiting ground for possible majors. But for me, that was a further reason for getting out of "Hum. 5," for it seemed to promise so much more philosophically than our departmental upper division curriculum was conceived to satisfy or, in many instances, even to countenance. Indeed, I well remember a number of able students who, having been seduced into philosophy through our course in general education, were bitterly disillusioned by the sequel.[2]

Before leaving the topic of general education at Harvard, let me make one or two further observations about the theory and practice, as well as the importance, of general education programs within the context of a modern graduate university. However

[*3 9*]

poorly conceived or implemented in the past, general education represents the one great recent effort to reconstitute liberal education within that setting. No sustained alternative is anywhere in sight. Merely to abandon it, therefore, would be unthinkable. Certainly general education is meant as a countermovement to the prevailing specialism, professionalism, and scientism that afflict all graduate universities in America. But properly conceived, this does not entail, as some of its critics seem to think, a quixotic effort to check legitimate specialization and technicality, to depreciate the learned professions, or to block the advancement of scientific knowledge. Its aim is, or should be, enlightenment, not obfuscation or dilettantism. As I conceive it, general education has two interrelated positive aims: (a) to cultivate all of the differential faculties required for a civilized life in the modern world, and (b) to enable the specialist, the technician, and the professional in any sphere to comprehend more adequately the significance of his own work and hence its relations to the other main forms of life upon which it impinges. Thus I should argue that any member of the intelligentsia who lacks a sustained and continuing general education is to that extent no less improperly prepared for his career than he is for the still more exacting enterprise of trying to be a human being. Plainly, these aspirations have been inadequately served by rigid Great Books and Great Tradition programs. And the snobbism, cultism, and archaism too often embedded in them are part of an ideology with which liberal education has nothing to do. To a degree, the Harvard scheme suffered, especially in the beginning, from these faults. All the same, its very inconsistencies, its miscellaneousness, and vagueness helped in practice to offset them, and in that respect it represented some improvement upon its predecessors at Columbia and Chicago.

One other feature of the Harvard plan marks an advance in educational principle and policy upon most of its predecessors. From the outset there was envisaged a series of optional upper-division general education courses through which new ventures could cut across departmental or even divisional curricular lines. Some of these courses, to my knowledge, have had great merit. Nor has their educational value been limited merely to students; many a professor's own general self-education has been revitalized in preparing and teaching such courses. Unfortunately, Harvard no more than its sister universities has ever contemplated extending the aims and practices of general education beyond the College level, and so "G.E.", at Harvard as elsewhere, has never remotely succeeded in liberalizing the university as a whole. Nor, for a great many students, has it provided either at the college or the graduate level a sustained educational environment within which gifted young men and women would be continually helped to relate their specialized and professional studies to their wider human experience.

For this reason, liberally-disposed teachers themselves have often felt that general education, at even the College level, is for the most part a waste of time, energy, and money. Accordingly, some have argued that "G.E." should be confined to the secondary schools, where, in fact, the equivalents of the ordinary lower-division general education courses, particularly in the humanities and the social sciences, are now widely taught. Increasingly their point of view tends to prevail. In consequence, bright students who want to get on with their "work" and hence to avoid spending time reviewing books they think they already know and listening to lectures that regurgitate ideas with which they are familiar, are now permitted, or encouraged, to enter college in "advanced standing," a convenient device for enabling them to bypass general education in the college, along with diluted survey courses offered by the various departments.

The result has been predictable. Fewer and fewer professors care to teach courses under general education auspices: fewer graduate students seek teaching experience as section leaders in such courses; and ever-increasing numbers of students both at the graduate and the undergraduate levels devote their energies almost entirely to subjects that serve their professional careers. In short, at Harvard as elsewhere, although vested interests in general education itself made it impossible to abandon the program altogether, it was clear from the early sixties on that general education had entered upon a period of retrenchment. And the dull, ill-written report of the so-called Doty Committee, whose task it was to propose reforms for the improvement of general education at Harvard, implied that henceforth "G.E." was not a domain where academic gold braid would be distributed in large quantities.

[*41*

So there, it seemed, was another dead end, for Harvard as well as myself. The report of the Doty Committee, as it stood, was not accepted by the faculty, but the meetings at which it was discussed were dispiriting. The aggressive opponents of "G.E.," though in a minority, offered devastating though largely negative criticisms of the program. Its exponents seemed discouraged and their own arguments were defensive and concessive. Nor did anyone so much as suggest that the reform of general education should mean not its curtailment but its extension into the highest tiers of learning in the university: that is, the graduate school itself. I have come to the conclusion, however, that until such a view prevails, liberal education at the University level is doomed, and that students who seek such an education and teachers who care to participate in it may do well to avoid the "great" universities altogether. Fortunately, as I came to see, other options remain, many of them immensely exciting. But of that, more presently.

One last aspect of my prolonged leave-taking from Harvard remains to be mentioned. During his last years at Harvard James Conant, who himself had been a largely absentee president during the years of the Second World War and who had been deeply involved in our war effort, as it was called, repeatedly warned the faculty against unforeseen entanglements that would inevitably follow were the university to become too dependent upon the largesse of government grants and contracts. Stressing the importance of free and basic research (its technological, including its military, potential was not mentioned, as I recall), he made it clear that the government, no more than industry and business, gives something for nothing. He insisted that we ought always to be prepared (as America's wealthiest and most liberal university) to go it alone should the Congress deny us its "foreign aid" or the Department of Defense find that its own specialized needs were better serviced by the research facilities of the great industrial and paramilitary corporations than by those of the universities. Well do I remember the faculty meeting at which it was proposed that the School of Engineering should be dismantled and replaced by a new Department of Applied Science. When someone raised the question whether applied science wasn't simply engineering under another title, Mr. Conant replied in effect, "Well, what we're really proposing is a department for the theory of applied science." Years later, upon reading President Eisenhower's famous farewell address, warning of the consequences of any uncontrolled military-governmental-industrial (he might have added educational) complex, I thought of his distinguished academic precursor whose own warning had also come too late.

In advance, one might have supposed that under the dispensation of President Pusey, who came to Harvard with a well-deserved reputation as a strong defender of academic freedom during the era of Joe McCarthy, Conant's endeavors to protect the university from ties to an ever more powerful nation-state would receive additional support. But the freedom of the university, like that of other complex institutions, has many facets. One as rich and powerful as Harvard may preserve the formal liberty of the members of its faculty to teach, study, and write as they see fit, and yet, by slow stages, create an ambience within which that liberty is subtly but effectively eroded. A university may protect those pure scholars who seek to get on with their basic researches come what may, yet at the same time tolerate or quietly encourage the grantsmen, the well-paid consultants of industry, and the advisors to the Prince who receive in the form of influence a compensation more gratifying than money. In so doing, it may reinforce a conception of academically public service which is in practice highly restrictive.

That is just what happened at Harvard in ever intensified degree under President Pusey's auspices. But the qualifying phrase must not be forgotten, for here as elsewhere Mr. Pusey was less an initiating than a conserving force in matters of university practice and policy. In a recent article, "The War Against the Young," Professor Richard Poirier has acutely observed that only at Harvard have American college graduates regularly been turned out who, like their English counterparts at Oxford and Cambridge, were imbued from boyhood with the belief that their "careers" meant something not to themselves alone, but to the wider historical and political careers of their country. On the whole the point is well taken. "Harvard men" (and most Harvard faculty members are, or quickly become, Harvard men; as if to make sure that they will, every new permanent member of the faculty who comes without a Harvard degree is automatically awarded an honorary M.A.) are constantly encouraged to think of themselves, even when they intend to spend their lives as private citizens, as in some sense public men who are to serve as exemplars of institutional and social responsibility. In this respect, Poirier at least is half-right in saying that at Harvard, to a lesser extent than at other American universities, is education "a combination of utilitarian course work and playacting: 'getting ready' to be an adult. . . ." However, it is doubtful whether this sense of public obligation normally carries with it, in any great depth or truth, an "historical self-consciousness." On the contrary, such self-consciousness has too often been provincial and conventional, stopping short at boundaries that circumscribe one's class or profession or one's town and country. In my experience at least, the self-critical historical consciousness, of which Hegel and Marx and Nietzsche spoke, has been rather less common among Harvard men than, say, among students and teachers in the university complexes of New York City or the San Francisco Bay area. Furthermore the sense of public service or mission engendered at Harvard results not from what the student learns in his classes or the faculty member from discussions with his colleagues, but from a pervasive collegiate atmosphere which itself encourages a great deal of genteel, in-groupish playacting. In short, the issue is not whether one is or is not getting ready to be an adult at the university, but rather what sort of adult one is getting ready to be. My strong impression is that the forms of playacting Harvard instinctively encourages by no means include preparation for developing roles of sustained dissent from the going concerns of the American national society. On the contrary: Harvard men are intended to be inside men and rarely do they turn out otherwise unless something else in their educational background serves as a prod or trigger.

Quite visibly, during the fifties and sixties, Harvard's ties to the big money and the big power in America grew ever tighter and more complex. The point was underscored when, after the inauguration of John F. Kennedy, a number of highly-placed professors and deans, including Schlesinger, Galbraith, Kaysen, and most saliently, McGeorge Bundy, took advanced posts along the New Frontier. Reactionaries like William Buckley professed to be worried about the liberalism of a Schlesinger, but the presence of Bundy as a key figure in the same operation was the tip-off that no rowdy doctrinal brawls would be tolerated except on Saturday night. And when I expressed doubts whether an administration full of such academicians could be expected to bring us more than a half-step closer to the New Jerusalem, I was informed (which was quite true, of course) that they had no such interest and indeed deprecated all talk of New Jerusalems as millenarian nonsense.

No, those were years, not of stringent liberal, social, or political criticism at Harvard, but of companionable accommodation to the predominant movements of American corporate power since the Second World War. In other universities and colleges during the period, there was a recrudescence of genuinely radical liberalism which demanded an end not merely to the Vietnam War but to the entire foreign policy of which that war is such an appalling example. The more influential Harvard liberals offered no principled opposition to American militarism and imperialism, with their calamitous effects upon our domestic life; just the contrary, they themselves were shapers of that policy. From my point of view, their liberalism—if, indeed, that word can seriously be applied to them—was and still is centrist and hence conservative to the core. Almost to a man, its exponents have preached the gospel of neo-pragmatic compromise at home and national self-interest abroad. They have accepted without demur the indefinite extension of presidential power with its ever-larger military and paramilitary establishments and budgets, as if it were a law of nature. And from few of them does one hear a word of serious concern about the obvious threat to the remains of our liberal democracy from the *de facto* shift in America from a congressional to an essentially presidential system of government.

Along with this conservative counterideology of hand-to-mouth social planning and unstructured but basically elitist welfare-statism went a corresponding interpretation of American social and political history which was no less depressing. According to this interpretation, which systematically minimized the significance of the American Revolution as well as all subsequent native radical movements, we were from the start an essentially anti-intellectual people of the center—any center that happened to exist—immune to all forms of "extremism" whether political, economic, ethical, or religious. To my mind, such a reading of the American past left the present generation unprepared to understand, not to say cope with, the deepening self-divisions, the destructiveness and brutality, and the ruthless egoisms that now seem so suddenly and unaccountably to threaten both the stability of our institutions and our unity as a people. At the same time, by suavely brushing aside great movements of dissident and sometimes rebellious idealism in earlier American social and political thought, it deprives our own intransigents of any sense of continuity with their domestic historical antecedents. In so doing, its authors must bear some responsibility for the tendencies among many members of the New Left toward a know-nothing contempt for liberalism and toward an amorphous politics of topical resistance that leaves it vulnerable to demagogues who offer their followers little more than a prospect of nihilist impotence and self-immolation. To those who have eyes to see, such anti-ideological new leftists are themselves inverted images of the very pragmatic centrist-liberals whom they excoriate. Were they by a miracle to come into power tomorrow, it would shortly be impossible to distinguish them, save by their rhetoric, from the crowd that preceded them.

During my later years at Harvard, the news had not yet reached me that a new generation of scholars was already emerging with quite different perspectives upon American history. And it was impossible for a mere philosopher to do more than express his doubts about the underlying premises of more erudite colleagues. Brought up on Parrington and Beard, I had never swallowed their respective simplifications of our American historical experience; in fact, I found the later writings of Beard thoroughly repellent. Yet each in his way was aware that there existed deep cross currents in that experience and that Americans of enlightenment and integrity have never been content to let our history simply take its course. They were ideologues—quite openly so. But their ideological positions at least made them aware of active ideological attitudes at work in the social thought and action of their forebears. Their critics, at Harvard as elsewhere, professed a more neutral approach to their subject. Wasn't it possible, however, that their very neutrality made them color-blind, so that, although they saw many things on the landscape that people like Parrington and Beard didn't know were there, what they perceived was an endless stretch of grey on grey? Indeed, wasn't it clear that the same neutrality, applied to the task not merely of establishing but of interpreting and weighing the historical data, is itself implicitly ideological in its effect if not in its conscious intention? And, in sum, weren't the neutralists participating in the great end-of-ideology sell which in its own way provided a rationale for the policies and practices of the dominant government-industrial-academic consortiums that were already forcing dissenters into a darkening mood of resistance, and resisters, in desperation, into forms of open rebellion?

Within the universities, the agony of Columbia was still a few years ahead. But at Berkeley, the graffiti were no longer confined to toilet walls, and any passerby could discern their meaning. In their "Introduction" to *The Berkeley Student Revolt*, Seymour M. Lipset and Sheldon S. Wolin, no boon companions of the young rebels, said: "Against this backdrop [of incessant student debate which from '56 through '63 had passed from the internal issue of student political rights and privileges to the wider issues raised by the civil rights movement] the student revolt of the fall of 1964 seems less like a sudden and surprising explosion from within the body politic of the university, but rather the natural outgrowth of eight years of expanding student political involvement. . . ." [3] That same year, on a periodic visit to the University of Michigan, I found that the involvement of students was matched by that of faculty members who had recently organized the first teach-ins in America. Everywhere one was made aware of a newly sophisticated attitude which related questions of students' rights and civil rights to larger unsolved problems of governmental policy, external as well as internal, that now create correlative problems within the university. Not everyone at Michigan by any means shared the apprehensions of the dissident activists; some, hitherto untouched by rapid changes in academic as well as in the national life since the Second World War, remained determined quietists, appalled at the "politicization" of institutions of higher learning. But in spite of themselves they too were caught up in the great debates that raged about them. On my return to Harvard, however, the New Frontier euphoria still remained largely undisturbed. At the first faculty meeting that autumn, one could only marvel at the benign assurance and optimism of which President Pusey's unfurrowed brow had become a symbol. An-

[47

other year of solid contributions to scientific knowledge was in the offing; the budget was more or less in balance; and in my own large undergraduate course dealing with the conflict of ideologies in the West, I continued to receive the polite attention which Harvard undergraduates give all but the dullest of their professors. Only the struggling old elm trees, full of Dutch Elm disease, had a look of sickness unto death.

Thus, like Santayana and James so many years before, did I come by stages to see, after nearly three decades as student and teacher, that my own Harvard education had come to the end of its term. I still had great affection for my "most kindly nurse." But I realized that if I were to remain a teacher of philosophy rather than a director at collegiate dress rehearsals for plays that never would be enacted, a change must be made. What sort of change? It would not do at all to start playing a game of academic musical chairs. Why leave Harvard, were it merely to another, inevitably lesser Harvard that one would go?

3

Interlude: On Going to Brandeis:

The Promise

Until the winter of 1965, the question "why leave Harvard?" as we scholars say, remained academic. I still had no firm idea of trying to make a new career outside the precincts of Harvard Yard; on the contrary, I remained full of flickering night-thoughts about stoical endurance, underground resistance, classroom demonstrations of witty professorial disdain. Fantasies. Others have taken this route, but it leads nowhere save to a life of cynical accommodation. Then, as it happened, an overture came from Brandeis through Harold Weisberg, then Dean of the Graduate School and an ex-chairman of the philosophy department who had already helped to attract to the university a varied group of interesting philosophers. The possibility intrigued me. I had lectured once or twice at Brandeis and a few years earlier had taught a seminar in one of the short offbeat summer sessions. These were enjoyable experiences. But what actually would it mean to go to Brandeis? My first thoughts, predictably, showed how completely a Harvard man I had become. My mother, when I called her to say that I was seriously contemplating the move, put the point succinctly: "You simply *can't* leave Harvard." There were indeed stabilities and comforts to which I had long been accustomed, as well as the assured, if sometimes unearned, distinction conferred by a Harvard professorship. I recalled the generations of bright, friendly students who had attended my classes. And whatever my colleagues might think of the matter privately, I could, if I said the word, offer a course in the mysticism of

[*49*

Wittgenstein or in theories of revolution from Hobbes to Lenin: the latter subject, in fact, had formed a large part of my course in the conflict of ideologies. Beyond all this, Harvard rivaled Oxford and Cambridge as a sanctuary for academic eccentrics. Where else in America could one find so firm an institutional guarantee of the liberal's ideal of personal liberty? And if that liberty, in a society like ours, is based upon a principle of privacy which can be fully enjoyed only by the well-to-do, what better excuse could a university like Harvard make for the defense of its great wealth?

What could Brandeis offer in compensation for the loss of these very real goods which Harvard automatically confers upon her own? More generally, did Brandeis give any better promise of fulfilling my emerging notions of what a university should be? When I began to make inquiries—for, like most people at Harvard, I really knew little about the new university a few miles up the river in Waltham—it was hard to find my way out of the local rumor factory. Well-meaning friends "warned" that Brandeis was too new, too poor, too volatile, too much under President Sachar's sizeable thumb. It was represented, in effect, as a kind of counterimage of Harvard, and hence as everything a well-established, well-managed graduate university shouldn't be. But universities can be quite different from their images, and in this instance the image itself had some appealing aspects. A graduate of Reed, I prized a certain amount of volatility; newness could be a positive virtue, which makes possible fresh starts that are so hard to bring off in an ancient institution like Harvard; poor universities, like poor people, don't have to keep up a front, and so enjoy a kind of freedom which rich ones can't afford. I was reminded of my country, affluent and powerful beyond the dreams of smaller states, yet loaded down with world-wide responsibilities, real or imaginary, which in practice leave it very little freedom of action. Perhaps the very absence of national responsibilities such as universities like Harvard are committed to (we had it constantly dinned into us by the president in his annual state of the union address that though Harvard was indeed richly endowed, her far-flung activities left precious little free money for wildcat educational ventures), would leave Brandeis unencumbered by obligations that make new experiments impossible. And if nobody a few miles down the river knew or cared about Brandeis, didn't this suggest that Brandeis, like a foundling, was free to go its way without worrying about what its overpowering neighbors might think? Then there was the everlasting matter of size. Harvard, despite its house system, its tutorials, its large faculty, had been little able to overcome the educational and human problems that go with bigness: anonymity and impersonality; enormous classes especially in lower division courses where contact with the teacher is often more vital than it will be later when the student has adjusted himself to university life and knows how to conduct his own studies; large, self-contained departments which, like well-guarded baronies, need pay little attention to what goes on in the external world. The list of liabilities could be extended indefinitely. Justice Brandeis himself had warned the nation, many years before, about the "curse of bigness." Hadn't the small university bearing his name a chance to avoid that curse?

Such speculations needed testing. In the following weeks and months, therefore, I tried to determine what Brandeis was really about. For a start I discovered that Brandeis deans of the faculty were not famous for durability; they went in and out of office as rapidly as French Premiers during the Fourth Republic. On the other hand, Brandeis's President, for all his obvious problems of delegating power, was accessible—perhaps too accessible—to both faculty and students. To my astonishment, when the time came for an offer, I was interviewed at some length not only by the dean of the faculty, but also by President Sachar himself. It was evident, after five minutes of conversation, that whatever else might be true of him, the President was a man of intellectual power and learning, deeply concerned, according to his lights, that Brandeis should become an exemplary university *and* college. In sum, the very occurrence of our meeting, which was extraordinarily open on both sides, suggested a man who, at least in affairs that interested him, was bold, innovative, and indifferent to the matters of protocol that make it so difficult in most universities for members of the faculty to discuss freely with administrators matters of mutual concern.

No doubt such a president, whatever his merits, might become in the end a problem for the university when it had reached the crisis of identity which comes with approaching middle-age. All the same, as a number of Brandeis professors pointed out, an immense freedom was in practice enjoyed at Brandeis, both by the faculty and by the students. But liberty is one thing and equality another. Brandeis also appeared in practice more equalitarian than more tightly-run universities. I was reminded of Thomas Hobbes' contention that where one man rules, everybody else is more or less equal, and where everything is known, nobody's information gives him an advantage over anyone else. Furthermore, as Hobbes again pointed out, where the eyes and arms of the Leviathan reacheth not, as in every dark alley of London, there the state of nature reigneth. And since the Leviathan has no eyes in the back of its head—nor at Brandeis was there a secret service to supply the want—a sensible time-honored principle was this: stay out of the Presidential Enclave and do as you please. A year or so later when asked about the difference between Harvard and Brandeis in this sphere, I replied, I believe truly, "At Harvard the links in the chain of command are so fine that you can't find them; at Brandeis there is no chain of command." At any rate the prevailing informality within the Presidential Enclave seemed a welcome change from what prevailed at Harvard, where, in the ordinary course, one never requested a personal interview with President Pusey and so hadn't the vaguest notion, really, whether he was, as he seemed to most of us, a remote, wholly impersonal functionary, bereft of first-hand understanding of what dissident members of the faculty, not to say students, might think on matters of educational policy. No doubt, Harvard is so big that no president (or dean) can possibly maintain contact with most members of his faculty. But this is another excellent reason for keeping a university small enough that it may be called a "community" without derision.

The same informality pervaded the entire university. Before I had taught a class at Brandeis, I came to know a sizeable number of my future colleagues in a variety of fields, from English to Physics, from Sociology to Fine Arts. From our conversations it seemed that departmental lines at Brandeis were paperthin and that familiar exchanges between people of widely different areas of professional interest were taken as a matter of course. To be sure, as I discovered later, the endlessly fascinating subject of "Brandeis" amounts almost to a collective obsession, but the talk con-

cerns not simply questions of local campus politics, but also matters of genuine educational concern. My own preoccupation with
ideas of the university in our time was shared by many colleagues,
whose views often provided a useful counterpoint to my own. A
similar informality prevailed in relations between faculty and
students. In fact, during my first year at Brandeis I sometimes
yearned for the old days at Harvard when one held meetings with
students during biweekly office hours or else by appointment. At
Brandeis, where privacy is an abstract idea rather than a practice,
I found it impossible to prevent people from knocking on the
door of my study even when, in desperation, I would occasionally
put up a sign, "Do not disturb; man at work." And on reading the
never-ending complaints in *The Justice* (the extraordinary hell-
raising student paper) about the insufficiency of faculty-student
discussion, I sometimes wondered whether anything would satisfy
Brandeis students short of the whole university community living
together in one great academic Kibbutz.

But the Brandeis faculty evinced other virtues. Most, of course,
were professional scholars, some already famous, others distinguished or rapidly becoming so. The junior faculty in particular
was lively, independent, outspoken, and when its members disap-
proved with some university policy, they frequently took to the
pages of *The Justice* to make known their opinions. Distinguished
scholars can be dull, and not every self-assertive assistant professor
is a genius. Brandeis undoubtedly had its full quota of drags: men
whose highest aspiration is to be chairmen of their departments,
academic senators who adore being mentioned as possible deans, in
short, sound men for whom soundness is the only end of academic
life. But there were, conspicuously, "the others"; among them,
psychologists who grasped the all-important categorical distinction between intentional acts and behavioral processes; professors
of English who wrote excellent poetry and criticism; philosophers
who cared for wisdom; historians of ideas who were also abrasive
critics of the contemporary social system. Many others. What
most impressed me was that, until proven otherwise, members of
the intelligentsia were taken to be intellectuals, bent on making
their own "the best that has been thought and said in the world."
Indeed, the intensity of the intellectual life at Brandeis was like
nothing I had encountered since my undergraduate years at Reed.

Nor was this all. Whereas at Harvard, as I have suggested, there prevailed a general atmosphere of centrist liberal opinion and of readiness for established forms of public service, not merely through but to the state, at Brandeis one found a dialectic between those who, broadly speaking, shared the Harvard point of view and others who, from one position or another, were radically critical of it. To juxtapose such names as John Roche and Herbert Marcuse suggests a degree of ideological polarization that was, and is, untrue to academic realities. Even so, the students were exposed to an active conflict of educational-social ideals. This, however, was one side of a cultural ambience with which I first came into personal contact in the 1940s during the year that I taught at Columbia. For a variety of reasons, Brandeis had become, in some part, an outpost for New York intellectuals, a factor that gave the university a tone unique among New England universities.

The New York intellectuals have been described many times, and the descriptions naturally enough are not all the same. What I have to say about them here, vastly oversimplified, concerns only their impact upon the intellectual life of the universities with which many of them have been affiliated, including Brandeis. It is unnecessary to restate that the New York intellectuals are not and never have been a coterie, like the Bloomsbury set, that they have an immense range of interests and talents, and that their ideological positions have shifted, sometimes more than once, in accordance with the changing fortunes of men during the past decades. Many are of Jewish origin, but some are not, and their attitudes toward their respective ancestral religions and ethnic origins are as various as their politics or academic backgrounds.[1]

What New York intellectuals brought, or lent, to Brandeis were a living sense of history, a cultural outlook uncondescendingly trans-Atlantic and cosmopolitan, a passionate hatred of totalitarianism and authoritarianism in all their unlovely forms, and an awareness of the artificiality of the lines between the world of the mind and the world of action. Because of this they have usually recognized the necessity, however hard one may try to conceal it, of having a point of view, and most of them perceive the self-delusion involved in an ideal of splendid academic neutrality as well as the dangerous innocence, especially in our age of perpetual crisis, of the pure scholar, unaware either of the calluses on the hands that feed him or of the explosive uses to which his own labors may be put. Prizing conversation (New York intellectuals, unlike so many American scholars, are incessant talkers), most of them are also writers and editors, committed to the healthy European understanding that insidious distinctions between savant and journalist, poet and polemicist, academic journal and critical review are inimical to the cultural and social life not only of the intelligentsia, but the whole society. Partisans, in Lionel Trilling's familiar phrase, of "the liberal imagination," they refuse to acknowledge all the iron curtains which victims of professionalism and specialism have erected between the great provinces of human culture. But because they themselves are also workers and hence professionals, they are saved from the dilettante's fatal weakness of ignoring the necessary divisions of intellectual labor and function embodied in developed arts, sciences, and social institutions. In sum the mark of the classical European intellectual is impressed more deeply perhaps upon New York intellectuals than upon any other corresponding group in America: that is to say, while respecting their own distinctive talents and skills, they recognize and belong to one another as men of the mind. Hence, whatever affiliations some of them acquire with particular academic institutions, they are all in effect members of a great free university whose only rule of tenure is an enduring concern of each for the work of his fellows.

From the beginning, some of this same cosmopolitan intellectuality (not to be confused with that dreary intellectual*ism* which converts intellectuals into a self-centered social class) found its way onto the Brandeis campus. At Brandeis, accordingly, it has been generally assumed that scholarship is a natural adjunct of criticism and creation, and the entire academy belongs, temperamentally and by vocation, to the encompassing world in which, in R. P. Blackmur's fine phrase "the whole mind is engaged in the whole field of its interests." Other universities have their poets and critics, their composers and artists, "in residence." But usually they are isolated extra-curricular adornments that serve as conspicuous signs of cultivation and affluence. At Brandeis, they were accepted without fuss as teachers whose courses belong as naturally and inviolably to the curriculum as those of colleagues who represent more standard forms of higher learning. And if their "researches" result in works of creative literature or art rather than in scholarly commentaries upon the works of others, the result is rejoiced in just as it would be had they discovered a new source of physical energy. Accordingly, the humanities at Brandeis appeared to be true humanities and not mere "subjects" in which putative scientists who lack the instinct for mathematics may find their scholarly niche.

The following year, I was informed, an imposing new theatre would be opened and with it a department of theatre arts. In itself this was nothing unusual, and even Harvard had recently made diffident moves in that direction. But at Brandeis the school was from the beginning to be an integral part of the liberal arts faculty. And it was mentioned in passing merely as one of many similar evidences that within the humanities the higher learning progresses not only through deployments of the word, but also in gesture, in movement, and in action, without which the significance of the word itself is often diminished. More generally, I was impressed to find that the colleges of arts and sciences at Brandeis form a quadrivium which include, in addition to the usual science and humanities, a whole division of "creative arts." [2] The great thing was that the higher learning, in every sphere, was understood implicitly to encompass much more than men articulate (or translate) in and through forms of words. In our main academic tradition, the higher learning, over which the university serves as the presiding institution, has been a learning that fulfills itself in essentially verbal achievements even when their subject matters are nonverbal activities of men. It is as though no symbolic form belongs integrally to the liberal arts save those exemplified in some mode of discourse. But at Brandeis, this overwhelmingly verbal and literary conception of the higher learning, and hence of the higher modes of human understanding and culture, was being offset by an impressive (if illogical) emphasis upon "creative arts" that both require and contribute to forms of cognition to which linguistic expression is secondary.

Thus reinforced by nonliterary visual, auditory, and dramatic arts, the humanities may once more hold their own in an age of science and technology. The arts, including literature, draw strength from one another to the enrichment of all. This has been true in all the great ages of the past. It is even more so in our own era of unprecedented new media in which are emerging wholly new forms of expression of the utmost artistic and intellectual interest. Let me say here that I want no part of fashionable theories of the creative arts which depreciate literature. In fact the immense problems of literacy that now afflict our colleges and universities are a direct function not only of a degraded mass culture but also of the fact so many of our young people devote the greater part of their leisure time to entertainments in which the linguistic arts have a secondary role. The current tendency to apotheosize "the medium" itself is absurd. Taken literally, the dictum that "the medium is the message" is imbecilic; were it to prevail the new media themselves would become obstacles to human art and invention and hence to the liberal imagination. Art always involves a doing and a making. And while it can turn virtually anything, in context, to artistic use, including the media and the materials themselves, the latter, taken alone, revert to the status of brute "objects" to gape at, immobile, mute, and inexpressive. In another context much else would have to be said on this point. For there is a genuine danger that many young people, with their uncritical use of drugs, their passivity and their mindless receptivity, have fallen into a trap of sensationalist hedonism from which, as Jean-Paul Sartre might put it, the only exit is nothingness.

By its very nature the higher learning, no matter how broadly conceived, can offer no haven to those who do not care to acquire skills, techniques, forms of practice, and whose interests therefore offer no purchase for the work either of the creative or the critical intellect. At Brandeis as on many other campuses, some students and faculty are treating the campus as merely a great "pad." Such people are no more friends of the creative arts than they are of the sciences. Indeed they pose a far more serious problem for the contemporary university than activists whose role is to make the university more critical of its actual social and political roles in the modern world.

Furthermore the attractive stress upon creativity and contemporaneity can itself become faddist, shallow, and obsessive unless balanced by a developed historical consciousness. What impressed me was that people at Brandeis appeared to be making an extraordinary effort to bring into meaningful relation throughout

[57

the range of the higher learning an informed sense of the past with a participative awareness of contemporary life. For example, Brandeis maintains a strong department of the history of ideas which provides context and depth for philosophical, social, and political studies; there exists both a school of Near Eastern and Judaic Studies together with an institute in Israel for upper-classmen interested in Israeli history and political and social institutions; conventional language and literature departments are enriched by a center for the study of communications which, among other things, seeks to explore roles and uses of such new media as radio and television, film and the computer, in international relations, government, mass communication, and not least higher education itself; established departments of social science and psychology provide structure and background for the professional school for advanced studies in social welfare. Old and new, traditional and experimental, theoretical and practical, analytical and normative: everywhere, or so it seemed, lively minds might be put on the stretch through mutual confrontations of relevant opposites. And because Brandeis, unlike its great neighbors, is not yet an educational mastodon, it seemed possible for a philosopher as well as his students to make connections with any or all of these ventures, few of which had so hardened into official disciplines as to exclude all but full-time apprentices. Such possibilities were not to be scorned; nor had I had any impulse to scorn them. Just the contrary. For philosophy, of all forms of study, cannot survive in isolation. And when it seeks or is compelled by academic circumstances to do so, it shrivels into a scholastic ritualism of mummified "problems of philosophy" whose very point its votaries no longer dare, or think, to ask. The poverty of philosophy, upon which both Marx and Nietzsche had heaped their scorn, was not the poverty of a mode of thought, which those great anti-philosophers themselves superbly revitalized in their own times, but of academic disciplinarians who never pause to inquire what their subject-matter really is.

Here, once more, I was brought back forcibly to my own embattled profession. What were the prospects for philosophy at Brandeis, already so widely committed to the other humanities and to the blessed "creative arts?" The department already possessed some distinguished thinkers. The fact that two major deanships were occupied by professional philosophers impressed me in one way, though not in another. It meant that I would be joining a department which might play a significant role in shaping the educational fortunes of the university. Unlike Plato, however, I have never envisaged philosophers, any more than priests, as kings in their own right, and even philosopher-deans strike me as anomalies. Of all men, the philosopher must remain a free spirit, as he cannot do when he becomes a director or manager of institutions which then command his primary loyalty and concern. The example of the *idéologues* in post-revolutionary France should serve as a warning in this respect, like that of the priest or rabbi who sits too close to the throne of temporal authority and power. The astonishing prospect was that Brandeis would soon have nearly as many professional philosophers as Harvard. And since, as it appeared, deans at Brandeis are deans for a day, one could not be greatly worried about the lasting effects of academic power upon the minds of future colleagues. Nor was there reason to worry lest Brandeis might be converted into a kind of educational Republic; the dangers, plainly, were of the opposite sort: namely, that the university might remain too long in a state of nature for its own good. The great thing was that a systematic effort had been made to attract to the university men of varied philosophical styles, so that for once there might be a chance of breaking through the walls of isolation and misunderstanding which now so disastrously separate the philosophical schools from one another. What was, and is, wanted is the opportunity for sustained dialogue between technical philosophers and visionaries, between analysts and existentialists, between physicalists and dualists, and between logicians and "literary" philosophers. Moreover, I was assured that close ties would continue to exist between philosophy and the history of ideas program. Indeed, were I to come to Brandeis it was contemplated that I would have the title of Professor of Philosophy and the History of Ideas as would also the English philosopher, Stephen Toulmin who, it was hoped, would also come to Brandeis the following year.

All in all, then, the promise was a rich one, and the more I thought about it the more did it appear that going to Brandeis would not at all be a matter merely of leaving Harvard. Indeed it appeared that a philosophical rebel might play a part in this adventuresome new academy, different from the pointless adversary role to which I had been too long accustomed.

Still, I hesitated. I had heard the crack that the people at Brandeis were attempting to establish a "Jewish Princeton on the upper Charles." Were this true I wanted no part of it, partly because, as I have indicated, I had no intention of leaving Harvard for another, lesser Harvard. But it was the phrase "*Jewish* Princeton" that most disturbed me, for it suggested an assimilationist ideal that I had long since repudiated as evidence of a profoundly false consciousness, which, embarrassed by what it knows itself to be, offers itself to the putative assimilator not in humility but in humiliation. By an iron law of life the humiliated can neither trust nor be trusted, but one day, without self-knowledge, will seek revenge, not only upon the "oppressor" but upon themselves. For analogous reasons, I had become increasingly suspicious of the abstract universalism, so common among minority group exponents of "the Enlightenment," which would impose a uniform culture that would obliterate all deep-lying sources of historical self-identity among the peoples of the world. It was (I must now speak in the first-person) my own hard-won achievement as a Jew, born of a mixed marriage and none too clear about the loyalties I had thereby incurred, to believe that any authentic affirmation of one's humanity begins at home, moving out toward others in the form of a large-spirited hospitality which, in offering refuge or possible friendship to the stranger, can respect his inviolate being only if one honors one's own. In another age, however, it is problematic whether "home" would so clearly have included for me "being a Jew." For, of course, I have other basic loyalties as an intellectual, as an American, and above all, as one who has tried to make common cause with all victims of intolerance. Since the holocaust, however, these same loyalties have appeared to me inseparable from my Jewish ties, which I could serve only in and through reaffirmation of my Jewish identity.

How could this identity be certified? In my case, it was impossible to do so by participating in the life that centers around the synagogue. Nor, although I had acquired a commitment to the heroic people of Israel, could the State of Israel be for me more than a sanctuary for Jewish people, cast out from other, inhospitable lands. Life in the Diaspora was not a contingent reality but a quality of my being which I could never wish to overcome. I am a teacher and a philosopher. What was more natural, then, than the thought that my way of serving the Jewish people might be by teaching philosophy in a university established and largely maintained by American Jews who wished thereby to make a unique gift to the land of their own birth or adoption? The real question was whether in any significant sense Brandeis was, or would remain, a Jewish university. If not, then going to Brandeis, whatever else it might mean, would be for me, at least as a Jew, a quixotic act.

I confess I was not greatly interested in the facts that at Brandeis school lets out on Jewish holidays, that pork is not served in Brandeis dining halls, including the faculty club, or that those who wish to observe the dietary laws may do so. Yet, as I pondered the matter, I believed that though the future for Brandeis was clouded, it was unlikely to become in the end an ex-Jewish Princeton. This was in part because large numbers of the Brandeis community were of Jewish birth, for, as Jews everywhere have discovered in times of stress, that overwhelming fact can be a spiritual as well as a sheerly physical reality. Whether they liked it or not, their very presence seemed to ensure loyalties of which they might be as yet quite unaware. That Brandeis was formally non-sectarian and, in our characteristic American sense, secular, did not imperil such loyalties. "Secularity," in this country, is essentially a political concept, which primarily ensures religious freedom and an absence of any particular ecclesiastical domination. In this sense, all American Jews, whatever their religious attitudes, are secularists. Obviously, a university may be secular in this sense, yet not committed to irreligion nor indifferent to principles to which its original religious affiliations have hitherto committed it. To my mind, the very catalogue of educational attitudes and problems mentioned above form some considerable part of a description of the mentality associated with "the Jew." And if other peoples in the West have come to share these attitudes and problems, then this is an evidence of the degree to which our Western culture is permeated with Jewish values.

Here is not the place to engage in the indoor sport of debating the question, "What is a Jew?" My concern is not with quintessential Jewishness (if there be such a thing) but, *in part*, with qualities of being that are indispensable to the highest forms of learning and teaching to which education at Brandeis has been dedicated in principle and in promise. (Later on, I shall add to these qualities another that may have for some a more distinctive religious significance.) Can these qualities be identified in any relevant way? Let us see. To begin with, learning and teaching are, for most Jews, mixed goods: they belong to man's nature as human and so are in themselves sources of intrinsic value; to teach and to learn are delights in their own right as well as obligations whose fulfillment is an essential human virtue. But teaching and learning also, and more importantly, have ends beyond themselves. Virgil left Dante at the top of purgatory hill; if Socrates was the midwife teacher of Plato, Plato, for us at least, is the creator of Socrates; Moses abandoned his people at the verge of the promised land. The act of creation precedes the giving and teaching of the law, and the latter are themselves fulfilled in continuing creative actions. For the scientist, teaching and learning have no reality apart from research, and for the humanist, the same holds in relation to creative and critical works of the imagination. Teaching and learning are modes of being, nor can they have meaning unless something actual is already present in them.

Now this understanding of the dependence of learning, however high, upon a life both within and beyond it is inscribed in the source of all Jewish being: the *Torah* itself. And the enveloping sense of presence, the continuing concern for actuality and for the creative acts that give it substance, has always been, in my limited experience, a quality of authentic Judaism, although of course this in no way guarantees that particular individuals will share that presence merely because they happen to be born of Jewish parents. Thus I was prepared to believe not only that Brandeis was founded by Jewish grit, ingenuity, and money, but that it might also provide an academic environment in which the precious thirst to be near to the sources of one's being might be slaked. Was I a gullible romantic? If so, I could at least claim the qualities of my fault. I had learned all about realism in a hard school, and realism does not make a life. As William James asked in effect, why not be gullible, if it gives one spirit and the will to transcend the limitations of one's contingent history? It has been said that all institutions are heartless, and utilitarian liberals are all too prone to believe it. But is it true? If so, then all forms of organized human being, as most anarchists believe, are cursed. I could not, and do not, believe it. The task for us is to give them heart and in so doing to make good their promise. At Brandeis, I felt, it might be possible, partly because of the circumstances of its origins and the manner of its development, to build, as my alma mater Reed had done, a genuine sense of academic community in which students, faculty, and administration might participate. Community, however, is an integral concept for understanding the idea of peoplehood itself, so precious to Jews, especially since the holocaust.

Brandeis has never been intended as a kind of Yeshiva with a liberal-arts college attached. And few members of the Brandeis community would wish it otherwise. The presence of the three charming little chapels, one Jewish, one Protestant, and one Roman Catholic, so designed that the shadow of any one would not fall on the others, touchingly symbolizes Brandeis's readiness to welcome people of all faiths as full-fledged members of the university community. They also serve as emblems of the ineluctable particularity of all authentic religions. Whatever else might happen at Brandeis, I was sure, it would not fall into the vapid syncretism that now prevails on so many other secular campuses. The more serious danger was that Brandeis might cease by stages to have any authentic sense of religious being and would become in the end not merely a secular but a profane institution, from which would vanish all sense of the holiness of the reality which covers all human life.

One last aspect of this agonizing, and agonized, problem now requires mention. By many circuitous routes, I have come to think that the philosopher, when all his self-protective masks have been removed, is by definition a religious person for whom, in one way or another, the gods of the traditions and of the world are, or seem, dead or dying. So far may his sense of the meaninglessness of the traditional religions go that, like Nietzsche, he may actually proclaim that God himself is dead and so spend his life tongue-tied, unable to bring conventional names for divine being to his lips. Beyond this, he may be so thoroughly estranged from the traditional religions that he regards himself as an atheist or even as one who no longer has anything to do with religion. For a long time I found myself in this situation. Yet I have become aware that my predicament was nothing new to biblical religion, and gradually I have perceived that part of the fundamental religious genius of Judaism consists in its insistent assertion of the absolute transcendence of God together with its loving recognition of immanent manifestations of that being in history: in acts of creation, in the achievement of moral understanding and responsibility, in the covenants upon which community and peoplehood are based, in the self-renewing trust and hope of genuine prophecy, and, finally, in the yearning toward a world of brotherhood and peace. Cultivation of a sense of this religious genius, forever subject to fresh interpretation and application and hence requiring endless meditation and discussion, not only has an inviolable place within the very highest learning, but may indeed provide the vital center of one's continuing being. Paul Tillich, that least orthodox of Christians, once said something analogous to this at a dinner for the heads of the general education courses at Harvard. However, he made the mistake (for it was the source of much misunderstanding) of employing the word "theology" in his discussion and so was taken to mean that the divinity school should be the center of the university. Undoubtedly this was not Tillich's intention, nor is it remotely my own. The question here concerns an educational principle and an ideal, not a matter of administration. Just as most English departments are indifferent custodians of the incomparable literature of our language, and philosophy departments poor guardians of the love of wisdom, so in our time most schools of theology, whether Jewish or Gentile, are inadequately prepared for their full human vocation.

Could Brandeis find a way toward this enlivening religious understanding? More to the point, did it wish to do so? The answers to both questions were unclear. All the same, I felt that, given the auspices under which it was founded, given the attitudes I have already described toward and within the humanities and creative arts, and, finally, given its experimental approach toward most contemporary problems of higher education, there was a real chance of a much needed opening to the left in one of the most confused spheres of humane learning. If since the holocaust Jews everywhere in the Diaspora are aware, as Irving Howe has recently remarked, that ". . . blessing or curse, Jewishness was an integral part of our life," it is still true that for many, perhaps most, Jewish intellectuals and academicians, this has little, formally, to do with Judaism as a religion. But new soundings are being made and new bearings taken by men who, whatever their attitudes toward the traditional religions, including their talk of God, exhibit a sense of religious concern whose quality is authentically Jewish. Whether there was any basis at Brandeis for such an impression remained to be seen.

4

On Going to Brandeis:

ACTUALITIES

AS IT TURNED OUT, MY ARRIVAL AT BRANDEIS COINCIDED with the emerging time of troubles which has beset most American universities since the late sixties. In part, Brandeis's problems have been peculiar to itself. A new private university, no matter how thoughtfully managed, has a hard time of it nowadays. But, because of its distinctive origins, Brandeis has run into difficulties, financial and otherwise, with which other new universities are not directly faced.

Old donors, who disposed their largesse in the mistaken belief that miscellaneous philanthropy is a synonym for enlightened good will, have been rudely disabused of their illusion. Some of them have rethought the order of their philanthropies, not always to the advantage of the higher learning. Hard money follows hard interests and hard interests in America are frequently myopic. The major part of Brandeis's endowment comes from a minority religio-ethnic group which has many responsibilities to its people outside the borders of the United States. Those who fancy Brandeis to be a rich university are mistaken; it has always had a hard time making ends meet, and in recent years it goes ever more deeply into the red. Furthermore, funds now available from the foundations and from the government are a fraction of what they were in the fifties and early sixties. The financial problem in Brandeis's case has also been exacerbated by its bold and rapid program of expansion. Not only have its new science buildings, along with their expensive equipment, its enlarged facilities for the social sciences and the humanities, its magnificent new theatre, and its dormitories cost a fortune, it has no less spectacularly increased the size of its permanent faculty, paying its members salaries equal to those paid by the most affluent universities, and providing yearly across-the-board increases which the latter rarely try to match. It is indeed arguable that Brandeis's expansion has been somewhat manic. In a time of harsh retrenchments, the effect has been to increase the sense of vulnerability which every new Brandeisian feels as soon as he settles in.

This vulnerability is not the same thing as the "fragility" of the university as an institution so much discussed nowadays by those upset by the antics of student rebels who sometimes seem prepared to tear down the campus unless they have their way. Brandeis has had its share of student turmoil, undeserved as well as deserved. At least the partial burnings of two buildings make it clear that the "terror" is not confined to the old central urban universities alone. But Brandeis is also exposed in many uncommon ways. For one thing it is now trying in earnest to become a graduate university. And, as we shall see, this effort places unusual stresses on the innovative college upon which its reputation has hitherto been based. In consequence, a crisis of identity has been created of the sort resolved, whether for good or ill, at Harvard and Johns Hopkins three-quarters of a century ago. For another thing, a conflict has emerged between those who desire to establish at Brandeis a variety of professional schools in law, medicine, and business and those who believe, as I do, that until the problems of the central liberal arts university and its college are solved, such ventures will distract the university from its primary educational obligations and diminish its power to meet them. These problems, added to those created by Brandeis's often disguised but very real "Jewishness," thus make the university vulnerable in ways peculiar to itself.

But Brandeis is also involved in the wider educational, social, and political perplexities in which, willy nilly, all contemporary American universities are implicated. Every university, whether or not it acknowledges the fact, has become part of a set of enormous socio-political combinations of which it and its sister universities are now the primary educational suppliers. Nor are the services the university provides for the national society all of its own choosing. Government funds, not unnaturally, are given for services rendered. And when questions are raised within the university about the ulterior purposes of such services, correlative questions are raised outside it about the fitness of the university for governmental largesse. Accordingly, an intense controversy continues about the uses that are being made of government contracts, many of which are only marginally related to the ends of liberal education. Likewise, there has emerged a profound division within the faculty and between a large segment of the faculty and the administration over the position the university should take toward the spreading Vietnam War as well as other international and national issues that now divide our people. As elsewhere, so at Brandeis, numbers of scholars seem not to care what sort of polity exists so long as it leaves them free to get on with their researches; they are opposed to any sort of disruptive political activity on the campus, regardless of the cause. Nor do they care to examine too closely the sources of the funds that make their own investigations possible. Another group, most of whom actively support government policies abroad or at home, gladly accept governmental involvement in university activities and deplore determined opposition to it on the part either of the students or their colleagues. They don't mind, in effect, if the university is quietly politicized if only it serves what they consider to be the national interest. A third group opposes the war and the university's implicit involvement in projects which contribute to the war effort. But its members still believe that the university, as a corporate body, should not take official stands against the war. From their point of view, political activity on the campus is tolerable or even desirable, but it should be conducted by individual groups which speak only for themselves, leaving other groups to espouse opposing positions according to their lights. Finally, there is a relatively small group which believes that the war, and the military and industrial activities that make it possible, have now undermined the very conditions of liberal education. In their view, the university, as an institution, now has an obligation to condemn the war and to cut all ties which, even indirectly, have involved the university in programs contributary to it. These divisions now go so deep that, apart from other disagreements, the old-time presumption of a basic community of attitudes among teachers and scholars, not to mention students, has become exceedingly shaky.

Many other formidable problems, both internal and external, will be mentioned as we proceed. Taken together they have created a sense of uneasiness which affects us all. However, un-easiness also bespeaks an awareness of possibility and in the human sphere possibility is simply another name for freedom.

To someone like myself who newly comes to Brandeis from an ancient metropolitan university, locked into a decaying university city partly of its own making, perhaps the most powerful im-mediate impression is that of the actuality of place. Brandeis's place indeed contributes greatly, if largely unconsciously, to one's sense both of its newness and its freedom. And despite appearances freedom, at this juncture, is in increasingly short supply in the American academy.

Not every one, to be sure, views Brandeis's situation in the same way. Many of my colleagues commute *out* to Brandeis from apartments and, when they can afford them, houses in Cambridge and Boston. For them the central city is a kind of womb, dark but comforting. For students also, the virtues of a university located on the fringe of a great city remain unclear. If they come, as many of Brandeis's students do, from large urban centers on the East Coast, the psychological distance between the campus and the city center can create an acute sense of nostalgia for the buzz and hum, the variety and the novelties, which one finds without trying on the streets of Manhattan, Philadelphia, or Boston. In their eyes, as well as in those of some of their teachers, Brandeis's location sym-bolizes a provincial remoteness from the great world where, on the one side, one is aware (even if one does not continually par-ticipate in them) of exciting new movements in music, literature, and the performing arts, and on the other, of the absorbing urban conflicts which are now the daily fare of inhabitants of the central city. An interurban university such as Brandeis appears to them to exist in a cultural and social limbo: it is not close enough to the city for daily confrontations, yet it is not sufficiently removed, like Dartmouth or Williams, for the fine old country living which fosters uninterrupted contemplation and study.

What these people fail to perceive is that the relations of the suburbs to the central city have not gone unchanged in recent decades. Except for the slum dwellers who cannot escape it, the old city center and its immediate environs no longer occupies its once commanding position. What happened to Los Angeles two decades ago is occurring now in most American cities. Boston is an excellent example. No longer does one have to go "in to Boston" in order to discover what is going on. On the contrary, much of the "action," economically, socially, and intellectually, is now widely dispersed throughout the suburbs, or ex-urbs, where, not insignificantly, many of the advanced technological industries are now located. Tragically for those who, for social or racial reasons, cannot leave, American cities are now being turned inside out. Accordingly, many older urban universities which cannot change their locations have become weary, obsolete benches of desolation, overwhelmed by problems with which they are no longer able to cope.

Without question, ways must be found to change these scenes of desuetude and despair. But such changes are slow in coming and existing programs of urban renewal do not always benefit the urban university. Meanwhile, Brandeis, along with other inter-urban universities and colleges, offers a significant alternative in the new era of megalopolis. Indeed, the very term "megalopolis" implies that great cities no longer have uniquely important centers where the progressive intellectual and cultural life of the society is to be found. A few decades hence, it is entirely possible that Brandeis may be closer to the center of things, so far as metropolitan Boston is concerned, than Harvard, M.I.T., or Boston University.

In the space age, in short, centrality has become an exceedingly variable concept, as farsighted university administrators as well as city planners already realize. Sheer physical proximity, plainly, is not a breeder of community. The city must create room for its people or they will, almost literally, die of congestion and suffocation; and that holds true, in particular, of the university city. The suburbs and the suburban mentality are widely criticized by those who still live in the city. But no man can be faulted for moving to the suburbs in order to find for himself and his family a little living space, a breath of fresh air, and acceptable schools and playgrounds for his children. He can be faulted only if he turns his back on the city (as all too many suburbanites do) and regards its problems as none of his own. The same is true, even more poignantly, of academicians. They cannot survive unmutilated in isolation from the city. Nor can they survive without that modicum of quiet which is necessary, among other things, for open-ended second thoughts about the interlocking predicaments of the university and the city themselves. But serenity, like love, is not achieved by an act of will.

In education as in other spheres of cultural life, idealists often imagine that the life of the mind is independent of the physical circumstances in which it is conducted. This error is no less egregious at the university level than at that of the secondary schools where harrassed teachers and students have neither time nor energy to convert confrontations into occasions for mutual illumination. Peoples perpetually at war become warlike, whatever their motives. In consequence, the question of justification becomes an endless and hence pointless affair of recrimination and counterrecrimination. Deracination breeds deracination, and, among the deracinated, argument gives way to a nonfunctional autistic rhetoric whose real meaning, like referred pain, is merely symptomatic. In the university, those who desire most to avoid it—the scholar and the scholarly student—are themselves necessarily caught up in a maelstrom of confused political actions and reactions which are too often merely reflexive. The beleaguered university cannot avoid the mentality that afflicts all beleaguered institutions and individuals: self-pitying, they search neither for causes nor solutions but scapegoats; by rapid turns defiant and compromising, they search for peace, all the while undermining the very possibilities of peace; self-divided, they leave their faculties and students alike uncertain of their vocations and at a loss how, or whether, to relate themselves either to the university or to the larger society of which it and they are both a part. Genuine crises, when they become endemic, breed a crisis mentality which aggravates each successive crisis, leaving the victim incapable of consecutive thinking about the problematic situation at hand.

Such is the situation and such the mentality at many urban universities, where, on the one side, radical dissent becomes confused with disloyalty or even conspiracy, and on the other, where constructive minds are overwhelmed by a blind impulse to destruction or else lapse by stages into a disconsolate lethargy. At

Brandeis, my own tendencies toward deracination (and I am not atypical) have not disappeared, but they have diminished. Like many others, I have acquired a fresh sense of belonging to an educational venture valuable both in itself and as an exemplum to the whole higher learning in America. Scapegoating is no longer necessary; authority is something to be used and modified rather than blindly defied. And although, increasingly, I have had to take heretical positions in relation to those of the Brandeis establishment, I have not had the oppressive sense of being a party to a meaningless caucus or cabal.

The very openness of the place revives one's faltering sense of the openness of higher learning in America. Possibility, the human thing, is once more a reality, and each day the campus itself bears witness that frustration is not a law of nature but a problem to overcome. From my own first office in Olin-Sang, an airy building which was part of a then unfinished complex at the top of Brandeis hill, I overlooked a scene of fascinating and exuberant diversity. And as I huffed and puffed my way up the walks, past all the new buildings, I recalled, with a wry sense of pleasure, the *Boston Globe's* not unfriendly description of the Brandeis campus as an "academic Disneyland." The noise from the new construction was (and still is) deafening: in fact, Brandeis resembles nothing so much as a frontier town, and the view from the west and south of rolling New England hills lends a deceptive impression of a city being carved out of the wilderness by ingenious and energetic men, sufficiently remote from Boston (actually only five miles away) to ensure its freedom to go its own way. Wags have referred to all this hullaballoo as a manifestation of President Sachar's "edifice complex." Not every building, certainly, is a joy to behold or live in; some, especially the first ones built, were done cheaply and are already obsolete. And it is obvious that many things are needed besides more new buildings. All the same, as I more clearly realized after returning from a prolonged visit to the University of Michigan, where even distinguished professors share dingy offices with colleagues not of their choosing and lecture in halls that are too often antiquated, airless, and dirty, Brandeis on its breezy hill presents a very agreeable contrast to the ordinary university campus in America.

Like most outlying cities around Boston, Waltham is, as they say, a "mixed bag." Originally an old mill and market town, with rows upon rows of two- and three-deck multiple houses, many of them gradually falling into disrepair, Waltham is also a main center of the new industries which have given metropolitan Boston another economic lease on life. And the parts of Waltham surrounding Brandeis present a respectable contrast to most of Cambridge whose greatest slum, which stretches between Harvard and M.I.T., is a horror unsurpassed by any to be seen in Charlestown or Dorchester. The enveloping grime and smog is less dense in Waltham than it is down the river. So long, in fact, had I become accustomed to the squalor of Cambridge that I simply took it for granted that no alternative existed to the self-perpetuating academic ghettos in which most urban universities are situated.

Let me repeat: the new existence of a Brandeis does not solve for it the problems that beset a Harvard or a Columbia. But it at least presents an alternative which enables us reasonably to raise the question whether, as it stands, the old urban university is any longer a viable institution.

This question is by no means academic. The juxtaposition of Harvard-M.I.T. richness and Cambridge-Boston wretchedness is in some degree responsible for the mounting hysteria and violence which beset those institutions. And, by analogy, the same holds of other expanding universities which, however well-to-do, cannot create environments conducive to reflection and study without exacerbating the agonies of urban renewal. Planners at Harvard tell us, not unjustly, that even the richest universities cannot solve *their* own problems, for all the fact that they are in some degree self-created, with their own limited resources. Their duty, so it is argued, cannot be in the first instance to renew the city; their task is to make possible the research and to supply the housing that will provide their own teachers and students with the living conditions indispensable to the work of the scholar. Too often, however, such living space cannot be provided except at the expense of those unfortunates who happen to live in the vicinity of the expanding university. In short, the predicament of the urban university is a function of the predicament of the central city itself, which cannot, without immense outlays of money and far more imaginative planning than now exist, provide tolerable conditions of work and life for all its inhabitants.

[73

But if Brandeis is to offer a serious alternative to its sister universities, the boldness of Abram Sachar must now be emulated in different ways which make full use of the largely temporary advantages which its situation makes possible. It must not give in to the temptation, to which many of its conservative trustees, administrators, and faculty members are liable: that is, to establish a fringe Harvard. Brandeis must resolutely go its own way, both educationally and administratively. It must accept its vulnerability, not as a liability to be overcome by finding a secure position within the academic establishment, but as a chance for challenging the establishment. In sum the advantages of a new place mean little unless they are recognized as a source of useable freedom, for an advantageous location remains merely another abstract entity unless we recognize and treat it—as our own imaginative forefathers treated the location of the New World itself—as an educational principle: that is, an opportunity for experiments in living and hence of learning, from which the "old world" of the graduate city university may itself discover something about the nature and conditions of contemporary higher education. Make no mistake. The new world has had to learn that, however wide and rich its frontiers, it cannot escape the problems and responsibilities of the old world. Similarly, no university like Brandeis can start absolutely from scratch. Its possibilities are limited in large part by the "old world" character of its trustees, its administration, and its faculties. We all come to Brandeis with archaic preconceptions. Accordingly, we too are imitative, apologetic, and, in the wrong way, defensive. Brandeis must recognize that it cannot survive without disfigurement if the Harvards and Columbias go down. But it also cannot survive to any purpose if it weds itself to the educational practices which currently prevail in those universities.

It is time to turn to other no less exigent actualities of which the newcomer to Brandeis is soon made aware. These actualities also create the distinctive possibilities which make the idea of Brandeis so appealing. But they are also sources of liability and perplexity which increase one's sense of the university's immense vulnerability.

To begin with, Brandeis is one of the few distinguished private universities to have emerged since the Second World War. Like all its sister institutions, it depends upon continuing public support, both from the government and the foundations, which for various reasons has been radically curtailed in recent years. Available public money goes increasingly to universities which are not only well-established but amenable to the governmental and social conditions which acceptance of such money presupposes. Thus, Brandeis is subject to all the pressures, implicit as well as explicit, to conform to the practices and attitudes congenial to the nation-state and its supporting institutions. All the same, because it is private, it is not yet directly subject to the political controls to which state and municipal universities are continually subject. Hence it can, *if it will*, say "No!" to super-patriotic legislatures, governors, and commissioners of education when they institute their periodic purges of intellectual and educational deviants who have opposing views concerning the well-being of our people.

But Brandeis is not merely private; it is also young. This is a great advantage. Its relations to government and industry are still fluid. Its power to control, and hence to change, them is correspondingly great. At Harvard and Columbia, not to mention M.I.T., despite their wealth or more probably because of it, it has become exceedingly difficult for administrators and faculties to disengage themselves from services to the national society which are morally and educationally corrupting and which, for that reason, are direct causes of the disaffection and turmoil with which these universities have recently been afflicted. Brandeis has little to lose and much to gain from repudiating these services, which in her case are still marginal. Hence Brandeis is still free to establish a position of exemplary independence which older private universities, scarcely less than their public counterparts, find it increasingly difficult to sustain.

Brandeis's newness as well as its youthful temperament contribute greatly to its internal freedom. In my encounters with students and colleagues, with departmental chairmen and deans, not to mention presidents, I have learned at Brandeis something about academic institutions which was obscured during my tenure at Harvard, where the hierarchy has been largely accepted, until very recently, as a matter of inviolable fact. Well do I remember a remark of President Conant at a Harvard faculty meeting to the effect that, although he was formally at liberty to dismiss the entire faculty, if he were to do so in a moment of madness, he would be out of a job before nightfall. His point of course was that the freedom of Harvard's president is restricted in the ordinary course in a thousand ways by a complex and dissociated bureaucracy whose ways he might deplore but which he could not radically oppose save at immense cost to his own prestige. At Harvard, as at other great universities where I have taught, bureaucracy, though it helps to protect the freedom of the ordinary professor, radically limits possibilities for rapid, necessary institutional change. At Brandeis, the situation is just the reverse. In fact, during the ascendancy of President Sachar, the university was commonly regarded as an academic patriarchy. Such a regime has many bad aspects, especially in an age when even in ordinary families life with father is intolerable to everyone. In matters of preferment, presidential caprice has been a source of justifiable irritation and, on occasion, outrage. Up one day and down the next—not only deans and professors, but whole departments, remain uncertain of their prerogatives. They may propose, but the old man disposes. As I soon discovered, faculty committees, appointed at the drop of a hat, come up with fruitful and occasionally exciting recommendations for changes in educational policy only to find themselves complimented for their industry and then sent on their ways to brood upon their impotence. All the same, the absence of a large and entrenched bureaucracy has its advantages. Overnight new area studies and graduate programs are established. Lines of communication are easily established, and desirable appointments can be made, and programs of study modified with a minimum of red tape. Flexibility in dealings with students, including student protesters, is likewise great, and more than one imminent bust has been prevented because the president, aware of what goes on, is on the spot to hear and redress grievances, real as well as imaginary. In consequence an easy, if sometimes embarrassing, informality exists in relations between the president and his "family" which, to an old Harvard hand, seems both astonishing and engaging. Ghastly family rows are all too common, but they tend to remain within the family. And God knows what can't be done when the wind from the Presidential Enclave is in the right quarter.

Times are changing and with the departure of the old president, as we shall see, Brandeis's patriarchal structure is changing with them. Both faculty and student participation in the determination of academic policies increases every year. The effects of these changes still remain to be seen. In a period of radical retrenchment many unforseen conflicts of interest as well as of policy will occur. Yet Brandeis is young and resilient. And because it has been of necessity continually improvisatory in the conduct of its affairs, Brandeis has taught me a great lesson: Institutions, educational and otherwise, are not merely systems of practices but also organizations and congregations of men who can, when they will, radically alter the most venerable rules in order to meet changing human needs. No institution is a thing governed by immutable laws of nature: it only appears so for want of resolute, organized, and continual opposition. Dissent is the mother of opposition, and opposition, the condition of innovation. And of all forms of social organization, patriarchies, unencumbered by attendent bureaucracies, are most vulnerable to radical opposition.

More generally, because all institutions are systems of human activity, they belong not only to the domain of necessity but also of freedom. And even their necessities, which are combinations of customary authority, social and economic power, and the indifference bred by unchallenged authority, are at most historical necessities which courageous and determined men, acting in concert, can break. Universities, like other institutions, tend to regard themselves in times of adversity as mere victims. But none are victims unless they accept the role. If they refuse the victim's role, who knows, they may change the world. Refusal is a great strength. This is a lesson which the Jews, themselves victims of the most unspeakable necessities imposed upon any people throughout the ages, have always known.

But herein lies a fact related to another dimension of Brandeis's actuality and which is part of its youthful resiliency and strength. Brandeis is a private university; but it is private in a special way. By its very existence, it represents the power of a minority group, no longer merely defensive, to contribute in its own way something of unique value to the majority culture, which the latter refuses at its peril. At Brandeis, American Jewry has brought into being a university of high, conceivably of highest, quality. From the beginning, however, Brandeis has been a laical institution, established and largely maintained by Jews, not for themselves alone but for all people, poor and rich, black and white, foreign and domestic, Gentile as well as Jewish. In the contemporary American way, it is a completely secular institution, no less so, certainly, than Princeton or Brown or Harvard. Yet, as I have found, Brandeis differs essentially from the latter universities, even in its misbegotten efforts to emulate them. For it is, and remains, the creation of men and women who, however much they may desire to be assimilated into the majority culture, know, as well as the blacks, that assimilation for minorities is a one-way street which leaves them, and therefore the majority, correspondingly impoverished. By no means does every member of the Brandeis faculty and administration realize this even now. Their notion of academic freedom, cultural and educational, is the freedom that would accrue to Brandeis were it to become a Harvard manqué. The students, on the whole, know better. And the recent incursions of "unassimilable" black students have taught them the values, to themselves as well as to the university and the larger society, of clinging to the distinctive virtues and aspirations of the culture which they represent.

The point is worth developing. Just as whites cannot fully appreciate *how* white is the American establishment, so Christians, including ex-Christians and post-Christians, cannot altogether understand how pervasively Christian our American culture continues to be. The Jew, like the black, remains in some degree an outsider in his own country, no matter how passionately he yearns to become "one of us." Even a fully post-Christian society, like a fully post-white society, would still be one in which the Jew, like the black, is merely tolerated. Now, toleration is an essential liberal virtue. But, educationally, it represents at best a point of departure, not an end. From a spiritual point of view, that end has two aspects: on the one side, self-knowledge and self-fulfillment; on the other, knowledge of and, ideally, union with one's "other." The post-Jew himself is still a post-*Jew*, just as the post-Christian is a post-*Christian*. He needs to understand, in positive as well as in negative ways, what makes him "different." And he needs to understand this, not for his own sake only, but for the sake of his Christian and post-Christian friends. For they also, whether they know it or not, are different and cannot fulfill themselves as human individuals unless they come, by stages, to comprehend what it means to be a Jew.

This matter has still another aspect. The philosophers of the Age of Reason sometimes envisaged a "heavenly city," as Carl Becker used to call it, in which all religions, all sects and nationalities, all parties would disappear. In that city, no man would have a distinctive point of view and all men would be united, naturally and instinctively, by the universal principles of liberty, equality, justice, and fraternity. What the *philosophes* failed to perceive, however, is that such a heavenly city itself represents nothing more than an attenuated secular version of the ideals of Catholic Christianity itself. When one looks at it from the outside, it appears all too plainly as a point of view, an ideology, which, like so many others, was an ideology to end all other ideologies. Now, as I believe, there is nothing wrong with an ideology or "point of view" as such; on the contrary, every cohesive social group has an ideology and every coherent individual life represents a point of view. The danger lies in the assumption that such an ideology or point of view, being universal, is no longer in need of radical critique. And this danger is intensified exponentially when that ideology becomes dominant, and hence repressive in any social system or culture.

Ideally, of course, we would all like to believe that "the system" we represent is self-corrective as well as self-protecting, and most of the great ideologies, Christian and Jewish, liberal and socialist, have been assumed by their votaries to be so. But historically and concretely we know, or should know, that self-correction, especially in matters of principle, rarely comes from the inside. The great value of minority or, which comes to the same thing, deviant cultures is that they serve as prods to self-correction and self-development to the wider societies of which they remain an unassimilated part. They cannot serve this role, however, without corresponding institutions of higher learning, in which the historical bases and ideal meanings of the minority culture can be explored in depth by its own representives. Thus, as I have begun to see, it is esssential in a predominantly nonCatholic society such as the United States, that there should be vigorous, self-critical Catholic universities, and why, in a secular society, such as ours, there should be universities that represent an arduous religious point of view toward our contemporary human existence and culture. My criticism of the ordinary state university is that it is so skittish about the appointment and encouragement of professors who are not secularists and who are willing to defend in depth religious perspectives which are inconsistent with secularism, just as my criticism of Catholic universities is not that they are dogmatic, but that they have not made sufficient provision for sustained critique of their own dogmas.

Heresy is the condition of all spiritual growth. And minority groups, in relation to the dominant culture, are by definition heretical. The danger is that the minority group, lacking colleges and universities of its own, fails to grasp the full meaning of its heresy. The counterdanger is that, even when it has such institutions, they will lapse into an ingrown sectarianism incapable of conveying its message to the wider society of educable men.

In a double sense Brandeis undoubtedly represents a cultural and spiritual heresy in America. Brandeis remains a Jewish university in a predominantly Christian and post-Christian society, and it represents, at least residually, a religious aspiration in a predominantly secularist system of higher education. The trouble, in our case, is that the heresy seems so shallow, so covert, so apologetic. This is why Brandeis has much to learn from its own black students. No one learns anything from the mere fact that Brandeis does not hold "academic exercises" on Jewish high holidays. This is a mere academic oddity, and the holiday observance seems no less hypocritical to the devout and understanding Jew than the pre-Christmas pleasantries in the Harvard houses must seem to serious Christians. Rituals and ceremonies have their human uses. But in institutions of higher learning, they do so only when supported and illuminated by studies in depth of the cultural life without which they lose all vestige of religious meaning.

When I first came to Brandeis the support given by the administration to arcane Judaic studies seemed to me merely an academic eccentricity, defensible mainly on economic grounds. No doubt many of my colleagues, as well as our students, still consider them so. I was wrong, and they are wrong. For such studies, in a secular age and in an emulsified post-Christian culture, can give meaning and vitality to the perspectives of a minority group whose religio-cultural heritage is of immense value to the entire society. Not only do they provide an educational link between the university and the people who support it, of importance to both; they also give depth to a vision of human culture and well-being which keeps alive nonconformist ideals of civility, justice, and, above all, holiness, for lack of which our leveling American society and polity is continually impoverished.

Theological and cultural heterodoxy is never an end in itself. At best it serves to reinforce other liberalizing efforts which give sustaining power to new adventures in educational and human practice. Brandeis's Jewishness, such as it is, remains marginal and idiosyncratic, without educational significance either to the Gentiles or to the Jewish people unless it represents a moving perspective upon human life as a whole from which Jew and Gentile alike can learn. Pursued in depth, it becomes a source of liberation both to its own faculty and student body, whatever their racial or cultural origins, and an example to other universities regardless of their dominant cultural orientation.

The point is a delicate one. Nor is it easy to make it in a way that will be satisfactory either to my own colleagues and students or to their counterparts elsewhere. Brandeis should be open to all comers and its faculty should remain free from all inviolate theological commitments. Its "genius," which is the genius of the Jewish people in America, entails cosmopolitanism and encouragement of the diversity of cultural and religious attitudes. Nonetheless I am convinced that Brandeis's own form of cosmopolitanism, from which all of us have much to learn, would degenerate into a mere garden variety conformism were it not for the circumambient presence of a minority group outlook of which, to employ Matthew Arnold's term, "Hebraism" is the spiritual center. "Hellenism" (or rationalism), if I may continue the analogy, is now the predominant educational philosophy of our private as well as our public institutions of higher learning. An alternative is wanted which, while in no sense irrationalist, keeps alive educational values which are otiose to the pure rationalist whether Gentile or Jew. Brandeis, as I conceive it, is uniquely qualified to represent that alternative, and this for the reason that Judaism, in its historical as well as in its theological heart of hearts, embodies the spirit of an intransigent minority and hence dissident culture which at the same time is passionately opposed to any and all forms of spiritual idolatry. No other religion, as I have come to think, preserves the values of particularism and universalism and of immanentism and transcendentalism in such a marvellous tension as Judaism. Correspondingly, few universities are as apt as Brandeis both to represent and to interpret this spirit in the domain of higher education.

But here for the present I must let the matter rest. One final point, related to those already mentioned, remains to be remarked. By comparison with the other major private universities, Brandeis remains small. Within a year or so, all but the most retiring professors come to know many colleagues outside their own discipline and exchanges of ideas between them, although frequently harsh, are usually companionable. Similarly, relations between members of the faculty and the administration, although often acrimonious, at least exist, which is too rarely the case at large universities, private as well as public. More important, classes even in elementary courses are small and the faculty–student ratio (one to eight) is very low. This makes possible informal classroom discussions which, particularly in the humanities, are of far greater educational significance than I realized during my Harvard years. As will be explained in a later chapter, a large part of what is learned in the domains of the arts, literature, and philosophy, depends not only on formal explanations, but on ways of *showing* the student, by processes of question and answer, by the use of exemplary comparisons, by the employment of irony and other figurative modes of discourse, by style and gesture and even the very being of the compelling teacher. Much of this power to bring the student into the presence of the work of art, the poem or novel, or the philosophical problem is lost in the great lecture hall where showing too commonly degenerates into mere showmanship and unanswerable rhetoric. But in the small classroom, where communion between teacher and student may be established, these dangers gradually disappear as both student and teacher become absorbed in the imaginative effort to perceive what is really there.

These actualities connote freedom, and a new freedom, intellectually and spiritually, is most desperately wanted throughout the higher learning in America. Existing patterns of academic organization have become obsolete, and new structural principles are required in order to realize the educational possibilities now present in our universities and colleges. Above all the quality of life within the university, which, for many, has become so meagre, must be radically improved, so that learning will once more be understood as a good in its own right. Thus instead of being merely a point of departure or a vehicle of passage to other and better things, as it now appears to all too many students and faculty members alike, the university must be a place of habitation where some of the basic modes of consummatory life, natural to human beings, are fully enjoyed. In other words, existence in the university must be made to represent a principle of endowed being as well as of abstract becoming. At Brandeis, an immense residual power exists for exemplary change in higher education. But that power is at present only fitfully exercised.

The truth is that since 1965, when I came to Brandeis, the university has been ridden with crises, most important of which has been a complex crisis of identity.

From the beginning Brandeis was conceived by its founders as a university. Yet until the early sixties its reputation was based upon its distinction as a first-rate liberal arts college.

In recent years, however, Brandeis has become a university in earnest. The graduate school has proliferated and the prestige of the various departments and schools has become increasingly associated with their ability to establish graduate programs and to attract graduate students of high caliber. This has had the natural effect of converting the College at Brandeis into a conventional university college. This change has produced many strains. For one thing, influxes of research-oriented professors, many of them uninterested in undergraduate instruction, have been brought in at high salaries and occasionally with special prerogatives not enjoyed by their colleagues. Accordingly, older members of the faculty have been obliged to reconsider their own priorities, and the result, for the students, is a new distance and inaccessability on the part of their teachers. They were used to an open door policy; now the door is frequently closed except during office hours. The old informality is diminishing. Departments, now obliged to turn out accomplished preprofessional majors able to compete for preferment with their counterparts at Columbia and Princeton, now become reluctant to sponsor students whose programs of study cut widely across departmental lines. Within the humanities, the arts, and the social sciences, the emphasis on formal scholarship has the effect of reducing the prestige of the freewheeling intellectual, the critic, and the creative writer and artist. As at other universities, the higher learning at Brandeis is increasingly oriented towards scientific and parascientific inquiry. Forms of knowledge which cannot, nor are meant to, meet the tests employed in the more "exact" sciences, have come under severe criticism. Nor is any sustained countercriticism available.

All the same, the liberal pull of the College remains strong. Nor is the competition for financial and other forms of support between the University and the College entirely one-sided. During his brief tenure, President Abram insisted that more attention be given by the faculty to the mission of teaching, including the informal teaching that goes on outside the class room in the professor's study, at the luncheon table, and in informal discussion groups outside the precincts of the academic department. To many research professors, such demands were, and are, intolerable. They object, understandably, to what is in effect an increased teaching load which diminishes their time for independent study. Similarly, "teaching" professors, who have been obliged to return to their studies and laboratories, find themselves overloaded in both directions with new responsibilities which they simply cannot meet. Departments which are University-oriented complain bitterly when funds are rediverted into activities of primary interest to the College. What becomes of a graduate school which cannot provide a developing program of graduate seminars, which cannot increase the number and value of its graduate fellowships, and which is unable, or unwilling, to add new professorships for advanced study that would enable Brandeis to compete more successfully with other "knowledge factories" for first-rate graduate students for whom the interests and problems of the college mean little?

Other academic tugs-of-war have also become more intense. The pull of the University, in practice, is to reinforce the power and prestige of the departments and the presumptive discipline they represent. Accordingly, it becomes increasingly difficult for interdepartmental appointments to be made which, however valuable educationally, contribute little to the formal strength of the departments involved. Accordingly numbers of teachers who have secured a place within the College, owing to the unspecialized diversity of their talents and interests, are finding it difficult to acquire tenure or, having acquired it, to secure preferment as professors, since their departmental interests and loyalties are marginal. Exponents of the College are not without resources for defence, however. For one thing, there is a strong movement, originating within the College, to extend the principles and ideals of liberal education not merely beyond the earlier stages of collegiate study but to postgraduate education as well. Not only within the faculty but also within the administration, the effort to offset, or overcome, the counterliberal evils of scientism, specialism, and professionalism has many supporters. This effort, let me add, is gaining strength not only among undergraduates but also among graduate students who themselves realize how impoverished are graduate studies when directed exclusively to vocational and professional ends. It gains strength also among many junior faculty members who are closer to the students than most of their senior colleagues. And by "closer" here, I mean not only that they naturally see more of their students than their elders but also that they share the students' sense of the inadequacies of a university as well as a college experience which leaves the would-be educated person to fend for himself. Aware of the enormous pressures exerted by the demand for professional expertise and by the competitiveness which accompanies that demand, many younger faculty members begin to wonder whether an academic career is worth the candle if the conditions of life as well as preferment within the academy are in practice so little different from those that now prevail in business and industry.

A recent example of this situation is illuminating. During the past year, a concerted effort was made to reorganize the Educational Policy Committee which, at Brandeis, has hitherto been at once unwieldly, unrepresentative, and weak. Formally, this effort has been successful. By an overwhelming vote of the faculty and with strong support from the administration, a new committee was established in the winter of 1969 which reduced the size of the committee and provided both for a number of elected members from the faculty and the student body. Unfortunately, the committee's mandate remains unclear. Within the committee, a large majority initially construed this mandate broadly and in so doing was supported by President Abram in what, as it turned out, was virtually his last educational action as president. The interpretation of the mandate was as follows: the new Educational Policy Committee was to be regarded as the central academic agency, subject to faculty approval on crucial issues, for educational planning and review for the whole university. This meant that new proposals originating in the office of the President to establish new departments and professional schools were to be submitted to the committee for examination and approval. It implied also that questions of policy initiated by the Graduate School should not be settled exclusively by the Graduate Dean and his Council without consultation with the Educational Policy Committee, since in important cases such policies plainly have educational implications for the College and hence for the University as a whole. This implication was also supported by Mr. Abram. However, when the committee sought confirmation of this broad conception of its mandate from the faculty, an uproar ensued, not only (as was expected) in the Graduate School office but also in a number of departments, particularly in the sciences. The age-old conflict—or supposed conflict—between the liberal interest of collegiate education and the professional interests of graduate instruction and advanced research broke out once more with renewed intensity. Efforts on the part of members of the committee to explain that, in a rational university, the educational policies of the graduate school and of the college cannot be decided independently had no effect whatever. In a word, there remains at Brandeis, as elsewhere, little chance in the near future of a unified educational policy acknowledging both the indisputable claims of specialized inquiry at all levels of higher education and the necessity at every stage for an inclusive human education, aimed at the liberation and enlightenment of the whole mind of all students and faculty members alike.

Brandeis is thus caught, predictably but disappointingly, in the same intolerable bind which besets virtually all graduate universities in America. This is a great pity, since it precludes a meaningful educational dialogue between the "specialists" and the "generalists." In the modern age the liberal arts college which ignores the claims of advanced professional studies has become increasingly an institution for cultivated mandarins. But these same claims in their turn are destroying the university as the central institution for unified higher education. Existing programs of general education, at Brandeis as elsewhere, are wholly inadequate to their purposes. Least of all do they meet the universal need for *educated* specialists and professionals who can relate their own work to the overwhelming problems of men in the modern age. Unquestionably a year of summary general studies, with no follow-through, leaves the ordinary graduating senior, not to mention the promising Ph.D. (and hence the promising young professor), with little more than vestigial memories of the idea of an educated man. What is wanted instead is a continuing dialectic between what *should* be the "two cultures" of the profession or vocation and the fully human person. As matters stand, however, such a dialectic rarely leaves the committee room.

Closely related to the diminished dialogue between exponents of these two cultures is the narrowing spectrum of ideological attitudes at least within the senior faculty and the administration. As it happens, I arrived at Brandeis at the same time that Herbert Marcuse retired from the university. Obviously Marcuse had been a controversial figure at Brandeis, admired or at least seriously listened to by his own students, and opposed by a number of influential colleagues who wept no tears when he was not retained on a year-to-year basis after the date of his statutory retirement. At that time, it should be emphasized, Marcuse had not yet emerged as a cultural hero of the New Left, and his special form of Marxist, or post-Marxist, radicalism posed no immediate threat to the conservative centrists on the faculty. At most, he represented an articulate, learned, and cultivated alternative, or antithesis, to pragmatic anti-ideological liberalism which increasingly prevails in the higher echelons of the university.

Now, I have never been a great admirer of Marcuse's writings. His most original and interesting book, in my view, is *Eros and Civilization*. His books on Hegel and Marx, although learned, are turgid and, for me, less illuminating than many other more recent works on these subjects, and his latest book, *One Dimensional Man*, strikes me as both simplistic and philosophically retrograde. His attack on linguistic philosophy is both ill-informed and stupid, for he fails utterly to understand the great advances which linguistic philosophers in our time have made toward differential understanding of the major forms of human thought and of life. Accordingly he is incapable of apprehending the uses of the analysis of linguistic as well as other symbolic forms in removing deep-seated conceptual misunderstandings which everywhere result in correlative confusions in the practices of ordinary life. Indeed, Marcuse seems oblivious to the historical continuities between the inquiries of the linguistic philosophers and the successive critiques of reason initiated by the great German philosophers whom he himself admires. However, these and other philosophical reservations do not gainsay the fact that Marcuse's departure left a large hole in the ranks of the senior faculty which has not been filled.

The functional result has been to widen the gap between student and young faculty radicals and their more conservative and frequently uncomprehending elders, both on the faculty and in the administration. The educational consequences of this mutual alienation are calamitous, for the assumption on both sides is that nothing is to be learned from the adversary. The adversary now becomes increasingly, a *mere* adversary, an alien, hostile, and inscrutable thing, which can be "objectively" analyzed and perhaps manipulated but never accepted as a fully human "other" or "alter ego." In short, there is at present not only little meeting of minds between egos and alter egos but no active movement of thought between them. The consequence is not an ideologically varied university but merely a bifurcated one. And bifurcation, among men, means an incapacity for discourse and hence for mutual educational relationships. Formal education of course continues at Brandeis as elsewhere, but its range, especially in domains whose concerns are normative, has been constricted. Students on the middle left, including in particular black students, ask themselves what is the point of debate when their remarks fall upon uncomprehending ears; dissident junior faculty members, concerned not unnaturally with complex problems of preferment, increasingly keep their deeper thoughts about the society and the university to themselves or else express them only in those parts of the shadow university where they will receive a sympathetic hearing. And members of the old guard merely reinforce their own preestablished ideological commitments. This is a pity. For in matters of ideology, as the cold war has taught us (if it has taught us nothing else), education is impossible when adversaries avoid genuine controversy and merely confront one another with endless countereducational recriminations.

In another way, the intellectuals at Brandeis who, as I have already remarked, have given the university its own panache and distinction, feel, with some justification, increasingly isolated from the rest of the academic intelligentsia. For them, the old European cosmopolitanism is threatened by a new highly-skilled but essentially unreflective and uncultivated scientistic and technologically-oriented provincialism. They want to talk and write about literature as well as its history; they want to discuss works of art, not merely the subject matters which provide the source materials of art; they want to examine the religions of the world as varieties of religious experience rather than as historico-social phenomena. And the continuing supplanting within the university, conceived as an educational world of political thought by supposedly "neutral" sociological analysis, deprives the intellectual of one of his traditional reasons for being. Accordingly, the loyalty of Brandeis's intellectuals has been attenuated, and numbers of them have already moved elsewhere.

The result is in part a gradual erosion of *cultural* radicalism within the permanent and semi-permanent cadres of the faculty who take for granted the priorities of the graduate university. On the whole, then, Brandeis has become more conventional as a university and thus more ordinary. Hence the reasons for coming to, or remaining at, Brandeis discussed in the preceding chapter, are now less compelling than they once were. And this is unfortunate, not for Brandeis alone, but for the whole higher learning in America which so desperately needs real alternatives to the standard versions of the graduate university. Indeed, if the truth be said it became a question during the last years of the sixties, whether Brandeis may not actually be falling behind Harvard and California as an innovative force in higher education.

Another crisis, or series of crises, at Brandeis has followed the first changing of the presidential guard. The fact is worthy of extended comment. At many universities, where the president is a distant figure unknown to most of his faculty and to virtually all of the student body, such a possibility would until very lately have seemed remote. In ordinary times the president of Harvard or Columbia exerts his power gradually and indirectly, and whether he exerts it wisely or foolishly is usually realized long after the fact. So true is this that many academicians have the impression, which recent events have shown to be radically mistaken, that in practice actual presidential power within the academy is not very great and that it makes little practical difference who occupies that office. At Brandeis, only the most indifferent or self-absorbed professor could fall into such an error. Abram Sachar, let it be said, may well have been the last of a vanishing breed of "great" university presidents in America. Admired by some, loved by few, "Dr. Sachar" (I have never heard a member of the faculty address him by his first name, a remarkable achievement in itself in this country) was ignored by no one. His faults and his limitations, like those of Ben Gurion (of whom he somewhat reminds me) are in part functions of immense resources of imagination, energy, and determination without which, it is scarcely too much to say, Brandeis would not exist. But by 1967 his founding work was done, and not least among his gifts to the university was his acknowledgment of the need for a change of venue which would inevitably be accompanied by modifications in Brandeis's whole administrative structure.

One thing at any rate is certain: the patriarchy has come to an end, even though not every member of the Brandeis board of trustees as yet fully appreciates or accepts the fact. Academic authority must now be dispersed and regularized, and a meaningful form of representative government must be created, supported by a governing board, which is no longer remote from the educational work and life of the institution. Provision must be made not merely for rotations but also for reversals of roles. Such changes in fact are beginning. The problem is to make those upon whose beneficence Brandeis depends understand their necessity and, if possible, to rejoice in the fact. Philanthropy, though essential, is never enough. Love and trust are functions of community, and community exists only where there is participation and hence shared responsibility.

Brandeis's second president, Morris B. Abram, very wisely did not try to fill his predecessor's shoes. His was a different task in what amounts to virtually a new epoch in the history of the

American, and more particularly, the private university. My own initial impression (which I confess is now somewhat clouded owing to the astonishing manner of his resignation after merely three semesters in office) was that the trustees had chosen well. The one deep reservation in my mind concerned the question of whether one who had not lived and worked in the university could quickly acquire the kind of loyalty, patience, and insight so desperately needed in its time of troubles. For the rest, I was prepared to believe that Mr. Abram's lawyer's instinct for order and due process, together with his civil libertarian's respect for human rights, his articulateness, and his evident desire to share his problems as an administrator with other members of the academy, would stand both him and the university in good stead. From the outset, it was clear that he meant to be his own man. Many of us thought that Mr. Abram's strength would be that of an administrator aware that his virtues, so far as the internal governance of the university is concerned, must be primarily those of a negotiator, conciliator, and, when necessary, just arbiter; educational initiatives, henceforth, would have to come increasingly from the faculty and the students.

As it turned out President Abram came to Brandeis with limitations which, as matters now stand, have proved well-nigh disastrous. The ways of the academy, even by one who is well-disposed, cannot be learned in a day. The outsider who comes to the university is likely to be caught on the horns of a series of dilemmas. On the one side, if he is a liberal, as Mr. Abram appeared to be, he is likely to be sympathetic to student demands for better and more dedicated teaching, better housing facilities and food, a less improverished cultural life. On the other side, he is faced with strong institutional priorities and vested academic interests within the faculty which are heavily weighted in the direction of research and hence of new academic appointments aimed primarily at strengthening its facilities for graduate study. He may perceive the need for structural changes in the university's administrative organization to increase student participation and faculty power. But, because his own authority derives from a board of trustees, many of whom know little about the existing situation on the university campus, he can scarcely press openly for a reduction of his authority or of their largely self-perpetuating power. He may wish to implement desirable innovations. But, for want of a developed philosophy of higher education, he is bound to be impressed by the contention of other professionals that the great task is to increase the number of professional schools and, even at the expense of the existing academy, to seek new funds for their maintenance. This impulse is intensified, in Mr. Abram's own words, by the fund-raiser's effort to increase the university's "luminosity." And luminosity, as the examples of Harvard and Berkeley make clear, is most easily brought about by appointing star professors, establishing prestigious institutes for advanced study, and founding expensive schools of law, medicine, or business, too often marginally related to the work of the central university. In sum, he has to cater, whether he likes it or not, to existing images of the "great" university.

Thus the brief period of President Abram's administration was not one of searching educational reappraisal and reconstruction at Brandeis; on the contrary it was a time of nonfunctional rhetoric and facile compromises. In the pinch the idealist too often gave way to the politician, the man of business and of affairs. Not unnaturally, those who hoped for an educational new day at Brandeis have begun to wonder whether more can be done than to shore up the ruins of the old days.

To be fair, a large part of the problem is *money*, which in the middle of a disastrous war abroad, is in increasingly short supply in all universities. And this financial crisis, to which the private universities are particularly vulnerable, has proved a near catastrophe for Brandeis. For the private funds, upon which Brandeis has always largely depended, come mainly from one ethnic group which in recent years has been burdened with heavy obligations, economic as well as moral, to the State of Israel whose very existence may well be in jeopardy.

Neither the Brandeis faculty nor its student body, it should be added, has begrudged this diversion of a largesse of which they were formerly principal beneficiaries. This fact became immediately evident at the onset of the so-called Six Day War when we were informed by President Sachar that during the period of the emergency all new construction would be stopped, all salaries frozen, and other economies instituted that would enable funds to be freed for Israel's support. Nor did I hear a murmur of dissent. On the contrary, when faculty members were invited to make appropriate contributions of their own, the response, among Gentile as well as Jewish members, was overwhelming. The same was also true among the administrative staffs and students. For the moment at least, we were all proudly aware that Brandeis remains indefeasibly a Jewish university and that Brandeis's fortunes are tied indissoluably to those of the Jewish people everywhere. And to most of us, I believe, the reaffirmation of Brandeis's vocation as an institution dedicated in particular to the advancement of learning among afflicted and disadvantaged minority groups was profoundly exhilarating. Perhaps we would be poorer now. But the Jewish people, even in America, have always known poverty. Nor has their passion for enlightenment been diminished by the possibility that this year's soup may be less rich than it was a year ago.

It is not too much to say, then, that most Brandeisians took anticipated austerity in good spirit, as a portent that our university might not "become just another nondescript 'secular' university" which desires merely to forget its origins.

But in education as elsewhere human beings are rarely capable of sustaining the awareness of primary values which comes in times of adversity. Since 1966 the new austerity has lost most of its compelling moral significance. Old routines have once more reasserted themselves. And again the drift continues toward the conventional pattern of the ordinary graduate university, despite the protests of some faculty and many student members who find Brandeis's capacity to serve as an exemplum of radical educational innovations extensively diminished. The sense of the virtue, for American education generally, of minority group attitudes and sensibilities has generally declined. For the same reason, there is now little effective awareness, particularly within the higher echelons of the Brandeis hierarchy, of the immense educational advantages of cultural diversity within the higher learning in this country. In short, liberal education, where it is most needed—in the graduate schools—is once more curtailed, and the vices of professionalism and scientism continue to spread throughout the undergraduate college itself.

President Abram, who at this writing has abruptly resigned in the middle of the academic year (1969–70), provides a striking instance of this failure of educational seriousness and devotion. As we shall shortly see, Mr. Abram's inaugural address, whose main thrust was a plea for "depoliticizing" the university, showed naïvete concerning the meaning of liberal education as well as extraordinary ignorance of the history of the American university, especially since the Second World War. His own conduct, as it turned out, proved a painful example of how self-deceived are those who most loudly denounce their more radically politicized colleagues and students. All the same the address was a harbinger of other and better things. For one thing, it showed an understanding of how deeply the Vietnam War has divided the academic community, and his own unequivocal condemnation of it in such a setting was inspiriting. Mr. Abram did not appear to grasp that his own condemnation of the war was a political act. But others did, and, according to their lights, applauded or criticized him for it. His avowal of liberal principles was large-minded and antiformalistic. He made a sound point in asserting their importance both to Jewish and to Gentile culture, to political democracy, and to institutions of higher learning. Furthermore, he showed an acute awareness of the idealism and the moral power of young people in a time when their elders, especially those in high places, have been systematically engaged in what Henry Adams called "the degradation of the democratic dogma." Mr. Abram rightly acknowledged how much our people owe to the young in showing the great moral wrong of a draft which tilts the scales of justice against the poor and the black. He applauded them for compelling us "to face the question, who shall protect the citizen when police act outside the law?" He went beyond this. "Today's students," so he said, "are emotionally and educationally more mature than . . . [my] generation at the same age." They have become "perceptive social critics of society." And he concluded that "there is little reason to suppose that students at a university such as Brandeis, if given the opportunity, will not infuse good judgment into decisions about the rules governing their lives in this community."

Those were brave words. The fact is that during his administration the roles of students in academic affairs were impressively extended. Expanded programs for educationally deprived students have been introduced, and dozens of new courses have been added to the curriculum dealing with problems of men which rightly preoccupy enlightened young people. In some courses, moreover, innovative faculty members, ready to try out new forms of pedagogy, now treat the classroom as a seminar and their students as junior colleagues for whom the teacher-student relation is a two-way process at the undergraduate as well as the graduate level. This serves to blur the distinction between the College and the University. But this is as it should be. More boldly, the classroom in numbers of courses, at all levels, now begins to open out upon the city and its people, to the advantage of both. The numbers of black students admitted to the university, nearly all of them on scholarships, have virtually doubled despite the university's tightened budget. The blacks, to my knowledge, have added an immensely valuable leaven to the educational mix at Brandeis, as elsewhere, and all of us, whether we as yet realize it, are greatly in their debt. We begin to understand what the Medieval scholars knew, that moral and theological education, properly understood, belong at the very heart of the higher learning. For unless one continually refines one's understanding of what is truly holy and just, one's technical expertise becomes a false god for whose worship, not oneself only, but one's people will accordingly suffer.

Such attitudes, it goes without saying, are not universally applauded by members of the faculty, some of whom, being schoolmasters, are still unable to distinguish the university from the school. For that gentry, the organizational term "department" is too often accepted as a synonym for a "discipline," and ability to meet the departmental requirements is confused with the virtues of an enlightened mind. The concerted power of such academic Pharisees is great. Unfortunately it accumulates as the graduate university increases in strength and prestige. And the mentality behind it afflicts even some of the ablest scholars at Brandeis. How should it be otherwise? Narrowly trained in other graduate universities, all of us remain at the same time the beneficiaries and the victims of an ideology of higher learning from which, as it sometimes seems, we can be liberated only by main force. This is a great pity, for the same individuals, when one meets them outside the precincts of the academy, are, not uncommonly, men of great, if dissociated, cultivation, who can be brought to tears (as I have observed) by a performance of *Antigone*.

Learning in any subject, is not readily transferable. Nor is its relevance to other forms of understanding appreciated, unless the student (and hence the incipient teacher and scholar) acquires the habit, which must be continually reinforced, of searching out boundary problems which have no meaning if he has no sense of what lies beyond the perimeters of his chosen discipline. Herein lies a temptation and a danger. Return to the old elective system naturally appeals to the libertarian. With the breakdown of general education, the elective system thus provides at once a covering ideology both for muddleheaded libertarians who want all students to do just as they please and for those who want their "serious" students to get on with their work. The libertarian opposes required general education on principle as a limitation of the student's freedom; the disciplinarian opposes it because it diverts the student's attention from his major. Thus all sadly, does the demand for liberty conspire with that for necessity to make teachers and students alike virtuously indifferent to, or contemptuous of, possibilities of an integrative university education.

Mr. Abram, so far as I could discover, had no settled point of view regarding such educational problems. Like many another administrator, he was temperamentally a libertarian but by long training essentially a negotiator. In practice, therefore, he applied in the university the same unstructured ideology of pragmatic liberalism which dominated American politics in the sixties. Those conservative alarmists who imagined that he was about to turn Brandeis into a participatory democracy were therefore as much deceived as those who took his rhetoric at its word. In the long run, had he not himself acquired a self-deluded political itch, he probably would have proved to be a traditional academic middleman, following by instinct rather than sustained conviction the line of greatest resistance. In the years just ahead the greatest resistance, my own guess is, will come from the "respectables," as I shall call them, who want nothing more from Brandeis than that it should be "normal." And in abnormal times, despite the rhetorical cough syrup, normality means conservatism and educational, as well as financial, retrenchment.

Inklings of such a style of action—it scarcely deserves to be called a philosophy of education—were implicit in Abram's inaugural address with its emphatic archaistic call for the depoliticizing of the university. To one, like myself, who had observed with dismay over many years the increasing entanglement of the universities in the ruinous affairs of the militarized and capitalized nation-state, such a call could mean in practice only one thing: a nostalgic plea for the *status quo ante*. Doubtless it did not occur to President Abram that his most articulate philosophical allies on this score were men like Sidney Hook, about whose views concerning academic freedom something more will be said in a later chapter.

What Abram failed to see, just as many academicians also do not see, is the crucial distinction between objectivity, conceived as a principle of sober second thought in any sphere of activity whether political or otherwise, and "value-free" neutrality which defeats the very meaning of liberal, or human, education. In the sense defined, it is entirely proper for the university to be objective and to require objectivity of its members. Neutrality, however, implies an abdication of judgment as well as of human concern. For the neutralist, were he consistent, would convert himself as well as the institution he serves into a mere object of inquiry.

A value-free academy, which is precisely what a university depoliticized in depth would try to be, is a contradiction in terms. At the least, the search for truth itself involves a commitment to the value of knowledge in every form, whether factual or normative. And an institution systematically committed to the search for and communication of truth in all its forms cannot in the nature of the case remain apolitical. Not every local political issue, of course, is a matter of immediate academic concern; nor am I contending that the university is obliged to take a stand on every matter debated in the state legislatures or the congress. But this does not imply either that members of the university, in their capacity as scholars, or that the university itself as a collegial body, must remain aloof when, as in Nazi Germany, actions and policies of the state undermine the very possibility of liberal learning or when, as in some of our own Southern states, prevailing

[97

social practices and prejudices radically limit the freedom of the academy in deciding policies of admission, appointment, or instruction.

But even if there were a serious move to detach the university altogether from political life, it could not succeed. Established professorial and administrative entrepreneurs would bitterly oppose it, partly from conviction and partly because their own research projects, consultative activities, and prestige presuppose close, as well as remunerative, ties to the state. Nor, in virtue of their own needs for academic expertise and support, would the state or federal governments tolerate systematic efforts to depoliticize the academy. Like Othello, the American university since its inception has continually "done the state some service, and they know't." Unlike Othello, however, the university has no stomach for the role of tragic hero. Like all institutions, it means to survive, which it cannot do by suicidal gestures. Depoliticization, bluntly, is not in the cards. For its service, our governments have shown their gratitude in financial ways. But that gratitude is based upon calculated *quid pro quo*, as recent events should make clear to all. In short, it is not the politicizing of the university which is the real issue, but the counterestablishment politics of students and faculty members on the left who refuse any longer to acquiesce in a politics of war and privilege, and their attendant forms of economic, social, and political repression.

Scholarly naïvete can no longer be pleaded as an excuse for failure to perceive what the demand for depoliticizing the university would mean. Especially when that demand is made by such thoroughly political men as Morris Abram, it plainly smacks of disingenuousness. As was proved so decisively during the era of the infamous Joe McCarthy, neither neutrality nor objectivity in the classroom will save a man from punishment or even outright dismissal if his political opinions are sufficiently unorthodox and his political activities, though conducted off the campus, are deemed by the "authorities" to be inimical to the American system.

The professorial grants-man and the conciliatory administrator doubtless feel as free as the breeze to say what they think and to do as their conventional consciences dictate. The reason is that it has never occurred to them to resist. But feeling free and being free, as David Hume long ago pointed out, are not the same thing. A man may feel free simply because it never occurs to him to make an issue of a right he comfortably enjoys. A free man— and it is the whole task of liberal education to make men aware of their freedom as men—is one to whom the exercise, and not merely the somnolent presumption of freedom, is a constant mental habit. In one sense, any truly free man is perforce a radical, since in behalf of others as well as himself, he cannot conscientiously acquiesce in the continual faulting of rightful liberties in the name of manifest destiny, national interest, or unjust compromises. Thus it is the free man, in full possession of his liberal educational endowment, who really understands how deeply politicized the university already is. And he knows this by the resistance he faces when in good faith he makes a move against the accepted order.

The question is thus not whether the university should be depoliticized but in what ways and under what circumstances it or its members should engage in political action. At Brandeis, as elsewhere, one finds no consensual answer to this question. Few of us, I believe, are prepared to accept physical violence on the campus on the part either of fractious students or of the "pigs" who so indiscriminately and unmercifully beat them. So far Brandeis's record on this score has been exemplary. During the bleak winter and spring of 1969, President Abram set a remarkable example, unfortunately not followed at Harvard and other universities in the Boston area, by refusing to resort to the admittedly uncontrollable counterviolence of the police in order to cope with the take-over of Ford Hall by black students. During the great national strike of students in the spring of 1970, there was also little violence at Brandeis. The faculty, with the support of Abram's newly appointed successor, President Charles Schottland, expressed its collective sympathy with certain of the demands of the strikers, including in particular the demand for an end to the war in Indochina, along with its corrosive internal effects upon the American political-social system. Yet, again unlike some other nearby universities, Brandeis managed to remain open, and those who wished to continue with their studies did so unmolested. Individual professors remained free, in practice, to follow their own consciences in the conduct of their courses. Formally, classes were held for the most part, though, as in my own case, they were sometimes converted, with the consent of those students who attended, into workshops at which the great issues symbolized by the strike were discussed soberly and in depth. Nor were those teachers who participated more formally in the strike penalized by the administration. This is not to say that perfect harmony prevailed. On the contrary, faculty meetings were acrimonious and considerable numbers of faculty members bitterly opposed any corporate expression of opinion on the political questions at issue by the faculty. But it would be a mistake to conclude from this that such corporate action served only to polarize the university. The fact is that the university, like the country, had long since been polarized. Most of us felt, I believe, that there had emerged a new solidarity which included a large number of the faculty and administration, as well as the student body.

In the face of such stresses indefinitely prolonged, Brandeis could conceivably go down. Its vulnerability is probably greater than that of any private university in this country. Its debts are huge, its usable resources diminishing. But if, God forbid, this should happen, a light would go out both in American Jewry and in American education. For the intellectual perspective of the Jewish people uniquely combines reverence for learning and a sense of history, with a passionate thirst, born of countless ages of repression, for justice and for equality. The very name "Brandeis," as I am reminded by my wise colleague and friend, Professor William Goldsmith of Brandeis's new Department of American Civilization, uniquely "symbolizes this marriage of intellectual preeminence with a sense of human obligation." That is a precious heritage we will do well to remember whether in times of prosperity or as, at present, of peril.

New experimental urban studies programs, which will take teachers and students alike into the city for participative observation, the flourishing Lemberg Center for the study of violence, promising moves to use the facilities of the biological and natural sciences for much-needed ecological inquiries, the massive effort of the department of sociology toward unorthodox investigations of contemporary forms of social conflict and alienation, which involve extremely unorthodox pedagogical procedures—all embody efforts to provide at Brandeis an experimental laboratory for exploring the conditions of human survival on this planet. These are straws in the wind, and none of them is unopposed. Undoubtedly some will fail; some may deserve to fail. But they are aspects of a new academic revolution which demands an entire reconstruction of prevailing notions of the higher learning in America. "Subjectivity" is no longer a dirty word among all responsible academicians. Some of us at least begin to see that subjectivity and objectivity are not always antonyms, and that there is a difference between human concern and autism. Lack of resources and energy, as well as lack of philosophical understanding of the diverse forms which the life of reason may take in the academy, continue to hobble all such endeavors. But such difficulties, if we persist, are not insuperable.

As a last-ditch stand, it is argued sometimes that the academy, by its very nature, must be an institution which serves primarily as a repository of accumulated knowledge and hence that it cannot engage actively in the advancement of learning in any sphere. This argument has no force. Research is a settled function of the modern university; scholarship can have no vocation within the academy unless the scholar is free to press forward on all levels toward the frontiers of human knowledge and to raise limiting questions that always appear meaningless to the conventional academic mind. The progressive university thrives on paradox and heterodoxy. And unless Brandeis continues resolutely to be progressive, it has no distinctive vocation or reason for being.

5

Coda:

Outward Bound

In the introduction to part i, i mentioned a number of factors that have made possible, and now indeed urgent, its writing. I have reserved one factor for a conclusion, for it places what has already been said in a new perspective in which I am now obliged to view both Brandeis as a young university in crisis and myself as a professor implicated in that crisis. This, as I mentioned, concerns an encounter in the summer of 1968 at the Danforth Foundation Workshop in Liberal Education where I conducted a seminar on the situation of the humanities in higher education. My fellow seminar leaders, let me say, included a number of distinguished teachers in a variety of subjects, some from universities, one or two from colleges, including San Francisco State College, embroiled in the student revolt movements sweeping institutions of higher education both here and abroad. Our "students," if that is the name for them, consisted of college administrators, deans and department heads, as well as professors in many different ranks and subjects, purposely brought together from a wide spectrum of American institutions of higher learning: universities and colleges, public and private, secular and religious, white and black, great, less great, and in some instances barely "accredited." A number were from the system of "university colleges," as Messrs. Jencks and Riesman call them in their book *The Academic Revolution;* [1] that is to say, colleges whose primary business has been to prepare students either for graduate or professional school or else to improve their social and economic status within the

American system. But the greater percentage came from colleges which, as yet, have no such conscious aspiration or else view it as a hope indefinitely to be deferred. It is fair to say, however, that the aims of most participants included a strong commitment to something they envisaged as "liberal education," though many were unclear as to what these aims now involve or even indeed whether they are viable in the era of the graduate university and the university college.

Some were frankly discouraged; others wondered whether they were not already educational mandarins, defending intellectual and cultural aspirations to which the American intelligentsia is now largely indifferent. Nonetheless, the great majority were dedicated men, with minds far more open to ranges and possibilities of humane learning at the higher level than colleagues I have generally encountered in the "great" universities. To me, this was all the more surprising and interesting since, as I have said, many were involved in administrative work whose academic problems, one might suppose, lie in a different direction. Most important of all, virtually everyone at the Danforth Workshop was, or appeared to be, committed to the four-year college as an indispensable educational institution, which represents values, now inadequately sustained by the leading universities and by the university colleges that serve and emulate them.

Let me emphasize that in my own seminar, whose problem concerned the nature and conditions of teaching and learning *in* (and not merely about) the humanities, were a number of scientists and social scientists as well as administrators, who well understood the great need, not only to break the hold of professionalism within the higher learning but also to find ways of bringing the resources of the college or university into the service of educating whole men, able to cope in their various stations in life with the immense problems of deliberation and choice forced upon them by our perilous post-industrial society. And they seemed well to understand the erosion of the sense of meaning that afflicts many reflective persons in our time. In sum, it had been many years since I had met in one group so many dedicated and cultivated academicians, proud of their vocations, quite as certain that their own institutions were as important to the higher learning as the great national universities.

But then, at our concluding general session, at which all members of the Workshop were present, and led mainly by a group of black teachers and administrators, we became involved in a prolonged discussion of the "upward bound" movement. At once on all sides repressed anxieties emerged that involved questions of status not only for the students but also for the colleges, their faculties, and themselves. Indeed, the whole "upward bound" idea had come to serve as a compelling image not for a group of students, but for the colleges as well. In principle they might be content to remain four-year colleges, convinced of the intrinsic worth of their own distinctive educational programs, and many of their best teachers might be happy to continue indefinitely in their careers in unacclaimed schools, whether black or white, religious or secular, private or public. At the same time, they very much wished that their abler students, at least, might succeed in precisely the terms that apply at prestigious university colleges such as Harvard or Columbia. Plainly the hold of the contemporary university college and the university which it serves has become very strong in these schools, in spite of themselves. In sum, despite all their previous affirmations to the contrary, their minds were deeply divided about the future roles of their institutions as well as their own responsibilities as teachers.

Who could be unsympathetic? Did they not in their various ways provide paradigms of the deep self-divisions that exist in all institutions of higher learning and, correlatively, in the wider social order to the maintenance of which such institutions are now so necessary? All the same, as I listened to the recital of their problems of soliciting really upward bound students and of eliciting among their abler students upward bound attitudes and aspirations, as well as of recruiting young members to their faculties likely to be imbued with and to promote such attitudes, I was dismayed. How vain seemed all our earlier professions of a truly pluralistic ideal of American higher education and how weak the thrust, after all, of the variant forms of liberal education implicit in that ideal!

At last I rose to speak, I confess, in some anguish. My purpose was in part to bring to the surface the implicit contradictions in all our well-intentioned educational philosophies which automatically are communicated to our students. More important, I sought to show how deeply, if unconsciously, elitist the whole system of American higher education is. Not only have all, or almost all, of our colleges become, or are trying to become, university colleges, which seek to bring their "best" students up to scratch so that they may be able eventually to make it at graduate school; worse, they convey to "the others"—the great mass of students who cannot, or do not seek to, "make it"—a sense of their essential second-rateness and their inability to perform roles of distinction within our post-industrial national society.

Thus I contended that the "upward bound" incubus must be shaken off and replaced, not just within the four-year colleges, but within the universities as well, by truly liberal ideals of men and women, teachers and students alike, who are at once inward bound—directed, that is, toward self-understanding and self-fulfillment of their whole personalities as human beings—and outward bound—directed toward forms of activity and work that will serve to make the whole world a more tolerable place for human beings to live in. In particular, I urged that responsible leaders of educational movements within the black community should strive, not to inculcate attitudes that merely lead their abler students into an homogenized society that deprives them of their own identity, but to bring them to a steadier view of their own vocations as educated black men. I argued that leaders within the church schools, whether Catholic, Protestant, or Jewish, should, among other things, attempt to preserve their distinctive religious identities so that they may contribute their own characteristic forms of spiritual insight to a culture desperately in need of religious and ethical, and hence of social and political, dialogue. Such dialogues must probe beneath prevailing ideological formulas to the sources of spiritual perplexity that turn many of our choicest young people indiscriminately against all hard-won forms of human understanding inscribed in the great testaments of our fathers. By "testaments," however, I did not mean only the Bible, but indeed the whole complex and various literature which belongs to our Hellenic and Judeo-Christian heritage. That heritage, so I maintained, can acquire a living significance for present-day students only when it is brought into honest and open confrontation with its "antitheses"—the post-Jewish and post-Christian and post-Hellenic thought that has emerged by stages since the Renaissance and which has reached flood-tide in our own age. However, *if* a true dialectic, undidactic and wholly free of cant, can be sustained, then it seemed to me possible for the church college, like its secular counterpart, to perform a cultural service, not only for members of the sect it represents, but for the whole range of human understanding. In this way, without losing its own identity, it may contribute in its own authentic way to the preservation, or revival, of human education in the present era.

Finally, I urged that the nonsectarian colleges must view their own educational activities, not merely as preparations for something else still higher, and the years of undergraduate life not as a kind of academic "passage to India," but as a time of developing experience, of intrinsic value to human beings already in command of their youthful powers of imagination, empathic perception, and sympathy. Young men and women, who may never again have such a bright perception of their own indefeasible being, require far more from the college than the development of skills essential to success in their later careers; they need a sense both of the gladness of learning and of the daily enlargement of their own subjective reality; the worth, that is to say, of their present existence, their moral intuitions, their aspirations for all their kind, their awareness that they belong to, and are part of, an encompassing Presence, which the pathos and the tragedy of human existence can darken but never destroy.

Saying all this, I was not unmindful of that trap which Wordsworth, knowing all too well whereof he spoke, once described. "Readers of moral and religious inclinations," said Wordsworth, "attaching so much importance to the truths which interest them . . . are prone to overrate the Authors by whom those truths are expressed and enforced. They come prepared to impart so much passion to the Poet's language that they remain unconscious how little, in fact, they receive from it." [2] All teachers are prone to rhetoric, especially when they talk about aims of education. How great is the distance, and how difficult the journey, from our talk to its embodiment. Then, once more, I bethought myself of my own university, Brandeis. How much, like Wordsworth, have we at Brandeis, wanted to believe in a ". . . hope that can never die,/ Effort and expectation and desire,/ And something evermore about to be." [3] But wanting to believe is not doing, and hope can indeed die when it is not translated into sustained action. How little, in actuality, do we—administrators, teachers, *and* students alike—impart our passion, or its rhetorical simulation, into a more significant work. As elsewhere, our true crisis of identity at Brandeis is a continuing crisis of integrity, which of course is part of the crisis of being itself. Once the Israeli war was over for the moment, how many of us, heaving a sigh of relief, went back to building an ex-Jewish Princeton on the Charles? And, more recently, how many, gratified that we have for the moment resolved our Negro problem "without violence," are already moving back into our little cubicles hoping that the black revolution will move somewhere else. How little, in substance, have we changed! We have not deeply pondered, or debated, as a faculty what our continuing dependence upon government contracts entails. We have not rehabilitated the merely *pro forma* committee to reform and reinvigorate general education to which I was appointed in my freshman year at Brandeis. Nor have we done a thousand and one other things which we promise ourselves on commencement or on crisis day. Versions of the dialectic between the departed Marcuse and the returned Roche have been submerged. And in sum, like a hundred and one universities and colleges, we lack a continuing impulse toward our own collective educational development. The actuality has become diffused and chaotic. A few are angry; more seem merely tired. We have a variety of rhetorics to offer prospective students, faculty members, or donors. But it is increasingly a question whether, in a phrase which T. S. Eliot borrowed from Santayana, they are matched by any genuine "objective correlative": a university, that is to say, which is itself "going to Brandeis."

I have been told that this is a "literary" question. If so, the reply must be that literary questions, taken in full seriousness, can bring us, as few things else can, to an awareness of our predicament, which is simply the absence of a persistent concern for our vocation. Too often our professional jargon, our shop talk, our largely meaningless faculty meetings, our rounds of conferences, the very products of our research, are so many symbols of our thoughtlessness and heedlessness, our constant search for distractions to palliate the overwhelming fact of our indifference to the

quality of the care we give not only our young, but ourselves—
ourselves! It is we who are the real sufferers; our students at
least have their youth, their capacity for self-education, their own
encounters as junior teachers and learners in the shadow university which so many of us, faculty as well as administration, shun
and fear. As far as I am concerned, the question at Brandeis is no
longer whether we still aspire to do something distinguished, but
quite simply whether we really wish to *be*. With the thousands
of other universities and colleges able to absorb us, what does it
matter whether Brandeis survives?

But of course the same question is now being raised at many
other universities and colleges throughout the land. If I castigate
my own university, it is in part because I believe that useful
criticism, like loyalty, must begin at home. But it is also because,
despite everything, the immense promise of Brandeis remains; nor,
in going to Brandeis, was I deluded. That promise, whether at
Brandeis or (as I discovered at the Danforth Workshop) at dozens
of smaller colleges and universities in every part of America, is
something for which it is very much worth leaving any overgrown multiversity, whether its name be Michigan or California—
or Harvard. But only by endlessly converting that promise into
new actualities can we present a serious alternative (which is part
of our vocation) to the multiversity itself.

My seemingly paradoxical conclusion, then, is this: The fulfillment of Brandeis's promise matters at least as much to Harvard
as to Brandeis itself. More generally, making good that promise,
"the Brandeises" can initiate a reformation throughout the higher
learning in America which "the Harvards" will then be unable
to resist. This is not rhetoric. An impressive analogy, admittedly
imperfect, has already been provided in England, where young
provincial universities, by going their new ways, are forcing Ox-
bridge to change its own desultory old ones. Many ex-Oxford
and ex-Cambridge dons, to my knowledge, have discovered that
the educational action is now taking place in the provinces or
indeed in the burgeoning universities of the British Common-
wealth: in Canada, in Australia, in New Zealand. The same sort of
thing can and should happen in America, where the curse of
bigness has turned our great universities into unmanageable con-
glomerates, whose rates of intellectual profit, since the mid-sixties,

have been declining at such a fearsome rate. So what I have called "going to Brandeis," in my view, remains our best, possibly our last, hope both for ourselves and our students, and therefore our country.

Part II

THE UNIVERSITY IN CRISIS:

Some Commentaries

6

Enter the Multiversity

In the spring of 1963, the then president of the University of California, Clark Kerr, delivered at Harvard the Godkin Lectures which were subsequently published under the title, *The Uses of the University*.[1] It was immediately acclaimed, and, as the chapters which follow indicate, its influence has been great. The reasons are evident: its manner is at once analytical and authoritative, its style crisp, its pervasive attitudes optimistic. Intellectually, Kerr exhibits all the characteristic attitudes of the intellectual leaders of the age. He is anti-ideological, finds his acquiescent norms in "the logic of history" rather than in a developed theory of human need and aspiration; he takes both society and institutions pretty much as they stand, hoping only to manage them efficiently so that they can continue to expand along the lines which history has already established: he cheerfully accepts change as both inevitable and desirable, but shows little impulse to make changes that are more than accommodative. Accordingly, he eschews definition like the plague, and, indeed, takes particular delight in the fact that the "multiversity" (Kerr is a coiner of apt catchphrases), unlike Cardinal Newman's university, is based on no governing idea or principle. The problem, as Kerr sees it, is simply to preserve some sort of "balance" between the ever-expanding pressures of teaching and research, general and professional education, science and the humanities, scholarly independence and the services which the American government expects of its public universities.

By themselves none of these qualities, however, would have made Kerr's book in any way remarkable. What distinguishes it, within its range, is its often devastating realism. He understands thoroughly the essentially elitist structure of the multiversity, despite its sprawl, and he accepts the fact that its motivations are overwhelmingly economic, not only administratively but educationally. The university is an "industry" whose business, which is knowledge, has become "a prime instrument of national purpose." This point of view is perhaps most tellingly summarized in the following remarks about the location of the university. "An almost ideal location for a modern university," he tells us, is to be "sandwiched between a middle-class district on its way to becoming a slum and an ultramodern industrial park." The reason is simple: the students may live in the one and the faculty consult in the other. The university and segments of industry are becoming more alike. And "as the university becomes tied into the world of work, the professor—at least in the natural and some of the social sciences—takes on the characteristics of an entrepreneur." Indeed the two worlds of the university and industry are now merging "both physically and psychologically." Like any other enterprising business, the university must create an image which will enable it to sell its products—in this case knowledge and people who possess it. Thus the universities which seek to rise in the academic hierarchy can most quickly and easily attract national attention by hiring great and visible "academic stars," both athletic and professional. "The former do little studying and the latter little teaching and so they form a neat combination of muscle and intellect."

Is there not, perhaps, a touch of irony here? Kerr, within his range, is something of a wit. But his ironies, as readers of his concluding chapter on "The Future of the City of Intellect" will discover, are mostly inadvertent. As the saying goes, he simply "tells it like it is," take or leave it. He has no objections to professional football stars on the campus. Just the contrary, they too are workers in the weedpatch of the multiversity.

This last figure, let me stress, is my own. Kerr's "workers," academic and otherwise, are inhabitants (except in the evenings) of the industrial park. His perspectives, like those of his professors, are essentially entrepreneureal. The primary differences between him and them are differences of power and status.

On this subject, let me add, he wears no camouflage. Accompanying the merger of the multiversity with other industries, there have occurred corresponding changes in its governance. Once upon a time, faculties were much concerned with, and had considerable control over, at least educational policy. But, beginning with Charles W. Eliot's introduction of the elective system, the whole point of faculty concern with, not to mention control over, educational policy, disappeared. The elective system, which, following the decline of general education is once more resurgent, came increasingly to serve the interest of the professional entrepreneur rather than the student for whom it was intended. In short, educational policy, except within the individual department, which was, and is, concerned primarily with turning out first-rate professionals and preprofessionals in its own discipline, simply disappeared. What was left of it was turned over to various administrative boards presided over by deans who have become fixtures in an endlessly proliferating academic bureaucracy. And so, the managerial revolution has come to the university with a vengeance. Not unnaturally, in contrast to the "new universities in England," there has been in recent decades "remarkably little faculty discussion of general educational policy." To this I should add only the qualification that by Kerr's own showing there is nothing "remarkable" about it at all. More important, however, is the fact, as Kerr says (and he should know), "organized faculty control or influence over the general direction of growth of the American multiversity has been quite small." In the multiversity it is the benevolent bureaucracy of administrators who usually make the basic decisions about academic policies.

This bureaucracy, however, is itself largely a servant. Residual power, whether for innovation or resistance to it, originates in large part off campus—assuming that the distinction between on campus and off campus still has any functional meaning. Trustees and legislatures, foundations and federal agencies, have combined with the great industrial powers to exert influences upon the university which faculties and students alike are largely helpless to resist.

Such, with qualifications, is—or was—the multiversity. Kerr accepted it, sometimes one feels, a bit stoically. But his successors, singing their respective variations on the themes to which he had given the names, were enthralled.

The Uses of the University was first published in 1964, the year of the great Berkeley bust which, a little later, was to cost the balancer, Kerr, his job. In Kerr's book it must be said that there were vague premonitions of some of the things to come, though he failed entirely to sense either their intensity or their depth. He mentioned that undergraduates are "restless," and spoke indeed of "an incipient revolt of undergraduate students against the faculty; the revolt that used to be against the faculty *in loco parentis* is now against the faculty *in absentia*." He went on to mention the blanket of impersonal rules for admissions, scholarships, and degrees. "The students," he said in the understatement of the decade, "also want to be treated as distinct individuals."

But all this was said in passing. "Change," as Kerr put it, "comes more through spawning the new than reforming the old." It has not turned out that way, as James Perkins, ex-president of Cornell, perhaps Kerr's most distinguished disciple, has learned more recently at a cost more bitter than Kerr was made to pay. Perkins, as we shall see in the next chapter, also stresses the "mission" of service. But unlike Kerr, he came eventually to see that the public service which the university must learn to accept as part of its corporate responsibility to the people includes forms of "social justice" (as he puts it) profoundly at variance with those hitherto rendered, without demur, to the government and great industrial corporations. More recently, during the great student strike of 1970, other conservative administrators like Kingman Brewster of Yale have also discovered that even the formal political neutrality of the American university may have to be sacrificed when the nation-state adopts policies which undermine the very existence of the university as an institution of liberal learning.

Thus a scattering of our educational leaders begin to understand that since the Second World War the multiversity has become a golem, huge and mindless, a creature of necessity rather than a continuing creation of free men. And they are learning the fundamental lesson that when institutions, including those dedicated to the higher learning, become objects their members, in spite of themselves, come to regard themselves as objects. Such a lesson, as we know, can also be quickly unlearned. Unfortunately, Clark Kerr's characteristic remark that the university is "a mechanism led together and powered by money" still fits the mentality of all too many highly-placed academicians who believe with him that the multiversity is part of an inexorable national and social "process [which] cannot be stopped." And once the pressures of student protest are reduced they will be all too ready to accept his laconic advice: "It remains to adapt."

The hope which lies behind the criticisms of Kerr's followers and successors to be found in the following pages is that the American university will not continue simply to adapt. It is a sometimes despairing hope, as I make clear in the concluding chapter of *Part II*, to which I have given the title "How Late is it?" Many of our national leaders are already demanding a "return to normalcy." And this means, in terms of the slogan which also obsesses many millions of their followers, frightened by internal strife that has reached a pitch not witnessed in this country since the Civil War, little more than a return to the adaptive system of "law and order" of which the multiversity is a natural product.

As I bring to a close this preliminary discussion of the controlling forces which dominate the multiversity, I have before me a highly symptomatic essay by a well-known liberal jurist, Professor Alexander Bickel of the Yale Law School whose title is "The Tolerance of Violence on the Campus." [2] During the strike Yale, he concedes, "has by and large kept its head." In New Haven, "violence and disruption are not a regular feature of our lives." Professor Bickel, let me emphasize, is by present standards a man of enlightenment. Like other liberals he deplores the "appalling use of deadly force at Kent State, in Augusta, and in Jackson, Mississippi, which we must punish as criminal and which we must bend every effort [sic] to prevent in the future." He insists that racism and "the debasement of values by commercialism" must stop. Admitting that the society is "flawed and gravely troubled," he accepts the fact that as the nation goes so must the university. However, he tells us, "the young are right about the war in Indochina." and, more bravely, that "the majoritarian process does not legitimate a war." Indeed, unlike Sidney Hook who so vehemently deplores something called "the minority veto," when it goes against the prevailing order, Bickel contends that "large and intense minorities have, and of right should have, a veto against war, and that there is no higher national interest than the speedy liquidation of a war that has been so vetoed."

To all this I say "Amen!" But Bickel says other things that reflect a point of view which leads us by stages back to Kerr. In Bickel's view, the Indochinese war is not only a symptom but the primary cause of our social and academic disorders. In his view, if only the accursed war is stopped we can get on with the lawful piecemeal, adaptive changes which a decent progressive society requires. Even now, so he says, "The society is free and open. . . ." And what repression there is is imposed, as often as not, by the young in the universities "where their pressure for ideological orthodoxy and a kind of emotional solidarity threaten to achieve what Joe McCarthy never did."

And lest we have any doubts about his meaning, he asserts in his concluding paragraph that "The place to begin restoring order in speech and action [forget not his contention that our society is "free and open"] is the university. . . . The *heads* of leading universities should convene publicly and reassert standards of speech and conduct. Instead of commiserating with each other under various auspices about a supposed crisis of irrelevance in higher education, they should announce their intention to institute a reform which is the precondition of all other reforms: the use of disciplinary power to keep discourse and action within the bounds of order." (italics mine)

How does this lead us back to Kerr? The answer should be plain: the first item on the agenda is a restoration of prevailing law, order, and decorum. "No more vandalism; no more assaultive, vicious speech, no more incitement to violent action, no more bullying, simulated or actual." Who shall establish the guidelines? The students in concert with their friendly teachers? Not at all. It is the heads of the multiversity who will reestablish disciplinary power. What Bickel demands, in effect, is a return to academic normalcy, with its decorous and largely meaningless faculty meetings and polite student requests for better housing and better teaching and its rules of rational speech and action defined in advance by academic gods from the machine.

My devout hope is that it will not turn out that way. Of course the university must have order, but it must have an order established not by "heads" but by elected representatives of the whole company of scholars, over which neither presidents nor trustees shall have an overriding veto. Such an order must be accomplished by a continuing effort to formulate a meaningful philosophy of higher education in the light of which the anti-philosophy of the multiversity will be repudiated. For the multiversity, as Clark Kerr has made abundantly clear, is not a human institution but a behemoth with not a single corporate idea of its own. It adapts by necessity to necessity, and the necessities to which it adapts are money and the managers who control the money. And by this time we all know who they are.

These are strong words. But strong words, as Luther understood at the onset of an earlier reformation, are required if the secular city, whose academic church the multiversity has now become, is itself to be restored to its own human vocation. Kerr calls the multiversity itself "the city of the intellect." But by his own description, it is not a city of the intellect but an accommodative information center. He believes that there is no alternative. But there is an alternative, though none of the eminent authors whose influential works we have now to consider knows where to find it.

Kerr is certainly right when he tells us that Newman's idea of the university as a cloister which has nothing to do with that "deal of trash" he called "useful knowledge" will not do in the contemporary world. But, as we shall see, Newman was merely overstating an important point in order to make it. Newman was right, now and forever, when he said that "Knowledge is capable of being its own end. Such is the constitution of the human mind, that any kind of knowledge, if it really be such, is its own reward." Like most eminent Victorians Newman was not a playful man, and it did not occur to him to say that things done for their own sake are, like dancing, always a delight to the soul. And like Mill, whom he resembled in more ways than he knew, he was also a trifle muddleheaded. Accordingly, he formally contradicted himself when he went on at length to emphasize the important human uses of liberal knowledge in "raising the intellectual tone of society," in "cultivating the public mind," and purifying the national taste," in "supplying true principles of popular enthusiasm and fixed aims to popular aspirations," and in "facilitating the exercise of political powers, and refining the intercourse of private life." But these *are* central and important uses of true universities, all the more important in a democracy in which everybody rightly aspires to go to the university. The contradiction is easily removed, and Newman himself might have removed it had he, remembering his Plato, stated more simply that liberal education belongs to that great category of "mixed goods" which are all the more delightful, being as they are, interesting both intrinsically and in prospect of their uses to humankind. Newman did not oppose useful knowledge, so long as it is useful not only to its possessor but also to his fellows. Nor did he oppose the politicizing of the academy, so long as the politics it espouses are fundamentally the politics of free men. What he condemned in his own age was essentially the mentality of commercialism, industrialism, and statism which, as he foresaw, would turn the university into a great trade school, a technological institute, a think-tank for bureaucrats—in short, a multiversity. And if, as a convert, he had been touched more deeply by the human wisdom of the southern Church, he might have perceived more clearly that the true university, by its very nature, should be a gay and festive place, whose rituals commemorate, not a life of endless service to Leviathan, of endless bickering and jockeying for preferment, of grading and being graded, but of glad and self-renewing development by students and teachers alike of the qualities intrinsic to man both as worker and spiritual being.

Unlike Newman, I happen not to be a convert to a church. And I am sometimes fatigued by the effects of his own conversion upon his later writing. At times the polemical spirit of the convert has the effect of diminishing the sense of the holy which he meant to celebrate. That sense, for me, is better conveyed by Kierkegaard and Nietzsche than by Newman. But cultivation of religious knowledge which supports the cultivation of artistic moral and political understanding, should indeed be a central function of the university. Nor can it be treated as a mere elective for those who seek a diversion when the professional work of the day is done. By a not-so-strange paradox, it is the complete and utter secularism of Kerr and the educators for whom he speaks, which, even when they make some passing acknowledgement of the educational values of the "creative arts," deprives them of any power to raise the anti-idea of the multiversity above the level of an historical social and political necessity. The creative arts and the creative sciences, by their nature, are enemies of necessity and adaptation. They belong to ideal orders of the mind which yearn for reconciliation and mutual involvement, not externally but internally in the minds of the men who pursue them. And in concert, their exponents, also by nature, find that in their various confrontations with the ordinary ways of the secular city they are invariably disruptive and revolutionary. The academy is not a utopia. But it must have a utopian and transcendental dimension which makes it impossible for it to adjust comfortably to the practices of the secular city. The ancient conflict between town and gown has natural and proper justification. And when the university submits its arbitration of that conflict to the governors of the nation-state or its campus representatives, the freedom essential to its usefulness to mankind is thereby destroyed.

The graduate university is now paying an exorbitant price in student conflict and faculty dissension for its forgetfulness of this fact. Not only does it invite destruction by wild men who mean to level it to the ground, but also disablement by men of ordinary civility and good order who, to their own amazement, find themselves obliged to go on strike against the institution to which, not always thoughtfully or courageously, they have given their lives. Men like Sidney Hook, and now Alexander Bickel, offer us an unreal alternative between "academic freedom" and "academic anarchy." Unreal, for it is based upon notions of academic freedom (and order) that in practice protect and give preference to the entrepreneur, the grantsman, the consultant, and the public man, while leaving the critic, unless he is compliant, at liberty merely to make a speech or two at committee and faculty meetings and then return, disconsolate, to a rereading of Newman—or Marx. It is unreal because, by Kerr's own admission the multiversity is already an educational anarchy whose only basic ground rule is adaptation. The academic freedom we now have is the freedom of the market place because it is nothing but an adjunct of the market place. And just as the work of art is now valued as an expensive adornment for the houses of the managers of the affluent society, the university finds an ornamental place for the humanist, the philosopher, the poet, the creative theologian, as long as he keeps his place in the museum where the university preserves its glass flowers. We can even find jobs for Marcusean revolutionists because they are properly recognized, not as exciting and moving writers of educational manifestos, but as lumpish Hegelians who seductively envisage the Absolute as a total erogenous zone. Marcuse no more threatens the multiversity than Shelley. He adds to it merely a piquancy and zest, like the plays of Pinter done in the round, responsive readings from the poems of Allen Ginsburg, or, if it comes to that, a day at the circus with the other Marxes.

We have had enough of mere piquancy and zest. It is time for something more drastic that gives the full lie direct to the multiversity. As I shall presently argue, it is the graduate university which is the bane of the higher learning, *not* because it concerns itself with serviceable professional studies, which are greatly needed, but because it is concerned with nothing else and because, as matters now stand, it effectively determines the practices as well as the aspirations of the university college. The whole ambience of the university college and, through it, the graduate and professional schools, must be changed. For the graduate university, strikes and all, continues to be dominated by an ideology of miscellaneous specialism, professionalism, commercialism, and subservient service to the national society. The educational changes I envisage must permeate the whole university, including the graduate and the professional schools. Unlike so many others, including, unfortunately, Newman himself, I do not want these schools to be peeled off from the central university and converted into elitist institutions of advanced special studies. The result would be a calamity for the whole so-called higher learning. This is why I am not content with Daniel Bell's makeshift recommendations for general education. It is also why, in my discussion of the Jencks and Riesman book, *The Academic Revolution,* I argue that the "revolution" they describe, already an all-too-accomplished fact, must now be followed by a second revolution of whose meaning they have but the vaguest notion. These are the idea-men to whom the heads of the multiversity will look for necessary changes once law and order are restored. We have had a surfeit of such necessary changes. We must now move, unaccommodatively, toward the establishment of universities, governed by ideals of the higher learning, in which *all* of us participate, lettered and unlettered, and the form of order that will then emerge will be a true order for educated men in a free society.

7

The American University:

IT IS A SOCIOLOGICAL COMMONPLACE THAT WE HAVE been moving into a post-capitalist, even a post-industrialist era in which, along with much prestige and money, residual power now passes to the university men. From this one might infer that we also are witnessing at last the decline of the nation-state. But the nation-state remains a powerful institution, and those who serve it or receive its aid, even on a *per diem* basis, generally wind up as state's men. This is as true of academicians as of lawyers, corporation presidents, or poets. It is arguable indeed that the academicians have given the nation-state a new lease on life: they make possible, for the first time, the conversion of a mode of government into a politico-social organism, a true Republic as it were, whose educator-guardians supply the rationale, the training, and the continuing fund of personnel for its maintenance and protection. All this and the open society too. For all his worries about alloys, Plato, the ur-academician, would have been enchanted.

Such, in effect, is the premise of Professor Daniel Bell's influential book, *The Reforming of General Education,*[1] a work that offers by far the most articulate presentation by a university state's man of the problems and possibilities of liberal education in the university age. Bell regards self-consciousness as a proper benefit of liberal education; he himself is also more conscious of his premises and of the terms of his own guardian's role than are most other members of his class. What they casually see, his sociological eye automatically places in a selective historical context; what they take for granted, his ever-available pen explicitly affirms. Because of this, certain chapters of his book, which is formally preoccupied with problems of undergraduate education in one great national university (Columbia) provide a useful preface to the whole spate of writings by still more highly placed leaders of the university set who are concerned with the unprecedented situation of the American university as the central institution for higher learning and the indispensable service agency for the American "national society."

The concept of the "national society" deserves the italics which Bell gives it in the following statement, for it provides the implicit frame for much establishmentarian thinking about feasible reforms in the great American universities:

> . . . within recent decades . . . the United States [has] passed from being a nation to becoming a *national society* in which there is not only a coherent national authority, but where the different sectors of the society, economy, polity, and culture are bound together in a cohesive way and where crucial political and economic decisions are now made at a "center." [2]

Remembering the day, some may feel that, construed as sociology, this statement is overdrawn. But there can be no question as to its usefulness as a thesis of centrist educational ideology. And anyone who hopes to save something from the wreck of general and liberal education in our universities must confront it as a pervasive over-belief of our university leaders.

Professor Bell describes a palpable fact when he points out that more centralized power has lately accrued to the state than has ever before existed in this country, and that as this power increases so do its ties to the nation's scientific technology become stronger and tighter. And as the national government becomes the mainstay of our ever more technical and expensive scientific research, so reciprocally the university, where so much advanced research and teaching occurs, becomes a new force to reckon with in our national polity. For it forms the base of a whole new intellectual class whose "leaders," as Bell carefully phrases it, are accorded "both national importance and moral authority."

Here an interesting parallel comes to mind. What Oxford and

Cambridge were to England in the time of its greatness, so Harvard, California, Columbia, and other national universities are now to the world-powerful United States. The all-important difference is that the forms of education in which the English universities excelled—the individual tutorial, classical studies, humanistically-oriented history and politics, and philosophy—are precisely the areas which seem least useful and relevant to the going concerns of our present national society. Where the English university tended to produce cultivated nonspecialists whose gifts were those of developed critical common sense and judgment, and acute if informal logical sense, the contemporary American university characteristically, though by no means always, turns out highly-trained scientific technicians, sometimes capable of contributing to the advancement of learning, but only within a restricted sphere of inquiry. Where the Englishman received, so to say, a common law education that led him from case to case, from precedent to precedent, developing along the way his sense of analogy and relevance, the American, within the range of his specialty, is trained to be methodical, exact, and systematic. Outside his professional range, he remains rather clumsy and impressionable, likely to be opinionated in a speculative way, but where something is to be done, curiously indecisive, ready to place the burden of obligation on someone else who can supply a more "informed" judgment.

From many converging sources, the impression emerges that, whatever may be their importance, our academic leaders are unprepared for the moral roles that have been thrust upon them. Yet it is precisely these same leaders whose limiting attitudes and aptitudes at once set the tone and determine the aims and functions of the contemporary university itself. Everywhere within the university, including the humanities, their influence and their example are as pervasive as their sufferance is indispensable. There seem to be exceptions: for example, President Pusey of Harvard is distinguished as an educator for his rehabilitation of the Harvard Divinity School and for his support of the study of religion within Harvard College. But this emphasis has not seriously modified the drift of things at Harvard, as the recent review of Harvard's general education program by the so-called Doty Committee illustrates.[3] And at California, at Cornell (as we shall

shortly see), even at Columbia, where the idea of general education originated and where the emphasis on liberal studies in the
College has always been vocal, the pull is overwhelmingly in the
direction of the forms of specialized research and instruction
which are useful to the national society and which therefore receive the government's bounty.

To a nonleader or antileader (in Bell's sense) it may be dispiriting, though it should not be surprising, to find that, of the many
prominent university spokesmen who have written about the
"crisis" of the university, few (Jacques Barzun is one erratic and
strangely self-defeating exception) have any fundamental objection to make to the way things are going there. Nowhere among
our leaders can one find a president or dean with the radical independence and crusading zeal of Hutchins, the imaginative cross-
fertilizing passions for language, poetry, *and* science of I. A.
Richards (at the top of his form), or the leonine philosophical
imagination of Dewey, with its interlocking educational concerns
for logic *and* history, for nature *and* experience, for settlement
houses *and* Cézanne, for methods of resolving problematic situations *and* the consummatory activities that can make a life worthwhile or a civilization significant. Nowhere today, if it comes to
that, can one find someone bold or strong enough to assert as
Paul Tillich did, that without a relation to the ultimate concerns
of genuine religion the modern university cannot possibly be
the educational center of an acceptable human culture. How
serviceable, and how undistinguished, are the words of our present-day university leaders. How barely distinguishable from one
another are these foxes, these well-meaning inside men, whose only
thought as educators is to advise the prince, to be of use to the
national society.

This does not mean that what they say is of no consequence.
Just the opposite. Because they instinctively know what is "possible" within the context of the national society, it is to them we
must turn in order to learn what may become of the university,
and hence of us all, in the years ahead. And when they describe
—as, for example, Clark Kerr did, the "uses" of the "multiversity," as he called it, we are forewarned that, if there are none
to oppose them, such indeed will be the uses of the university in
our time.

It is in this spirit that we must take *The University in Transition*,[4] by James A. Perkins, ex-President of Cornell and a Bellean national society leader if ever there was one. Perkins's pedigree is impeccable: it includes everything from a Ph.D. and assistant professorship in political science to the assistant directorship of a "School" of Public and International Affairs, and from government service to the vice-presidencies of a distinguished liberal arts college and of a great foundation. The names of the national governmental and educational advisory bodies on which he serves read like a catalogue of great problems for a course in Contemporary Civilization. When he informs us, therefore, that the distinctive feature of the American university is its commitment, not only to the accumulation and transmission of knowledge, but also to its application as a public service, we do not have to reach for his idea of "public service." By public service he means, essentially, service to the national society and its government. Nor are we in doubt that the service rendered may include the person of the applicator himself.

President Perkin's account of that knowledge worthy to be impressed upon the minds of university students holds no surprises. Homogeneous with the prose that invests it, it reads like the précis of an entry on "Knowledge" from the University Administrator's own Book of Knowledge. President Perkins may be called a rationalist and a gnostic; for him, that is, all knowledge is a product of "reason," and human good is an emanation from knowledge. He dutifully reaffirms "the Greek affirmation" of man as the rational animal, declares knowledge to be the result of "reason's application to the results of observation," and confidently states that knowledge, so viewed, is applicable to "the whole range of human experience." He does not spend himself in definitions of "reason"; so often, however, is "knowledge" equated with the products of "research," that one feels that, even without research, one knows what he has in mind. Nor does he plague us with uncertainties about the ranges or limits of the life of reason, much less with the possibility that reason and the standards to which "reasonable men" hold themselves liable may be subject to critique. President Perkins, so to say, takes a positive view of reason just as he takes a positive view of science. And he takes the American university, at least on the side of its research, as a going cognitive concern, as of course within limits it un-questionably is. My quarrel is not at all that he raises no doubts about the validity of scientific research or the importance of its transmission and use. Rather is it that he seems not to see that there may be precious forms of knowledge, possibilities of human study and learning, worthy of a great university's concern, which simply are not products of "research" and which do not fall reasonably within the purview of most American academicians' notions of reason.

To be fair, President Perkins, himself trained as a political scientist, would probably not wish to be held to strict interpreta-tions of such concepts as science and reason. Undoubtedly he would repudiate the notion that all knowledge, or science, must be formulable in mathematically exact terms. Yet what he says about "the humanities," and it isn't much, suggests that he con-ceives them, at least for university purposes, primarily as those products of historical and philological inquiry which would be publishable in the *Proceedings of the Modern Language Associa-tion*. It does not include the sort of informal critical and philo-sophical reflections upon literature and the arts that one en-counters, say, in the prose writings of Coleridge, or Arnold, or Nietzsche and, in our time, in the essays of Eliot, Camus, or, particularly in his earlier period, Lionel Trilling. In its current usage, the cant word "research" is a perfectly apt term for the work of the behavioral psychologist or comparative linguist, and hence for the preliminary investigations that are often invaluable to the man of letters, the humanist, and the philosopher. It is not, I believe, a word that is appropriate to what the latter are doing when they finally close with the "objects" of their concern, nor is it the word for what they are doing in performing their own characteristic jobs of work.

President Perkins fancies the three primary activities of the American university as "missions." If his account of the first mis-sion is an academic stereotype, one part of what he says about the second mission—which he habitually calls the "transmission" of knowledge—is not. Indeed, his is the first published expression I have encountered of a powerful trend among those members of the academic establishment who would streamline the whole university curriculum so that it can more readily serve the interests of research and public service. For nearly a decade not only general education but also, in its older senses, liberal education have been under increasingly severe attack in the universities. And the rash of reexaminations of general education—which scarcely two decades ago was regarded as *the* educational reform of our age—is in fact less a function of an understandable desire to improve, let alone expand, existing general education programs than to curtail their role in the undergraduate curriculum and to make it easier for "bright" students to avoid their requirements.

Now it must be acknowledged that many "G. E." courses are uninspired (so, by the way, are many departmental courses), boringly taught to phlegmatic students who want to get on with their careers. Further, the better secondary schools, and particularly the private schools, are currently giving students great lashings of general and liberal studies. The average freshman from Choate or Loomis sometimes reminds one of T. S. Eliot's Prufrock, who has "known them all already, known them all," from Plato's dialogues to the plays of Genet, and from set theory to the dark night of the soul. What really remains for such a creature but to move on as rapidly as possible to graduate school? The device in many universities of admitting precocious freshmen to "advanced standing" has many justifications, among them the avoidance of an expensive fifth year of high school at Harvard or Cornell, another prolonged course, that is, of general and liberal studies. Moreover, as President Perkins and Professor Bell both ask, in effect, "Who nowadays wants to teach General Education?" (Young Ph.D.s with their careers ahead of them go where the prestige, the security, and the hard money are, and at most universities this is *not* the office of the Committee on General Education.)

Not, certainly, James Perkins. His argument has force. Like Kerr, Perkins is a pluralist about higher education, but he would achieve the ends of the multiversity by different means. Kerr, an imperialist and a federalist, would let the university diversify its activities more or less as it will within one great academic union. Perkins, however, belongs to the Ivy League. He wants to maintain a greater internal coherence within the university so that none of the missions he ascribes to it will be overwhelmed by the rest. This means, in practice, that the job of transmitting knowledge must be constantly geared to the demands of advancing research and service. Perkins's ploy is thus to "break the lock step that would keep all institutions and students working in the same patterns and at the same pace."

In a university, undergraduate instruction "can and must be different . . . than in a college, and . . . it can and must appeal to a special category of student." This difference, as Perkins describes it, is a direct consequence of his thesis that the university is *the* place, among institutions of higher learning, where the advancement and application of learning in the interests of society are primary missions. Such an institution may "hold fast to the ideals of a liberal education." But it must "recognize that, in the face of rapidly improving secondary education and the multi-concerns of the modern university, the style of liberal education will have to be adapted to its environment." Hence, for the student "who wants to specialize"—clearly the university, as distinct from the ordinary college, student-liberal education will have to be provided either by the secondary school or by "a special program that includes liberal along with professional studies—or a combination of both." "After all," as Perkins blandly says, "a liberal education is the objective of a life time. Why assume it should be crowded into the first two post-secondary years?"

Why indeed? The only trouble is that, like many others, Perkins himself obviously would shed no tear if liberal studies were conducted mainly in the secondary schools or else in four-year liberal arts colleges, which would thereby become glorified finishing schools run by professor-masters for whom research and service are not true missions. Plainly, the university is here being unveiled by Perkins as America's great center for advanced studies, which admits into its precincts only clever young apprentices whose interest in learning is, from the beginning, entirely professional. President Perkins only slightly blurs his tracks. "There can be," he reminds us, "a liberal and professional way of treating any subject." Yes. In a university where the missionary pressures on student and teacher alike are wholly on the professional side, "it becomes particularly important that the research-oriented professors have as broad a view of their subject as possible." Yes. But how is this to happen in a context where there is only a "special program" of liberal studies, and when even this per-functory hat-tipping in the direction of liberality is at once forgotten? We are warned that "the flexibility and independence of graduate-level work will have to characterize a larger pro-portion of undergraduate education too." Already this is hap-pening in the junior and senior years; for those "who are ready for it—and there are many more than we think," it doubt-less will have to be extended into the first two years. Obviously the next step must be to get rid, not of the Ph.D. degree (as some have argued), but of the B.A., at least as a university degree. This done, the incoming freshmen can proceed, without ado, to the work that will enable them shortly to swell the ranks of the professor-missionaries of the American university.

President Perkins's formula for preserving coherence and bal-ance within the university in the face of its "multi-concerns" has a certain plausibility; formally, it preserves the identity of the university as an educational institution of sorts, as Kerr's multi-versity does not. The formula is this: ideally each of the missions should positively *strengthen* the other two; that is, no training for public service that doesn't reinforce research, no research (presumably) that fails to strengthen the curriculum; but also, note well, no curriculum and no teaching that fail to strengthen research and service. In practice this implies that no additions should be made to the university staff which do not strengthen the research and service corps, no courses added that fail to pre-pare students for their work as protoresearchers and servicemen, no "extracurricular" artistic, literary, or intellectual activities which can't be justified by the power they add to the missions. Not a word is said about those dimensions of teaching whose only justification is the enlargement of the human imagination, the quickening, in part by subtle processes of emulation and identifi-cations, of the student's impulse to become a more fully *human* being. President Perkins talks of the mission of service, but he quite ignores that service which a university ought to render its own members—students, faculty, and administrators alike—the provision of an example of a community of mutually-developing persons, at once learned and cultivated, dedicated to their own work but responsive to achievements of orders different from their own. Why is it that virtually a whole generation of the choicest students and junior faculty are so revolted by the grubbiness, pretentiousness, and vulgarity of the multiversity, by its remoteness and impersonality, by its deadly "functions," including, among others, its incredible "commencement" days with their honorary degrees for retired generals, and the ghostwritten speeches in justification of some manifest destiny or other? Having read several books about the Berkeley student revolt and having witnessed something of the sort in my own university, I am convinced that what animates these uprisings is not so much a demand for greater political or social freedom, or a desire to participate in the day-to-day running of the university, as a desperate, angry reaction to the meagerness and meanness of so much ordinary university life.[5]

President Perkins remarks that young people who "keep looking for a kind of faculty-student relationship that can best be found in an independent liberal arts college" are involved in a fruitless search which merely adds to the problem of internal cohesion (never forget the missions!) in the university. And he tells them that if they need a sense of security that comes from being a member of a smaller, tighter community, "they should not come to the university." But, then, who should come? Youthful computers, already programmed for research and service? What he does not, will not, see is that *everyone*, whether student or professor or administrator, suffers from the anonymous life of anxiety-ridden specialized and professionalized missionary work to which the university anticommunity commits its members. The brutal fact remains that for all too many of its inhabitants, including its students, the central institution of higher learning in our time is not remotely a "mission" (to update slightly Newman's image of the university as an "active cloister") but a factory town whose industry (to employ a characteristic figure of the university leaders themselves) is a kind of knowledge.

Such reflections are further darkened as one follows President Perkins's later ruminations on the universities' struggles for internal coherence and self-control in the face of mounting external interference, particularly by the national government. But I have no space, even if I had the heart, to do more than mention his suave defense of the burgeoning, immensely costly administrative bureaucracy, with its lunatic hierarchy of trustees, presidents and vice presidents, chancellors and provosts, and department heads, its subtly influential administrative and secretarial assistants for whom frequently not only the student but the ordinary faculty member are figures in a committee report. Nowhere is there a touch of irony, a note of self-depreciation, an awareness of the appalling menace of full-time university executives and their appendages, who indeed make a mission of administration and whose relations to what goes on in the classroom or the laboratory, not to mention the dormitory or the common room, are not sufficiently developed to be called ceremonial. Not even vaguely does President Perkins intimate that a distinction might be drawn between something called "institutional management" and "educational leadership"; that in fact the kind of institutional life American university managers must lead usually insulates them from the educational life of the university. It is no accident I think that, as *Time* magazine cheerfully pointed out in a recent issue, leaders of business and heads of universities have become interchangeable parts. In fact, as our universities move, in Perkins's phrase, "from autonomy to systems" (as the University of California has already done), the president of a multiversity is nothing but the executive officer of a knowledge industry." [6]

If one cares to learn something about the actual ways of university administrators, more is to be learned from Herbert Stroup's sardonic *Bureaucracy in Higher Education* [7] than from a dozen books of apology by national university leaders such as Perkins and Kerr. Stroup, a sociologist as well as Dean of Students at Brooklyn College, reminds one at times of Veblen. His book is uneven and offers no real alternative to existing trends. Indeed, Stroup defends academic bureaucracy as "a stabilizing and regularizing influence on the social body," whose very existence "tends to stave off haphazard, quixotic and even irrational efforts on the part of powerful minorities." He also argues, following the political scientist C. J. Friedrich, that bureaucracy *may* be a positive help to the maintenance of a democratic society.

Nonetheless in the case of the university, Stroup himself contends that "the college worker" is not less but "more amenable to the dictates of interest groups than are others in society." He reminds us of the melancholy fact that of all groups composing the Nazi party, teachers were the best represented, and he quotes approvingly a statement of Hans Gerth and C. Wright Mills to the effect that scientists and technicians just because of their narrow training and limited knowledge are the most easily manipulated of all groups in modern society. For my part I do not know this to be true, but on general grounds I find it believable. The very organization of the American university, with its absentee owners (trustees) and quasi-military chain of command, at once relieves the ordinary professor and student of responsibilities for what happens to the institution itself and systematically unfits them for sustained political action in spheres outside their immediate fields of professional interest. For most of us academicians, in fact, major decisions and policies adopted by "the university" are like fate, and we uncheerfully accept them as such.

If it is true, as M. E. Dimock remarks in a statement quoted by Stroup at the end of his book, that "an institution tends to take on the character of its leadership," those concerned with the quality of academic life in our universities have reason to be alarmed. For our top university leaders, as Stroup demonstrates, are largely and effectively insulated from that life. They may know something about it by description, but they do not share it, any more than the captains of other industries share the ordinary life of workers. Invariably this separation is reflected in their public utterances. Indeed, the fatal limitation of the books, and minds, of university hierarchs like James Perkins, who so gladly preach to the rest of us about missions in which they themselves participate —perhaps can any longer participate—only ritually is their utter remoteness from the educational process. What their discourses really amount to are managers' briefs for those parts or aspects of the national industry over which they preside but which, even as presiding officers, they understand only imperfectly. The rest— and it is a very great deal—is not their "business."

James Perkins, no more than Clark Kerr, offers a remotely acceptable account of the *idea* of the university. But if I have to choose between them, I will take Kerr's account, both because it is more accurate as a statement of fact, and because, construed as prescription and prophecy, it at least leaves open the possibility that the university may include something more than an advanced technological institute. A multiversity may be an educational department store with attached service stations of various sorts, but, like Sears, it sells everything, including, conceivably, a half-liberal education.

Admittedly the sort of undergraduate education which a university makes possible differs in important ways from that afforded by even a first-rate liberal arts college like Oberlin or Swarthmore. For undergraduates as well as graduate students, a range of educational possibilities, informal as well as formal, exists within the environment of a university, even of the second rank, which the most richly endowed four-year college cannot match. Correspondingly, the university college has liabilities which not all undergraduates are able to offset. But "getting lost" is not, as Perkins contends, by any means the whole problem. An undergraduate can get lost at Oberlin as well as at Cornell, and many students at smaller universities such as Brandeis have readier access to what is left of their teachers' minds than they do at large city colleges. The point is rather that the university college itself is subject to both intellectual and moral strains, and has peculiar problems of identity and integrity that arise from its being embedded within a university whose academic departments and institutes have educational commitments that frequently (although by no means always) lead away from the concerns of liberal education. Quite apart from the existence of the professional schools, which can in principle enrich the undergraduate curriculum, there are the graduate school and the graduate students whose presence is felt, often for the better, throughout the college. Further, in a university college, the opportunity, as well as the pressure, to specialize and to do it quickly is commonly greater than in most other colleges. For these reasons, the issue of liberal education—what it is and what it is worth, especially to the exceptional student—may be more keenly felt in the university than in the four-year college. And partly because of this, the general education movement itself and most of the current proposals for its reform have originated within the universities.

But the significance of liberal education, and hence of the problems of general education in the era of the multiversity and the university system, is unlikely to be intensely felt by anyone not directly involved in the primary educational life of the university college. This is true enough, God knows, of many research professors, anxious to "get on with their work." How much more so must it be of professional administrators, bemused by the incessant demands of all the far-flung missions over which they preside. This is a question, not of good will or personal endowment, but of experience and of the focus which experience alone makes possible. To write significantly and imaginatively about what is at stake in the contemporary crisis of the university college—and this, I have come to think, lies at the very heart of the wider crisis of the university and of the whole higher learning in our time—one must be constantly involved as a teacher, writer, and person in the fundamental work of the intellect. Only so can one realize what an incomparable endowment a truly liberal education can be for young people just coming into full possession of their powers. But only so, also, can one appreciate the sense of divided loyalties and aspirations, and the feeling of attenuation and loss, which pervade the contemporary university college. Plainly, the task is, in the full etymological sense of the term, a philosophical one, well beyond the range of interest or experience, I should add at once, of most academic philosophers. It requires someone who, like Daniel Bell, is himself (if he will not mind my saying so) caught in the crossfire between the scholar and the intellectual, and who, one suspects, finds it impossible to satisfy all the aspirations of his own commodious mind within the limits set by even so sprawling an academic discipline as sociology. In the next chapter, we shall consider with what success Professor Bell, a philosopher now almost in spite of himself, has coped with the monumental job of work to which he has been called as historian, critic, and (conceivably) reformer of general education in one great university college, Columbia.

8

The American University:

A PRIMARY MEASURE OF THE CONDITION OF OUR UNIversities at the present time is the increasing uncertainty among its leaders, even after several decades, about the success, or even the aims, of general education. Of course there are technical reasons, as Daniel Bell explains in *The Reforming of General Education*, why it has been increasingly difficult in an age of competitive specialization and spreading bureaucracy to staff general education courses with first-rate teachers. Again, who wants to teach general education? Nor have cleverer students, dazzled by professional and material opportunities that are open to students who distinguish themselves in their major subjects, been quick to acknowledge, or perceive, the virtues of courses that lead nowhere and anywhere and that because they are nonprofessional, seem not quite serious and respectable. But apart from all technical problems, profound ambiguities in regard to the leading aspirations of general education have, from the beginning, made it difficult to decide what standards are appropriate in judging the success or failure of general education.

In part, as I suggested earlier, the aim of general education in the university has been to preserve at least some of the values traditionally ascribed to liberal education. But there are also other often quite extraneous reasons both for the rise of the general educational movement and for the forms it has taken. As Professor Bell emphasizes in his account of the "original assumptions" of the movement, ". . . general education at Columbia was the result of a curious mixture of parochial, sociopolitical, and philosophical motives." What was true at Columbia, where many of the early experiments in general education occurred, was true elsewhere. At Columbia John Erskine's famous General Honors course, in which students read and discussed one classic a week, became the prototype of humanities courses later given on a hundred campuses. Its quasi-humanistic aim was to "enculturate" students who had not hitherto been exposed to "the great tradition." On the other side, the course which at Columbia was later called "Contemporary Civilization" had as its progenitor two courses, one in "War Issues" and the other in "Peace Issues," that were introduced during the First World War by politically-oriented members of the philosophy and history departments. Courses of this type, now usually taught under social science auspices, were, as Bell says, "an open and frank acknowledgement of the direct responsibility of . . . [the colleges] to the stated democratic needs of society."

More surprisingly, the Great Books course also had a predominately social and political bias, although in contrast to the embryonic "C.C." course it presented, according to Lionel Trilling, "a fundamental criticism of American democratic education" and, presumably, society. This sociopolitical emphasis persisted as the general education movement spread, first to Chicago and, after the Second World War, to Harvard. Bell fancies, however, that both sides of the dialectic were strenuously presented only on Morningside Heights. At Chicago the prevailing Aristotelianism and Thomism imparted to general education "the flavor of an aristocratic critique of the democratic," whereas Harvard's program was a response to the obligation, assumed in the name of democracy, to provide young citizens with "some common and binding understanding of the society which they will possess in common." Perhaps there are grains of truth in all this, although to someone like myself who has taught courses in general education both at Columbia and at Harvard, it seems a vast oversimplification of reality. For one thing, even when conceived politically, the attitudes conveyed through courses in "the classics" are both more various and more complex than Bell suggests; more important, their concern is frequently with quite different dimensions of individual or collective life. It is true, for example, that Aristotle believed that tragic heroes must be well-born, but it is also true that what happens even to Aristotelian heroes (and their kin) is a humanly fearful and piteous story of calamity, of communal guilt and personal expiation, of fatal passion and wasted good, of reconciliation and catharsis. And if Aristotle at times is a snob, Euripides, for one, is not. What the devil have wild women like Phaedra or Medea, or their still enthralled audiences, to do with social questions anyway? The primary interest in many general education courses in the humanities, including the one at Columbia, is not, at least in my experience, "ideological" at all (the term is Bell's, but it is employed in this book in a common nonpejorative sense at variance with his practice in his writings on "the end of ideology"). And I can vouch for it that although official theories of general education are often full of crass ideological directives, many teachers in the humanities happily ignore them. What concerns them are the durable intrinsic interests of literature and philosophy themselves: with their power, that is, to delight the spirit, to enliven the imagination, to refine and clarify discourse, and to bring to the whole mind a fuller sense of its inventiveness, singularity, and freedom.

Bell's account of the development of general education at Columbia, Chicago, and Harvard is inevitably flattened out in his recapitulations of the "original assumptions" which he ascribes to all three programs. He is aware, moreover, that there has always been a discrepancy between the statements of those who formulate educational programs and the practice of those who teach in them. Nevertheless, Bell's recapitulation remains a useful point of departure for discussions of prevailing tendencies. In the case of an historian who is also a reformer, such a summary of working principles also sets in relief what he regards as of abiding importance. And for a reformer who is in no sense a revolutionary, it provides a useful context for his own proposals for change.

The first two of the four traditional assumptions which Bell ascribes to general education have objectives that lie well beyond the customary round of scholarly activities. The leading assumption, which he identifies as "ideological," is that university students should not only be made aware of the unifying needs and common practices of American society but also that they should be instilled with "a sense of common tasks, though not necessarily a single purpose." Here, says Bell, the operative term is "consensus," a word, he carefully tells us, which was in use at Chicago long before it became a hallmark of the Johnson administration. But for general educators also, be it noted, the concern is with a national consensus; nor, despite the reference to unifying needs and common practices and tasks, are any specific limiting terms placed upon it.

Does this mean that, in Bell's view, exponents of nationalist ideological consensualism in general education have been prepared to instill in their students a respect for every deep American consensus, regardless of its content? Some part of the answer to this question may be implicit in Bell's account of the second extramural assumption which he lists simply under the heading of "Tradition." This assumption, whatever else may be said for or against it, plainly contravenes the blank-check consensualist ideology which is all too prevalent. What "the tradition" has represented is an effort to inform students with a better grasp of the history of the wider Western civilization and culture of which our own remains a variant. But the concern of general education with that history is by no means the historian's own professional interest in it. On the contrary, its highly selective aims, as Bell describes them, are to develop the student's sense of "recurrent moral and political problems of men in society," and more particularly to chart for him "the travails of the idea of freedom" and to "instill" in him the idea of "civility."

Bell curiously neglects to point out that such a use of "history" and "the tradition" is itself largely ideological. But even ideologically, how many aspects of the tradition, recurrently emphasized in "G.E." courses, are inadequately comprehended in terms of liberty and civility? Consider for example the pervasive rationalism and scientism which, since Plato, has dominated our academic ideas of learning and knowledge. How deeply reflected are these attitudes in the preoccupation with general ideas of liberty and civility? And consider the countertraditions of fideism and anti-rationalism represented by such names as Augustine and Luther, by Rousseau and (on one side) Hume, by Dostoievski, Nietzsche, William James, and the existentialists. In many general education courses, I believe, it has been the developing dialectic between the conflicting attitudes or ideas represented in these traditions which for many students has proved the truly instructive and civilizing thing.

Again, consider the revolutionary ideals inscribed in the terms "fraternity" and "equality," and in the troubled aspirations commonly ranged under the head of "romanticism": specifically the passionate yearning for all that lies beyond city life, the whole "mighty being" of Wordsworth, and behind it the idea of nature variously associated with such names as Goethe, Rousseau, Spinoza, the Stoics, and *Ecclesiastes*. Such phases of human culture, admittedly ambiguous and often blurred, are deeply veined through the whole Western tradition. And they also are represented in the syllabi of general education courses everywhere. Nor are they treated by all exponents of the tradition as merely its underside, covered with festering sore spots of rebelliousness, primitiveness, incivility, and mysticism which well-groomed students are to understand only in the way in which certain liberals have understood their critics. Many teachers of general education believe, I think rightly, that such concerns and affections are irremovable aspects of the dialectic of human existence.

But of course the main virtue of "the tradition" for many of us has always belonged to another level of educational interest: its immense virtue, that is, as a repository, not just of "ideas," "ideals," and "commitments," ethico-political or otherwise, but also of artistic, literary, and religious, as well as philosophical and scientific achievements—actualizations and consummations of the mind's powers of creation and invention—which are perennially absorbing on their own account to any teacher or student worth his salt.

But this is not all. Professor Bell knows the difference between understanding of the idea of liberty and an actually liberated person. And elsewhere he remarks upon the substantive liberating effect of studies in which interest is recurrently raised from the particular theory at hand to the more general conceptual or methodological issues which it may raise. Yet, in this crucial resumé of the common assumptions of general education, it is only the ideas of liberty and civility and the recurrent ethico-political idea of "man in society" which come to his mind.

From a moral point of view, the virtue of the entire tradition of liberal education has been in principle to liberate the mind and soul of the student himself. In fact, one's whole feeling about Bell's summary could change if the concern for consensus and for ideology were put (where teachers, confident of their own vocation and of the inherent dignity of liberal education, instinctively put it) in its natural and legitimate second or third place, and if first place were reserved for the actual development of free and civil beings, capable of making up their own minds about the value of national societies, ideas of liberty and civility, and the rest. What interests us in the case of Socrates are not just his highly ironical discussions of the golden ideas, but a personal embodiment of them, which, through Plato's art, takes possession of us as it took possession of Plato himself. Again, from the standpoint of extractable doctrines of civility and freedom, Montaigne offers us even less than Socrates. Nor does it matter. What Montaigne presents to us, through his continually shifting discourse with himself, is not an idea of civility but a highly civil mind struggling toward its own true freedom. When all has been said and done, what "we" hope for, what makes our impossible task one worthy of a Virgil himself, is that when we withdraw we will bid farewell not just to a scholar or idea man, but the semblance of a free human being. Is this not the one commencement in which alone we teachers have any deep wish to take a part? And after all, is this not the true reason why we have refused to turn general and liberal education over to the secondary schools? One hopes so.

Bell discusses the third and fourth assumptions of general education, in more intramural terms, under the headings of "Contra-specialism" and "Integration." Now "Contra-special*ism*" is an accurate enough term for the purpose, and indeed correctly conveys a major intention of general education. But it can be misleading and certain weaker manifestoes have undoubtedly confused specialism with something very different: the concern, that is, for exact knowledge or for detailed understanding of a particular science or art. In this latter sense and at a certain stage, as Bell acknowledges, specialization is both necessary and laudible, and any general education program which opposed it would be doomed, and rightly so. Like scientism and professionalism, specialism is another thing altogether, and it is a profound malaise that afflicts both teachers and students in the humanities quite as much as it does their (other) scientific brethren. In the form described by Bell, specialism is that "religion of research" which German universities bequeathed to their uncritical American emulators in the last decades of the nineteenth century. Intensified by the inducements of technological industry and the insatiable demands of the national government, it is indeed the only religion now visible on most campuses.

Against specialism, as Bell himself puts it, "The rallying cry . . . [has been] *humanitas*." Because he describes the evil of specialism, against which liberal education as a whole is a continuing protest, in too narrowly academic terms, the rallying cry is deprived of its full meaning. Actually, the religion of research in our age is but one form of the vocationalism and professionalism that pervade our entire educational system. It is also a manifestation of that narrowness and exclusiveness which we object to in "the bureaucratic mentality" which blankets our whole institutional life. Liberal and general education are attempts, all too feeble, to make teachers and students aware of human concerns, as well as responsibilities and rights, more ultimate and more pervasive than those defined by any special job of work, academic or otherwise. And it has been the endless, often thankless, task of college and university teachers committed to liberal education to illuminate and, if possible, to strengthen all those primordial forms of action, of speech and art, of sympathy and passion that serve to offset the myriadic sources of alienation of men from their lives and from one another which the term "specialism" symptomizes.

A closely related point has to be made regarding the fourth premise of general education which Bell places under the rubric of "integration." In fact, Bell's way of describing the demand for "integration" (which is accurate enough) as well as his own suggestions for meeting it, illustrates some of the very evils which the antispecialist aims of liberal education are intended to correct. Certainly integration, of some sort and of something or other, is wanted. The question is, *what?* In Bell's account the sources of disintegration are also conceived intramurally as the fabulous increase of scientific knowledge and the accompanying proliferation of fields, subfields, and nonfields of scholarly inquiry. Correspondingly, the remedy has been sought in an "interdisciplinary approach" which, at least in general education courses, "emphasizes the broad relations of knowledge, rather than the single discipline."

Hence Bell's emphasis on "the centrality of method" as a way of understanding "principles of disciplines." But a concerted understanding of methods of inquiry, while it may serve for integrating the scholarly activities of the academic man, may still leave him, even as an intellectual being, a complete shambles. What is so curious, if Bell's account is right, is that exponents of liberal and general education have here played directly into the hands of those for whom the university is a scientific institute, a place for the integration of master problem-solvers.

The fact is that no one with a voice sufficiently commanding to make himself heard has deeply questioned prevailing notions concerning the nature of educational problems of integration, of which the modern university is merely the most conspicuous breeding ground. Nor is the reason far to seek: most of us who participate either occasionally or regularly in general education programs are university men ourselves, that is to say, academicians who, however reluctantly and unbelievingly, have been trained to be, and are, functionaries of the very system which general education is meant to mitigate and to counteract. All our manifestoes, "Red Books," and reports on the need for the reform of general education everywhere, bear witness to this fact. We too— we scholars—have conceived the educational problem of integration as the problem of integrating professorial minds of the sort we know all too well. Nor are we alone in this. From Plato to Whitehead, who himself once claimed that a sufficiently thorough study of mathematics and logic could itself provide a liberal education, our academic sages have continually sought to counter specialism and disorder with a more methodical understanding of the foundational ideas, the conceptual schemes, and the methods of inquiry at work within the curriculum of academic studies itself.

What we must return to, however, is the Socratic assumption that an integrated mind, fully aware of its own more ultimate concerns and possibilities is, at all stages of its educational development, more than an intracranial meeting place for the disciplining of disciplines. Knowledge of forms of scholarly inquiry and learning will serve at best only to relate those same investigations themselves. But the contemporary university student needs and demands something else as well. To be sure, he wants help toward an understanding of the connections between, say, the methods of physical science and those of sociology or between the findings of the economic historian and those of the historian of English literature. However, he wants also to know the wisdom that may lie in the study of such connections. He wants not only to tie the academic strands together, but to tie his knowledge of them and their methods back into his developing experience as a human being. He wants to know what they portend as forms of life, both for him and for his kind. What he gets is mainly an integrative ideology for the social class into which he is being initiated; a system of rules for the self-identification and unification of the university men themselves. This has its virtue; among other things, it provides the emblem of a great potential collective power. But this is a lesser virtue, I believe, than a university should aspire to. And it is for this reason, among others, that the original assumptions of general education demand reexamination and revision.

Bell himself is by no means uncritical of these assumptions. In particular, he opposes the contention that there is an inviolable core—whether of great books or values—which every liberally educated person must know, and, knowing, make his own. Unlike the original general educators at Chicago, he has no preformed notions either of the good society or the good life. And he would replace indoctrination in a bogus *philosophia perennis* with the polymathic sophistication and self-consciousness that come from a developed sense of history and method. Bell puts it succinctly when he says, in defense of the liberal arts college against those advanced thinkers who consider it a waste of time, that the college "can be a unique place where students acquire self-consciousness, historical consciousness, and methodological consciousness." In a world in which all mooring places have been washed away, what the student needs nowadays is not an anchor, for which he no longer has any use, but a pair of compasses, a strong keel, and a first-rate set of pumps.

The only trouble—and it is a weakness that may be inherent

in all such points of view—is that Bell's memory is so short. He defends the self as the subject of a liberal education. Yet in practice the self always seems to disappear in a field of historical-methodological orientations. Consider the following statements culled from the same page as the preceding quotation: "What I shall argue . . . is that in this day and age, and even more in the coming day and age, the *distinctive* function of the college must be to teach modes of conceptualization, explanation, and verification of knowledge" (my italics). Or again, "I strongly believe that historical consciousness is *the* foundation of any education . . ." (my italics). Such pronouncements recur again and again. Meanwhile, what has happened to consciousness of the self? Well, an account like Bell's gives us only a kind of advanced sociological consciousness whose educational need is to "balance" the abstract with the concrete, the general with the particular, the method with its applications, but which avoids like the pox anything resembling a developed philosophy of human culture or of life.

It is not, I surmise, mere modesty or caution which leads Bell at the outset of his long discussion of "The Need for Reform: Some Philosophical Pre-suppositions" to disavow any claim to present "an ordered philosophy." When he tells us that what he offers is not an exploration of "the 'ultimate grounds' of belief about the nature of man and society," nor "an exercise in dogmatics—theological or pedagogical," but only a sketch of "pre-suppositions" that have guided his own educational investigations, the impression conveyed is of one who has not only put away vain and childish things, but who has felt no stronger philosophical need than to "make explicit the compound of prejudices, opinions, and values that have guided this inquiry." Sufficient unto the day is the inquiry thereof.

But if Bellean self-consciousness tends to be dissipated into historical and methodological consciousness, historical consciousness itself tends, in a manner that would have delighted Hegel, to be absorbed into methodological consciousness. Bell, who has a positive horror of thoughts about last, or first, things, wants history, but he wants it without laughs or tears, without birth or death, without any of the finalities of which it is also a record. What he seeks, for educational purposes at least, is a history of middle distances that keep their place as contexts of inquiry and do not distract the student—or teacher—from the bustling foreground of contemporary institutional life upon which his own inquiring eyes are trained. Perhaps this is why, despite his laudible demand for the "wider vistas" which the study of histories and cultures other than our own can give, the perspectives of history in his treatment always seem foreshortened. And it is partly for the same reason that he sometimes imputes to academic arrangements and programs of fairly recent origin a deeper significance than they really had at the time, yet also, paradoxically, fails to perceive in them possibilities of reconstruction that might occur to someone less preoccupied with the immediate context of scholarly inquiries and procedures.

Nowhere is this tendency more strikingly in evidence than in the educational significance which Bell finds in the grand trivium of the latter-day American university: the (natural) sciences, the social sciences, and the humanities. For many academicians, including Harvard's reforming Doty Committee, this trivium is merely a matter of administrative convenience (reinforced perhaps by the accumulating pressures of academic power politics). Accordingly, they treat it with scant respect as an educational principle. For Bell, however, there is lodged within the trivium an implicit rationale which not only justifies the traditional triadic division of general education courses (of which students are commonly required to take at least one in each main area), but the basis for a proposed reform of the whole modern liberal arts curriculum. This rationale, needless to say, is methodological. Thus, in Bell's view what the trivium represents when properly understood is three grand "strategies" of inquiry, from which he derives three characteristic principles of learning with which all university students should be thoroughly familiar.

Bell's major innovative idea, therefore, is that *the* indispensable education which a liberally-endowed university college alone can adequately provide—whether in courses conducted under general education auspices or in the more specialized offerings of academic departments—should be a continuous, increasingly sophisticated training in the methods of inquiry and learning which the (natural) sciences, the social sciences, and the humanities respectively exemplify. Bell's account of these strategies is admittedly impressionistic. The strategy characteristic of mathematics and the natural sciences is said to be "sequential" or "linear," moving from axioms to theorems, from hypotheses to their deducible consequences, and from simpler ideas and subject matters to those that are more complex. In part, what Bell has in mind here are developed scientific systems like those found in Euclidean geometry and Newtonian mechanics. In part also he has in view such organized sequences of studies as the young mathematician runs through in moving from algebra, geometry, and calculus to differential equations and the rest.[1] In the social sciences, on the other hand, both inquiry and learning move crab-wise by something called "linkages" in which "the understanding of one kind of phenomenon cannot be self-contained but is possible only by an understanding of linked contexts within a social system." Thus, to take one of his examples, elements of economic policy can be grasped only in a political context, the understanding of which, in turn, involves a conception of the social community. In the humanities, the method of knowledge is said to be "concentric." Here, as he puts it, a few major themes—the nature of tragedy, the varieties of life, the discovery of the self—are returned to again and again for ever more enlarged comprehension of their "meanings."

In this instance, however, some of the difficulties of Bell's scheme begin to emerge. At times the aim of learning appears to be the enlarged appreciation *of* imaginative literature and art; at other times, however, his emphasis is upon scholarly learning *about* such works and, more particularly, upon historical and critical writing which may give "the student a sense of how an imaginative work relates to its own time and how its enduring qualities transcend that time." Just what qualities *are* these? Are they still essentially, or primarily, qualities of felt experience, qualities that exist for the delight and rejuvenation they may directly yield? Or are they qualities which are significant to the savant, the social scientist, or the historian interested in recurrent patterns of culture and social organization? One is a bit disturbed by such a statement as the following: "If the *intellectual* need of the Humanities course is for historical context, the intellectual need of a Contemporary Civilization course is for 'historical explanation' " (italics mine). By Bell's own admission, the student of the humanities, or his professor, resorts perforce to the extrinsic linkages of social science and history. But are these the only intellectual needs or forms of learning which Bell takes to be involved in our recurrent "linked" encounters with literature or art or music or philosophy? If so he is simply mistaken. Not merely the senses and feelings but the whole cultivated mind is continuously involved in the primary recreative act of appreciating the line of action in, say, *Hamlet* or *The Divine Comedy*, in the modulations, thematic transformations, and the returns of a Mozart sonata, or in the complex, interactive spatial and functional relationships of a great building. I agree with Bell (and, behind him, Trilling), against certain of the lesser "new critics," that if you don't from time to time go "outside" the poem you are likely to miss indispensable clues as to what is "inside." For what is inside is not a perdurable open-faced "object," but a system of meanings, a symbolic action, a movement of words, the sense of which is not "given" in the way that some foolish philosophers have supposed "sense-data" to be given.

Still, if Bell's reforms succeed, the student's work of art will be absorbed increasingly into a great chain of sociohistorical links, and by the end of his senior year he won't be able to tell *Hamlet* from the strategies of interpretation which scholarly inquiries about the play presumably illustrates. And if the reply is made that literary and critical-historical concerns are both legitimate— as indeed they are—and, in principle, mutually reinforcing, Bell's emphasis, so far as collegiate education is concerned, remains heavily upon "the centrality of method," "the strategy of inquiry," and the now fashionable "meta-" studies which constantly analyse but never face the forms of artifice that shape our existences as men.

Compared with the inert, simplistic rationalism of someone like James Perkins, Bell's pluralist account of methods of inquiry and learning is a pearl of great price. But when one looks closely, he continues to wear the stigmata of the rationalist and the academician for whom knowing about things, rather than knowing *them* ever more appreciatively and discriminatingly, is the main achievement to be hoped for from the higher forms of learning. Most of his specific innovations, it seems to me, would reinforce attention to contexts of inquiry rather than to experienced realms of being. To talk continually about strategies of inquiry and methods of knowledge is entirely appropriate to the content of the existing trivium, *all* of which, including the so-called humanities, are dominated by the religion of research. But it will not do at all for a liberated trivium in which, *especially* at the highest levels of learning, the knowledge to be sought is not entirely a technologically useful theoretical knowledge about correlatable and manipulatable objects, natural, organic, or social, valuable as this can be. Nor will it do for a philosophy of learning and knowledge, and hence of education, which has worked itself free from the rationalist's obsession with the logic of scientific explanation and with methods of theoretical problem-solving, illuminating as these can also be. What is wanted, I suspect, is not a theory of knowledge, in the sense which has largely prevailed since before Descartes, but something quite different that begins by talking of modes or ways of knowing, in quite ordinary senses of the term, which represent, not only the achievements of positive science alone, but all of the characteristic ways of handling and doing things which, when they succeed, we call knowledge.

To such a view, let me add, Professor Bell, who is a pragmatist to the tips of his prose, should readily assent. Here and there, in fact, Bell himself provides us, although only in passing, with some clues to the approach I have in mind. For one thing, he sees in part that the issue, even in the university, is not simply that of teaching versus research, but also of one form of teaching (and hence learning), which is geared to the forms of achievements over which scientific research presides, versus others which are geared to other forms of achievement, such as moral, aesthetic, and (I should add) religious and philosophical understanding. These too are modes of knowledge. But the virtue of moral understanding, for example, does not consist in an ability to describe and predict, and hence to manipulate things, but to guide our choices and actions in our dealings with persons. Again, Bell sees, and indeed insists, that the achievement which humanistic knowledge may represent is the achievement of those fulfilled and significant experiences of reality, including works of art, which often goes by the overworked term "appreciation."

The point is simply this: such forms of knowledge are correlated not with "subject-matters" or classes of phenomena, with which the existing trivium is largely preoccupied, but with different ways of relating ourselves as knowers, and hence as learners, to that which we "know." Thus the sort of knowledge, of which theoretical natural science is the paradigm, relates primarily to activities concerned with our relations to (what we regard as) *things*. The same is true, of course, of much that goes by the name of knowledge in the more "behavioral" branches of the social sciences and in the humanities, although still perhaps confusedly and unsystematically. However, the sort of knowledge with which social scientists and historians like Bell himself are mainly concerned is precisely *not* a knowledge of men as "phenomena," as Kant called them, but, something entirely different: a knowledge (as Bell puts it, albeit inadequately) of "the differentiations and variations of human actions." Here the knowledge aspired to is an understanding of the reason why, and not merely how, human beings *act* as they do, individually and in groups, together with the characteristic forms of motive and the recurrent modes of practice that pertain to their work, their experience, and their lives as men: that is, as actors, office-holders, sons and lovers, and above all as persons.

The task of reconstruction, so far as liberal education is concerned, is indeed to discern within the trivium different modes of knowledge, and hence of learning. But these are not properly based upon strategies or methods of scholarly inquiry, much less upon classifications of subject matters which invariably wind up conceiving their "objects" as phenomena. Accordingly, the forms of sophistication which higher-level courses in general education ought to provide is not just a better grasp of modes of scientific concept formation and theory construction, meta-theoretical studies of the logic of explanation, and the like, all of which have as their aim a better comprehension of ways of coping with phenomena of various sorts. They should seek, first of all, to differentiate those major forms of activity that serve to absorb and delight the minds of men: our dealings with physical objects, our relations with human (and other) persons, our engagements with those creations of the imagination, of which works of art and literature are merely the most conspicuous. Only in relation to them do we then begin to see what the point might be in giving an account of those specific forms of achievement that go by the names of knowledge and of learning. And only then does it become worthwhile, or even possible, to distinguish accurately the skills required for the explanation and prediction of phenomena, including the human organism regarded as a phenomenon, which, in their most exact and systematic forms, are called scientific methods; the powers required for determining the various ends of human action and for appraising the conditions of their fulfillment that pertain to what we call moral or practical knowledge, or, more simply, wisdom; and, finally, the abilities required for discerning those moving possibilities of experience inherent in "objects" of human consciousness which, in one form, albeit misleadingly, is sometimes called critical or aesthetic understanding. Such forms of knowledge are not all, or exclusively, products of inquiry or "research," but they are none the less precious for all that. Nor, in their higher forms, can they be readily acquired without the help of informed and gifted teachers, able to guide perception, to develop attitudes and enlarge sympathies, and to impart skills, as well as to explain facts.

To understand what such activities of the mind entail, however, and what is involved in the forms of knowledge required for successful participation in them, nothing would be more useful, in my opinion, than an enlightened philosophical study of the primary forms of human utterance, the "logical" geography of the several main "universes" of discourse, and, accordingly, the characteristic sorts of things we do, not only with words, but with other important modes of expression, in talking and thinking about natural phenomena, in our responsible conduct toward persons, and in forming and appreciating discussions of things worthy of our attention, our admiration, and our love for their own sakes. Such a study, however, is a far cry from courses in "logic, methodology, and semantics" which are sometimes taught under the auspices of departments of philosophy.

Reading Bell, I sometimes have the sense that, save when his professorial mind is moving in orbit around the idea and the problems of the national society, he is essentially an eclectic or mannerist, an historicist collector of notions and ideas who has no spiritual homeland to which he wishes to return, no shore of light that he hopes eventually to reach. Like many other polymaths, he is a world traveller, but without a destination. This impression is also reinforced by his fatal invocation of John Dewey's idea of education for education's sake.

In the end perhaps the reason why Bell reverts so obsessively to notions of inquiry and method as binders for his proposed reforms is that he really has no educational ends beyond the higher, more serviceable learning, of which the existing national university is the repository. But this may also be why, when it comes to the content of his reforms, he instinctively turns to those linkages and sequences with which he identifies the social and natural sciences. In the humanities, for example, his proposals seem invariably to direct the student's attention to the historical and social contexts of art, to contexts of criticism, to contexts of those contexts, and so on into the night. Of course he hopes and expects that the student will return to a more discriminating, knowledgeable experience of *The Marriage of Figaro*. But my impression is that what the Bellean sophisticate is more likely to return to is a search for still wider and subtler contexts, that he will become in the end only another, more omniscient scholar. Poor Figaro.

Thus, sequence after sequence, link after link, but never really centering, never *landing* or *settling* anywhere, Bell's philosophy of education is for scholars-in-flight whose only home is an international airport. At moments Bell himself seems aware of this danger. But only toward the end of his final chapter, "A Reprise, with Some Notes on the Future," does he broach the idea that from the university experience there might emerge human beings, not only conscious of having sampled the best that has been thought, said, and done in the world, but aflame with a passion for active, creative, perhaps revolutionary emulation. Bell speaks of two "orientations towards the future that divide the intelligentsia today—the technocratic and the apocalyptic." And he proposes that we educators should at once try to "humanize" a scientific technocracy that seems to have lost its soul and to "tame" the apocalypse. But how? By more suggestive chat about "strategies" of inquiry; by further study of study? Who can believe it?

In sum, I am bound to say that the idea of a liberal and hence a general education for the university student finally eludes Bell, just as the idea of the university in our time eludes Perkins and Kerr, and for related reasons. Still, as we have seen, there are intimations in Bell's compendious book of something better than he actually manages to deliver. I usually find myself on his side when, for the nonce, he opposes the attitudes of those who view the university college as merely a way station on the road to the graduate school. And some of his specific proposals for reform seem to me wise. Wherever he complains against the parochialism and provincialism of the existing system, I am on his side. The study of Western civilization no longer suffices for those who would understand not only the ideas but also the practices of civility and freedom that abound in the contemporary world. Into the main stream of general education must be introduced courses which answer to this want. Nor does the study of "the classics" suffice in literature or art or philosophy, any more than it does in the sciences. Into the humanities programs must be introduced courses dealing with recent, or even with contemporary, works of distinction. Further, the Humanities programs must include, more centrally and insistently than they have in the past, the study of nonliterary arts. Finally, in the sciences, courses should be made available in which the students may become aware of the revolutionary techniques which contemporary mathematical logic, theory of games, and computer science have made available to the theoretician and the scholar. One day, no doubt, these will be a part of common human understanding. All this plainly requires that general education must not be restricted to the freshman and sophomore years. On the contrary, as Bell rightly insists, it must be continuous if it is to be of any permanent benefit. And his proposal for a "third-tier" scheme, in which each student in the senior year would "brake the drive toward specialization" by trying to generalize his experience in his discipline, has merit, even though his particular ideas concerning its implementation seem to me to suffer once more from the same methodolatry which I think is the besetting evil of his book.

Who will make the next try? Someone, I hope, with a wiser philosophy, a more adequate understanding of the wide diversities of human practice, a more constant passion to relate what he understands to the ultimate concerns of human existence. It should also be someone less preoccupied than any of the writers we have hitherto considered with the affairs of the national society and more attentive to the spiritual and intellectual disorders within the American university itself.

9

The Revolting Academy

A SPECTER OF REVOLUTION HAUNTS THE LAND. OR, rather, a congregation of revolutionary specters. For it is a major problem simply to sort them out and then, when possible, to relate them to one another. There seems to be general agreement that the working classes, for the present at least, are out of it; their conservative unions, for example, belong as firmly to the established order as Hubert Humphrey, and for the same reason. To this extent, certainly, Marx must be updated by anyone who still finds him relevant. One major revolt (we may as well begin by distinguishing revolts, which are, as the term implies, active and intentional, from revolutions, which, in their loose common usage, may not be) is that of the Black Power movement. Like the revolt of individuals involved in the resistance against the war in Indochina, it concerns us here tangentially: in so far, that is, as it relates to the student-young faculty revolts now occurring at universities here and abroad. However all these revolts, in one way or another, are effects of the sophisticated scientific-technological "revolution" which has converted the university into the indispensable supplier of manpower to the immensely rich and powerful post-industrial national society of which Daniel Bell and Zbigniew Brzezinski, among others, are exponents. The latter revolution, in turn, was made possible by the products of the "academic revolution" which preoccupy Professors Jencks and Riesman in their book, *The Academic Revolution*: [1] the revolution, that is, initiated in the last decades of the nineteenth century, which transformed the old sectarian liberal arts and land grant colleges into modern "graduate school universities."

As it turns out, Professor Brzezinski has lately published in

The New Republic an essay—or a position paper—"Revolution and Counter Revolution" [2] which, despite the ironical disclaimer in its parenthetical subtitle "(But Not Necessarily about Columbia)" directly forces upon us the central issues which, I believe, connect these revolts and revolutions. Accordingly it helps to bring into common focus both the problems which concern Jencks and Riesman and those discussed in Professor Kenneth Keniston's recent book, *Young Radicals: Notes on Committed Youth.*[3] The relevance of Brzezinski's article owes much to its author being at once a major prophet of the new epoch, which he calls the "technetronic society," an acute typologist of revolutions and counter- or pseudo-revolutions, and a harshly realistic strategist for establishmentarians. In Brzezinski's view, the future belongs to those who have mastered the scientific-technological and administrative methods and tools upon which the governance of the technetronic society depends. He and his allies are benevolent elitists, for whom "participatory democracy," as young radicals now call it, must recall the Brook Farm experiment, itself the gesture of an archaistic American dream of an era that had already disappeared by the middle of the nineteenth century. These academicians accept as a fact that democracy in our time is not really a major issue, and they prefer not to discuss it. Although opposed to ideologies of all sorts, they do not explicitly repudiate the values and ideals of liberal education, even as reinterpreted by apologists for the multiversity. Rather do they prefer to let dead issues bury themselves in the academic committees and reports in which the futile ideologues of bygone traditions fritter away their energies. The technetronic academicians, meanwhile, collect their grant money, do their research, and ply their way back and forth between Logan, La Guardia, or San Francisco airports and Dulles Airport in Washington.

So much for the prophecy. Now for the typology and the strategies of revolutions and counterrevolutions that don't necessarily apply to the situation on Morningside Heights. True revolutions, such as the industrial revolution and the revolution now producing the technetronic society, according to Brzezinski, must always be genuine "responses to the future." In many instances such revolutions are already being carried out more or less adequately by existing institutions—which in the present situation of course includes the great graduate school universities described by Jencks and Riesman. But institutions such as the contemporary university are not always entirely adequate to their occasions. Significant revolts may occur which, however intended, may be taken to be implicit efforts to remove existing forms of institutional obsolescence. Such revolts are properly handled by the established authorities first by immediate isolation of the rebels through effective violence, and then by reforms that automatically take any remaining wind out of the shredded flags of the rebellion. Thus such revolts, properly handled, may implicitly serve the true revolution.

On the other hand, Brzezinski tells us, counterrevolutions such as the peasant revolts that occurred during the transition from feudal agrarian societies to modern industrial ones (as we can now see) are "responses to the past," and hence lacking both in historically significant ideological content and sustained power. Their "violence and revolutionary slogans," as Brzezinski puts it, "are merely—and sadly—the death rattle of the historical irrelevants." The only question, as it applies to the current student-faculty revolts, is, of course, whether, or how far, they are merely counterrevolutionary reactions by expendable misfits to academic life in a post-industrial age or evidence of a genuine need for institutional reforms that must be made if the universities are themselves to respond adequately to the demands of the new technetronic society.

It is no accident that Brzezinski fails to tell us what to do about counterrevolutionaries—for (one may argue) only after the fact can it be known for sure who really represents the wave of the future. Presumably competent authorities, who can tell an old dog from a young one, will throw the old dog a bone and then get back to work. But there is another way of interpreting Brzezinski's point of view: just as establishments which manage to put down true revolutions are bound to fail in another way since they must institute reforms roughly equivalent to the aims of the revolutionists, so counterrevolutionists who succeed must fail in the end since they will have to do the work of the establishment in order to survive. Either way the significant outcome is much the same.

Applied to the present situation in the universities, Brzezin-ski's argument might go like this: the wave of the future lies with the sciences, the forms of research, teaching, and academic orga-nization that serve the technetronic society. No doubt the existing establishment does not fully understand this and on the whole is not doing its job very effectively. In any case, fracases of the sort that occurred at Columbia and later at Harvard are properly to be viewed as latter-day peasant counterrevolutions. In short, the noise we hear is merely the death rattle of a historically irrele-vant part of the academic "community" that is, students and faculty who, for one reason or another, have been unable to ad-just to the forms of life essential to the university in the tech-netronic age. No doubt they will have to be put down, but then, one hopes, as gently and quietly as possible, and with no fret about the outcome. On the other hand, to the extent that the revolutionists' grievances indicate malfunctionings that must be removed if the technetronic university is to do its work, then the authorities, again having put the fires out, are bound immediately to inaugurate the necessary institutional reforms.

Only two things are wrong with this (highly schematic) argu-ment, but they are fatal to it. For one thing, the argument as-sumes in advance that the revolting students and their allies among the teaching fellows and professors are latter-day "peas-ants," unable to make the required intellectual and social adjust-ments to academic life in the new era. This is an error, as we shall soon see: many revolters are first-rate students who well under-stand the advanced methods of scientific technocracy; they and their older sympathizers in fact include some of the most sophisti-cated minds to be found anywhere on university campuses: that is, not merely dull-witted English majors and historians but mathematicians, logicians, linguists, advanced students of com-puter science and game theory. If this gentry is, in the current vernacular, about to opt out of the multiversity, it knows where-of it opts. More importantly, this very fact suggests that within the technetronic society there are already emerging deep-lying contradicitions that, understandably, first appear in the university. However outmoded are the specifics of Marx's analysis of nine-teenth-century capitalist-industrial societies, it may be true that the more advanced social systems of our own era may well be caught up in unprecedented dialectical conflicts of their own that threaten their internal stability. Societies consist not of classes and institutions only, but of the human beings who give them substance: if institutions systematically frustrate the needs and aspirations of considerable numbers of their ablest and most valuable functionaries, then a quasi-Marxian analysis may still be appropriate. To my knowledge, no one has disproved such a possibility in the circumstances that concern us here. Indeed its reality appears to be confirmed, almost against their authors' wills, by Keniston and by Jencks and Riesman. The fact is all the more arresting since the angles from which they conduct their investigations are so divergent.

As he is at pains to make clear, Professor Keniston is neither a young radical himself nor even a professorial fellow-traveler. He is, at most, a well-disciplined diagnostician. It is nonetheless fascinating to find a youngish professor of psychology in the Department of Psychiatry at the Yale Medical School, whose academic credentials are impeccable, bearing witness to the attitudes of many young radicals as being evidences not of counter-revolutionary obsolescence and maladjustment, but of a highly developed sense of moral responsibility, a compassion, a maturity and openness of spirit that contrast sharply with the falseness, inconsistency, and in the end always violent "realism" of academic authorities who sometimes forget what it means, in Keniston's homely phrase, "to help people be people."

Keniston has made it his business to learn, within his limits, whereof he speaks. His work is the product of a study of a number of students who worked from June to September, 1967, for Vietnam Summer, an organization of young radicals opposed to our military adventures in Southeast Asia. By stages he was made acutely aware of the connections between the young radicals' opposition to the Vietnam War, their sympathy for radical movements among black irreconcilables, and their mounting indignation at the arid forms of life offered them and their fellows on the best American campuses. In short, Keniston has come to understand (though not, I think, in full depth) how far so-called young radicals in America are alienated from the presumptive future which our national society professes to hold open both for its own citizens and for victims in "underdeveloped" areas of the world.

Like many other commentators, Keniston says (some of the time) that while the New Left is strong on integrity and sensibility, it is short on relevant programs. Nor does its emphasis on participatory democracy, of which he evidently approves, make up for the lack of meaningful ideology such as Marxism supplied an earlier age of young intellectuals in the West. Young radicals, it appears, care more for informal, improvised forms of social change than for explicit programs for reconstructing the social order. And while they show the pragmatic passion for the *ad hoc* that typifies most forms of native American radicalism (as well as conservatism), they suffer from corresponding faults of instability and instinctual distrust of organized authority and power.

So they may. What then? Perhaps Professor Brzezinski would regard these traits as proof that the young radicals are really expendable counterrevolutionists whose counterideology is moribund. Keniston does not. What he brings out, ironically, is their affection for and dependence upon their usually upper-middle class parents, from whom they have largely absorbed their own formal ideals. He implies, in effect, that they are merely trying to make a traditional American dream come true in a new time in which their elders have abdicated their own responsibilities. So conceived, many young radicals thus could be viewed not as revolutionaries but as true friends of a half-fulfilled but self-divided social order who are trying to show their elders what has to be done in order to realize ends which their elders share. Looked at through Keniston's own thoughtful but unideological eyes, "young radical" might thus better be construed to mean "progressive" which is to say "true conservative." But this seems merely to confirm the view of Daniel Bell that all informed and decent people really do now live at the end of the age of ideology in which, labels aside, everybody pretty much wants the same thing. The only differences concern questions of means, ways of getting things done, or, in the language of the Kennedy movement, "styles of action."

I for one remain unconvinced. As the last great pragmatist, John Dewey, taught us long ago, means and ends tend to interpenetrate as "lines of action," which in practice must be taken as wholes. In problematic situations, whether personal or social, we find that means and ends can radically diverge from one another. Those who, however reluctantly, acquiesce in the Vietnam War, and those who view it as a form of collective murder which can be atoned, if at all, only by repudiating the primacy of all conceptions of the national interest, do not share a common anti-ideology. Similarly those who really are committed to "participatory democracy," and hence insist on participating directly and fully in all forms of social life that can rightly command their allegiance, are separated by an ideological abyss from those traditional exponents of "representative democracy" who believe that it is all right to commandeer young men into military service so long as it complies with a draft law passed by an elected Congress whose members "represent" their constituencies.

The same holds for those who accept the existing institutional organization of the American university, with its absentee owners and governing boards, its chains of command, and pre-established "missions," and for those who are convinced that the university itself, like the national society which it reflects and serves, must be radically restructured. The former, including large numbers of faculty and students who want simply to get on with their careers, are generally "reasonable" men. They are often prepared to acquiesce in gradual changes, even of a quasi-structural sort, but the only academic revolution which they consider legitimate and are willing to defend is the one described and half-defended by Jencks and Riesman: the graduate school university which, in the era of technetronic society, means and can mean nothing but the main training ground for that society's managers. Moreover, when party lines harden, those who accept the existing organization find that they have no alternative but to oppose any attempts to transform the university in ways demanded by the young radicals. Often they are ready to "negotiate" with the latter, just as their counterparts in the State Department are ready to "negotiate" with the government of North Vietnam. But they are not remotely willing, as it were, simply to "pull out": that is, to renounce the system which has forced them into educational conflict.

However, if by a miracle they chose to do so, they would, as the exponents of the technetronic society themselves imply, automatically alter the orientation of the national society and, in consequence, the future of man on this planet. This, I have come to think, is precisely what the more astute young (and old) rebels on our campuses realize. It is also why they regard the university as *the* place where the wider human and social revolution in our time must begin.

But it is just here, it seems to me, where Keniston as well as Riesman and Jencks fail to probe deeply enough the various forms of rebellion and revolution which they describe. Keniston veers away from the issue, in part because his own approach is too purely psychological and clinical; Jencks and Riesman do so, as we shall see, because theirs is too purely sociological. Keniston takes the psychological alienation of the American college student seriously, but not the student protest movements. He doubts that "culturally alienated students are much interested in 'political protest,' " and goes so far as to suggest that "alienation, *as I have studied it*, and the current phenomenon of student protest seem to me two quite distinct, if not opposed, phenomena" (Italics mine).

Perhaps so. But here it seems necessary to remind Professor Keniston that "alienated" behavior, whether on the part of young radicals or their parents, covers not only a multitude of oddities and self-destructive follies—from long hair to drugs and perfunctory, emulative scholarship—but also immensely significant forms of social action, of which Vietnam summers are themselves productive instances. Perhaps because of the limitations of the methods of "clinical research," preoccupied as it is with the correlations between the emotional lives and ideologies of alienated students and their early family situations (parents fail to live up to their "promises," etc.), he tends to view "politics," so far as young radicals are concerned, as something largely peripheral or external.

In fact it is not, I think, unfair to say that all forms of alienation, whether social or political, are assumed by Keniston to be rooted in, or perhaps masks of, parent–child tensions in which their parents' ways of accommodating themselves to the worlds they live in—worlds of professional or business activity, of suburban home life and conventionally progressive but ineffective political actions—appear to the child as sell-outs that violate the principles they profess. In short, from Keniston's point of view it is the failure of the parents in their daily lives to practice what they preach that breeds in children an often unconscious hostility to those to whom they are most deeply attached and wish to emulate. Indeed, it sometimes seems to be implied that if this hostility could be removed through the young radicals' understanding of the sources of the parents' sell-out, the radical impulse itself would either disappear or take forms that are merely more "progressive" than those taken by the parents themselves. So he fails to perceive that student alienation not only manifests itself in a variety of forms, of which the political seems to him the least significant, but that in some important instances it is in its very nature a function of a developing political or political-social understanding which conceives of on-campus revolt as a political act *continuous* with other student-faculty protest movements that are all aspects of a more general social upheaval.

Keniston admits in his concluding paragraph that "cultural alienation among a segment of our most talented and sensitive youth is . . . an almost inevitable consequence of the kind of society we live in." He adds that the task is not to "cure" alienation, since alienation is a condition that in itself neither seeks nor needs cure, but to help young alienated people to find "personally meaningful and culturally productive ways of focussing and expressing their alienation." Just so. But why does he exclude, or ignore, radical politics, whether on campus or off, which is precisely the mode of action many gifted and informed youths have discovered to be culturally the most productive way of articulating their alienation? Indeed why, for that matter, should they not see that only through political action on and off campus can they redeem their parents' broken promises? The family itself, I need hardly remind Professor Keniston, is part of a political-social system; parents fail their children, as the latter may eventually understand, because they have been pressed into the service of a leviathan which has betrayed its own promise to them.

The move from the psychological to the sociological, as the Jencks-Riesman book makes evident, ensures a wider perspective, but not necessarily a clearer vision. In fact, the very range of matters discussed in their book seems to involve a dispersal of

[*165*

their attention and a corresponding blurring of their insights. Though they are explicitly (and, in my view, properly) normative as well as descriptive in their approach, their norms are as pliant as their descriptions are varied. In substance, what they offer us, both normatively and descriptively, is an extended set of variations on the theme stated by Clark Kerr in his book on the "multiversity." This is no accident, for their admiration for Kerr's "much maligned but marvellously perceptive study," *The Uses of the University*, is quite explicit.

Undoubtedly ex-President Kerr perceived more than did some of the faculty members who, as Jencks and Riesman remark, "reacted with horror to the mirror he held up to them." Undoubtedly he perceives still more now that he is no longer burdened with the chores of his presidential dealing with a myopic faculty. All the same, I am not reassured, whether by one who has been through the presidential mill or by amiable and knowledgeable professors, that the "top management" in the academic world, i.e., the university presidents, who themselves still largely start out as members of the academic profession, really represent the interests of "middle management" (the faculty), both to their supposedly "ceremonial" trustees and to the world. It would be unfair to recount here events that have occurred, at Columbia and elsewhere, since *The Academic Revolution* was written: everything written these days seems out of date before it goes to press. The point is that even if the academic revolution described by Jencks and Riesman has succeeded beyond the wildest dreams of its initiators, this serves only to underscore the urgency of the question: why does that success which has made the university so indispensable to the technetronic society dispose so many of the university's own choicest spirits to revolt so passionately against it?

This paradox is where all relevant reflection on the question of academic revolution has to begin. But Jencks and Riesman seem as much to illustrate as to illuminate the trouble. Consider the matter of style. One of their contentions, for which they are prepared to supply evidence, is that the nostalgia of certain aging academicians for the good old days of the liberal arts college is unfounded. In the "meritocracy" wrought by the graduate school university and the university college, professors and students alike are better informed, more clear-headed, and more literate than ever before. Now Jencks and Riesman themselves can reasonably claim to be well above average representatives of this admirable state of affairs. Yet in a single chapter, concerned with the "bifurcation" of higher education between public and private colleges, the already overworked phrases "public-sector" and "private-sector" recur over and over in a fatuous litany which ends by obscuring the crucial point that, as the authors themselves put it (so help me), "the public and private sectors [have] increasingly similar objective methods, and . . . the major differences between them today [reflect] differences between the students who chose one sector as against the other." Such figures as "handwriting on the wall," "the sky seems the limit," "pays the kitty," "defense mechanism," strewn throughout their book, convey an impression, all too often justified by the argument, of a weary recital of obvious, if ill-sorted, truths mixed with doubtful observations.

Jencks and Riesman's book has been called "a mine of information." That is part of the trouble. Much of the information has by this time a rather stale smell. Nothing new emerges in their account of the sharp break with the past that occurred with the founding of primarily graduate universities, at John Hopkins and Clark, in the late nineteenth century, the establishment of graduate schools, first at ivy league and then at leading state universities, the breakup of the university and college faculties into departments, and the organization of professional schools for medicine, law, education, and business. They describe the accompanying transition from colleges whose values, "in Talcott Parsons' terms," were "particularistic" and "personal" to those that are "universalistic" and "meritocratic." And they single out for special emphasis the important development of "university colleges." By the "university college," it should be added, Jencks and Riesman do not mean colleges in the graduate school university, such as those at Harvard and Columbia, but also the first-rate four-year colleges such as Amherst, Swarthmore, or Reed, whose faculties are recruited from the graduate school universities and whose educational programs are largely geared to the requirements which their students must meet in order to succeed in graduate school. But there is too little scrutiny either of the quality or relevance of the curriculum of contemporary university colleges to the lives of the faculty or the student body.

Jencks and Riesman by no means accept *in toto* the academic revolution as it has filtered down into the university college from the graduate and professional schools. And their unoriginal contention that the graduate schools are where significant educational changes must *begin* if the university as a whole is to be improved, is a bit like saying that it is in the insane asylum where we must begin to make the changes that will revolutionize society. Actually the significant changes must be instituted by rebellious *and* imaginative teachers and students on all levels. Wonderful to say, they are in fact already occurring everywhere in "the shadow university," where young scientists talk to one another about their public responsibilities as scholars and teachers, where young social scientists and historians discuss the differences between "behavioral" investigations of the featherless biped and the study of man as an active, purposeful human being, where young students and teachers of literature refuse any longer to settle for lives of pure scholarship in which reading and writing for pleasure and instruction have been long forgotten, where young theologians at once ponder the real logic of "god talk" and refuse to accept knowledge about religion as a substitute for the possibility of a higher understanding, and, finally, where young philosophers not only explain the distinction between what is and what ought to be but are no longer ashamed to seek knowledge of what really might be and ought to be.

Everywhere, in fact, many of the cleverest, most sensitive minds in and about the university are already conducting a new revolution that concerns the whole life of the mind—which if it is to be meaningful requires at the same time a correlative transformation of our whole elitist, imperialist, militarist, national society—and not simply that part that has become sanctified, both in and out of the graduate schools, as "the higher learning." But the glimpses of this revolution are rare in *The Academic Revolution*, which, I regret to say, is all too accurately named. What is perhaps most appalling is that much of the time Jencks and Riesman seem scarcely aware that both young and old radicals, who are dedicated to the reforms necessary to make our post-industrial society a fit place for human beings to live in, are laying on the line their reputations, careers, and, in some instances, their lives.

According to Jencks and Riesman, even Sarah Lawrence, Bennington, Reed, and other "off-beat" experimental colleges have largely fallen into the post-revolutionary goose-stepping of the contemporary university college. But there remain "sectors" where the academic revolution has been frustrated or else has scarcely begun: as might be guessed, they are those underdeveloped or underprivileged areas of so-called higher education where superstition, ignorance, or poverty (or a combination of the three) still prevail. In their chapters on Bible Belt Protestant, Roman Catholic, and, most notably, Negro colleges, the authors have things to say that are illuminating as well as disturbing. Like most good liberals, they applaud pluralism in education as elsewhere. But, for all their praise of diversity in the domain of higher learning, they constantly take the nonsectarian, secular, national graduate university, with all its accompanying gear, to be standard for higher education of the better, more progressive sort. Where this standard can't be emulated, no doubt other ventures must be made. But in such instances the assumption nonetheless prevails that it is a pity that the primary academic revolution can't occur first.

Their discussions of the Roman Catholic colleges are typical. Now it is undoubtedly true that sectarian, parochial, and pietistic influences have too often hobbled the graduate school academic revolution in Catholic schools. Indeed faculties in those institutions all too often are inadequate to their distinctive religious, as well as to their ordinary secular, educational responsibilities. Furthermore church colleges are participating in the "identity crisis" which, Jencks and Riesman say, the Church as a whole is now undergoing. Perhaps something immensely useful to the standard universities themselves might be learned from closer scrutiny of that crisis. For it provides an instructive contrast to the unmentioned identity crises through which our secular national society in America and all its service institutions are themselves passing.

Throughout the national universities, there is a groping toward a recognition of the religious dimensions of existence. Correspondingly, in some of the departments of religion and the theological schools attached to the national universities, revolutions of thought and attitude are emerging which have proved of absorbing interest to secular academicians for whom, for partly irrelevant reasons, God—or at least "god talk"—is as dead as the great auk. What if a genuine educational dialogue were initiated between the Catholic (and Protestant and Jewish) institutions and their secularist adversaries? What if they entertained the idea of pooling their energies in behalf of educational ventures that neither of them, alone, seems able to carry through in depth? In an ecumenical age, this should give no one the willies. No doubt "The Church (and hence its schools and colleges) may . . . have to move even faster than most institutions if it is to retain the loyalty of its most talented and innovative spirits." But what about the nation-state itself, and what about the industrial-political-military complex which Harvard and California and M.I.T. so prosperously serve? One can only agree that the "breakdown of the Catholic ghetto" is a good thing, but the breakdown of intellectual ghettos at M.I.T. and Harvard might be, educationally, an even better thing, and conceivably the religious colleges could offer aid in this direction.

I am quite ready to believe what I am told when Jencks and Riesman assert that the "best young religious" teachers, Catholic and Protestant, "do not seem to have the temperament of empire builders." But maybe we have had too much empire building in America's institutions of higher learning. At this stage, it is arguable that what is wanted is a host of anti-empire builders, abrasive educational iconoclasts and anarchists. As usual the attitude of Jencks and Riesman toward all this remains confused. They tell us,

> while we ourselves are less than enamored of the secular graduate schools as models, we find it hard to see how the Catholic universities will invent acceptable alternatives. Under these circumstances we must return to the question of whether a *reputable* college or university can really be Catholic in any significant sense [italics mine].

But what *is* reputable? In short, what Jencks and Riesman seem to offer with one hand they casually take away with the other. So, despite their informal sociological commentary on the predicaments of Catholic collegiate education, they evade the overwhelming issue: what, in a fully human—and this must mean of course religious and moral as well as scientific and technological —sense, should a really "reputable" college or university be? At the risk of being misunderstood, I must go further: precisely because their whole approach is so flatly, undeviatingly "sociological," and hence naturalistic and positivistic, their analysis remains at once one-dimensional and circular. Never for an instant does it occur to them to look above the heavens or below the earth for sources of educational renewal or self-transcendence. Meanwhile they go on endlessly not liking what they like, and approving of what they disapprove. Perhaps what they need is an identity crisis of their own.

To my mind, the long, detailed chapter on "Negroes and Their Colleges" is the most interesting part of their book. It is also heartbreaking. Once more, alas, the "better" Negro colleges, even more than the Catholic ones, are faint images of their whitish counterparts, with Negro Ph.D.'s, together with some white missionaries, trying to bring the "academic revolution" to black campuses. But too often, especially in the deep South, it is, or appears to be, a case of the blind leading the blind in impoverished church schools, many of them not accredited, and many more on the verge of losing accreditation. And, although plenty of white colleges are no better, ". . . it is true that the great majority of Negro institutions stand near the end of the academic procession in terms of student aptitudes, faculty competence, and intellectual ferment." Exceptions exist, such as Fisk, Hampton, and Tuskegee among the private colleges, Texas Southern and Morgan State among the publics, and "that peculiar hybrid," Howard. But, despite a few brilliant professors and students and some lively programs, even these institutions "would probably fall near the middle of the national academic procession." In 1964 the ten or so leading private colleges had a combined endowment of only 100 million dollars, about half that, for example, of affluent Connecticut Wesleyan. At one time, at least, the leading foundations were reluctant to help these colleges "on the understandable ground that their help would mean perpetuating segregation." And here precisely is the terrible bind: integration doesn't seem to work, but segregation means, in most cases, the perpetuation of incompetence, dreariness, lethargy. Hence the white money, "understandably" afraid of doing the wrong thing, leaves the black institutions to make it as they can—or can't.

The integration problem itself has two aspects. According to Jencks and Riesman, the wealthier private colleges, such as Tuskegee, are likely to maintain the integrated faculties they now have and to attract some professors, both black and white, with good academic training. But integrated faculties do not make integrated student bodies, and the trickle of liberal white students from the North who are attracted by the idea of attending a predominately Negro—or "black"—college is small and likely to remain so. But this is only one side of the story. As the authors observe, the situation of white members of faculties in black colleges is very hard. Those who go to them with the "romantic illusion" that the oppressed are more radical, more idealistic, or more "teachable," than affluent students in the North are soon disillusioned. Their black colleagues and administrators are often pleased to see them leave, both because they are sources of political and pedagogic "trouble" and because their departure confirms the assumption that whites care about blacks only for neurotic and missionary rather than for more authentic reasons. And, as I can attest from many talks with a number of immensely intelligent, dedicated, and resilient white professors at a black college which I visited for several days, most black students would rather be taught by less well trained teachers of their own race than by white instructors. The result was, I was told, that a good many white professors, for psychological reasons of their own, come to regard their tenures in the Negro colleges in spite of themselves as "tours of duty." It *was* disheartening, God knows. And evidently *nobody* was, or is, to blame.

What are the alternatives? The black colleges are likely to survive. They will continue to recruit their students largely from all-Negro Southern high schools, and to send many of their graduates back to teach in those high schools. Circles within circles. For this reason, among others, Jencks and Riesman are not optimistic about the success of programs to "upgrade" the weaker black colleges. One possibility they consider is that of converting black colleges into authentic "community colleges." But the problems, economic and otherwise, remain overwhelming. They also mention efforts that have been made and could be made to establish something like "free universities" where unsophisticated students, unresponsive to "high culture of the kind that dominates most liberal arts curricula," might come to it "step by step from an imaginative treatment of the 'popular culture' in which incoming students are already immersed." Here, by way of illustration, they refer to "the sports, the pop music, the comics and pulp fiction, the TV shows, and the cars that interest the young. . . ." But, as these all too casual examples suggest, their minds, if not their hearts, do not really seem in it.

In fact, the whole idea of the free university leaves Jencks and Riesman cold. "Like most faculty members," they disdainfully observe, "we have been unimpressed by the supposedly free universities established on the periphery of major universities, since these seem for the most part to have encouraged self-indulgence and cultism. What is wanted are really new ways of learning, not additional courses taught by Marxists and acidheads." Nor does the establishment of the Free University of Mississippi, instituted by the black students of Tougaloo along with some white students from neighboring Millsap College, qualify their judgment. In fact, they do not consider this university to be a genuine example of a "free university," and one reason appears to be that it has faculty support from both parent colleges which could help it to become a truly creative forum for inter-racial confrontations. Moreover, the durability of the innovation remains uncertain. Possibly so. But, as always, it is for them the presence of a faculty, itself the product of the academic revolution toward which their attitudes are elsewhere ambivalent, which seems to provide the saving grace in Jackson. Thus it is not only the black colleges that seem forever to move in circles, but Jencks and Riesman themselves who in effect can really envisage educational possibilities initiated only by enlightened representatives of properly "accredited" institutions in which their academic revolution has already occurred.

What Jencks and Riesman have to say about the free university movement, both here and elsewhere in their book, is both imperfectly informed and imbued with the very attitudes which repel the faculty as well as the students participating in it. One does not have to be, or approve of, an acidhead or Marxist in order to recognize the significance of this movement as a commentary upon the monumental inadequacies of the formal curricula and

[*173*

modes of inquiry that prevail not only in struggling Southern Negro colleges, but also in the national universities. Nor does one have to be a romantic utopian or anti-intellectual to understand that what many free university advocates object to is not the hard, disciplined work which they must do to win legitimate B.A.'s and Ph.D.'s, but the combined irrelevance of conventional, establishment-oriented social science and boring "scholarly" humanities programs, at fifth remove from their primary literary, artistic, philosophical, and religious subject matters.

In many cases, what people in the free university movement object to is not research but the ordinary academicians' sense of what is useful, relevant, desirable. Dozens of teaching fellows and junior faculty who are as bored by Marx as they are leery of acid find in the free university, whatever the quality of its performance in particular cases, an absorbing educational idea. Whatever may be its promise, the restless, protesting educational activism behind it is animated, as Professor Keniston observes, not by self-interest but directly or indirectly by concern for "alleviating the oppression of others."

So it goes. In their concluding chapter, after a variety of timid and limited proposals for reformation of the graduate schools and, through it, of the gradual correlative changes in the university college system, Jencks and Riesman close with the observation that

aside from nuclear war or a wave of national repression brought on by racial conflict or the defeat of imperial ambitions, generational conflict seems the major threat to stability and growth of the academic system.

It takes at least two generations to close a generational gap, and, if I may match impression with impression, it is not clear that the academic authorities who occupy the executive suites and laboratories of our contemporary universities are any more willing than their predecessors to do what is necessary to convert the most emulated institutions of higher research in America into habitable cities of the human mind. Neither at Columbia nor at California is there a sustained all-university attack upon "the critical problem of graduate instruction in the social sciences [which] is to narrow the gap between individual students' personal lives and their work."

As it stands this statement no doubt is open to the reply that no university can, or should try to, solve each student's identity crisis for him. A contemporary university, it has been truly said, is neither a family, a mental hospital, a brothel, nor even a *community* of scholars. Nor is it a church. But, save us, this certainly is not what Messrs. Jencks and Riesman of all people have in mind. Here, let them refute themselves.

> The graduate school must somehow put the student in closer touch with himself, instead of making him believe that the way to get ahead is to repress himself and become a passive instrument "used" by his methods and his disciplinary colleagues. This is no mean task. The difficulty of the job is not, however, an excuse for the present situation, where the student's subjectivity is not even regarded as a problem.

There are other ways of saying this, and other things to say about it. My quarrel with Jencks and Riesman here—aside from their lack of ideas about the nature of "subjectivity" and hence about the ways in which men may learn or teach something about it— is that they never have the courage of their own criticisms. For no more than six pages before the indictment just quoted, in a concluding warning against "the pitfalls of nostalgia," they managed to say, "When we turn from the narrow question of academic competence to the broader question of human growth, the academic revolution again strikes us as a progressive development." Indeed, they remind us, "there is more of everything now," outstanding teachers and all. Yes indeed—more of everything. What "everything" includes, let us not forget, are forms of research that result in ever more lethal forms of weaponry, in violent or merely repressive modes of "pacification"—whether in the form of domestic riot control or projects whose primary function is to reconcile disaffected ex-colonials to the policies of their new imperial masters—and, not least, in the folding back into the technetronic society of young radicals who can be mollified by participating in "accredited" forms of urban renewal.

Here I find it useful to return to Keniston and his young radicals. As Keniston puts it, as if anticipating—and forestalling—

Brzezinski, the young radicals "seek an orientation to the future" that recognizes how the adoption of dehumanizing and destructive means can turn professors of the noblest ends into monsters. At this point, however, I shall not dwell on their search for new ways to personal development which are responsive to these qualities of youth—of creativity, yearning, openness, and intransigence —which our whole culture, and its central educational system, seems bound to frustrate. I am more impressed by what Keniston, himself half-contradicting what he seems to have said before, refers to as the search for "new ways of learning," "new formulations of the world," and "new concepts of man and society." The educational ventures germane to this revolution have many aspects: for example, new forms of extra-curricular activity that would replace Big Ten football with education programs conducted by college students and faculty in ghetto high schools; unconventional do-it-yourself courses by concerned teachers on problems of race relations and on the deadly imperialist politics of the technetronic societies; experimental work not only in creative writing, but in all forms of artistic and intellectual activity that do not fit established canons of the "higher learning"; offbeat interpretations of recent and contemporary history that are not afraid to acknowledge the "revolutionary" assumptions from which they proceed; and, not least, efforts toward cross-generational dialogue in which it is not assumed in advance that only the teachers have professional rank. In my view, this is the most exciting and promising aspect of the *second* academic revolution now, however falteringly, already in process. The multiple forms of research involved in it (it is arguable) could become the highest learning of all.

Here lie problems not only of delicacy but of amplitude, not only of amplitude but of the subtlest relations. The ablest minds are scarcely able to cope with them. However, as a *social* achievement, the venture will not succeed so long as the effort remains marginal, concessive, or begrudging. But so it will remain, alas, like other poverty programs, until leaders of the national society, both inside and outside the academies, are ready to say "No more!" to all forms of imperialism, whether political or educational.

IO

Guardians of Law and Order

IN THIS CHAPTER WE ARE CONFRONTED WITH ACADEMIC positions and attitudes quite distinct from those examined in earlier chapters of Part II. Neither Kerr nor Perkins, neither Bell nor Jencks and Reisman, show any profound anxieties about the future of the American university system. In the cases of Professors Sidney Hook and Daniel Boorstin, however, one detects at once a new shrillness, mounting at times to something close to hysteria, in response to the rising tide of radical criticism and action on the part of a significant fraction of our students and their faculty supporters. Boorstin and Hook write as men with their backs to the wall. And, especially in Hook's case, it is plainly a part of their purpose to encourage a conservative rally which will protect our establishment, academic and otherwise, against the young intruders. In Hook's view, the politicization of the university by radical student movements is a completely new thing in America. It is also, he believes, an unmitigated disaster.

What makes the cases of Hook and Boorstin all the more interesting is that, as they tell us, they themselves began their own careers in the twenties and thirties as radicals in their own right. By stages, however, they have identified themselves with what they now conceive to be the great traditions of liberal democracy in America. Unfortunately it is hard to distinguish them any longer from those arch-conservative exponents of "law and order" on the campus and elsewhere who treat all established patterns of educational, social, and political authority as god-given. Both of them come on strongly as advocates of sweet reason against the dark forces of irrationality, anarchy, and violence that now prevail on the left. To hear them tell it, were it not for the atrocities perpetrated by student and black activists, we could, and would, cope systematically and promptly with all malfunctioning of our institutions, academic and otherwise, the decline in the quality of life on our campuses and in our cities, and the progressive abandonment of the underlying principles of truly liberal education by the managers of our colleges and universities.

In recent days Professor Hook has emerged in effect as President Nixon's man in the academy. His writings have been widely circulated by the President and his advisors, and his recipes for restoring law and order on the campus are now hailed by the Nixon administration as deliverances from on high. His testimony before the Presidential Commission Inquiring into the Causes of Campus Unrest has received much publicity. He has also headed up the so-called Coordinating Center for Democratic Opinion (more recently renamed The University Center for Rational Alternatives) with which many distinguished conservative academicians are now associated.

There are all the more reasons, therefore, to examine with some care what he and Boorstin have to tell us about the anarchistic tendencies which, in their view, are currently undermining our academic and cultural establishments.

Hook's work, *Academic Freedom and Academic Anarchy* (New York: Cowles, 1970) and Boorstin's book, *The Decline of Radicalism: Reflections on America Today* (New York City: Random House, 1969), are not, it should be emphasized, part of any sort of unified plot or counter-conspiracy. They are addressed ostensibly to different questions; they also exhibit different professional talents and draw upon partly different funds of information. On his own level, Professor Hook is still a polemicist to be reckoned with. If he wins fewer campaigns than battles, it will not be for want of trying. He directs his brief against the confusion, current among certain professors and administrators as well as students, between academic freedom and academic license, which in his view has now reached the stage of anarchy. Like Plato, the ceaselessly active counter-activist Hook can be a very practical man of affairs indeed. He also remains a philosopher who bases his case upon an updated theory about the natural *telos* of the university which treats all students as underdeveloped apprentices and places—or seems to place—responsibility for the governance of the university in the shaky and unwilling hands of the faculty.

Hook has no patience with student demands for structural changes, but his own scheme would require scarcely fewer drastic changes in the organization of the American university. Professor Boorstin, on the other hand, lacking any discernible theory of institutions, either factual or normative, offers no premise for social reconstruction. As an Americanologist whose specialty is such image-making happenings as presidential world tours and national wars against poverty, Boorstin has a cataloguer's eye for some of the more conspicuous unrealities of contemporary life in America. As a social and political moralist, he induces his own ideals rather casually from the less troubled dreams of the fathers up to, but not beyond, the sainted FDR's New Deal. But even these ideals are non-functional. Consequently there runs through his book a corrosive nostalgia for the dear dead days when communities really were communities, whose members shared common needs and goals, and which regarded themselves as parts of a cohesive national society.

Boorstin's evidence shows, if anything, that the national society is now a thing of shreds and tatters and that the sense of community is less real in the suburbs than it is in the city slums where black power festers and hatred of white America has become, not unnaturally, a racial obsession. In the circumstances, I should have thought that the conclusion to be drawn is that the conservative power elites in America are now incapable of leading our people a step closer to the promised land of equality and justice. Boorstin vents his wrath entirely upon the New Left cop-outs who, unlike the sturdily loyalist radicals of yore, are merely, in his view, engaged in a desperate struggle for personal power and privilege. To Chernyshevsky's great question, "What is to be done?" Boorstin, unlike Hook, has no explicit answers. Hence, unlike Hook who is both shaker and mover, Boorstin is only a shaker.

Such differences are superficial. More significant are the converging attitudes which Hook and Boorstin share with the ever more virulent counter-resistant forces of the social and academic center in America of which both authors are unrepentant spokesmen. The issue for them, no less than for their opponents, is power. When the rhetorical camouflage is removed, they have one message for their brothers: hold on to your own.

Once upon a time, as they insistently remind us, Boorstin and Hook were genuine intellectuals and radicals. That time is long gone. Now they are conventionalist inside-men who have abandoned the intellectual's arduous critique of reason, which, from Kant to Marx, and from Nietzsche and William James to Sartre, has always been at the root of sustained radical reflection.

Not only do they deplore the antics of particular wild-men on the New Left, they condemn the entire movement, intellectual and anti-intellectual, lettered and unlettered, white and black, young and middle-aged, nonviolent as well as violent. The causes of deracination mean nothing to them, nor have they any interest in removing those causes. To hear them tell it, one would gather that violence exists nowhere in America except on the lunatic Left. Purblind, they deplore the ever-deepening polarization of opinion throughout the present decade, while never giving a passing thought to the fact that they themselves are already polarized.

Initially, I was disposed to think that Hook's and Boorstin's purpose is to divide still further the already tragically divided radicals in America. I was mistaken. By neither style nor tone nor argument are these books intended to convert any of "the New Barbarians," as Boorstin calls them, to the ways of traditional American civil society, scholarly decorum, and right reason. Just the contrary: Hook and Boorstin take it for granted that these barbarians are unregenerate outsiders against whom the gates of the open society and its liberal academic institutions must now be closed by main force. For them the time has passed for the characteristically American practices of pragmatic compromise and negotiation. Who can negotiate with those who present us with "nonnegotiable" demands? Who can compromise with power-mad deviants who scribble their nauseating graffiti on the sacred halls of American learning and defense? Such questions are now academic. These books, make no mistake, are addressed exclusively to "us," the confused insiders who must be made to realize (which is true) that the radical students and their faculty camp-followers cannot be appeased by self-taught courses in the new "relevance" and that the blacks cannot be bought off with free paintbrushes, bigger hand-outs from the welfare state, or the substitution of Senator Brooke for Agnew as Nixon's next vice-president.

Do I exaggerate? Then consider the books themselves.

In the first part of his book Boorstin provides a commentary on the many new communities which are the products of "Our new ways of thinking about and classifying ourselves, our myriad new products and services offered in unimagined quantities, our new ways of advertising and distributing, our new institutions for promoting philanthropy, the arts, and education, our American Standard of Living—almost everything most modern and most American [that] has drawn us together [and apart] in unprecedented ways."

Most conspicuous among our new communities are the "consumption communities" whose members are drawn together by a common taste for Scotch, three-button-suits, sports-cars, king-sized cigarettes, or Doublemint chewing gum. Naturally enough, such communities are thin, volatile, and transient. Unlike more traditional communities in America, they are held together not by "a shared religious or civic dogma, not a shared booster-enthusiasm, not even a shared economic interest [sic], but something much vaguer and more attenuated."

All the same, Boorstin has kind words for them. For a consumption community still "consists of people who have a feeling of shared well-being, shared risks, common concerns. . . ." Above all, there is the high standard of living which, because it is a public fact, has become a public benefit. Says Boorstin, "You can become *rich* without my becoming richer. But it is hard for you to have a high *standard of living* without incidentally raising mine" (italics in text). Booster enthusiasm, it seems, is not dead after all, even if there are not as many as there once were to share it.

Throughout this discussion of consumer and average-man communities, what most intrigues me is Boorstin's systematic inattention to those who do not, or will not, belong to them: the unemployed and unemployables, the rural and urban slum dwellers who have to scrounge, not for a standard of living, but for a living itself, the people who are not deluded by laws of averages.

In the second part of his book, Boorstin suggests how some of the very agencies "which draw us together also stir Americans to fear, to distrust and even to hate, one another." He remarks, in the book's best chapter, "The Perils of Indwelling Law," on the dangerous tendency to derive rules for the interpretation of the law from general notions about the manifest destiny of American society. Yet even here Boorstin draws inferences which are, to say the least, ambiguous. He tells, truly, that "The conviction grows—and is expressed in the curricula of our best law schools—that the lawyer must not only know the law. He must know the facts of life, the facts of our society, the laws of social behavior inherent in the society itself."

But the conclusion he draws is not that these facts may enable our lawyers, as they enabled Brandeis and his successors, to resist the tendency to find the imminence of the law in the supposedly inevitable tendencies of the society itself, but, on the contrary, that they lead them into "the temptations of social narcissism" that convert statistical averages into rules of law. Boorstin blandly ignores the strenuous efforts now being made in our more enlightened law schools to overcome the dangers to the whole society of a narrowly trained legal profession and judiciary bereft of any rules for interpreting and applying the law except for hand-me-down social, political, and moral prejudices which, at any time and place, pass for common sense.

He tells us nothing about the brilliant young professors of jurisprudence who, making use of the new philosophical techniques of semantical analysis and the knowledge of the world which they have gained in and out of the classroom, show us how our grand old constitutional and common law can still be used as powerful vehicles of justice and common good. "One of the most difficult problems in our society today," says Boorstin, "is to get a message in from the outside." Yet when outside news comes to us from our own people, Boorstin ignores it or else rejects it as a manifestation of the new barbarism.

In a shallow chapter on "Dissent, Dissension and the News," Boorstin draws an invidious line between "disagreement," which produces debate, and "dissent," which merely produces dissension. He reminds us that some of the greatest American champions of the right to disagree, including Thomas Jefferson, Oliver Wendell Holmes, Jr., William James, and John Dewey, "were also great believers in the duty of the community to be peacefully governed by the will of the majority." Yet he seems to have forgotten Jefferson's revulsion against flaccid, unenlightened majorities, James's disgust with the popular imperialist progressivism of Theodore Roosevelt, or Dewey's insistence that majority rule becomes a tyranny when large numbers of men are denied access to the political processes whereby conventional majorities are formed.

In fact, Boorstin is less concerned with the problems of improving the quality of American democracy than with deriding "the rise of minority veto" as manifested above all in the conduct of black power leaders and student rebels who, although they represent "a group which is not very numerous," know that they occupy crucial positions in which they can exercise inordinate power. Boorstin writes, making a point which Hook more loudly echoes, "Small groups have more power than ever before. In *small* numbers there is strength."

Indeed so. I can still remember, with pleasure, the widespread disillusionment with the Vietnam war that forced Lyndon Johnson to retire from the presidency after a single elected term in office, the grass-roots peace movement which supported Senator McCarthy's campaign for the 1968 Democratic presidential nomination, and the continuing spread of that movement during the past year when a president, elected by the barest plurality, is obliged in desperation to appeal to a mythical "silent majority" for support of an endless war that he has now made his own.

All of these were outgrowths of pitifully small movements. The veto-power of small numbers, I agree, is very great. But the veto-power which most impresses me, alas, is not that exercised by black and student dissidents, but that continually exercised, for example, by jingoistic and segregationist Southern senators, by university trustees and presidents whose "formal" powers can be reconverted into overbearing real power in a single day, and, not least, by the lobbyists and confidence men who have such ready access to the suites of those who pretend to rule in the name of the people.

Boorstin rightly deplores the influence of the polls and the media upon public taste and opinion. He does not, however, make an issue of the silent majorities upon whom poll-minded presidents rely for support of their wars and their discriminative deflationary policies of welfare budget-cutting and "acceptable" rates of increase in national unemployment. Again, Boorstin's target is the "Professional dissenters [who] do not and cannot seek to assimilate their program or ideals into American culture." And he criticizes the media for the dramatizations of these dissenters and their unholy works. So he says, ". . . expressions of disagreement may lead to better policy but dissent cannot. The affirmations of differentness and feeling apart cannot hold a society together. In fact these tend to destroy the institutions which make fertile disagreement possible and fertile institutions decent."

He tells us nothing about significant dissent throughout the land which is not a creation of the media but an awareness of systematic injustice and apparently irremediable inequality in our country. To be sure, the media do show us the ghastly effects of "a sniper's bullet"; they also, thank God, provide eloquent witness to the incredible frivolity of high-placed ladies and gentlemen whose example to the rest of us is merely one of all-too-conspicuous consumption and self-aggrandizement. I am not over-addicted to commercial TV, the national news magazines, and the front pages of the metropolitan newspapers. Yet even they let us know, one way or another, not only how divided are the infractious dissidents from the great majority of the American people, but how that majority too often accepts the domination of established bases of institutional power in government, in the armed forces and the police, and in education. Boorstin does not even perform that service.

The era of the Great Depression—in the days of his own intransigent youth, Boorstin tells us—witnessed a host of bona-fide radicalisms which included large numbers of our academics, intellectuals, men of public conscience, many of them dominated by Marxist ideas. These dedicated people, convinced of the necessity of a general reconstruction of corporate social life in America, helped to promote a new and wider labor movement, helped FDR to popularize the welfare state, and sought to persuade their fellow-citizens to join in the war to stop Hitler. They had their faults: they fenced in American social scientists by new orthodoxies, and many of their (socialist?) policies were misguided. All the same, they did much to awaken the lethargic American conscience to facts of life which had been swept under the rug by the prosperous manipulators of the American economic and political system.

"That," says Boorstin, "*was* radicalism. And those who were part of it can attest to some of its features. It was radicalism in the familiar and traditional sense of the word. The word 'radical' does, of course, come from the Latin *radix*, meaning 'root,' and a radical, then, is a person trying to go to the root of matters" (first italics mine). To be sure, "those radicals never were quite respectable." But they shared in common with their forebears, going back to the Antinomians of Massachusetts Bay and the Quakers of Pennsylvania, a search for meaning, a doctrine with a specific content, and, above all, an affirmation of community and of the awareness that all of us share the same root problems and are implicated in the same social crimes and evils. These radicals and radicalisms (as we know) do not always succeed in their wider social or political aims; all the same they served as a "tonic" to the whole society.

What then is the paradox? Of course there is none. Nowadays, according to Boorstin, there is a lot of talk about new radical movements in America. This is a hoax. The new so-called radicals are not radicals at all, but barbarians, bereft of ideas, a sense of purpose and community. Who are they? "Student Powerites" and "Black Powerites," who merely "preen . . . the egoism of the isolationist self." Ever and ever it is "Students [who] seek power for 'students,' Negroes [who] seek power for 'blacks'— and let the community take the hindmost."

One might go on indefinitely quoting in this vein, but I shall not. How dare Boorstin tell us that our contemporary radicals have (to employ his own three standards of true radicalism) abandoned the search for meaning, that they have no specific ideas or "subject-matter," that they have no concern for community? True, many contemporary radicals, who have been reading (among other things) the writings of the younger Marx are more profoundly disillusioned than Boorstin with the shibboleths of conventional Marxism and the socialisms based upon it. But they also demand a reconstitution of American institutions so that all the people may participate more justly and equally and freely in a meaningful communal life. And this is no less true of most advocates of student and black power than it is of the thousands of artists, writers, clergymen, academicians, jurists, *and* business men who have joined the resistance movement that is now awakening considerable numbers of Americans to the infamies of which the Boorstins, in their turn, seem so heedless.

Sidney Hook, in his tragic way, is more impressive. He has an articulate point of view. He hates what Boorstin hates, but more systematically and more ruthlessly. As they say, he has also done his homework. His quotations from Tom Hayden, Mark Rudd, Hal Draper, et. al., not to mention such elder statesmen of the New Left as Herbert Marcuse, and such alleged sell-outs as James Perkins, former president of Cornell and (of all people) Judge Charles Wyzanski, are no less effective (if one is making points) than some that the reader will recall from such notables on the other side as, say, Boorstin and Hook, not to mention the latter's new-found allies and supporters, S. K. Hayakawa and Spiro Agnew.[1]

Hook is a master of the polemical case study, and he uses it here persuasively, at least for those already prepared to be persuaded. His lengthy appendices which include his "second thoughts" on what happened at Berkeley in the fall of 1964, his accounts of "some recent incidents at Columbia and New York University," and his treatment of "the case of the University of Colorado" are full of facts, although there are many other facts he fails to cite, and although, as he knows, no facts, uninterpreted, can lead us to a responsible conclusion. At Berkeley, for example, he tells us all about faculty self-division and indecision, but little about the incompetence of the then Chancellor Strong and the vacillations and false statements and false promises of other administrators, including Clark Kerr. The abusive language and violent actions of students and nonstudents are richly cited. Yet the violent police, as well as those who make use of them, are unfailingly treated as well-disposed agencies of proper law and order.

Indeed, I do not fault Hook for his harsh criticisms of book burners, of ex-student weirdos who tell the students to abandon their studies, of faddist admirers of the antilibertarian rhetoric of Herbert Marcuse, of witless people who deride our bill of constitutional rights without pondering the human uses to which it continues to be put. Like Hook, I too want liberal democracy to survive in America, though I have very different notions of the terms of its survival. Not least, I want activist-philosophers to survive, though I hope they may not all suffer from the counter-conversions that afflict philosophers like Sidney Hook. Like Emerson, and still more Thoreau, I would be my own man, ready to speak out for repressed minorities, fearful of great unmanageable governmental industrial combinations, anxious about property rights that no longer represent human rights, harsh in criticism of those who place the security of institutions above the well-being of men.

This is not to argue that liberalism, whether old or new, has ever provided a fully adequate philosophy or ideology. In every age even the greatest liberals have lacked a certain depth, an adequate sense of history. They suffer from a curious obliviousness to forms of intransigence which the characteristic agencies of the strongest liberal democracies in the West seem powerless to remove. As Boorstin points out, the ideal of community has not been wanting, but it remains at best somewhat abstract, and those who adhere to it lack that strong sense of collective responsibility for the removal of palpable causes of want, suffering, and alienation which drives desperate men to apparently gratuitous acts of lawlessness and violence. Most liberals expect too much of time, good will, and the arts of discussion. Or rather they fail to see that what seems so eminently reasonable to them appears to their critics and adversaries as mere manifestations of vested interest which can be coped with only by acts of resolute disobedience, defiance, and rebellion. There is a sense of existential peril of which William James alone among American liberals seems fully aware.

But I do not quarrel, here, that Hook lacks the imagination of a James or a better power to give it articulate expression. My quarrel with him is that his liberalism is so attenuated, so *formalistic*, so dominated by hostility toward "the others" and by the manias of the counterconspiratorial mind. How diminished is his sense of freedom and justice, his passion for equality and fraternity. How accusatory is his logic, how rigid is his concern for established forms of decorum, no matter how invidious.

Hook's doctrine of academic freedom is a version of the doctrine of *Lehrfreiheit* developed in the essentially graduate universities of nineteenth century imperial Germany. According to him (*n.b.*), academic freedom is "the freedom of professionally qualified persons to inquire, discover, publish and teach the truth as they see it in the field of their competence. It is subject to no control or authority except the control or authority of the rational methods by which truths or conclusions are sought and established in the respective disciplines."

The definition is worth pondering. In the first place it applies to no one but research scholars and teachers. Learning as such is not mentioned among the activities covered by academic freedom. Nor is this an accident. The rights it confers are limited exclusively to *professionally qualified* persons; it protects no one, either to teach what he believes to be true or to seek the truth save within the field of his "competence." And, although in principle it admits of no authority, apart from that of "the rational methods" by which truths are sought and established in the various disciplines, it serves only those who have a "discipline" and who do not range adventurously beyond it. Finally, it assumes without argument that all reputable disciplines have authoritative rational methods.

In this book Hook at times seems to hedge his bets about the universal authority of something called the "scientific method," though elsewhere he still treats science as the paradigm of human understanding. Perhaps one day he will come to see, with Santayana, that the life of reason itself may be essentially pluralistic. Even so, the qualifying phrase "rational methods" raises doubts about the academic propriety of all forms of creative thought and insights for which no methodology can be provided. And (to go no further) this places all imaginative literature and art in a precarious position, except as *objects* of study for scholarly inquiry. But even if we grant him the doctrine of rational methods, Hook's notions of academic freedom, and the idea of education behind it, remain singularly old-fashioned and, in this age, illiberal. Many disciplined philosophers, for example, have grave doubts whether their own problems and subject matters comprise *a* discipline at all; indeed when one is *doing* philosophy rather than recording its history (and that in a not very deep way), disciplinary questions scarcely arise.

The plain fact is that Hook's notion of academic freedom is both undesirable and inapplicable. Its legalism and formalism, were they seriously invoked, would turn academic freedom, not into a charter of educational liberty, but into a virtual criminal code against undesirables. Unfortunately this is just how Hook himself appears to conceive its use. He tells us in an expansive moment that "the very nature of free academic activity implies an openness to all points of view, provided only that they express the conclusion of honest inquiry." But this does not mean, he goes on at once to say, that teachers who enjoy tenure (not to mention those who don't) are licensed to think and say what they please.

Here Hook invokes his pat inquisitorial distinction between "heresy" and "conspiracy." "Conspiracy" is here defined as "a deliberate act in violation of the canons of professional ethics and integrity" which, of course, is itself defined recursively by Hook's own formula for academic freedom. One may agree, to take one of his own examples, that after very thorough investigation a university may be obliged to reprimand professors of mathematics who, "seized by one or another variety of religion," insist on denouncing sin or socialism or capitalism before their classes.

However, such examples merely distract the reader from a central issue at stake in Hook's underlying theory of higher education and, behind it, of knowledge. He makes a great point of the contention that while academic freedom entitles a man to seek the truth it does not thereby entitle him to teach it. He admits, or rather insists, that this thesis runs counter to all thinkers—from Augustine to the present—who have thought they had *the* truth. The conclusion is plain: If academic freedom is the right not to *teach* but to *seek* the truth then teachers "must enjoy freedom from any ecclesiastical, religious, economic, or political dogmas that would bar the road to further inquiry."

Now I am aware of no dogma that makes further inquiry impossible in any absolute sense, including those which Augustine came to accept after much soul and mind searching. Dogma and interpretation are in fact inevitable parts of a continuing human dialectic to which the writings of the magnificent Augustine bear eloquent witness. Dogma is not the enemy of thought, but its progenitor. And the medieval universities, whatever their limitations, are proof of the fact.

No one, Hook included, is free of dogmas (nowadays we call them "points of view"). But the dogma of the open mind, which Hook professes, is not only a myth; it is a bad myth which leads only to self-deception. The great evil is not dogma but the refusal to recognize one's own dogmas for what they are. Hook's principle looks liberal, but in practice it is just the reverse. It is not a defense of inquiry, but a principle for academic inquisitions such as occurred during the McCarthy era when professors whose work has long since earned, and justified, their academic tenure were summarily dismissed because their political convictions happened not to conform to established views concerning the nature and conditions of a decent society.

What intrigues me here is Hook's own forgetfulness of the details of his own doctrine of academic freedom when adherence to them suits his own purposes. "We are not," he tells us later on, "restricting the university to an impossible purism and absolutism." Of course the university may justifiably sponsor research in areas of military defense "if its staff is willing and qualified to undertake it, and the nature of the research project does not interfere with its strictly educational functions. . . ." Nor, when classified research is in question, does Hook raise close question about the correlation between qualifications for such research and those which established a scholar's competence within a particular discipline and which presumably provided the basis of his academic tenure in the first place. On the contrary he now tells us that scholars "*must be free to determine their own field and line of inquiry*" (italics in text). That this plays hob with his formal thesis about the conditions of academic freedom gives him no qualms whatever.[2]

It is time, however, to turn to the question of *Lernfreiheit*, the freedom of students. This freedom, once more, is not included in Hook's original definition of academic freedom and, as we shall see, for a very good reason. For him, the freedom to teach and to do research (at least within the precincts of the university) is neither a civil nor a human right; it is in short a corporate right, earned by the teacher and researcher, and granted to its members by the self-perpetuating governing bodies of the university. The freedom to learn, on the other hand, is treated as a purely human right which everyone has, so to say, by nature. A brave thesis. But what is its relevance to higher education where students are also expected to earn their right to continue simply as learners by passing entrance examinations, keeping up with their studies, and paying attention when there is something to be learned from their instructors?

The point of this question becomes clear when new questions are raised about the rights, not merely of abstract learners, but of *students* as an academic class. For if, unlike his teachers and preceptors, the student's own well-earned accomplishments leave him, academically, forever in the position of the mere learner, then it follows that he can claim no right to participate, except in a purely dependent and "advisory" way, in any of the basic decision-making processes of the university. But this is precisely the position into which he is locked by Hook's analysis. For in Hook's view, the academic freedom of students derives entirely from the natural freedom to learn. This freedom, so he claims, entitles the student accordingly to freedom of certain curricular choices, freedom to doubt, challenge, contest, and argue within the context of "inquiry."

Beyond this, Hook concedes, students are justified in presenting three kinds of "demands" wherever a situation exists that makes these demands relevant. They are justified in demanding "educational participation" (in matters of policy) in the form of *"consultation"* (italics in text). But this includes no right to participate in the decision-making process which rests, or should rest, with the faculty and the administrative officers who presumably represent it.

Second is the right to "the individualization of the curriculum as far as possible within the resources available—and where not available, the right to *request* the reordering of educational priorities to make it feasible."

Third is the right "to *expect* those responsible for their education" to maintain "a central and continuing concern with the character of teaching on the college level, and the corollary right to evaluate their teachers on the basis of their classroom performance" (italics mine).[3]

This *sounds* tolerably liberal. But even if we grant that these rights of students derive from the human right to learn, Hook does not thereby establish his more important thesis that, *in the academic context*, a student is, or is to be treated as, a mere "learner." The rights of the learner are one thing; the rights of the students, especially in institutions of higher learning, include or should include much more. Many of them, to my knowledge, are wiser and have more liberal notions of higher learning than their instructors. Many of them have learned far more about the common realities of academic life than have university presidents closeted in their executive suites. Many, in fact, are better teachers than their professors, and know more about their subjects, not to say about what it means to be an educated man, than the professional grantsmen preoccupied with theoretically low-grade problems of scientific-technology. To be sure, not every student is a light to the world. But Hook's applications of the doctrine of *Lernfreiheit* in contemporary America are based not less upon intellectual distinctions than upon institutionalized class distinctions which many conservative academicians now regard as indefensible.

Why should students not enjoy the same freedom to seek the truth as their elders, especially when their elders refuse to seek a truth which all of us most desperately need to know? Even if *Lernfreiheit* depends entirely upon *Lehrfreiheit* it by no means follows that students must learn only from their teachers or that teachers should not be obliged on occasion to learn from their students. Why in practice—and *praxis*, as Marx and Dewey have taught, is the great teacher—should not all the academic classes (including administrators, professors, and students, not to mention trustees) participate in all the essential enterprises of a true community of scholars?

If they did, in my opinion, everyone would benefit. What a welcome change it would be if every trustee were obliged to assume the position of student from time to time, or if professional administrators should have to return to the classroom every year or so. Similarly, how useful to everyone concerned would be a recognized practice that would ensure the participation of both undergraduates and graduate students in teaching and administrative functions.[4]

But it is pointless to continue in this vein. Plainly, Hook's theory of academic freedom, were it consistently enforced, would increase the very anarchy he deplores. Why does he fail so completely to see this? The generic reason, I believe, is that Hook's own mind has lost its old power of thinking problematically and concretely. He announces principles which, abstractly considered, have an air of reasonableness, but which, when applied, merely intensify the issues they are presumed to resolve.

More specifically, Hook cannot, or will not, relate the problems of academic freedom to the realities of academic power. He writes, indeed, as though nothing much had changed during the last quarter-century either within the university or the other social and political institutions to which it is now umbilically tied, save the eruption on the campus of a small but determined group of hostile undergraduates. He might see matters differently if he took into fuller account the extramural pressures exerted upon the university by industry and government and their profound effects upon the contemporary functions of the higher learning in America. He deplores student power, as we know, because it interferes with what he understands by *Lehrfreiheit*. But the effects upon *Lehrfreiheit* of the enormous accumulations of administrative and extra-administrative institutional power that now exist are never faced. In his view, both students and faculty members have never enjoyed so much freedom as they do now. Why then do both groups feel so profoundly frustrated? To this question Hook gives us no intelligible answer.

It is illuminating in this connection to compare Hook's position with that of Clark Kerr whom he so much admires both as an administrator and as an educationist. In his book *The Uses of the University*, of which curiously Hook makes no mention, Kerr candidly admits that the university and other industries are becoming more alike. Says Kerr, "As the university becomes tied into the world of work, the professor—at least in the natural and some of the social sciences—takes on the characteristics of an entrepreneur. . . ." This requires freedom of a sort, but it is certainly not, in any traditional sense, academic freedom. According to Kerr, the two worlds of industry and education are in fact merging both "physically and psychologically." Where does this leave the old-fashioned academic knight of curiosity, especially if he lacks tenure and depends for his preferment upon some professorial entrepreneur whose only interest is in getting on with his grant-covered project? Kerr is at least candid. But Hook gives scarcely a thought to the bearing of corporate academic science upon the problem of academic freedom in America.

Again, Kerr acknowledges (and he should know) that in the new multiversity, it is not the teachers or their students, but the benevolent bureaucracy of administrators who often make the basic decisions about academic policies. Never, to my knowledge, does Hook rebuke Kerr for acquiescing in this doctrine of academic power; he simply bypasses it. On the contrary, he reserves his wrath for Kerr's disciple, James Perkins. Perkins, who having contended in his own writings that "public service" is one of the primary "missions" of the American university, briefly employed his own administrative power, in a time of crisis, in the "service of social justice" to the black students, at some expense to Hook's doctrine of *Lehrfreiheit*. Well, what about social justice? That, in Hook's view, is no part of the university's concern. He simply assumes, without argument, that some invisible hand of human progress guarantees that "the quest for social justice cannot conflict with principles of academic freedom. . . ."

Faced with the importunate demands of students for fuller participation in educational policy-making, he conveys the impression that the authority of the faculty is a kind of inalienable Rousseauean general will that can be shared with no one. But *vis à vis* wise administrators, trustees, and state legislatures, he leaves no doubt that the authority of the faculty, even in central educational matters, is eminently alienable.

But of course the issue is not one only of authority, but of power to enforce it. Hook remarks upon the long-suffering administrators who "have been goaded into summoning police because of the demoralization produced by prolonged occupation of university buildings or because of threatened acts of vandalism and violence. . . ." Imagine what would happen if the students or even the faculty were to summon the police because of the demoralization produced by still more prolonged occupation of university buildings by the R.O.T.C. or by government agents engaged in classified research. Or imagine what would happen if they phoned the governor to summon the state militia to protect them against the threatened acts of violence of administrators who announce that they will call in the local police if a student (or faculty) sit-in is not terminated within the hour. Merely to ask such questions is to answer the question where the lines of actual power lie. Kerr does not need to ask such questions, for he has already provided the answers, whether he likes them or not. Hook does not ask such questions because, on the whole, he wants the power, regardless of the authority, to stay where it is.

Like Boorstin, Hook is quick to denounce students who, as at Harvard, "frankly want power" and who have the temerity "even [to] demand . . . that research projects be dropped in areas related to defense." But we hear not a word about the passion for power on the part of professorial entrepreneurs or administrators and, behind them, the industrialists, the militarists, and the other politicians. Who curbs *their* power? To this question, Hook has no answer nor does he, presumably, need one. But the question of academic freedom, especially from the point of view of the student rebels and their faculty sympathizers, is, as we say, academic, unless it is related to the question, "Who rules?"

In his book, Hook's answer is muffled, but in an article in *The New York University Alumni News*, we gain a clearer view of his position. There he tells us that in the building of a great university, including a great faculty, administrative leadership is essential. No doubt this is true, but what if, like Hook, we should reply with the students and the faculty, "Leadership yes; power, no!" Hook's implicit rejoinder is this: "In the affairs of the mind and in the realm of scholarship the principles of simple majority rule or of 'one man one vote' do not apply. The most 'democratically' run institutions of learning are usually the most mediocre." This statement is not uncharacteristic. Hook has nothing but kind words for "unhappy administrators" who, when "called upon to make important decisions in many fields in which [they] can only guess," are unable to count on the gratitude, and "in the pinch of crisis" even the confidence, of their faculties. And his book, make no mistake, is a call to arms against every form of resistance to legitimated power.

I will not further tax the reader's patience with a recitation of

Hook's own nostalgic memories of what well-bred and well-disposed student radicals were like in the days of *his* youth. I will also spare him the further evidences of Hook's and Boorstin's ghoulish gentility which matches anything I have heard from Richard Nixon. For them, as their writing shows, the new gentility is a creature, not of the cultivated mind, but of an established power so brittle that it cannot abide, let alone comprehend, such pitiful affronts to its dignity as the ancient American cries "bullshit!" and "motherfucker!" If this is the language of violence, then its habitual use by cops as well as by students, by generals of the army as well as by buck privates, and by white elephants as well as by black panthers is simply another proof that we Americans are a people given to violence on every level of our power-driven society.

Possibly President Pusey of Harvard knows no better; he appears to have been born on the top floor of Massachusetts Hall. But Hook and Boorstin know better. Once upon a time they were intellectuals, partisans of new ideas and forms of discourse, passionate critics of the possibilities of progress offered our people by the power elites. What has happened to these ex-radical conservatives that they should be so full of bile and so full of animus against anyone who dares to tip the boat of our all-too-national society? What makes them so endlessly permissive when conventional institutions reassert their own terrifying power? And what makes them so unimaginative and unfeeling when new radicals of whatever age challenge both the authority and the power of those institutions?

I do not know the answers to these questions, for I do not know what makes one man keep the faith and what makes another, in the same circumstances, lose it. But I know this: if their own constituencies listen to Hook and Boorstin, then the American Republic is in for some much grayer days than it has known during the troubled decade of the sixties. For either, in the face of overwhelming power, the "others" will simply go underground, as until now most of them have not done, or else they will lapse into a disconsolate lethargy, as some of the weekly magazines now predict. Both ways, the republic loses incalculably.

II

How Late Is It?

I HAVE, AS I MENTIONED PREVIOUSLY, HAD THE RATHER special benefit of participating for two summers as a seminar leader at the Danforth Foundation Workshop on Liberal Education at Colorado College.[1] The brief but hectic weeks of the Danforth Workshop provide a useful synopsis, as well as simulacrum, of the drift of events in the American academy, as well as in the social order—or disorder—of whose health the academy has become at once a sensitive symptom and a determining cause. All the more impressive, therefore, are the astonishing changes in temper and in attitude which I have discovered among the membership of this workshop in the space of one academic year.

In 1968, when no students were participating members and no black teacher was a seminar leader, serious divisions of opinion existed within the workshop. But no conflicts of attitude emerged which precluded belief in a residual consensus about the ends of higher education; the essential worth of the academic establishment, despite its many obvious limitations and faults; or the benefits to be derived from an education in any of our great national universities.

In 1969, a few students were added to our ranks, and although the small number of black teachers among our lay membership remained about the same, we acquired a particularly brilliant and dedicated black professor as a seminar leader. In general, however, the composition of the membership was not radically different from what it had been in previous years. But in that year, not only was there a sense of mounting tension throughout the workshop, rising in some instances to open hostility, but more significantly, there was little common faith in the reality of a working consensus either about the values and aims of higher learning or about the forms of organization and governance proper to an acceptable university. Often, old colleagues and friends were barely on speaking terms, and efforts to conclude the workshop with at least an appearance of mutual confidence and good will were largely unsuccessful.

Some depreciated the significance of these oppositions. Others sought to "cool it," either by pretending that the divisions didn't exist, suggesting that they did not really involve any considerable number of the workshop membership, or by reminding us that, after all, life at the workshop is brief and their commitment to it relatively low, at least in their own order of academic priorities. But such efforts to minimize the importance of the changes in character which the academic experience of one year had wrought in the life of the workshop were, in my opinion, unavailing. In fact, precisely because we were a varied and carefully selected group of teachers, administrators, and students, the depth and intensity of our disagreements must be of the very greatest interest to anyone concerned with the significance of existing power conflicts within universities and colleges and their relations to prevailing patterns of value in our society.

Employing my experience at the Danforth Workshop, I will define some of the shifts in the developing power conflicts within the academy and in the educational and sociopolitical outlooks which I have observed among my fellow academicians during the past year. I shall also try to relate these changes to developments within the larger society.

Many more of us are now aware that, throughout our system of higher education, time is rapidly running out. While we continue to believe in the virtues of rationality, reflectiveness, and impartiality, we are obliged by the ominous circumstances to come directly to terms with the great issues that confront us. These issues include:

1. Student participation in the educational and administrative affairs of the academy.

2. The peremptory demands of black people for studies that reflect their own interests and their own historic experience within a predominantly white country.

3. The incursions into the universities and colleges of increasing numbers of "disadvantaged" students, ill-prepared for the highly technical studies now required for professional competence in most disciplines.

4. The precipitous decline of liberal education and the correlative demand on the part of the dissident groups for better, updated, more relevant studies concerned with the problems of men in contemporary society.

5. The unsatisfactory quality of life in the academy, not only for student and faculty radicals who employ unconventional means to secure their ends, but also for conservative faculty members and administrators whose subservience to the demands of the nation-state is now criticized by their fellow academicians.

6. The predicaments of the urban university in an environment which is hostile to its traditional educational activities and forces it to reconsider and to reconstruct those activities virtually at a moment's notice.

7. The pervasive awareness of malaise throughout the academy and the consequent speculations about the academy's sheer will and power to survive in a society in which many of the tasks of professional and technical education can be as well or better performed in the para-educational institutes and laboratories now maintained by industry and government.

Everywhere the time available for deliberation appears to be radically foreshortened, and scholars, like everyone else, find that they must make the best of it. On the more positive side, however, they now increasingly recognize time as a *value* in its own right whose exigent demands can no longer be postponed indefinitely.

I am impressed by the general hardening of opinions and attitudes in every stratum of the university—the "left," "right," and "center." Those who are satisfied with the existing organization of the university and with the correlative roles, functions, and ends which that organization implements, are now far more determined than they were even a year ago to protect it. This determination is reflected in their increasing readiness to resort to the overwhelming power of civil and legal authorities, even at the expense of the cherished principle of academic extraterritoriality, in order to put down forms of student- and faculty-supported protest that directly threaten the organizational *status quo.*

The fact is reflected in their increasing acceptance of violence or counterviolence as indispensable adjuncts of educational policy. Whereas violence had hitherto been decreasingly accepted as part of the educational process, it is now taken for granted as a necessity, especially within the precincts of the higher learning itself. In short, violence and repression are no longer generally regarded as primary disvalues in the academy. In the eyes of many realists, violence is now construed as a positive support of "rationality" itself, just as many radicals have contended since the time of Karl Marx.

The same point may be made even more saliently concerning the concept of authority. The "conservatives" as I shall call them, are increasingly impatient with radical students and faculty members who challenge on principle the existing provenance and governance of the university. In their efforts to maintain their own authority and power positions within it, they find themselves increasingly alienated from large segments not only of the student body but also of the faculty and, in some instances, the administration.[2] To this extent they become, in spite of themselves, symbols of repression to their critics. For the same reason they are regarded by their adversaries as primary sources of violence or counterviolence, determined to maintain their own established positions at any cost.

Because the formal authority of trustees and, behind them, the legislatures has been so readily reconverted into peremptory actual power, that authority is automatically challenged by its victims. Indeed, the latter are commonly driven, however mistakenly and futilely, into anarchistic positions which impugn any form of authority on principle. The movement symbolized by the phrase "participatory democracy" can in part be construed, both on the campus and outside it, as a counterresponse to a misapplied and divisive authority whose actions are now interpreted by dissidents as little more than a naked display of arbitrary institutional power.

The authority and power of trustees and, behind them, legislatures must in daily practice be largely delegated to academic administrators, including not only presidents and deans but also department heads and senior committee men. Accordingly, the latter find themselves caught between their colleagues and students, with whose attitudes and conduct they often personally sympathize, and the still higher authorities whose agents and representatives they are. Unfortunately, the administrators appear to their critics no longer as honest middlemen and negotiators, but rather as servants of the powers to whom they owe their office.

This fact serves to exacerbate the sense of misunderstanding and alienation between the administration and many senior faculty on the one side and students and junior faculty on the other. On both sides questions of priority become increasingly exigent. Opponents of the existing system demand that its exponents fish or cut bait; in their own foreshortened view, those who are not with us are against us. On the other side, exponents of the system, whatever their private reservations, are now obliged to give first priority to the defense of the existing university, along with its authority and power structures, and hence to view all deep criticism as evidence of institutional disaffection.

The increasing determination of university leaders and spokesmen to preserve and to protect the existing university as an institution *ipso facto* increases the prevailing conflicts. Influential exponents of the system, such as McGeorge Bundy, are ridiculed when they tell us that the real authority and power of the university resides, as they believe it should, in "the faculty." For the same reason, those who contend that the power of trustees is merely formal are regarded as hypocritical sycophants. The ready reactivation of that formal power in critical situations makes clear, at least to those against whom it is directed, where the real power within the academy lies.

Rigidity breeds rigidity, just as violence breeds counterviolence, and the exercise of power creates its own opposition. It is no accident that just as the attitudes of the conservative forces within the university have hardened, so have those of their adversaries. In a classic sense of the term, we are now witnesses to an all too real *agon* whose dialectic must be understood before it can begin to be resolved. Disaffected students now present non-negotiable demands.[3] Dissenting faculty members condemn their colleagues and the administrators whom the latter defend. The occasional administrator who is determined at all costs to preserve the principle of extraterritoriality on the campus, even if it means allowing fractious students to occupy university buildings indefinitely, is obliged to resign.

However, necessity creates strange bedfellows. Those who are prepared finally to stand on a principle find that their own priorities force them, often against their will, into the camp of the dissenters of whom they may otherwise disapprove. The principled administrator or faculty member sometimes finds himself drawn into the ranks of the radically dissenting academy. In the same way, the dissenting academy itself becomes by stages a rebellious academy, some of whose members are now girding themselves to accept the demise of their own institutions for the sake of what they esteem to be its proper educational ideals.

Thus the range of negotiable issues, or the willingness to negotiate, has plainly diminished during the past year. And those who are still committed to the principle of negotiation (which they sometimes mistakenly identify with rationality itself) are caught in a no-man's land between opposing activists. Of these, not many have moved by stages into the camp of the dissidents. More frequently they find themselves drawn in spite of themselves into the camp of hardened conservatives who contend that the time for negotiation is now passed and who are prepared to call in the police at fifteen minutes notice to clear their campuses of obstructors. Thus, by a tragic irony, professors of reason and argument find themselves committed in practice to the use of pre-emptive academic, legal, and political power in order to force the dissidents to "listen to reason." And their resort to force in turn makes the latter ever more intransigent.

I am not saying that we have actually reached a point of no return within the dissenting and counterdissenting academy. Nor do I profess to know where such a point lies. But everywhere there is an increasing sense that it now lies within the range of existing possibilities, and hence that irresolvable conflict within the universities and colleges may be an impending reality. Thus, as I discovered at the Danforth Workshop this year, there exists on all sides a pervasive mood of stoical resignation regarding divisions of opinion and attitude.

In another way, those who still profess to believe in the fine old ideal of mutual trust and liberal consensus no longer strive ever more patiently to realize it in their own actions. In fact, those who talk of such things as "trust" and "community" commonly seem ever more abstract and remote from the actualities of university life. As it turns out, unfortunately, their own conduct constantly belies their ideals. They yearn for community, but act in ways that diminish the possibility of genuine communities of attitude and feeling. They nostalgically recall the good old times when there was a deep underlying trust among students, faculty, and administration. But in practice they are no less mistrustful of their colleagues, their students, or their academic superiors than those dissidents who tell each other that there are none to trust any longer but themselves.

All of the major power conflicts within the academy seem to turn on the question of its structure. However, all of these conflicts are not of the same sort. Initially, at least, it seems possible to range them under two main heads. Whether they can all be so classified is unclear. Indeed, it is by no means certain whether in the end even these types of conflict are themselves distinct.

The first type of conflict concerning the existing structure of the university does not appear at first to involve basic disagreements about the ultimate aims of the higher learning. For example, many students who demand greater participation in the governance of the university, especially in matters of appointments and curriculum, often seem initially to share with their elders the same broad attitudes concerning the aims of the higher learning.

Thus I have found very few student activists who deny that the university should concern itself with the advancement of learning through teaching and research in all the main departments of human inquiry and culture. They may demand that more of their teachers' time be devoted to teaching, but few deny that regular independent study is essential to successful teaching and that without such study teachers become drudges and hacks.

Moreover, not many student activists, in my experience, deny the importance to themselves of rigorous pre-professional and professional studies arranged around a field of major interest. They merely insist that such studies take into account all relevant contemporary phenomena and that they be effectively integrated with comprehensive studies that place them securely and discriminatingly within the wider contexts of human life and culture.

A very considerable majority of their elders very likely share this view, however obsessed they may become in practice with their own professional investigations and activities. The drifts toward professionalism, specialism, and scientism in the university seem not to be matters of individual intent but of institutional factors, both within the academy and the society which put a high premium upon professional distinction and which accordingly direct tendencies toward competitiveness and emulation into increasingly narrow channels of inquiry. The prevailing systems of institutional and social rewards and penalties make it difficult, even for men committed in principle to a more liberal conception of higher education, consistently to act in accordance with their beliefs. It is precisely for this reason that many student activists oppose existing patterns of academic organization. For the same reason these students are likely to be political and social radicals who demand corresponding structural changes in other institutions within our society.

Many faculty members, including especially junior members, who demand wider faculty participation in the basic decision-making processes of the university, do not seem at first to differ radically either from the trustees, the administration, or their more compliant colleagues concerning James Perkins's primary "missions" of the university—instruction, research, and public service. They complain rather about their own incapacity to play a continuing and decisive part in establishing policies designed to implement such missions or ends. Their complaint is based upon the contention that the trustees, the administrators, and senior research professors, largely reponsible to themselves or their own superiors, continually subvert the very ends which they profess. Once more the assumption is that existing structures of authority and power preclude forms of effective participation and review on the part of the faculty at large that might result in policies more consonant with the proper missions of the academy.

According to the present hypothesis, dissident students and

faculty members demand a restructuring of the university in ways that would give them more effective power only because they believe, rightly or wrongly, that the existing modes of governance within the university make it difficult or impossible to implement the professed purposes for which the academy exists. But such a view of the matter is superficial. For when such conflicts over the existing structure of the university are more deeply probed, it soon becomes evident that the consensus concerning the ends of the university described above is abstract and unreal. It is simply not true, in the view of more thoughtful dissenting members of the academy, that substantive agreement concerning the ends of higher education any longer exists.

For example, many students demand a greater role in the decision-making process because they consider the existing curriculum, especially in the social sciences, history, and the humanities, largely irrelevant to their own historical predicaments and their social and cultural aspiration both as students and as human beings. And faculty members are profoundly repelled by prevailing conceptions of public service according to which they themselves are expected to participate. Many are angered by the ties between the university as an institution and the governmental-military-industrial combinations. They condemn academic practices that, in effect, place the facilities of the university, including its faculties, at the disposal of institutions of whose own goals and policies they passionately disapprove.

To shrewder members of the dissenting academy it begins to appear that supposed disagreements over structure are frequently ways of concealing disagreements over basic educational policy and purpose which in their view should be debated in their own terms. They demand increasing power precisely in order to modify the ends now pursued by the academic establishment.

The second type of power conflict within the university mentioned above also concerns questions of governance and organization. But it does not at first glance seem to be concerned with issues about the ulterior ends of higher education. At least some of the power conflicts seem to concern the structure of the university as an end in itself. Thus some students oppose the existing structure because it excludes them from effectual control over university affairs. Like their elders, whom they not unnaturally emulate, they also want to run things and are disgruntled when they cannot do so. The will to domination is very strong in a society such as ours, and those excluded from the corridors of power often contest the order which excludes them merely because it leaves them out. In some instances the profession of supposedly higher motives appears to be nothing more than a mask.

However, many students and faculty members demand a restructuring of the university which will give them greater power in the determination of its policies for better reasons. They sincerely believe that their own presence on the governing boards and committees of the university will of itself insure a better chance for a genuine community of scholars. They argue that the application of the principle of participatory democracy, or community, within the classrooms, within archaic self-serving academic departments, as well as within the overarching administration of the university is a positive human good, desirable on its own account. As I understand, what they demand and are prepared to fight for is, in sum, a truer polity or city of the mind within the academy so that all its members may better fulfill themselves as liberated human beings.

For much the same reason, academic dissidents also demand basic structural changes in the governance of the university which will, in their opinion, radically reduce the psychological distances that prevail among members of the major classes within the university. From their point of view, such forms of psychological distance are both symptoms and causes of human alienation which are inherently divisive and destructive. Nor are they content with the reply that some forms of psychological distance and alienation may be necessary or even desirable in the university as elsewhere, for indispensable divisions of labor, differentiations of function, and accompanying systems of authority.

Stated in these terms, those who accept such a reply as sufficient remind one of conservative Catholics within the Christian church, just as their opponents remind one of radical Protestants who regard the historical church as paradoxically corruptive of all who aspire to live a Christian life. Similarly, the former remind us of those who, in more obvious political terms, maintain that even within a liberal democracy, established aristocratic principles of hierarchy and authority are necessary to the administration of justice, just as their opponents remind us of classical revolutionists who contend that the only just polity must be one of institutional liberty, equality, and fraternity.

Once such analogies come in view, another issue that divides members of the academy is forced upon us. "Strict constructionists" like to remind us that the university is essentially a place for teaching, learning, and study. They are fond of telling us that the university is not and cannot properly serve as a church or state. They warn us that, unless the university limits its conception of its functions, it will involve itself unnecessarily and at great cost in wider political and social conflicts that are not and cannot be its concern. Accordingly, they accept the university, like the legal system, as an institution which can no longer be, or pretend to serve as, a community either of scholars or of men.

This contention has some strength. Yet it fails to satisfy dissenting "loose constructionists" for whom the university must now assume historic social functions and roles whose importance short-sighted formalists fail to appreciate. The former contend that in an era of prolonged cultural crisis, when other institutions are no longer adequate to their occasions as carriers of central social and human values, the university is obliged to assume at least some of the functions of a church or a polity. They believe that only by accepting such an enlarged sense of its educational and social missions can the university justly claim the position of centrality which its own functionaries themselves ascribe to it. Such a contention is easily misunderstood. It does not entail that ordinary officers of the university must in any literal sense assume the roles of priests or statesmen. Patently this gentry is unprepared for such roles.

What is asked for is an enlarged sense of the whole university's contemporary vocation as a repository of human culture and learning, a new determination on the part of academicians to serve as independent critics of manifest cultural confusions and institutional inversions, and, more generally, a readiness on their part to assume a more active role as conscience to the society. In the name of these roles and purposes, it is contended that the university must first clean its own house by cutting off its subservient services to the military establishment and its industrial adjuncts, and by assuming its proper responsibilities for rehabilitation of the university city over which, in so many cases, it now presides as an oppressive landlord.

Undoubtedly students and faculty members who take this view tend to regard themselves, in effect, as a new "elect" (in the traditional Protestant sense of the term) which may serve as a carrier of a revived and relevant idealism to which their elders—the grantsmen, the vocationalists, the old-pros, and the pragmatists—now pay only reluctant lip service. It is not so much that their ideals are different from those professed by their elders. They mean in all seriousness, by their actions as well as by their words, to rejuvenate an imperial sociopolitical order, including its acquiescent academic knowledge factories and service stations. They understand, however, as did their Protestant forbearers, that they cannot fulfill their mission without power and hence, on occasion, without risking the possibility of violence. Jean-Paul Sartre wisely reminds us that such violence is always to be understood as a counterviolence or retaliation to the violence of "the Other."

Their critics, who are legion, charge these would-be Luthers with *hubris* or *chutzbah*. They call them romantics, utopians, chiliastic visionaries who would replace the university, with its traditional finite educational ends, with something else which in anticipation might gratify their own infinite yearnings for union and redemption but which is no longer a proper or manageable institution of patient study, research, and learning.

These critics, to whom I listened endlessly this year at the Danforth Workshop, charge such dissident students and their faculty supporters with generating a sense of unstructured totalistic crisis which, because it is objectless and devoid of empirical content, is therefore incapable of meaningful resolution. In the name of justice, some of them admit to a certain admiration for the passion and courage of the "rejuvenators," as they may be called, but ridicule them for failing to provide any acceptable plan for orderly institutional and social change.

More generally, they charge such idealists with being both victims and manipulators of general ideas who lack the factual information required for consistent and systematic institutional improvements. Other critics are even less generous. They imply that, like most other malcontents and incipient revolutionists, the underlying motivation of such academic idealists is sheer resentment. These dissidents, incapable of either instruction, discipline, or the exercise of authority essential to all great achievements of civilization, and lacking more useful outlets for their aggression, seek by any means at hand to humiliate their betters and to bring them down to their own wretched levels of unexamined protest and violence.

Perhaps there is something in this. Resentment, like aggression, is a universal sentiment and, when deprived access to an authority that continually works to our disadvantage, we all are subject to the destructive impulses it may occasion. Resentment, which is by no means always self-interested, also has another name: the sense of justice or reciprocity. And though resentful men may not understand the cause of their affliction, just as the man who demands justice may not always know how to realize it, they still deserve to be listened to.

Here use may be made of a striking medical analogy first suggested to me by Professor Donald Larsen of Texas. This is the concept of "referred pain"; that is, pain which crops out in places that may be remote from the source of bodily disorder. Referred pain is not illusory even though it cannot be removed by remedies applied directly to the painful organ; rather it is an associated symptom of genuine and potentially lethal malfunctioning elsewhere in the organism. Something has gone wrong which must be located and remedied if the organism is to be restored to health.

Thus, what we have to consider, even if we do not accept at face value the dissenters' descriptions of the source of evils either in the university or in the larger body politic, is the question: what is it that *now* disposes them to acts of desperation in the absence of any one justifying cause? More generally, what are the deep-lying maladies in the organization and economy of our universities and colleges that result at this time in so many diverse forms of referred pain everywhere in the academy?

The answer to such a question cannot be simple. A part of it undoubtedly concerns long-standing internal malfunctionings within the university. For example, we have now to reckon with the consequences of a hundred years of infatuation with the nineteenth century ideals of the German university, with its Ph.D. system and its rigid academic hierarchies of ordinary and extra-ordinary professors, its conscienceless commitment to "pure" re-search, and its indifference to the claims of liberal education which was henceforth delegated to the *Gymnasium*.

Our own universities have indeed become knowledge factories dominated by graduate schools interested exclusively in forms of study and training necessary to specialized and professional scien-tific or parascientific inquiry. Accordingly, our universities and colleges are now institutes for the training of pre-professional and technological elites. And their faculties are themselves systematic-ally deprived of the forms of training and experience required for rehabilitating the entire university as an institution of relevant hu-man learning. They themselves are victims of referred pain who are forced back in times of stress on conventional formulas for re-storing order and continuity so that they can get on with their scientific and professional work.

In a larger sense the entire university is dominated by the bane-ful ideology of "rationalism" which puts a premium upon the theoretical-explanatory conception of knowledge and hence auto-matically downgrades all forms of understanding that do not con-form to this model. The whole domain of meaning and value, re-course to which is indispensable for all practical reflections and decisions of policy, is disposed of as something purely "subjec-tive," "emotional," of interest to scholars only for what it symp-tomizes. And teachers or students who concern themselves in depth with this side of the life of the mind are treated as pariahs who, lacking any proper objective subject matter and method-olgy, therefore have no proper place in institutions of higher learning.[4]

At the Danforth Workshop this past summer the effects of this ideology were everywhere apparent in the widespread refusal even to consider the possibility that knowledge of vital importance about the quality of life in the university has been directly re-vealed in the confrontations of disaffected students and their fac-ulty allies with the authorities who preside over our mills of scientific-technological knowledge. But what if these students and faculty members should really understand something not only about themselves but also about us which can only be learned in and through such confrontations? What chance have we to acquire, not to mention make use of, such knowledge when we systematically discredit its possibility? Accordingly, what can we scholars make of the contention of the single black seminar leader at the Danforth Workshop, Professor Charles Long of the University of Chicago, that the sheer presence of increasing numbers of black students in our institutions of higher learning will make the meaning of "the relationship of the liberal arts to the liberation of persons and society" more intense and significant?[5]

Such questions have their obvious analogues when we turn to the situation within the national society whose wider conflicts of power and patterns of value, or disvalue, are everywhere reflected in the academy itself. It is my entirely unoriginal contention that virtually every important issue concerning the existing structure of the academy has its direct counterpart within the larger society.

The fact is evident in the systematic refusal of most national leaders in politics, government, and industry to take seriously the insights of oppressed minority groups and to rely rather on the presumed learning and expertise of ex- or absentee-professors who confess that they have no general theoretical knowledge of the problems they are called upon to solve. It is evident in the almost pathetic struggle on the part of young men and women, powerfully supported by their parents, to gain admission into the more prestigious university colleges and, from an early age, to confine themselves to courses of study in the secondary schools that may give them a chance of admission to such colleges. And it is evident in the very conception of "upward-bound" programs that will presumably enable "disadvantaged" students, including especially black students, to make their way through these same institutions of higher learning into remunerative positions of prestige and authority.

However, the forms of referred pain that afflict our universities have other by no means unrelated causes in the national society. Once specific cause, of course, lies in our inability to conclude a futile, bloody, debilitating war in the Far East. Another lies in the devastating side effects of that war within the society, including the uncontrolled buildup of an overwhelmingly destructive military power and the increasing readiness of civil authorities to use it on the "home front" in order to preserve law and order, and the continuation of a national selective service, or draft. But the war as well as the ever more influential and extensive military establishments are themselves functions of an imperial and counterrevolutionary foreign policy which appears not only to many people in South America, Africa, and Asia, but also to our own youth and above all our black population, as inherently repressive and warlike. What is worse, the latter, who not unnaturally regard this immensely costly and enervating policy as something which is maintained largely at their own expense, are thereby further alienated from the government to which they must look at the same time for economic assistance and for the protection of their existing rights.

A correlative source of the same malaise lies in the patent inability of an overwhelmingly affluent society, or else an unwillingness on the part of those who control its wealth and scientific-technological expertise, to cope effectively with any of our national disorders: the blights that afflict our cities, the waste or misuse of our national resources, the contamination of the air, water, and land, the deep pockets of corrosive poverty and misery among all "disadvantaged" peoples whether in the cities or in rural areas. These evils are not only material, but also cultural and spiritual, for they give rise to the widespread conviction that those who have effective control over our resources are committed in practice to maintaining their own power positions at any cost, even to themselves. In such a society, so it is argued, men no longer regard themselves as human beings but as things or artifacts to be used and manipulated simply in order to maintain the system.

To my mind the most distressing aspect of this situation is that the traditional aims of a government that calls itself liberal and democratic are no longer taken seriously by those who have little or no share in the determination of its policies. And the ideology of liberal democracy, with its commitment to a rule of law, now stands discredited in the eyes of the very people it is meant to benefit. Thus they become in turn advocates—and victims—of a counterelitist ideology of separatism and sometimes of violence whose own inevitable consequence would be a form of dictatorship for which ideals of justice and legality no longer have meaning.

Unfortunately the "Others" offer the people no meaningful

alternative. On the contrary, their own elitist attitudes are disclosed in their fashionable but empty doctrine (derived, of all things, from Karl Marx) of the "end of ideology," which barely conceals their own counterideology of political "realism," pragmatism of the day, and low-budget social engineering. Indifferent even to existing constitutional forms and restraints, they talk endlessly about "national society" and the "national interest," of whose prevailing power structures they themselves are the primary beneficiaries.

The net result is the general sense of disillusionment and drift and of an unwillingness to take seriously the belief of idealists in our capacity as a people to make necessary radical changes in our institutional life. In more metaphysical and religious terms, one finds an increasing attenuation of the faith in man's capacity for self-determination and self-transcendence.

However, these very terms are discredited by anti-ideology intellectuals who serve as apologists and frontrunners for the existing establishments. As they repeatedly tell us, morality and religion themselves belong to the domain of ideology. Those who continue to speak in ethical and religious ways are thereby discredited in advance as "extremists" and "alienists" who have nothing to say to sensible men of business and affairs. Thus, systematically self-deprived of any language save the languages of science and power, do they themselves provide their opponents with formal as well as substantive justification for their own cynicism regarding the principles of our American system.

It would be instructive at this point to chart in some detail the development of what, from an educational as well as a more general sociopolitical perspective, is probably the most important chapter in the story of our emerging value patterns in American society as well as the conflicts of power attending them.

Unfortunately there is space only to make the barest mention of the situation of our black population and the forms of referred pain that everywhere afflict them. Among black leaders, the idealism of Martin Luther King, which provided the main hinge of the great civil rights movement in the fifties, is being replaced by a black power movement whose separatism, sometimes reinforced by a mystique of despairing counterviolence, now leads black people into head-on collisions with their white adversaries. Indifferent now to belated and hypocritical appeals to principles of democracy, the rule of law, and the ideal of an integrated polity of equal and free men, these leaders treat self-interested white elitists and sincere white liberals alike as a common enemy which nothing will move but determined manifestations of brute force and power. Ours, as they claim, is through and through a racist society and culture which they must combat by every means, physical and ideological, at their disposal. And the admonition that they thereby become victims of a tragic ideology of black racism falls on ears now as deaf as those of their adversaries.

This ideological decline, however, can only be understood as a function of the disarray of our whole society. Until this is understood we will continue to misconstrue the forms of referred pain from which so many black Americans, regardless of their economc and social positions, so deeply and grievously suffer. Meanwhile, the havoc thereby wrought upon our entire educational system is incalculable.

However, it is not all havoc. Let us now return to the situation in our confused and revolting academy. In the preceding remarks, I have deliberately overstated the point in order to make it. Black students and teachers, like the people from which they come, are by no means merely pathetic victims of an ideology of racism and counterviolence: Like the white student-activists from whom they have now unfortunately but understandably dissociated themselves, they are not only well aware of their own dignity as human beings but also of the immense value of the moral, social, and educational perspectives they have reached through long centuries of enslavement and oppression.

Black students tell us, as can no other group in America, what are the concrete meanings of such universal concepts as community, justice, and freedom, and in so doing they already help to restore our badly eroded belief in moral and, behind them, religious realities. Indeed, their very presence in the academy is a constant reminder of the primary services of the colleges and universities in a democratic society: the fitting of *all* citizens not only for forms of work which will make use of their own best intellectual energies, but also for an encompassing *human* existence in which the whole mind of man may at last fulfill itself.

But there is another more practical lesson to be learned from the ever increasing numbers of self-disciplined black insurgents on our campuses. With their various "nonnegotiable" demands, for the sake of which they are prepared to sacrifice themselves in order to tie up the daily routines of whole universities, they show the rest of the academic community many things it needs to know about its own power and the human uses to which it may be put. They show us, for example, how the power of the entire academy might be used for wider educational purposes through organized, if sometimes unconventional, activities like their own.

Who knows, if we stood together and were willing not only to form lobbies but to organize our own sit-ins or even general strikes against punitive legislators and governors, not to mention a reactionary congress and president that care more about "law and order" on the campus than about the quality of the education offered there, we might well effect a new understanding of the higher learning as well as radical reconstruction of our conceptions of its services to the national society. Were we ourselves exigently to make our own nonnegotiable demands, no doubt at considerable cost to ourselves, for far larger grants-in-aid and scholarships for disadvantaged students and for better, more extensive nonelitist "upward-bound" programs for those now inadequately prepared for college, who can say that we would not bring about a regeneration of ourselves as teachers and a reinstitution of that sense of community which is so sadly missing from the contemporary campus? It is not inconceivable that we might thereby re-establish our right to an authority and leadership as educators which our dissenting students no longer acknowledge.

One thing is clear: such possibilities, or hopes, will not be realized by scholars who simply stand and wait. We are told by conservative members of the academic establishment that the university must now be depoliticized for the sake of its perennial ends of disinterested learning and teaching. To heed such advice would be a disaster. On the contrary, just as our insurgent academy, both black and white, has taught us that significant liberal learning must concern itself with the liberation of human beings, so it has helped us see, by its own example, how academic mountains can be moved by concerted, dedicated, disciplined political action. A liberated university, in short, must liberate itself; there is no one else to do the job.

This is not to say that all the bold tactics and strategies mentioned above are practicable. Nor, certainly, is it for me to vouch for them. Like most of my kind, my knowledge extends only as far as my experience, and that experience, as I am well aware, is still far too abstract and literary. But this at least I have learned and do know: political action on the part of academicians can be a force for good as well as evil. I have also learned from my juniors in the dissenting academy that, from an educational point of view, politics can be a great "mixed good." It can serve to protect and to advance educational values, but it can also serve in the process to create them. In the domain of the higher learning, as elsewhere, men learn mainly from participating, by acting and doing. Spectatorial minds contribute nothing to the advancement of relevant human understanding.

The title of this chapter is "How Late Is It?" The inescapable answer is that it is very late indeed. The power conflicts both on the campus and in the society have made it clear that, unless we academicians display more care both for the protection and the enlightenment of *all* our kind, including our dissenting students and faculty, our sacred academy will not be worth saving and that its demise will not be deeply mourned by those for whom the exploration of the moon means more than the rehabilitation of the planet Earth.

Our student activists have taught us the inestimable lesson of refusal and the immense liberation that comes from refusal. It always remains within our power to say "No!" to militarists and industrialists who employ our services in defense of a national interest about whose ends we have not been consulted. And it is within our power to say "No!" to their academic lackies. Should we say it together and with conviction, I am convinced that simple "No!" would do more to revitalize the higher learning in America than a thousand grants-in-aid from the government and the foundations.

Part III

NEW APPROACHES IN THE HUMANITIES

12

Analytical Philosophy and Educational Development

1. Philosophical Analysis and Its Educational Uses

BEFORE CONSIDERING WHAT THE CONTRIBUTION OF ANA-
lytical philosophy to educational development may be, it is essential that something be said about analytical philosophy itself,
its history, its varieties, its development. If the expression of my
views sometimes seems peremptory and dogmatic, that is merely
the result of an effort to be concise.

Let me say to begin with that I do not consider analytical
philosophy to be more than an adjunct of philosophical activity.
The often-concealed business of all philosophy is with the wisdom
and hence with the conduct of life, and especially with that form
of education which is the condition of self-knowledge, self-development, self-transcendence, and self-control. Philosophy is not,
properly, a subject or subject matter, not a discipline, not a
science, not even an art. This does not mean, of course, that
philosophical reflection should not be disciplined. Nevertheless,
all philosophical inquiry that achieves its end of liberation must
constantly move beyond the reach of all previously acquired disciplines, for philosophy, which is constantly preoccupied with limiting questions and with what lies beyond pre-established limits,
finds existing disciplines insufficient to its purposes. By nature, any
discipline, including the disciplines of science and established
religion, is inadequate to the aspirations of the philosopher toward

self-knowledge and self-control. In attempting to deal with philosophical problems, we invariably find that our pre-existing discipline and our disciplines are constantly breaking down, having to be repaired, supplanted, or even, on occasion, dispensed with altogether. Indeed, no discipline can be adequate to the endless crisis of human existence, which is the only perennial problem of philosophy.

Analytical philosophy is nothing new. In the *Euthyphro*, Plato makes all-important distinctions between questions about the meaning of piety and questions about the genesis, the uses, and finally, prevailing standards of piety; in the later dialogues, in which he attempts systematically to distinguish and to relate the concepts of being and nonbeing, of limit and the unlimited, of particular and universal, of appearance and reality, and of change and the permanent, Plato raises most of the questions which have occupied analytical philosophers since his time. What distinguishes Socrates and Plato is their sense of the relevance and even the necessity of such conceptual and logical analyses to the conduct of life. But as Plato shows, the philosopher is not, in one sense, a pure or disinterested analyst of ideas. In the *Parmenides*, for example, the concept of mud is considered, but only for purposes of illustration. What concern the analytical philosopher are the forms of thought that guide our major forms of action. What constantly preoccupy him are the notions of the good, the true, the valid, the beautiful, the ideal and the real, the noble, and the holy, by means of which all of us articulate the ideals, standards, and procedures that govern our activities.

Plato, of course, did not and could not have the last word. If, as Whitehead contended, all subsequent philosophy is but a series of footnotes to Plato, the footnotes, which get longer with every issue of *Mind*, are now more illuminating than the text. In short, analytical philosophy has had a long and extremely varied development, full of false starts and misconceptions, but also full of fruitful insights and fresh beginnings. Plato raised the major analytical questions, but he rarely succeeded in answering them; indeed, it is doubtful whether he or his followers grasped the nature or point of the questions they were raising. The philosophical analyst, to his sorrow, always finds that chief among the difficulties created by his predecessors are those arising from their preconceptions about the nature of analysis itself. In consequence, he is inevitably drawn into queries about the nature of nature, the analysis of analysis, the meaning of meaning. Here again, the opening moves were made by Plato. Philosophers have since gradually begun to work themselves free from Plato's own pre-conception about natures, analyses, and meanings, but they have done so laboriously and at great cost to the subsequent and inter-locking histories of both philosophy and education.

Until the end of the nineteenth century, few philosophers un-derstood that analytical philosophy must become, or acquire, a theory of expressions. Inevitably analytical philosophy, as it be-comes more fully aware of what it is up to, turns, at least in part, into a linguistic philosophy, and this for the simple reason that, as Charles Sanders Peirce put it, "thought and expression are one." To understand a concept is to understand the meaning and the use of a form of expression. Peirce, however, also rightly insisted that not all forms of expression are linguistic, and hence that a general theory of expressions, which he, following Locke, called "semiotic," must make provision for many different types of signs, of which linguistic signs, such as they are, are only a special form. Where Peirce went radically wrong is in his assumption, inherited from Plato, that all meaningful expressions are signs, and hence that signification is the paradigmatic form of expression. In sum, like most philosophers since Plato, Peirce was guilty of a pervasive and crippling error which might well be dubbed "the semanticist's error," that is, the error of supposing that the only, or proper, use of expressions, and particularly of verbal expres-sions, is to signify objects and to specify their characteristics and relations. This error is closely related to another, which in its turn may be called "the epistemologist's error." This is the mistake of supposing that the primary, or only proper business of discourse, and hence of thought, is to assert truths abut the nature of things, and, correlatively, that the primary concern of the human mind itself is with the intuition, or else with the verification, of such truths. If anything has been learned from recent linguistic philoso-phy—although in fact it could have been learned long ago from George Berkeley and David Hume and Immanuel Kant—it is that human utterances have many characteristic or conventional roles, of which description, prediction, explanation, and analysis itself are merely the most conspicuous in a culture and in a tradition which, since Plato, has placed such an overwhelming emphasis upon cognition in general and theoretical science in particular.

Two tragic and consequent spiritual errors have attended the semanticist's and the epistemologist's errors. These may be called the errors of rationalism. One of them is the mistake of supposing that religion, art, morality, and philosophy are either putative forms of a super-science of being or reality or else, as it were, primitive protosciences which, in due course, will be replaced by genuine positive sciences, ready and able to give verifiable accounts of what there is. The countermistake of rationalists is to suppose that since, or in so far as, religion, art, morality, and philosophy are not sciences, or else are incapable of becoming sciences, they are at best peripheral or ancillary cultural activities and at worst sources of mythology, obscurantism, superstition, and irrationalism.

These attitudes are widely and often unconsciously shared not only by the intellectuals and by men of letters who serve to propagate and to popularize the technical theories of the great philosophers, but also by educators at all levels of instruction, both formal and informal. To this day, as I have found to my cost, they dominate, or else confuse and distract, programs of general education that aspire to do "something more" than the various special sciences can decently provide, but are misled into supposing that the "something more" in question must in principle be capable of justifying itself, if not in scientific ways, then in the superscientific realms of rationalistic philosophy, theology, and ethics. They are responsible for conceptions of liberal, as distinct from technological and professional, education that reflect the classical view that the proper concern of a free man, i.e., a citizen and a member of a leisured class, is with the cultivation of reason and, through this, with the contemplation of theoretical truth. It is from this standpoint, as it has developed in our own time, that the liberal arts are still regarded as ancillary to the aims of research and the advancement of learning. And it is for this reason that the so-called humanities have become increasingly, and particularly on the side of academic prestige, departments of literary and cultural history, of linguistics, semantics, and logic, and that departments of fine arts and music have become departments of archeology, art history, museum science, and musicology. Within the humanities, the cultivation of the imagination remains incidental and accidental, and the concern with appreciation is left to young instructors who have not yet fully outgrown their amateur status as lovers of literature or art or music. Religion, where it is not relegated to the divinity school (which itself still remains in bondage to intellectualistic and scientistic theologies, the effect of which is to breed either skepticism or soft-headedness), becomes the province of a standing committee, usually comprised of historians, sociologists, and linguists, with perhaps an epistemologist thrown in to sweeten the pot. In most liberal arts colleges outside the Bible Belt, the cultivation and development of substantive religious understanding and concern remains *infra dig*, something which, because it is viewed either as not seriously concerned with what exists or else as concerned only with suppositious or supernatural entities beyond the range of scientific or historical scrutiny, has no proper place in the formal academic curriculum.

There remains, however, an uneasy feeling on the part of most educators that while the "facts" are pretty well taken care of by the various special sciences, something called "values" is not. But how to take care of them without embarrassment in an academic context except "objectively," i.e., through the respectable methods of historical, anthropological, sociological, and now logical and semantical analysis, remains a question to which our committees on educational policy have found no satisfactory answers. Curiously, the one type of school which, to its own satisfaction at least, provides an alternative to the diffident eclecticism of our public and secular schools, namely, the Roman Catholic university, is itself the victim of a classical semanticism, epistemologism, and rationalism which in their own ways reduce, or aspire to reduce, values to facts and moral principles to a kind of natural law. Such an alternative, I am convinced, cannot survive the scrutiny of contemporary philosophical analysis. And where an attempt has been made to introduce that sort of alternative into the nonCatholic university, as happened for example at the University of Chicago during the era of Hutchins and Adler, the result has served merely to discredit the whole effort to provide responsible ethical and evaluative instruction in the schools of higher learning.

[*223*]

Meanwhile in the secondary schools, desultory, insensitive, and dogmatic programs of instruction, or indocrination, in the civic values and virtues of the existing political and social esablishment leave the student quite unprepared for the arduous tasks of moral and ideological reconstruction upon which depend the possibility of orderly, progressive social change. In an age of unparalleled technological development, of social and political revolution that involves whole continents, and of murderous ideological conflicts, the average high school graduate, for all his learning, is wholly untrained for the continuing work of individual and collective deliberation, without which democracy itself remains merely another form of oppression, and civil liberties merely protective covering for the advertiser and the propagandist.

These remarks must not be misunderstood. I have no illusions about the ability of analytical and linguistic philosophy alone to offset the monumental intellectual confusions and spiritual disorders inherent in our major Western cultural traditions. The analytical philosopher, like his great progenitor, Socrates, remains essentially a midwife; he offers merely the possibility of a clearer head, a freer imagination, a more receptive sensibility. He does not offer salvation; he cannot provide a faith; he cannot remove the economic and social causes of human alienation and oppression. Let me also emphasize, that, although I think it is indeed one of the functions of a wise linguistic philosopher to offset the errors of the semanticist, the epistemologist, and the scientific methodolatrist, it by no means follows that he is, or should be, hostile either to science itself or to knowledge, or to those forms of discourse which are indispensable to science and to the inculcation and spread of knowledge. Linguistic philosophy should refine and clarify our conceptions of the life of reason, not oppose it. It is the business of the linguistic philosopher to state the terms and the limits of rational judgment and action, not to propose alternatives to them. Irrationalism is as profound an error as rationalism, and the mind that despises science is unfit for philosophy itself.

2. *Educational Development: Its Meaning, Conditions, and Limits*

Now I must come more directly to terms with our subject. What I propose to do in the pages immediately following is (1) to offer an account of the concept of educational development— its use, its range, its varieties, and its limits; (2) to say something about the idea of the teacher—what he must do, what he can and cannot do within the process of educational development; and (3) to indicate some of the logical conditions of learning—what it is to learn and not to learn, and what perhaps cannot be learned and hence what falls outside the range of educational development. In the course of my remarks I hope to show how limited is an education which confines itself to the purveying of information—what William James called "knowledge about" and Gilbert Ryle calls "knowing that"; I hope also to show how much, even within the sphere of theoretical education, generally depends upon the acquisition of skills and the development of aptitudes —in short, upon much that goes, somewhat pejoratively but without justification, under such headings as mere "training," vocational education," "professional education," or "technological education." The greater part of all education, as I shall argue, is and must be a matter of training and of forms of teaching and learning that now pass as merely vocational, professional, and technological. At the same time, I intend to question the value to the learner of an information-oriented education, even within the domain of science itself.

When we glance at the etymology of the term "education" we are immediately confronted by the question whether the phrase "educational development" is not pleonastic. It is worth recalling that the Latin root of the word "education" and its cognates is the verb *educere*, which means simply to lead or to bring forth, and hence, in at least one obvious sense, to develop. And it is significant that our word "educe" is also derived from *educere*, for initially "education" seems simply to be a virtual synonym for "development." From this point of view, one is tempted simply to say that a person's educational development and his education are one and the same thing, and hence that an analysis of the idea of educational development would simply be coordinate with the analysis of the concept of education itself. Nor, up to a point, is the temptation to be resisted, for, as we shall see, the word "education" covers a lot of ground, from which, initially, nothing pertaining to the rearing of the young, or at any rate the undeveloped, can reasonably be excluded.

Upon reflection, however, one perceives at least a distinction between educational development and other forms of development that is germane to our purpose. For one is bound, I think, to resist the suggestion that the concept of education applies naturally to the maturation of the organism, and in particular the physical body, through ordinary ineluctable processes of growth and assimilation. It may well be, therefore, that a main point of discussions of educational development should be to underline the central differences between education as a developmental process and other modifications or changes to which organisms, and particularly human organisms, are subject. For example it would be entirely pertinent in a study in depth of the process of educational development to examine the ways in which other developmental processes set limits to, or else positively impede, what can be accomplished through education. Or, again, it might be worthwhile, in certain contexts, to elaborate the ways in which the levels of natural development or maturation must be carefully taken into account in intelligently planning the formal educational development of men from kindergarten, through the secondary schools, to the college, the university, and the graduate school. Despite all this, however, the primary fact remains that there can be no form of education which is nondevelopmental, and that any teacher who leaves the minds and hearts of his pupils just where they were has taught them nothing at all.

In my view the sphere of education and hence of educational development is coterminous with that of mental action. Even so-called physical education, which by definition involves the training and the manipulation of the body, would not, I think, be called a form of education were modes of mental action, and hence of mental aptitude and skill, not also essentially involved. A child who has a tendency to be pigeon-toed can, in a sense, be "trained" to walk normally. But in so far as this involves merely the exertion of mechanical pressures with corresponding bodily changes, one would, I think, be properly disposed to resist calling such a process or development "educational." Hence, I shall contend, as a general thesis, that all education whatever involves, if indeed it does not implicitly aim at, some form of mental action and the acquisition of the skills and aptitudes, as well as the achievements, essential to such forms of action.

If this is so, the term "education" and its cognates themselves belong to the sphere of what the English call "psychological," as distinct from purely physical, or physicalistic, expressions. I myself prefer simply to say that "education" and its cognates can be fully explicated only within, and in the light of, a general analytical philosophy of mind. From this the important consequence follows that any analysis of educational concepts which attempts to define them in purely bodily or physical terms, or, alternatively, which supposes that the theory of education could be part of, or else reduced to, something which is nowadays called "behavioral science," is systematically misguided. The reason for this, however, has nothing to do with the metaphysical doctrine, of which I, at least, wish no part, that implies that the mind is a ghostly substance to which the individual consciousness alone has immediate access and which other persons can penetrate only symptomatically, if at all. The claim I am making is not, in the first instance at least, ontological, but logical and semantical. For I am contending only that the development of minds, and hence educational development, cannot be properly discussed or understood exclusively in purely bodily terms. And I argue that although certain physical changes are normally or typically correlated with mental changes, and although, therefore, there are certain physical conditions of mental and, hence, educational achievement, it is a radical error to suppose that mental changes are nothing but physical changes or that meeting certain physical conditions simply as such is all that we mean by mental or educational achievement. Education per se is a mental process, and the logic of meaningful discourse about education and educational development, accordingly, is not and cannot be discourse about mere bodily changes. And it is precisely for this reason that the whole philosophy of educational testing, including not only the testing of actual performance but also testing for aptitudes, is in need of a complete conceptual overhaul.

There are also other directions in which it is supremely important to oppose reductivistic analyses of the concept of educational development. Here I have in mind particularly the tendency in some quarters to reduce the educational process to that of formal and informal instruction. Educational development, or, more simply, education itself involves not only formal and informal instruction of the learner by a teacher, but also what the anthropologist calls "enculturation." By "enculturation," I take it, the anthropologist has in mind the processes, in large part passive and unintentional, through which most individuals acquire the attitudes and propensities, linguistic or otherwise, that characterize them as mature members of various social groups. As we say, "experience is a great teacher." What this means, among other things, is that by the ordinary wear and tear of living in societies, through an immense variety of what we somewhat animistically call "agencies," human beings learn, and learn to adapt themselves to, the myriad rules, laws, and principles, the learning of which constitutes the greater part of "growing up."

For our purposes, the notion of enculturation is useful precisely because it enables us to correct not only the common tendency to overintellectualize the process of educational development, but also to overstress the role of purposive and intentional action even within the sphere of informal education which occurs outside the school. As such, educational development properly involves not only the results of specialized courses of instruction in particular subjects or subject matters, or even of thoughtful parental training that results in the acquisition of skills, linguistic and otherwise, without which formal education itself could not even exist; it encompasses also the results of enculturative processes of identification, of uncontrolled suggestion and association, which not even the most perfect totalitarian system could conceivably control. Indeed, it is largely through a study of the concept of educational development, as I have lately come to see, that we are enabled to overcome the nightmare of a society of human robots, "educated" by their masters to do, think, and act in certain routine ways from which every "outside" influence is excluded. Once we realize, in fact, how little of what we all learn depends upon instruction, we are freed from the gratuitous worry that a system of instruction, beginning with infant toilet training, could, even in principle, turn out a class of creatures capable of nothing but following the rules which their teacher-masters have set for them. The learning process necessarily outruns any process of instruction, whether formal or informal. And for better as well as for worse, the educational development of no man can ever be exclusively a matter of deliberate, institutionalized routines. Accordingly, the term "educators" must include not only human instructors and teachers but also institutions, practices, and indeed all of the agencies, personal, interpersonal, and impersonal, that serve as media for the formation, development, and reformation of the mind. In other words, education is a process before it is an agency, and it remains a vehicle of self-developing long after the last course has been taken and the last examination has been passed.

But now I want to propose a second general thesis which is implicit in what has already been said. The thesis is this: the sphere of a person's educational development is virtually coterminous with the development of his sensitivity to meanings. Whatever serves to structure a person's awareness of meanings or to enlarge the range of meanings to which he is responsive belongs distinctively to his education, and hence to his educational development. In short, wherever there is a mode of meaning, there is a corresponding possibility of educational development. Accordingly, failures or blockages in the educational process are all in one way or another failures or blockages of the process of assimilating the meanings or modes of meaning that the environment offers our minds for understanding and use. If this is so, however, the limits of the educational process are reached whenever one passes beyond the domain of meaning into spheres of purely instinctual reaction, of unalterable bodily change, and of organic insensitivity or unresponsiveness.

3. *Teaching, Telling, and "Enculturation"*

From what has been said, a basis has already been provided for seeing why those who are concerned with the whole idea of education and with the educational process as a whole must at once realize how much of the education of any person or group proceeds, and must proceed, without benefit of teachers, of schooling, or indeed of instruction of any sort whatever. This may have its saddening, or even frightening, aspect when one thinks of the inescapable educations afforded by life in a city slum or in a country rent by the savagery of war. But it also has its happy or at least its hopeful side when one bears in mind the ways in which a progressive culture, enlightened institutions, and an open, amiable, and peaceful social milieu may itself serve in innumerable ways to educate the human spirit and to compensate for the limitations under which, for one reason or another, the formal educational system may labor.

Either way, we see why the teacher is something at once more and less than the "educator," and why teaching, no matter how skillful or extensive, can only be a part of education. For education may go on without a teacher or even, as we have seen, without any person to do the educating. Or to put the point in another way, if we agree at least for the sake of discussion, to treat the concepts of teacher and student as coordinate ideas, so that every teacher must have a student and every student a teacher, then we may see why only a part of our education is owing to what we are taught as students, and why teaching must always remain only a special part of education, even in the most abundant society endowed with the amplest supply of skilled and dedicated teachers.

Except in an incidental, metaphorical sense in which, inevitably, we personify any educative factor as a "teacher," teaching is something done by individual persons. Plainly, there is no teaching without a teacher, and no teachers except individual organisms. A dog, as well as a man perhaps, may teach, but, strictly speaking, institutions, cultures, societies, or natural environments cannot. We must distinguish, however, not only between those teachers who do their teaching within the framework of the formal educational institution which we call the school and those who teach more informally outside such a framework, but also between forms of teaching in which what is learned is a consequence of what the teacher aims to teach, and those forms in which what is learned (and taught) is not such a consequence. I may teach you something more, or less, than I mean to teach. Correspondingly, you may learn from me, as a teacher, what I never meant to teach, and I may teach you more, as well as less, than my tour of duty as a teacher permits or requires.

But now we have been provided with one way of distinguishing between teaching a subject and teaching a person. Any teacher must teach somebody; unless some person or persons are instructed, teaching cannot occur. But there may be teaching, and indeed powerful and important teaching, without a subject. Socrates was a great teacher, but he had no subject to teach. Few of us, unfortunately, are disciples of Socrates. But all of us teachers who do have subjects to teach, organized information to impart, and methods to inculcate, may nevertheless teach much more than our subjects or disciplines or methods include, and indeed more than we mean to teach or even imagine ourselves capable of teaching.

Here we begin to trench upon what may well turn out to be one of the central issues of an analytic philosophy of education. Professor Israel Scheffler, who has perhaps done more than anyone else to advance interest in the analytical philosophy of education, makes a sharp distinction not only between teaching and enculturation but also between teaching and telling. Without going into details, I think that the central point of Scheffler's position is that teaching as distinct from enculturation or mere telling (and hence education in the broad sense) involves something more than what psychologists call "conditioning," as well as something more than making students aware of ideas or meanings. That is to say, a teacher not only shows something to his students, he also explains, or is capable of explaining, what he has shown; a teacher not only tells but gives, or is capable of giving, reasons for believing that what he tells is true or valid or correct. In a word, the teacher, as distinct from what may be called the mere "teller" or even in the broadest sense, the mere educator, always provides, or is capable of providing, a rationale for his instruction. And when the teller or the educator, as I shall call him, is incapable of giving reasons, of providing a rationale, of invoking a method or a way of doing things in order to justify what he says or shows, he fails by that much to attain the stature of teacher.

For the sake of discussion let us, a bit tendentiously, call this the "rationalistic" theory of teaching. And now, by way of contrast to it, let me briefly describe what may be called simply the anti-rationalistic theory of teaching.[1] By this I have in mind the point of view which not only does not regard the giving of reasons, or even the capacity to give them, as essential to or inherent in the activity of teaching, but which depreciates the preoccupation with reason-giving, or justification and explanation, of method-mongering, as positively inimical to the aims of the teacher, at least along the higher reaches on which he may aspire to move. Thus, for example, the teacher who seeks to inspire his students, whether by his eloquence, by his example, or by his general comportment, is perhaps bound to be an antirationalist and thus to depreciate the whole tedious, discursive side of formal education. And in justification of his own work, he, like William James, is likely to stress (or overstress) the happy improvisations, both of word and gesture, which the particular topic or circumstance happens to suggest.

I think that although the issue between the rationalist and the antirationalist may be clarified, it cannot be settled entirely by the methods of logical or semantical analysis because the issue between them is not, at bottom, entirely a logical or semantical issue. As far as I can see, the concept of teaching does not positively require that the teacher be capable of providing a rationale or explanation of what he seeks to impart; further, it may well be that certain forms of teaching can proceed only by way of example, by a process of "showing," for which there are no linguistic equivalents and for which no reasons are available. To this extent I think that logic is on the side of the antirationalists. But when he goes beyond this to contend that "true" or "real" or "significant" teaching, or teaching of the most significant or important subjects, cannot proceed discursively, or else that discursive explanations provide a positive hindrance, he is claiming more than the logic of our discourse about teaching requires. Indeed, what he is doing is attempting to deflate (or else to inflate) a certain mode of teaching, or the sort of subject matter to which that mode naturally lends itself, under the guise of philosophical analysis.

How does this happen? Is there not some important feature of the notion of a teacher which has so far escaped our notice and which, for whatever reason, positively invites those of us who have educational or pedagogical, and hence developmental, axes to grind, to grind them into the very texture of our thinking about educational problems? The answer, I believe, is that the term "teacher" and its cognates, particularly in cultures which, like our own, set great store by the institution of the school and by the teaching process both as a means and as a model for achieving desirable social ends, are not purely descriptive terms that serve to neutrally characterize ordinary things or processes. Built into the notion of the teacher is the idea of someone who does something desirable or exemplary, of someone who serves an important cause or end, or who performs a function of merit or value within the community. To say that one is a "teacher," in short, is not merely to describe one's occupation, what one does for better or for worse, but also to lay a flattering umbrage to one's soul, to claim for oneself a certain status together with the privileges or rights pertaining thereto. Likewise, to say that someone is not a teacher is, in at least certain contexts, automatically to disparage him or his work. And if it can be "shown" that he is not a "true" or a "real" teacher, then automatically he is declassed.

In saying this, however, I do not claim that the word "teacher" and its cognates serve merely as terms of praise or that their meaning is merely "emotive." Indeed, the whole concept of emotive meaning seems to me to be at once too coarse and too misleading to serve any longer as a useful rubric of linguistic analysis. What I contend is only that in ascribing or assigning the teacher's role to a person one is, at the same time, laying upon him certain responsibilities and entitling him to certain rights or prerogatives.

4. The Learner: "Learning That" versus "Learning How": Modes of Meaning and Modes of Learning

So far we have dealt only in passing and by implication with the primary object, or product, of the whole process of educational development, namely, the educatable and educated person. In concluding these remarks, it is essential to say something about him, partly in order to distinguish aspects of the process that have hitherto been neglected and partly in order to make clear what lies beyond the process of educational development. Here, among other things, I want to deflate the importance for educational development of merely "learning about" or "learning that." Even for those who seek instruction in the most advanced and abstract reaches of theoretical science, learning how and learning why are continually indispensable.

This is not to say that education should be exclusively concerned with questions of method. For the study of methods is meaningless and pointless save in so far as the methods are actually used in making significant inquiries that lead to the formation of hypotheses, theories, and doctrines. Moreover, there is a great danger in certain quarters that students may be led into that fatal sin of methodolatry, the worship of the procedure or routine, which itself can stultify the advancement of learning. Methods are to be seen as being in continuous interaction with the results they yield and with the ends they serve, and therefore as themselves subject to modification when they conflict with other no less exigent commitments. Again, nothing that is learned, or learnable, should be viewed as incorrigible, as beyond the pale of critique and of criticism. I like to think that an analogue of the so-called "naturalistic fallacy" hovers, or should be made to hover, over the whole *idea* of education as well as over the entire system of concepts affiliated with it. Anywhere, at any time, we may in all seriousness echo the ancient cry, "But is it, after all is said and done, really right, really valid, really proper, really true?" Of course, the open question becomes a silly question, which is to say, not a question at all, when asked idly or compulsively or tendentiously. Nor am I suggesting that serious people should raise it whenever they feel a minor irritation with "the system" as it stands. My contention is again that every a priori is so only for the time being and every preemptive certitude can be made to yield under stress. And, in a word, the stress here upon learning how is intended not so much to enthrone method as the only proper subject matter of instruction, but rather to underline the point that within the sphere of theoretical learning itself, learning about the nature of things is largely valueless, if not strictly impossible, unless one at the same time learns how such theoretical understanding is acquired.

But now we must come once again to cases. To begin with, just as we were obliged to distinguish teachers from mere educators, so also we must distinguish students from mere learners. If the end of education in a sense is learning, that end will not be served simply by trying to make students of us all. The student requires a teacher, the learner as such does not. Indeed, it may well be that the most urgent educational need is for teachers to enable their students to continue as learners, on their own, after their courses of instruction and of study have long since been forgotten. The point is obvious, but it is important both conceptually and practically. For the educational process has made a fetish of the student and with the studies and courses of study to which he is submitted. Not the instruction of students, but the learning of men is the overarching business of education. The learner, by definition, can only be a student part-time. But it is what he learns the rest of the time which usually matters most, both to himself and to his fellows.

The learner, we may say, is a would-be knower. His primary business as a learner is with knowledge. Unfortunately, however, this is perhaps the most misleading statement a philosopher of education can make. For the concept of knowledge has been so badly misanalyzed and misconceived in our western philosophical tradition that it might almost be better to say that the business of the learner is more with feeling or volition or sensibility than with something called "cognition." In the first place, knowing is not confined to, if indeed it has anything to do with what rationalistic philosophers call "intuition." In the second place, knowing as such is not a matter of certainty or of being certain. In the third place, it is not, as such, a matter of mere theoretical understanding. And finally, there is no such thing as the seat or faculty or organ of knowledge, nor is that seat or faculty or organ properly described as the intellect, the faculty of reason, or the faculty of judgment. Knowledge, above all and first of all, is an achievement. Secondly, as an achievement, it exists in degree, and hence in varying degrees. Thirdly, it is a form of achievement which is open not only to theoretical mathematicians, physicists, and sociologists, but also to people who can barely count, to people who play the flute, who make decisions, contracts, promises, judgments, who perform operations—in short, who do anything that involves what we call "know-how"—the acquisition of skills, the understanding and ability to conform to rules or routines, to enact, to engage in practices, to assume roles, responsibilities, and obligations, to adopt policies, and, in a word, to do all the things which are connoted by the phrase "knowing how," and hence "learning how." On this score, indeed, a large and fundamental point can be summarily made by saying that one great province of educational development, and that by all odds the most important and the most extensive, concerns the endless and endlessly various business of knowing and of learning how.

This is not in the least meant to minimize the significance of "knowing that" and hence of "learning that" in our educational scheme of things. My interest here is of another order. For, in the first place, when one fully appreciates how much of any person's education, even on its theoretical side, is concerned with, or depends upon, learning how to do things, one is then less disposed to overstress the importance of sheer "learning," as scholars rather curiously call it, within the process of educational development. But in the second place, when we attend more closely to what is comprehended under the concepts of learning how (and learning what and why),[2] we see more clearly how specious is the claim, reiterated by rationalists in all ages, that the only or primary business of education, and hence of the educated man, must be with the pursuit of truth, and particularly of theoretical truth. Indeed, we may see how specious and dangerous is the very notion that it is the business of education, including in particular the so-called higher learning, to advance theoretical learning, either individually or collectively. Learning how is indispensable, although not sufficient, to do anything well.

But it is precisely for this reason that an educational system which is directed only to the forms of learning how that are necessary to doing theoretical science is in fact neglecting three-fourths of its responsibility. The reason that our culture produces so many learned monsters and so many educated fools is very largely, in my judgment, the deep-rooted blunder of placing what my old colleague Morton White calls "the teacher of knowing," as distinct from "the teacher of feeling or willing," in the driver's seat of our educational system and of rewarding so heavily "the student of knowing" as distinct from the "student of feeling or willing." Or, rather, since this way of talking is itself so deeply misleading, let me return to my own point that even if, perhaps, all instruction aims at knowledge and all learning results in knowing, all instruction does *not* aim, directly or indirectly, at cultivating and informing the theoretical intellect.

The point toward which these remarks have been leading is simply this: if all meaning either is or involves expression, and if the meaning of all expressions and all modes of expression must somehow be *learned*, then plainly what learning (and hence educational development) covers is everything that essentially involves the use and application of expressions or what I sometimes call "meaning carriers." This means that the limits of educational development are set only by the limits of our powers of learning in regard to the use of expressions or meaning carriers.

What are these limits? In general, they are reached whenever we come to the performance of a particular act, to the making of a particular decision, to the adoption of a particular policy, to the composition of a particular poem or sonata, and to the whole sphere to which such words as "discovery," creation," and "invention" apply. After the fact, discoveries, works of creation, products of invention are proper materials for the learner's educational development. But one cannot learn to discover, to create, or to invent, any more than one can learn to live or to die.

The moral point here is not only that, like Virgil, all teachers and indeed all educators must finally bid farewell to their pupils, who must thereafter go it on their own, but also that the learner himself must not expect everything from his education or be perversely disappointed when it appears to fail him. Maturity comes when one has learned *both* the necessary competencies *and* the necessity of moving on one's own, beyond the range of competence. Learning can continue throughout life, but it is not life. Educational development can progress until senility sets in, but even in one's youth neither education nor learning can be all. What one must learn at last and above all is that one must cease, and continually cease, to be a mere learner. In America, where so much has been invested in education, both materially and spiritually, this last lesson should never be forgotten. The good society, like the good man, is something which not even the most affluent and resourceful educational system can produce on order.

[237

And this too is something which all rationalists since Plato have had a hard time learning. The school does not, any more than the military camp or the church or the music hall, provide a proper model for the good or the just society. For the good society, like the good life, has no models. And though a society might just conceivably learn how to be "great," according to the preconceptions of one pundit or another, its worth is another matter which only the gods are able to decide.

13

Learning and Teaching in the Arts

IN OUR TIME THE ASCENDENCY OF THE NATURAL SCIENCES within the higher learning has been no less spectacular, at least among the cognoscenti, than the monumental contributions of scientific technology which seem indeed to presage a new age of man. Their methods, as well as the characteristic attitudes of those who employ them, are everywhere admired. Where such methods are emulated, as in the harder behavioral sciences, the disciplines in question automatically advance in academic prestige. And where their applications have proved less successful as in the softer "sciences of man," such as history, depth psychology, and government, their very status as genuine cognitive disciplines is called in question.[1] As for the humanities, their place within the scheme of higher education is now totally confused and insecure.

On the one side, their place is increasingly preempted by scholar-scientists who seek to analyse works and movements of literature and art in terms supplied by relevant behavioral sciences. On the other, courses of instruction hitherto assigned to them are now incorporated within general education programs whose admittedly acculturative purposes appear to be as well (or better) served in secondary schools as in institutions of higher learning. In the former case the work of serious scholars might (in principle) as well be parcelled out among the behavioral sciences in question or else placed within certain "area studies" in which the respective resources of such sciences are pooled together for the sake of a particular common inquiry. And if, for reasons of academic accommodation and convenience, they are still largely conducted under the auspices of traditional departments of English and foreign languages or of fine arts and music, this in no way affects the nature of the findings in question or the methods by which such findings are certified. In the latter case, unhappily, humanistic courses of study are treated essentially as forms of "training" whose only function within the university is remedial. By the nature of the case, those who give such courses are regarded as having no cognitive subject matter and so as making no significant contribution either to the propagation or advancement of learning. In fact they are recognized as "teachers" only in the wide sense of the term which is sometimes applied also to religious leaders, moralists, and retired statesmen. Their role (so it is argued) is merely to arouse interests, to form attitudes, and to refine feelings. This is not to deny that the student usually picks up an assortment of information (or, more likely, misinformation) in the course of such cultural massages. For in order to focus and structure the student's attitudes his trainer is bound to introduce objective explanations and arguments into his discussions. But he does so only interstitially and for the sake of ends having nothing intrinsically to do with the forms of intellectual enlightenment to which the higher learning is properly and exclusively dedicated.

Either way the "humanist" is bound to find his situation unsatisfactory. If he elects to become a scholar the interests which initially attracted him to literature, music, or the fine arts are eliminated from his work as a scholar-teacher and must be cultivated during his leisure time. If on the other hand he insists on giving courses in the "appreciation" of literature or art, he finds himself in a kind of academic limbo, along with the football coach or the resident chaplain.

Everywhere, in short, it is taken for granted that the paradigmatic form of human knowledge is that which achieves its highest perfection in the "exact" sciences of mathematics and physics. From this point of view, and the educational ideology attending it, the only truly educational function of humanistic activities within the "house of the intellect," as Professor Barzun calls the university, is the propagation of some form of scientific knowledge and the methodological studies essential to its reception.

All else, no matter how appetizingly packaged, is an acculturative service. And if the term "education" is still applied in its own looser honorific sense to such services, the result in no sense involves a principled philosophical enlargement of our conceptions of knowledge and learning but only a dubious increase in the connotation of a term which serves merely to legitimate the miscellaneous enterprises to which the multiversity is nowadays committed.

The more general aim of this chapter is to make a further dent in this reigning educational ideology and the theories of knowledge, and hence of learning and teaching, that lie behind it. Here, however, my specific purpose is to help to restore to the humanities their own distinctive and integral positions within the higher learning, thereby returning to the house of the intellect one of the grandest of its mansions.

But if my purpose is normative, my argument is analytical. I contend, and mean to show with the help of a particular example, that, as the words "knowledge," "learning," and "teaching" are characteristically employed, both in the conduct of our everyday affairs and in our developing efforts to come to terms with the great achievements of the human imagination, of which the arts are perhaps the most conspicuous example, the sciences represent neither the only, the primary, nor essentially the highest form of knowledge. From this point of view, the knowledge about works of art and imaginative literature made available to us by scientific scholarship, although immensely useful in its way, can never take us to the heart of the matter: the illumination of the art object as a work of art.[2]

It is no part of my purpose, let me emphasize, to deny that the arts (like the sciences also) commonly afford gratifications that are noncognitive. But such gratifications usually, although not always, depend directly upon modes of perception and thought which involve the whole activity of the human mind. This is true, moreover, not only in the case of works in such genres as narrative literature and representational painting, in which apprehensions of what is stated or represented are necessary to understanding of the works as forms of art, but also of works in other genres where ordinary questions of so-called descriptive or representational (and hence, according to the prevailing jargon, "cognitive") meaning presumably do not arise. In all the arts, but perhaps most conspicuously in the case of the art of music, appreciation of their internal formal patterns of sound, volume, line and color, involve powers of discrimination, anticipation, and recognition analogous to those involved in the conduct of any inquiry in theoretical science. So much will doubtless be conceded by appreciative students of these arts who know intuitively that a Haydn quartet or a Beethoven concerto is inaccessible to those for whom all music is mood music and a classical recapitulation is nothing more than a second-go-round of the same old string of melodies. But I go further. For, as I now see, appreciation of what is meant, or intended, in works of art also constantly depends upon ways of "seeing the point" which have no close analogues in the case of apprehensions essential to scientific knowledge.

For example, the understanding of comedy requires, in its simplest form, the ability to see the point of a joke and hence that it is a joke. But jokes, although occasionally found in scientific writings and in lectures, are not an essential part of what they are meant to communicate. Likewise appreciation of a tragic drama requires that we understand the play as a tragedy, that is, as the awesome representation of a form of human misfortune. Such appreciations, however, have nothing to do with scientific inquiry, which concerns itself exclusively with correlatable rates of change in the occurrence of phenomena, including such curious phenomena as featherless bipeds. But we must now go a step further. For those who take a tragedy merely as an occasion for a good cry also miss its point as a work of tragic *art*. (They recognize it as the account of a calamity which therefore involves persons and not merely things. And this is why they cry. But it still does not exist for them as a work of art.)

Here we verge upon an insight which will be more fully developed in the sequel. At this stage it must suffice to observe that artistic appreciations always are concerned with what the artist is doing *in* bringing it into being. The artist's intentions in the act of creation, as I am now disposed to think, may well be something which is *sui generis*. And so, very likely, is our own discernment of his intentions in that act. As I read him, this point was first clearly perceived by Kant in his *Critique of Aesthetic Judgment*, where he makes the initially obscure distinction between "purposeful" and "purposive" activities and apprehensions. A purposeful activity Kant tells us, is, and is properly taken to be, a means or condition of some ulterior end. Hence it could just as well be satisfied by any other line of action that did the job. To this extent, accordingly, the thing done or the means taken has no individual actuality either for the artists or for ourselves. It acquires such an actuality only in so far as it is something done, and appreciated, as we say, for its own sake. This is why we are disposed to say, paradoxically, that it has no meaning, though, as a work of art, it is something which can only be understood in intentional terms. It is also why, no less paradoxically, that its intention is not to accomplish or become something but simply to be something. Kant sought to resolve the paradox by saying that the work of art, whose characteristic interest is internal to the life of the individual work itself, is not purposeful but purposive. And for this reason, as he said, we can never form a general concept of its meaning as we always do in our scientific description and predictions of phenomena.

Here it is easy to be misled. For it is a logical commonplace that no individual thing, as such, is ever exhausted in terms of the general properties ascribed to it. But for the scientist the uniqueness of an individual thing is of no interest; it concerns him only as an object of a certain sort which can be correlated with objects of other sorts. And even when, for the nonce, he happens to take an interest in it, and finds it engaging or even lovely, as in the case of a cloudy sky or a fall of snow, it still remains something inactive, inert, and incorrigible. A work of art on the other hand is never just a thing which happens on occasion to please or charm us. It is, and it is appreciated as, something created and something done, whose design is the unique product of a particular series of human actions. And these actions, as we perceive, sometimes go awry even though we have no rule for judging just how the artist made his mistake or what might be done to rectify it.

A work of art is thus something both intelligible and corrigible. Yet its intention can never be fully grasped in terms of other things, either natural or human. Concepts apply to it, but only by analogy and never definitively. It represents a human face, even a particular face, yet it is not that face, nor was meant to be. It bears likeness to natural phenomena, yet it is not a natural phenomena, not even the most exquisite or appealing, and terms applied to the latter provide merely a suggestive basis for its understanding. It is something done, but done to no purpose, and the purposes by which we may attempt to triangulate it invariably fall wide of the mark. Yet it is in no sense an oddity or, in the vulgar sense, a miracle. It is something to which we all have access, though not perhaps in earliest childhood. Quite humanly but wonderfully, it is something which means something and not, like a rock or cloud, merely is something; or better, its meanings, as they are revealed to us in our own active appreciations, *are* its being, and it has no other. When we lose sight of this, as our whole contemporary philosophy of higher education impels us to do, a great part of the dignity and power of humanistic learning and teaching goes down the drain.

On Knowing and Appreciating a Work of Art

But now we have to ask in some detail what that meaning and the modes of being it may contain actually come to. What are the terms and conditions of our knowledge of it? How and by what stages is that knowledge reached? And in what sense, and to what extent, can it be the product of human learning and teaching?

To take the last point first, it needs to be said that no matter how widely we may construe the concepts of knowing, learning, and teaching, there are some aspects of our experience to which those terms do not apply. Certain things simply happen to us. We are seized by pain; random sensations make their way into our fields of consciousness: unassignable pangs of uneasiness; flickering afterimages; the whole flow and jetsam of what C. I. Lewis called "the primordial empirical given": all this I take to be pre- or post-cognitive. Furthermore, even if we should agree that there are forms of knowledge which do not involve teaching or even learning, our only access to them, so to say, is inspirational. However this serves to underscore the point that most forms of knowing and understanding are *achievements* and that the concept of an achievement does not apply to everything that falls within the range of consciousness.

Granting, then, that not all forms of experience are cognitive and that some things may perhaps be known that are not cognitive achievements, we still cannot profitably proceed to the question of what must be learned for purposes of artistic understanding until we have first provisionally sorted out what in fact we have to know in appreciating works of art. To this end, as well as for the sake of concreteness, I propose henceforth to confine my remarks mainly to a classic example of visual art, about whose status as a work of art there is little question: namely, Giorgione's *The Tempest.*[3] The painting shows a young woman, sitting nude on her garment and nursing her baby, screened from passersby by a small thicket on the bank of a running stream. Opposite her in the lower left corner of the picture, a young man stands protectively, leaning on his staff. A little way behind him are some ruins partly overgrown by shrubs and trees. In the middle distance, a bridge spans the stream and the two sides of the picture; beyond it are buildings, increasingly white with an expanding sense of distance. Over the town a threatening sky is pierced by a bright bolt of lightning, and the whole scene is illuminated by that strange tinted light sometimes seen during a summer thunderstorm in which greens and browns seem to glow from within.

To start with, and at the least of it, we must recognize Giorgione's picture as a perceptual unity distinct from whatever else surrounds it in our field of vision. This is indispensable; but clearly it does not suffice by a wide margin. For one may observe a perceptual unity and still not recognize it as a picture. In order to identify *The Tempest* as a picture and what belongs to its pictorial unity, we must also perceive that certain things that may appear on its surface—specks of dust, shadows cast by inadequate lighting in the room where it is hung, overcoats of varnish that create extrinsic highlights, etc.—do not belong to it. Moreover, as a picture, *The Tempest* must be understood, not as a lovely thing, but as a human artifact, something done, for whatever purpose or reason, by a man or group of men. Recognition of this all-important fact still does not suffice, for we must also know that this picture is a painting which demands to be looked at in a way which is very different from the way in which we look at a billboard poster or an instructive illustration in a travel book. In short, we must know that this picture is to be treated by us as something to be appreciated, not necessarily without regard to, but at least

[*245*]

without concern for, whatever ends it may serve for the artist, his patron, the society in which he lived, and, above all, ourselves.

Here, however, we approach a problem of some delicacy which even those who stress, as I have done, the difference between purposive and merely purposeful activities in the arts do not always appreciate. Perhaps the first philosopher to consider it with some care was David Hume, who pointed out that our awareness of the utility of an artifact may have something to do with its beauty. What Hume had in mind (as I understand him) is the fact that our appreciations of a work of achitecture, for example, are not diminished or necessarily distracted by our knowledge of its characteristic functions as a building. On the contrary, our perception of the distinctive beauty of a house requires both that we recognize it as a house and not a temple or town hall and that we perceive its suitability to its appropriate architectural purpose. What makes this possible is on the one side our own freedom from immediate practical preoccupations with the house and on the other our imaginative delight in observing the fineness with which it serves its appointed ends.

The same holds, in analogous ways, of other works of art, including paintings. Our sympathetic sense of the decorative, instructive, or religious roles that are so beautifully served by first-rate Renaissance paintings is in no sense a distraction from our appreciation of its artistic value. In fact, it converts their incarnations in the noble work into indispensable aspects of its own complex artistic design and meaning. To be sure this conversion will not occur without subtle shifts in the psychological frames that directly return us to the picture itself as something which, as St. Thomas puts it, pleases when seen.[4] But what is seen and the manner of the seeing are immensely expanded by our awareness of its human functions in ways that the uninitiated observer would not understand and could not foretell.

But this is to anticipate. Let us, for the moment, approach Giorgione's *Tempest* more simplistically. A man from the moon, unacquainted with the forms of life, including especially human life, on earth would probably not recognize the simplest representational forms which immediately press themselves upon our attention when we look at the picture. For us, however, this picture is unmistakably a landscape full of a variety of figures, natural and human, which we recognize and are meant to recognize as likenesses of things we encounter in everyday life. These likenesses do not for a moment deceive us. We view them, and are meant to view them, only as likenesses no matter how true they may be to their originals. On the other hand, we do not regard them as vehicles of possible information about a certain landscape or type of landscape in northern Italy, with its characteristic contours, types of vegetation, houses, modes of apparel, and so on. This learning, by hypothesis, we *must already possess.* But here it lies exclusively at the disposal of the painting itself. And learning this is an achievement of no little difficulty in its own right. For it entails that one knows at once how to arrest one's attention so that the informative use of these forms never becomes dominant and to redirect one's attention to their interrelations to one another within the painting.

Yet anyone who knew this much would still by no means appreciate Giorgione's picture as a visual composition. What else is wanted? Well, one must appreciate also the qualities and relations to one another of line and color, of light and shade, above all the points of stress or emphasis, the organizing factors which bring into proper focus the other recessive or subordinate visual qualities of the painting as a distinctive artistic unity. But in *The Tempest* (and this is one of its virtues) such visual elements are never apprehended in isolation from the representational forms. Its composition is, so to say, a cohesive visual-representational design in which other visual elements continually interact with and qualify its representative forms. Our appreciation of *The Tempest,* therefore, cannot merely be a matter of attending to the representational and the sensory forms discursively, as it were, side by side. The painter forcibly demands that we perceive how they continually inflect one another: light and shadow setting off the natural forms that comprise the landscape, or on the other side, the placement of mother and child in such a way as to reinforce the linear relations and to draw attention to color relationships which otherwise might not be noticed or else would be seen in an altogether different way. For example, the color of the mother's garment is seen as the color of a garment, and this in its own way affects the felt quality of the color itself. And, in a word, visual relations that might otherwise be incongruous

[247

or even repugnant to one another acquire a quite different perceptual quality when apprehended in their characteristic representational contexts.

But one might perceive all this yet still miss levels of significance without which the work would lose much of its distinction and power as a painting. Let me resort to a weary word which is used here simply as a throw-away term: "expression." Both the representational and the visual forms, in their various combinations, serve at once to express or articulate certain ranges of emotions, feelings, and, not least, moods. The stormy sky, with its deep contrasting perspectives, introduces into the picture a dramatic element which threatens the repose of the lower part of the picture, thereby distinguishing it sharply from many other Renaissance paintings of similar scenes by, say, Perugino or Raphael. At the same time, this drama is qualified by the profound stability of the landscape with its nearby houses and other domestic artifacts, and above all by the protective presence of the young man standing quietly in the lower left-hand corner of the picture. This, as we realize, is not vaguely like one of Turner's tempests in which the very presence of a floundering ship merely underscores the interplay of elemental natural forces. What we recognize here, evidently, is a version, or semi-version, of the pastoral.

The very word "pastoral" calls attention to another characteristic feature of many works of art some knowledge of which is required for their full appreciation. This is the factor of genre. As a version of the pastoral, Giorgione's painting thereby establishes its place within an ancient artistic tradition whose conventions provide an inclusive rationale for much that we see and feel in the picture. Our awareness of it reinforces and gives point and focus to our happy sense of artifice, cultivation, and even learning. And at the same time the mental sets which it imposes save us from misadventures in our effort to understand why certain otherwise irrelevant objects are included in the picture and why its curious blandness (if that is the word) is in no sense to be regarded as a fault.

In art, however, we must also realize that the genre, with its conventions, is encompassed by the work and not it by them. Accordingly, there are aspects of Giorgione's *Tempest* which, as we should not be surprised to find, are not easily comprehended in terms of the genre of the pastoral. To begin with, the lower landscape impresses one less as a semi-rural retreat than as a private park which is virtually an extension of someone's property in the nearby town. For reasons mentioned in the next paragraph, the mother seems to be sitting with her nursing infant, if not on her own land, then on the land owned by some friendly *padrone* in whose house she can find, for the time being at least, a home. Thus, as we see them in relation to one another all elements in the picture reinforce a deep sense, not simply of natural affection and compassion and peace, but of profoundly urban civility. Every stroke of the brush, as it were, converts the whole imaginative world of the picture into a mode, not merely of human action, but of civilized and indeed civil human life and living.

This of course is a hallmark of much Venetian art: its continual expressive reminders of transforming domestic virtues of *la città*, the city. Here, as in the works of Titian and Veronese, the city becomes as it were an encompassing element or substance, which offers nourishment and hospitality to anyone who enters within its precincts. And Giorgione, no less than Titian, never lets us forget this fact.

But there is another, more important reason why *The Tempest* cannot be comfortably viewed as a version of the pastoral. This at once concerns its subject matter and the peculiar force and intensity of its treatment in the painting. As a Renaissance painting, which contains a mother, child, and attentive young man, *The Tempest* preserves, and trades on, a vestigial awareness of the iconographic meanings characteristic of religious pictures of the Madonna and Child and, conceivably, even of the Flight into Egypt. But this quality of Giorgione's creates its own fascinating uneasiness and tension. For *The Tempest* is probably not meant to be seen as a distinctively Christian painting, as are the Madonnas of Bellini, not to mention those of Fra Angelico or Giotto. And the intention is suggested by the picture's title, which is not "Madonna with Child" or "Flight into Egypt" but "The Tempest." Here, briefly, Giorgione is breaking out of one tradition which is called Christian into another which (misleadingly) is called humanistic. This is not so much a Mary with the Infant Jesus as simply a mother with suckling child; this is not so much a conceivable Joseph as an amiable young man who offers them protection against the elements. But the ambiguity remains; nor could we understand it without a knowledge of the religio-artistic traditions against which, as well as half within, Giorgione is working.

At all events, to call this a secular painting is to misconceive it, at least if the word "secular" is taken to connote "irreligious" or even "nonreligious." For *The Tempest*, no less than the great works of Rembrandt, is indeed a religious painting whose intensity the word humanistic does not convey. In this picture, the lady and her child, whether formally strangers or members of the town, are at home and at rest; nothing disturbs, or can disturb, their inner tranquility. They are not merely *at* home, as we say, but home. Perception of this quality transmutes the entire painting in a way peculiar to Giorgione among Venetian painters. And this is why we speak of his paintings not only as marvellously and magically lyrical but also as profound and inexhaustible. For there is embodied in them, as in *The Tempest*, those feelings of wonder, of mystery, and exhaltation, which are the benchmarks of that dimension of being that is known among religious writers as transcendence.[5]

Learning and Teaching

From this inadequate synopsis of what needs to be known in and for appreciating the various levels of significance in a great work of visual art, let us now turn to problems of appropriate learning and teaching in the arts. Heretofore I have argued that before we can even begin to understand these levels as levels of artistic *value* in a particular work like *The Tempest*, we must already know, and be able to identify and to determine, what a work of art is and what are the conditions of its appreciation. These aspects of our knowledge are immensely complex; nor can we suppose that the operations involved in framing and identifying a work of art can be performed without previous experience. Making full allowance for moments of insight in our fulfilled apprehensions of a particular work, which, so to say, come to us as gifts of the gods, such insights do not come to those who are unprepared. And preparation is a matter of learning, however difficult in many instances it may be to identify and to describe. Thus for example, we learn by stages not only to identify material objects in accordance with some general principle of classification, we also learn the vital difference between a natural object and an artifact. Having learned this, we learn also to distinguish among kinds of artifacts: what their distinctive purposes may be and how they serve their respective functions. Then we learn how to distinguish those intentions of an artist that may be realized directly in the productive actions themselves. For until we have learned this, we haven't yet come in sight of the artistic significance of any work of the human mind.

Plainly, we cannot succeed in the performance of these complex mental operations, in particular instances, if we come to them openhanded, out of a nondescript experience. For we must have learned in a systematic way the vital categorial distinctions between treating something as an object and treating it as an artifact, and, secondly, between treating it as an artifact that is to be used for some ulterior end and treating it as something, not purposeful but purposive, something whose artistic virtue is understood in the successive acts we perform in contemplating its own internal design.[6]

Little children, I have found, learn quite early to make many of these distinctions in a rudimentary way. But they do so gradually and playfully, partly by imitating their elders and partly from one another. And though it is true, as I believe, that play itself is an instinctual form of behavior, knowing when to play and when not to, how to play a game or play it well, are not things we do by instinct. Still less do we instinctively realize when others are playing and when they are in earnest. My point here, however, is not that learning to treat something as a work of art is so much a matter of learning when someone else happens to be acting playfully (although there is certainly an important core of truth in the play theory of art, just as there is also in the theory of art as mimicry or imitation); rather is it that what we apprehend in coming to recognize things as works of art, the result of which is learning, as it were, how to recognize something done in a semi-playful spirit and, accordingly, when it is appropriate to treat it in a like manner.

The reason why I have used the phrase "semi-playful" in the

preceding sentence is not, let me add, to hedge my bets. Rather it is to reinforce the point that learning what a work of art is, and hence to treat it as such, is a complex process which, as we will see more fully below, involves a variety of interacting and interqualifying skills and powers of transference. Thus do we learn by stages that actors in a play are not merely playing, or rather not literally playing, in the way gamesmen do, by learning at last that they are not involved in scoring a point or beating an opponent. And we are helped in this by learning to attend more closely to their gestures, verbal and otherwise, and in the process to permit our ordinary empathic responses to have their way—up to a point. In short, we learn to *combine* our understanding of play with our developing understanding of the powers of imitation in order to perceive expressive values without responding to them in an everyday purposeful way. At bottom, I am convinced, we are mainly aided in this process of transference by learning the nonliteral, figurative uses of words, and especially the use of metaphor. For metaphor, more than any other trope, serves at once to transfer the meanings of expressions beyond their customary ranges of application and to rivet our attention to the object to which they are so strongly and strikingly applied. In another way the metaphor, which is no ordinary analogy introduced for the sake of a new line of inquiry, simply invests the object itself with a new *being*. Metaphorical utterance in the normal course, is quite useless. And we see its seemingly absurd point only when we see that it is there for the sake of what it reveals to us. This, I am persuaded, is why Aristotle said that metaphor is the soul of poetry. In a larger sense, indeed, the whole poem is an extended metaphor.[7]

But now we have to ask whether, and to what extent, it is possible to teach what is involved in recognizing something as a work of art (that is, as something to be responded to in the manner appropriate to such a work). For it is by no means self-evident that wherever there is a learner there may also be a teacher. Especially in the case of natural languages, most learning is informal, and many things are learned from teachers that they do not intend us to learn. All the same, it seems clear that at least part of what we learn, particularly as we become more sophisticated in our responses to works of art, can be and is taught, often in a quite deliberate manner, with the use of skills, linguistic and otherwise, that have already been learned.[8] For example, young children are commonly taught by their parents to recognize in many situations that works of a certain sort, about which the child is easily misled, are *to be* accepted as forms of play and art. Implicit in this teaching are also rudimentary forms of instruction about certain archetypal genres. For example, the child is taught not only that a certain narrative is a story, but also that it is a fairy tale or fantasy. Again, he is taught not just to treat a play merely as a play; he is also prompted to view it as something comic and laughable, or else as something essentially serious which is therefore to be taken in a quite different way. And because the child often laughs when laughter is inappropriate, he is brought by stages to see that in this sphere as in others he (like the artist) can make mistakes. In short, he begins now to learn the important lesson that there exists a vital difference between free play or fantasy and art, the application of which involves a certain discipline, with respect to which his own unprompted responses are corrigible and hence subject to modification and control.

Here also we may see in another way how the significance of genres is so commonly misunderstood by both the teacher and his student. Genres do not impose, either upon the artist or upon his audience, set types or formulas which must be strictly obeyed mechanically in all situations. Art, as we gradually apprehend, belongs to the domain of subjective life, as Kierkegaard calls it, which is free in a way that the exact sciences are not meant to be. Yet the subjective life is not unstructured, not a mere ragbag of charms and oddities to be taken by the observer simply as he will. It requires that the subject relate himself to the work and achievement of his fellows with respect for their intentions, for he can miss a point vital to his own subjective life if he simply follows his own passing inclinations and perceptions.

In sum, the complex, yet indispensable preparations for appreciating works of art involve a great deal of prior integrated learning and instruction, much of it quite deliberate. Thus (to return to our example) the process of readying oneself for appreciating Giorgione's *Tempest* requires the antecedent informing of many powers of perception acquired by many stages and in many devious ways. Some of these will be further elaborated upon as we proceed now to give some account of the forms of learning and teaching required for appreciating the work which here is serving as the primary vehicle for our discussion.

In this instance I have deliberately chosen a work of representational art as an exemplum, not only because it contains levels of significance which may be absent from nonrepresentational art, but precisely because in a work of this type, the representational level is apt to be the first on which the ordinary person is able to make contact with it as a work of art. Only very gradually do we learn to attend closely to the less obvious interests in patterns of color and line and to their interactive relations to the representational form themselves.

The perceptions of the representational forms in a painting depend, of course, upon prior experience of their likenesses in ordinary life. And the initial recognition of these likenesses, in many instances, occurs without formal instruction. In Giorgione's *Tempest*, most of us identify at once the mother and her nursing child, the young man in the left-hand corner; then we notice the landscape of the rocks and shrubs and framing trees, the canal, the comforting background of houses receding into the distance, as well as the tempestuous sky. Other things in the painting, the little boats, the part of the mother's garment lying behind her on the grass, the precise position of her legs, we discern only by stages. Because they are stylized or abstractly represented, we may in fact not see them at all until they are pointed out by a patient guide. Above all we may fail, within the context of the picture itself, to see what the human figures are doing, *how* they are disposed toward each other, what are the functions of artifacts like the stone, the boats, or the bridge. Thus without a teacher we may fail to see the young man as a friendly observer-protector, that the mother is sitting quietly, gazing beyond any objects in the picture as if contemplating things to come. We may fail also to notice that the path and the bridge provide access to the nearby houses which could be reached immediately if the mother and her baby were in real danger of a drenching from the distant storm.

But just now we come in sight of a dimension of the work which can only be gradually learned through accumulated experience of other works in its own tradition: the general manner in which representations are stylized, and the characteristic reasons for this. Nor will all this be fully appreciated unless we perceive it imaginatively against the contrasting background of other, earlier styles of representations in the longer tradition of Italian medieval or Renaissance painting. Here there is space for mention of only one or two such factors. From one point of view, Giorgione, like Bellini before him, is a greater realist than say Giotto, whose linear landscapes are unconcerned with the purely visual values of perspective, and whose figures, themselves often highly abstract, are represented without regard to their natural relations of size. The interest and power of Giotto's landscapes, whose colors have a primarily symbolic and decorative significance, are directed especially to the stimulation of our sense of the tactile values, as Berenson calls them, of the objects in his paintings. Giotto seems scarcely to care how things simply look, but only how they might feel to a hand that caressed them. Like most Venetians, Giorgione is less a draftsman than a painter.[9] He wants, among other things, to open our eyes, to make us see more vividly how things look at a certain distance in their characteristic lights and shadows and colors in relation to other objects in the pictorial space. And to this end, his treatment of distant objects is perforce vaguer than that of someone like Giotto or even Bellini. Where Giotto's abstract trees seem almost to be iconographic emblems, Giorgione's, although less sharply outlined, appear immutably as trees in fact look at a certain distance. Moreover, whereas Giotto paints all his objects in his pictures in much the same degree of detail and clarity of outline, Giorgione sets in powerful contrast to the impressionistic background the more sharply focused figures of the mother and child, with her garments, her bodily position, and above all, the visual-tactile quality of her lovely flesh. In his own way Giorgione too gives us a powerful sense of tactile values; but because they are not dispersed evenly throughout the picture, they are stressed all the more dramatically as felt qualities of the human figures in the foreground.

In short, even when we restrict attention to the sheer matter of understanding what Giorgione is up to in his complex and varied treatment of representational forms, we are compelled to view them in their contrasting imaginal relations to the manner

[*255*

in which such forms are handled by other painters in the traditions within which, as well as against which. he worked. However the artistic value of these relations cannot be learned directly by such abstract descriptions and explanations as I have outlined in the preceding remarks, but, only with their help, by continual redirections of our eyes and minds to ways in which objects are presented in the picture itself. Our talk, descriptive and explanatory, can be useful, often even indispensable; but it must be supplemented in practice by sequences of instructed gestures which serve in effect as so many demonstratives. And these demonstratives do their own work only insofar as they in turn reinforce our attention to the salient stylistic similarities and differences which we are meant to hold in mind in looking at Giorgione's painting, and which, when we learn to do so, adds so much to our appreciation of the painter's art.

Full understanding of representational forms in a painting thus requires not only a heritage of common experience of the corresponding natural forms as seen in ordinary life, which are for the most part learned and taught informally; nor does it require merely powers of recognition which enable us to distinguish physical objects from human persons and their artifacts. It demands, further, that we learn, through informed experience of relevant artistic traditions, the specific quality of the treatment of representational forms by a particular artist in a particular work. For most of us however this learning is gradually acquired and its relevance established only with the help of a skilled teacher's explanations; descriptions, demonstrations, and gesturings, with the all-important aid of slides and recurring visits to galleries of art.

But, as we have seen, *The Tempest* is not simply a learned and sophisticated arrangement of representational forms. Just as the movements of words in *Lycidas* or *Ash Wednesday* carry with them a powerful beat and surge of sound, so in Giorgione's masterpiece, the representational forms are wondrously invested in all the qualities and dimensions of distinctively visual perception. Like his compatriots, for example, Giorgione is a splendid colorist, and he deploys in extraordinary ways all the various dimensions of color. But, like Matisse, he is never a mere colorist. He seems almost to be in love with space, of which he makes us aware through complex organizations and counterpoints of line and shape, of mass, volume, and perspective. Above all, he is a master of illumination, of light and shade, of sunny clarity and deepening shadow and obscurity. These visual qualities and relations are never presented as random miscellanies of "sense data" or "aesthetic surfaces." They pull and haul, press forward and recede, glance and glitter, divide and return, tense and relax, threaten and recompose within a moving and expressive composition.

How do we achieve this distinctive visual understanding and knowledge? The ways are many, and there is space here for schematic mention of a few. Our original discriminations of such relatively abstract sensory and spatial properties are of course automatically learned in the process of our developing differentiations of material objects. In the normal course, however, we regard them merely as characteristic and identifiable features of such objects: we don't see *them*, but the object through them. Something else is required to bring them forward as qualities and relations interesting in their own right.

We come to this understanding in two characteristic ways. In the first place, the artist himself, by his own powerful example, helps to teach us the difficult lesson of exercising our sensory and visual faculties without concern for the portents of good or evil that lie at the basis of most classifications of things in common life. But even Giorgione could scarcely accomplish this unaided. He belongs to a great line of artists who have already taught us, in our countless encounters with their works, simply to look and see rather than to identify, classify, and appraise in accordance with our workaday preoccupations. Cimabue and Giotto, for example, have already made us perceive the power of line and shape and the tactile values which are tied to them; from Piero della Francesca we learn the values of perspective and the monumental impassivity of things, abstracted for the moment not only from their ordinary representational meanings but also from the other visual interests of line and shape and color that may be embodied in them; we learn from Perugino the significance of space and air, from Michelangelo the vitality of bodily movement, of force, pressure and impending change; and we learn from Giorgione's own predecessors and contemporaries,

[257

from Bellini and Titian and Veronese, the fascination of color, of light and shadow, and the delightful decorative uses to which they may be put. Some teach in one way, others in another: some by way of contrast, others by similarity and variation.

Nor are we limited for teachers to the artist's predecessors. Rembrandt, Delacroix, Renoir, Cezanne, and Matisse serve, when we return to Giorgione, to illuminate his own vision in their own characteristic and distinctive ways. Had I the skill and sensitivity, I have no doubt that I could prove the use of a Pollock or a de Kooning in teaching us what to look for in the immanent abstract expressiveness of Giorgione's treatment of color and line.

But these remarks are overwrought. They suggest that "the artist" is a creature apart, set off from the ruck of ordinary and obscure Judes who, imperfect artists themselves, still have that impulse which helps us to see qualities of visual perception under the form of art. The fact is that before we ever come near a Giotto or a Piero or a Giorgione, a thousand lesser artists, both creative and recreative, have already taught us something about the values of line and color, of shape, perspective, and materiality. And just as the great artist is himself an apprentice who must learn his craft before he can be a master, so also for the appreciation of his art he needs many auxiliaries and associates, some of whom also possess the gift of tongues. For the artist as such is mute and teaches only by his example. And whether he likes it or not, knowledge of his art depends also upon those interpreters who know how to deploy the resources of language in order to make us see what he may be up to in his treatments of space and light and air.

Here indeed one is tempted to say that in learning to appreciate not only the representational but even the more abstract and sensory forms of art, language itself is the primary teacher. More properly in learning how to use and apply such words as "graceful," "lovely," "charming," and "garish," we are automatically taught to "bracket" the thing seen and to view it not for what it may signify in some practical or scientific scheme of things, but simply as something to be looked at. But these "aesthetic concepts" or terms, as Professor Frank Sibley calls them, have been badly overworked and misused by advertisers and other sensationalists.[10] They may arrest attention, but they reveal little. And what they do reveal reduces the thing seen to the level of a million other "beauties" about which there is no need, or time, either to instruct us or to praise. The man of words does far better, in the normal course, to stretch the applications of such commonplace factual adjectives as "cold," "flat," and "dry," which, in unusual circumstances, acquire the power to rivet our attention to the perceptual qualities to which they refer. He does still better to make figurative use especially of verbs of action and their participial and other adjectival derivatives which, unlike vague "aesthetic" terms like "handsome," and "comely," call specific attention to the "energy," "efforts," and "powers" displayed in a painter's "thrusting" line, his "shifting" colors, his "broken" forms and "pressing" masses.

In talking about works of art we have all been misled, I think, by the easy use of aesthetic terms which call our attention equally well to the delightful colors of a sunset as to the painter's deployment of them in a picture. Anyone can be charmed by a "pretty" sky, but the lines and volumes and luminosities present to us in a painting belong to an artistic composition whose controlled, intentional values move us in an entirely different way. We have also been badly misled by the blanket use of the word "contemplation," which better serves to describe our inactive ruminative gazing at the sea than our involved scrutiny of the perspectives and masses of a pictorial design. Giorgione demands that we be affected by his handling of colors, moved by his shifts from impressionistic backgrounds to sharply-defined lines of the figures in the foregrounds of his paintings. For him the purely "aesthetic" pleasures of the musing eye are always transformed and transmuted into expressive understandings of a painter's enlivening brush and mind. In art, mind is all. And where mind is, intention is. Nature lets us do with it as we will; the artist does not. Where we see the colorist's composition or the organization of a draftsman's lines and shapes, it is the artist who not only establishes the vehicle but sets the tenor for what we are meant to see and feel.

Here the teacher has a subtle and difficult task. He must do and undo; speak and then alter the meaning of what he has said in trying to make us see and feel what he himself understands. In order to lead he cannot avoid the risk of misleading. In *The*

Tempest he must call attention to the fluctuating red of the young man's jacket, the green on deepening brown of the rocky earth beneath the half-reposing lady and her baby. He must make us see the shadows and the lights as ways of bringing into relation all the pictorial forms present in the painting. But he cannot leave us with these enhanced perceptions. He must make us see them as aspects of a multi-dimensional picture whose whole substantial reality continually returns to the individual parts its own encompassing creative force and energy. And only for a moment, and always with a view to returning us to their values within larger compositions of the picture, can he pause to talk about the hues of the mother's skin or the bright surface of the broken pedestal in the foreground.

Moreover, the teacher will badly fail both Giorgione and ourselves if he leaves us with only a more vivid awareness of the rich sensory and pictorial values of *The Tempest*. He must forever recall to us that the lights and colors of the sky are qualities of that sky, that the lacy figures of the enclosing trees are indeed to be seen as trees and not as mere abstract decorations and draperies, and that the flesh tints of the mother's skin are meant as revelations of her bodily and human presence. And the special freshness and fragrance of all these wonderful visions will be still lost upon us unless the teacher disposes us ever and again to see them together as so many interacting perceptual and imaginal movements of an inimitable artistic concert.

But of course there are concerts and concerts. There are certain fugues of Bach, for example, whose intricate designs, however interesting in themselves, remain almost totally inexpressive. Their patterns of sound intrigue the ear and the mind, but nevertheless, as we say, they "leave us cold" or "unmoved." This does not necessarily mean that they are therefore defective or imperfect; it means only that the range of their artistic interest is limited. Indeed the interest of many obviously expressive works by a Sibelius or a Tchaikovsky is all too easily exhausted at a single hearing, whereas in many of his lesser works the formal counterpoint of Bach ever and again revives our attention. In the greater works of Bach, however, we find an energy, a ceremonial seriousness, a gaiety and pathos and exaltation, which are profoundly and wonderfully *moving*. And the same is true of

Giorgione's painting. Bach and Giorgione, in their very different ways, can bring us again and again to the point of tears, as (for me at least) Vivaldi and the lesser Venetian masters such as the father and brother of Giovanni Bellini almost never can.

Here we are confronted once more with another basic dimension of most great art which I have referred to under the heading of "expression." And just as the teacher can improve our understanding of the other aspects of a work of art, so also he can aid us in the appreciation of its expressive values. Here, I shall take my examples from the writings of distinguished critics whose command of the artifices of language is so beautifully matched to their capacities for imaginative identification and feeling. For example, in describing Michelangelo's nudes, which "so increase our sense of capacity," Berenson tells us how their "manliness, robustness, effectiveness," fulfill "our dream of a great soul inhabiting a beautiful body" and how in the Sistine Chapel Michelangelo creates "the type of man best fitted to subdue and control the earth and who knows, perhaps more than the earth." He is helping in his hyperbolic way to expand our awareness of the Promethean expressiveness of Michelangelo's extraordinary art. When Nietzsche, more succinctly, refers to the "golden seriousness" of Mozart's music, he defines precisely the very being of, say, the great E-flat major symphony and the haunting Clarinet Quintet. And when D. F. Tovey speaks of "the longing for the solo instrument" which is established in the opening ritornellos of Mozart's incomparable concertos, he makes us understand how different are the dramatic values of these works from those of the romantic concertos of Schumann and Mendelssohn. Finally, when T. S. Eliot refers to the "tough reasonableness concealed beneath a slight lyric grace" in the poetry of Andrew Marvell, we are brought summarily to an exact awareness of the unique and elusive expressive power of Marvell's best works.

It is not for nothing that all of these critics, with the possible exception of Berenson, are also men of art. Indeed Berenson himself, like Pater, may perhaps qualify as a symbiotic artist whose consuming passion to articulate what he perceives in the works of artists working in a wholly different medium converts him, at moments, into an interesting writer on his own account. As artists, these writers are completely unafraid of exposing the feelings and emotions which, as Santayana put it before Eliot, they find "objectified in the work of art." Moved, they in turn seek to move, and in moving us, by their choice of words, they reveal expressive meanings about which most of us are too inhibited to speak, if indeed we are aware of them at all.

But the great critic, who usually interests us as a writer on his own account, is likely to be for that very reason an imperfect teacher. As often as not, he reveals as much about his own character and taste and art as he does of the works about which he writes. The great critic is also likely to be more preoccupied with judgment than with analysis. And though judgment is indispensable to appreciation and hence to teaching, it exists in the sphere of art education never as an end but as a means to something beyond itself. Too often, moreover, the critic's "reasons" are tendered as evidences of *his* judgment and taste, rather than as remarks intended only to bring us back to the artwork itself.

The teacher's discipline and art are stricter, more austere. For his concern is exclusively to bring his students closer to the distinctive being of works of art. His stern and self-effacing task is not, like the great critic's, simply to call attention to individual strokes of genius or, like the learned art historian, sociologist, or psychologist, to develop or illustrate a general theory of the place of art in large movements of culture or the significance of an artist's work as a manifestation of his personality. Making continent use of all these sources of understanding, for what they may be worth, his whole vocation is to bring his students to fuller awareness of the continuous evidences in works of art of the creative life which comprise one primary level of every man's own subjective being or actuality.

No teacher can make this understood by his talk alone. And his explanations and descriptions, left to themselves, remain abstract "literary" remarks until he ties them back into the picture itself with the help of bodily gesturings and grimacings by which the inert student is at last forced to notice, and in noticing is moved by, the complex palpable reality of the painting or poem or sonata. Quite literally the teacher must himself become an actor of sorts, or, if you will, an interpretive artist who compels the student to see the picture, not as a sensitive connoisseur or voyeur or mere man of judgment might, but as a fateful action in which the observer himself for the time being is meant to become wholly involved. In their own ways, teachers are at once performers, actors, and reactors, and it is only as they act and react that anything happens to the student that results in artistic understanding. The teacher is thus more and less than a scholar, just as he is less and more than a creative artist, In his own way, the scholar does something and knows something, but its artistic relevance remains problematic. He scarcely knows whereof he speaks. It is for the teacher to put the scholar's knowledge to work and to establish its power to illuminate for the student some artistic quality of a picture or novel or building. The good teacher is learned; but he never intrudes his learning upon his students. He never drops names or drones on in knowledgeable —and meaningless—recitations of facts. On the contrary, he seeks always to avoid coming between the student and the artist, and on occasion, therefore, simply prefers to stand aside and let the artist teach his own lesson. In short, the teacher's only function is to bring the other two together in ways they might not be able to do on their own. And the degree to which he succeeds in this taxing enterprise is the sole measure of his achievement.

For the teacher as for the student of the arts it is also the continuing effort to discern the artist's intention in his work which distinguishes him from the talkative purveyor of "aesthetic" charms. In this effort he finds his true discipline, his work, and his honorable corrigibility, which is the mark of every form of teaching and learning. By some perverse irony, many critics, especially old "new critics," treat the artist's intentions as irrelevant aspects of a private soliloquy and the so-called "aesthetic surface" of the work as its only discussable aspect. Just the reverse is true. "Aesthetic surface" in fact is a piece of historical-philosophical flimflam whose very meaning shifts from critic to critic and from philosopher to philosopher. And disagreements about what is "there" aesthetically invariably wind up as unresolvable disputes about the meanings of a word. But the intentions of the artist, like those of the teacher and the student, belong to the public domain. And we learn what his intentions are, just as we learn about anyone else's, by his actions, by his performances, by his achievements, and his failures. And the knowledge we acquire of his intentions, in many direct and indirect ways, is never complete and always fallible. Beautifully, however, there are always his works to return to, as well as works of other artists, whose own related designs, with their varied and contrasting meanings, and their correlated successes and failures, provide clues to the controlling form of the artist's actions and intentions in *this* individual work of art. And just as the all-important intentions of someone accused of murder in a court of law are established by processes of examination and cross-examination, by skillful interpretation of analogies and precedents, and, finally, by that cummulative sense of judgment which it takes a lifetime to acquire, so the intentions of the artist are established by many stages and in many degrees.

But the murderer's action is purposeful, whereas that of the artist, as Kant says, is only purposive. And this is what creates the teacher's peculiar problem. For he cannot resort to analogies taken from common life which reveal intentions that are merely purposeful and which are established, as in a law court, only for the sake of further purposeful judgments and actions. The judge's task is to render justice, and justice imposes possibilities of punishment, retribution, and atonement. The art teacher's task however is only to inform and enhance awareness of a significant composition or design. And neither he nor his student nor the work of art has anything to gain (or lose) from his effort but an increment of being and (in the fine old-fashioned sense of the term) truth.

The work of art is not a practical achievement, though it may cost the artist, his student and interpreter much sweat and many tears to bring into being. Still less, one must never tire of saying, can it be identified with the physical object which provides its material ground. Its actuality consists, accordingly, of a network of uniquely moving possibilities which to the disciplined and imaginative observer are as indelibly present in it as its pigment or frame. But these possibilities must be selected from a multitude of impressions, many of which we are obliged to discard, precisely because they lead us away from actualities of form and meaning to which the work of art itself compels us, over and over again, to return.

A Return to Kant

But how shall we know which possibilities are real and what interpretations that purport to establish them are true? It is by facing this question, I believe, that we come finally in sight of the point, as well as the limitations of all our explanations and interpolations, our scholarly excursions, our emphases and silences, in our efforts to teach something that can lead us more deeply into a work of art. The answer to the question, in an age which worships method, may seem initially deflationary and dispiriting. For I am bound to say with all possible emphasis, that here, as in all the humanities, there is no science, no certain method or criterion, no "objective" or nonpersonal routine for testing what is really there, and hence what is finally relevant in our apprehensions and in our interpretations of a work of art. And this, I am convinced, is the penultimate lesson of education in the arts. The ultimate lesson, however, is that this is not an evidence of failure, either for ourselves or for the humanities. Rather it is a sign of their unique importance within the realms of spirit.

In a remarkable statement in his *Critique in Judgment*, Kant puts the point in the following way:

... genius is a *talent* for producing that for which no definite rule can be given; it is not a mere aptitude for what can be learned by a rule. Hence *originality* must be its first property . . . its products must be models, i.e., *exemplary* . . . genius is entirely opposed to the *spirit of imitation*. Now since learning is nothing but imitation, it follows that the greatest ability and teachableness . . . cannot avail for genius . . . we can readily learn all that *Newton* has set forth . . . but we cannot learn to write spirited poetry, however expressive may be the precepts of the art and however excellent its models . . . artistic skill cannot be communicated; it is imparted to every artist immediately by the hand of nature . . . There is therefore for beautiful art only a *manner* (modus), not a *method* of teaching (methodus). The master must show what the pupil is to do and how he is to do it; and the universal rules, under which at last he brings his procedure, serve rather for bringing the main points back to his remembrance when the occasion requires, than for prescribing them to him. Nevertheless regard must be had here to a certain ideal, which art must have therefore before its eyes, although it cannot be completely attained in practice.[11]

Kant's statement is worthy of a hundred pages of gloss, which I have no space here to make. I must therefore confine myself to two points, one in which, as it seems to me, he mistakes his own insight, and another in which he helps to reestablish the truth implicit in it. When he tells us that the genius of the artist is entirely opposed to the spirit of imitation, he means, I take it, not just that the creative act transcends any formulas which the artist may happen to use, but that the interest of his production, as an individual work, lies, not in its conformity or failure to conform to any rule, but ultimately in the design he achieves in the work itself. For us, his appreciative recreative admirers, therefore, any failure, either on our part or his, to conform to a rule is no test of its artistic merit or achievement. In another way, so to say, the interest is not in the theme but in its variations, not in the genre but in its handling, not in the style but its individual inflections.

But Kant contradicts himself when he says that learning is nothing but imitation and its success the accuracy of the imitation, and this for two reasons. In the first place, works of art themselves do provide models of a sort, exemplums, or as Matthew Arnold puts it, touchstones, of fineness or excellence. There is no rule to be educed from the works of exemplary genius, but nonetheless there remains a basis or ground for significant comparisons. Thus by stages, and with the aid of such exemplums, we learn that tact or judgment which enables us, in contemplating other works, to distinguish relevant from irrelevant possibilities of significant meaning that enhance the value of a particular work. Correspondingly, our critical communications, upon which depend the possibility of teaching, especially on their higher levels, is communication of a distinctive sort whose relevance, however, remains for each person to establish, according to his own developed powers of imagination and judgment. Accordingly, critical communication provides only a problematic match between what is asserted and what is apprehended. Within it, as in every domain of humane learning, an element of freedom, and hence a chance of misunderstanding, is forever possible. But this possibility is a function, not of our inarticulateness or incapacity for understanding; rather it is a quality of the "object" under discussion. Because its possibilities are open and available to us as teachers and students in a purely exemplary way, what we teach and what we learn can never be expected to correspond exactly to "what is there." Indeed, if it could, that very fact would show that we would not be teaching or learning something about a work of art, but about a phenomenon whose only significance lies in its conformity to some general scheme or classification or in its power to confirm or disconfirm some putative law of nature.

Put in this way, however, the basic power of the teacher of art is inadequately represented. For it is not so much a question of what the teacher cannot do, but of what he can do. For his best students he manages to illuminate and preserve the vital distinction between the instance which conforms to a settled rule and the exemplum which, in virtue of its exemplary use, does not. He also elicits imaginative awareness of artistic possibilities, and of their importance, even though, as Kant intimates, he can offer no formula for finding them. But, for the gifted student, he can do more. For at his best he himself provides an exemplum: a continuous presence who by his talk and his gestures, as well as his reticence, conveys an awareness of what it is to look for true possibilities in a work of art, what it is to find a significant artistic form, what it is to develop an authentic taste which at the same time respects the legitimate differences both between authentic readings of a work of art and between such readings and the uses to which individual persons may put the arts in compassing their own material ends. By his example, in a word, the teacher imbues the student with a sense of his own proper freedom as well as of the responsibilities which that freedom entails. His exemplary task is thus to awaken and sophisticate independent judgment, and in so doing, to make clear that judgment always has an end beyond itself which each student must realize in his own way.

At bottom, then, as Kant says, there can be no method or *methodus* of teaching the arts but only a *modus* or manner. But this remains a form of teaching all the same, as anyone who has pondered the writings of an inspired critic such as Arnold,

Eliot, Tovey, or Berenson well knows. In fact, it may well be the most difficult and demanding of all the forms of education.

One last word about the passage from Kant quoted above, which I shall use in a manner somewhat different from what he may have intended. Kant seems here to have in mind only the relationship of the master artist-teacher to his apprentices, who in due course may become artists in their own right. And his remarks about this relationship are just. My purpose here is different. For the sake of discussion, I shall assume that the student's interest is primarily appreciative and recreative, that he is not an apprentice artist, but, more humbly, one who aspires only to a richer understanding of works already in being. The point is that he, too, can learn, not only from the teacher's imaginative commentaries, but from directed forms of practice—drawing, composing, writing—which done can give his eye and ear and mind the special training they need for seeing and hearing and imagining with an instructed and focused mind. Drawing and playing invest the drawer and player with a sense both of difficulties and of difficulties surmounted; the hand, here, leads the eye, and, as Kant suggests, brings back to the mind a sense of the virtues of a fine performance which is itself the product of accomplished work as well as of genius. In a word, knowing something of *how* the painter draws and paints, the student (as well as the teacher) is enabled to discover in the individual stroke of genius the skill and the effort which makes that genius apt for its own creative intentions.

But there is a further virtue in this mode of instruction, implicit in Berenson's discussions of the tactile values which give such weight and power to the frescoes of a Giotto or a Masaccio. For these values are always apprehended concretely and not merely descriptively and illustratively. Because of this they are fully understood only by one who has taken a brush in his hand and discovered, with a teacher's help, how much has to be done in order to accomplish the far-from-simple purpose of mixing paints, drawing a circle, or converting a series of brush strokes into a painterly action that fulfills an as yet inchoate and unformed intention. *Praxis:* It is practice, and actions informed by practice, that give substance to art. And it is only through practice and its resultant achievements that we are enabled to see how and why the work of genius is not merely an "aesthetic" gift of the gods, but a human artifice, set in its own motion by the art and the work of the artist.

The point must now be generalized. The ordinary "lover of art" whose eye has no hand to steady it and give it point and focus, is to that very extent alienated from painting. He can overcome this alienation only by actions of his own that are fundable back into acts of perception which enable him to achieve a substantial awareness of what the artist has done. The "realistic" art so greatly prized in the Soviet Union does not in the least exemplify this principle implicit in what I take to be Marx's and, behind him, Kant's aesthetics. Just the contrary, it offers us only a static illustration through which we may conceivably learn something about the external circumstances of a worker's life, but nothing of his work. As art it fails because it degrades the artist, treats him only as a duplicating machine that turns out endless copies of historical, sociological, and ideological information. The true lesson of Marx is that the artist's achievement lies not in someone else's actions which he attempts unavailingly to copy, but in a significant action of his own. And for us, as observers, that action moves and exalts us only through the work that prepares us for our own congruent acts of recreative perception.

Here the artist himself once again becomes a teacher and we, his students, bring away from our experience of his work an exemplary fund of learning which serves us again and again in our efforts to find our way into other works of art. Teaching and learning, in all their various ways, are forms of work, and work is never a matter only of happy chances and insights. We learn by doing and by the doing of skilled and disciplined teachers who themselves are at the same time emancipated from the many errors of misplaced intention, including those of imitation, scientism, and mindless aestheticism.

And now for an all-too-schematic resume. What makes teaching and learning in the arts such a complex and arduous affair is that it amounts to a virtual summation of all the arts of education itself. For teachers of appreciation in any art require all the powers necessary for recognizing all the varied contributions which teaching and learning can make to artistic understanding and appreciation. First and last there is the guidance of eye and mind into the intentional object itself. This demands a developing ability to determine what properly does and does not belong to the many-leveled design of the work of art. And in turn this involves the ability to distinguish artifact from thing, and the purposeful artifact from the purposive design. It involves the ability to perceive the representational forms present in the work, and their complex internal relations to one another. Beyond this it demands also that we know how to convert raw sensations into discriminated perceptions of line or color, along with their attendant expressive qualities. It requires further the stretched and developed imagination, gained through previous encounters with works of art, which enables us to convert our understanding of genre and style into artistic metaphors for the illumination of a particular work. And finally, but not least, it involves that wide experience of relevant life which enables the free mind to apprehend some of the possibilities of human being of which every work of art is a celebration.

In the sphere of art education, as in education everywhere in the humanities, we at last perceive that every form of teaching and learning, from the explanation to the pointer, has its appropriate use. But we realize also that explanations as well as pointers subserve ends beyond themselves, and that education, although a delightful thing both for the teacher and the learner, necessarily moves toward a life beyond itself. We realize also how unavailing are all our explanations and gestures without tact and judgment, those indispensable powers for determining what is and is not relevant when, in one way or another, our existence is in jeopardy. And judgment, too, as we have seen, can be learned, though only by slow stages and with the help of exemplary models. But in acquiring judgment two other things are also learned: one, that only a small part of learning is a matter of following rules, the other that judgment is always a servant never a master. For judgment, together with all the preparation that lies behind it, is a hindrance unless it brings the judge himself back into the world of the thing judged and makes him an imperiled participant in its exigent actions and designs. In fact, the judge for whom judgment is an end is no judge at all, but an executioner whose first victim is himself. Nor can he succeed without the developed skills and sensibilities that enable him to appreciate what the man he judges has intended, how he has done his work, under what stresses he has acted and what precedents he has had at his disposal. For work of any sort, including above all the work of the artist, is always a serious, if also, on occasion, a golden thing, not an out-pouring of an automatic response to surface irritations, but an achievement which is the product of a long sequence of human actions.

In the end we are confronted, in this time and in this place, with a unique and perilous engagement with an act of creation which is all our own. The actuality of a work of art, like a life, is a fund of possibilities, and possibilities which exist only for beings who themselves are free. God, if God there be, may possess them all. For individual men the actuality of a work of art is always something less. But in understanding this fact, we are taught one thing more which is the great moral gift of all humane learning: that humility, that tolerance, that awareness of ambiguity, and that undogmatic assurance which is the priceless possession of the liberal mind. But here we verge on other dimensions of humanistic education that must be described in another place.

14

Art and Anti-Art

RECENTLY, AT AN INTERNATIONAL CONFERENCE CONCERN-
ing fashionable notions of "structuralism" in theories of literature
and language, a distinguished French academician offered the following theory: A work of literature, as distinguished from a sewing machine or a rock, is not something "objective," ineluctably
and hence finitely there for all who have eyes to see and know. A
novel or a poem is in its essential character something at once subjective, withdrawn from the public eye, and infinite in its possibilities of meaning and hence of interpretation. I replied that he
had not in my opinion adequately distinguished poetry from
sewing machines and rocks. After all, sewing machines placed in
museums become works of art, capable thereafter of every sort
of nostalgic or prophetic interpretation, rocks are as infinite in
their possibilities as novels, and finally, all too many poems and
novels, alas, are made to order, thoroughly finite, and as utterly
objective in their meanings and roles as so many hub caps. To all
this the reply was that sewing machines might become works of
art, but that he wasn't talking about works of art, and that he
never used the term in discussing literature. On the contrary, he
had an animus against the very notion of a poem as a work of art,
and what he was defending, and alone cared about, is the subjectivity, the uniqueness, the freedom of individual works of literature. Somehow he felt that in literature alone, in our modern
technological and scientific world of artifacts and things, could

man evince and express himself, do as he, and he alone, pleased or must.

A work of art is indeed something palpable, finite: Something is expected or demanded of it, if only the power to elicit a certain particular form of response; and it gets high or low marks according as it meets such set expectations. It is indeed a sewing machine or hub cap on parade. But the novels of Kafka, the plays of Beckett or Genet, and, he might perhaps have added, the poems of Allen Ginsberg, are not on parade; they belong to their creators and his friends, if any, whoever they may be; or, rather, they belong to anyone who wants them for such personal interest or involvement he may find in them. In a word, my colleague was contending that, at least so far as literature is concerned, "Art," and above all "work of art," stand for public, objective ideas and hence are dirty words. He didn't add, though others may do so for him, that even the terms "literature" and perhaps even "poetry," "fiction," "the novel," and the other genre words we traditionally use in talking about such works or things as the *Divine Comedy, The Red and the Black,* and *Howl,* are, in Nietzsche's phrase, "bad air." And in a word, he was the spokesman of a loosely knit movement which invokes such terms as "anti-novel," "anti-hero," and "anti-art" as slogans to express a shared intransigence, distrust, and alienation from the tradition.

II

It is worth reminding ourselves, however, that our avant-garde is not alone in its repudiations of traditions: every age worth its salt is a father-killer; to create something is to kill something else. No doubt this will provide little comfort: it is not meant to. We absurdists spurn comfort, along with soap and sobriety. Nor does it provide justification; we have all heard of the genetic fallacy, and we prefer quite simply to go it alone. We are not history's men; but our independence is qualitatively a new thing, for it is a gift of the historical consciousness itself, as Nietzsche discovered, and Marx, in his prophetic way, foretold.

If therefore I introduce my remarks by way of a few historical observations, it is not in order either to remove the curse from our newest literature and painting or to deny it its proper ration of freshness, intransigent oddity, or horror; it is rather with a view to understanding what it is that we may be faced with and how, for better or worse, we must approach it, as men facing the imponderable actions, or motions, of their fellowmen. For understanding, although it does not require that we should love its object, is required for judgment. And judgment is precisely what we lack. Every sleeper through Andy Warhol's latest film fancies himself to be entitled to proclaim it the greatest cinematic event ever, just as every government secretary considers her failure to understand Robert Motherwell's *New England Elegy* as evidence of its unworthiness.

Let me first remind you then that our concepts of art, and especially fine art and work of art, have been current for only a little more than three centuries. Plato had the notion of *techne*, but applied it to statesmanship as well as to music; and though he had an idea of the beautiful, he held that mathematics affords a far more beautiful art than sculpture, the dance, and the other mimetic arts. Poetry he regarded as a pseudo-art and therefore neither good nor beautiful: poets are too self-expressive; they stir up our emotions, and besides they are liars. Plato turned all true art into a mode of knowledge and treated artists who did not conform to his demands as perverts. The more prosaic Aristotle understood better than Plato that *mimesis* may itself be a source of pleasure, and that if you wish to find universals in poetry, it behooves you to look for them in the right place. Plato inadequately grasped the distinctive pleasure that miming gives or the way in which it may express the universal, the enduring, or the ideal. Aristotle understood also, in Santayana's phrase, that it is usually a long way around to Nirvana, and that happiness is not to be had just for the asking. You have to look in the right place and in the right way if you are to find the hair-raising exaltation that tragedy affords.

But even Aristotle, that classifier's classifier, missed a point in applying well-tailored Sophoclean standards to the judgment of such plays as *Medea* and *Hippolytus*. These strange and wild works, he said, were imperfect tragedies—since he too lacked the notion of the work of art, he was unable to add that they were imperfect works of art. And he felt that understanding their imperfection as tragedies was all he had to understand. But of course it was not. For our purposes, Euripides may be regarded as the first anti-tragedian—at least as the tradition of his age conceived the term. He demanded an understanding which the conservative author of the *Poetics* could not give. Then, too, he afforded a strange, outlandish thrill, or excitement, which might not be happy, and certainly was not good, but which, for him who is taken by it, can become a necessity. Euripides, I should add, was a neglectful mime; he had his mind and heart on something else altogether: obsession, compulsiveness, repression, the anti-rational or anti-human, perhaps even, in relation to his predecessors, anti-art.

After the Renaissance, ideas of art more conformable to our own began to emerge. And of course they were accompanied by a profound shift in the character and intentions of the arts we now, unthinkingly and tendentiously, call "fine" and in the attitudes of the "artists" toward their audiences. Now, the painter and the sculptor were no longer content anonymously to add their bit to the perfection of a communal house of worship, nor was the musician willing merely to provide an accompaniment to services that serve interests other than those we fancy as "musical." The Renaissance artists came to use biblical scenes as mere material occasions for their own newly-conceived painterly or sculptorial or musical ends. They refused to serve simply as illustrators, decorators, or commentators upon activities, interests, above all, ideas, to which their own exigent purposes are secondary. In a word "artists" decline now to be and to be treated as mere artisans, ready like Prufrock to swell a scene leaving the direction of the action to another. It is they who bless the patron, rather than vice versa; it is the church or public building that provides the occasion for the exercise of their skills and powers, rather than they who simply help to magnify it. And in short the artist, in our sense, now becomes aware of himself as an independent power, a destiny or fatality in his own right. No one can observe the difference, say, between a Cimabue and a Masaccio and fail to perceive, and to feel, what the new freedom must have meant to artists in the *Cinquecento*. This has nothing to do, let me emphasize, with question of intrinsic beauty or value, though it has a good deal to do with the question whether, and in what circumstances, questions of intrinsic value and beauty are, and are to be, raised. Similarly, one feels that the shift in character between the paintings of the early Bellini and the late, or more strikingly between Bellini's predecessors and Tintoretto, is not just a shift in style but also in the sense of what is permitted and expected of the painter *as an artist*. Tintoretto is certainly a religious painter in my judgment; conceivably he is a Christian painter, but he is not, save ironically and in passing, one who places his gifts at the disposal of the church or state. For him every occasion is one to disport himself.

All the same, throughout the Renaissance the freedom of the artist is still limited in many ways. This shows itself in matters of style as well as in subject matter. More to the point, for our purposes, it shows itself in the very commitment to a subject matter. Even the mannerist is tied to the tradition of subject matter in distorting the styles he stylizes. Art may no longer be viewed as a form of deception or illusion; but the artist is still a mime; an entertainer who amuses, commemorates, and who incidentally instructs through his imitations and illustrations. He may belong to himself, but, so to say, only secretly or covertly. In the case of Velasquez, one feels again and again that the painter, or rather the individual, is in hiding, showing himself only through the ironies implicit in his arrangements, his dazzling brushwork, his very absence, like Cordelia, from the scene. How terrifying are those magnificently decorated Hapsburgs, astride their toy horses, with their still, vacuous faces, their rich fatuities. Not even Goya, it seems to me, is a greater master of contempt. But whereas Goya openly mocks his subject, or merely uses him or her as an occasion for displays of his passionate grotesqueness, making it plain for all to see who is master and who is slave, Velasquez hides his superiority in the draperies, in a lower lip, in a dull complexion. Outwardly everything is sumptuous, just, marvelously elegant and craftsmanlike: in a word, courtly and subservient. Certainly no royal prince could imagine Velasquez as a rival, let alone a superior man about to turn the tables on his masters.

The emergence, in the seventeenth century, of the concept of "the fine arts" (*beaux arts*) at last seems to free the artist in the modern sense from the status of a mere craftsman whose works are merely to please when seen. The painter and sculptor, and gradually the poet and the musician, become the masters of a distinctive, specially designated kind of genus: the arts which, by definition or nature, are fine or beautiful. No longer, it seems, a merely attendant lord, a high-class servant, an illustrator, or teacher, he walks in beauty, not incidentally or by accident, but, as it were, essentially and by natural right. Unfortunately, however, the notion of the fine arts was tied at the same time to traditional notions of the beautiful such as harmony and symmetry, order and decorum. It was also confused with the notion of plastic arts or arts of design—arts, that is, which are distinguished by the interest in their shape, form, pattern, or outline. Viewed as such, poetry in particular plainly loses as much as it gains. As fine art it need no longer be instructive, but the genuine expressiveness and imaginative power which can go into first-rate instruction is in effect now denied the poet as a creator of "fine art." And, separated now from the merely useful arts, which not being fine are now automatically demoted to a condition of servility, the fine arts lose touch with the rest of life, with matters of necessity or common interest, let alone life, death, and ultimate concern. They are ready for the splendid palaces and glass cases in which, on Sundays, they may be peered at by observers who are not vaguely re-creative. Now, automatically, the principle is: *Nole me tangere:* do not touch me. The fine arts by definition offer us beauty; but beauty as such soon becomes threadbare, and the Pitti Palace can seem a hall of mirrors, of bric-a-brac, of lovely irrelevances—a palace, oddly, in which to celebrate, not the life, but the death of art. In another way, the fine arts become *objects* of art; of art, no doubt, but objects nonetheless, sweetbreads under glass, to be looked at, mincingly tasted, but never swallowed and digested. Accordingly, the lover of art now becomes a voyeur, a witness at a peep show, who overlooks, in all senses, what is really going on. No wonder that toward the end of the eighteenth century the creative poets, musicians, and painters want no part of fine art, no more of beauty, no more of that art which conceals itself in the form of an object which wishes only to be seen and, on Monday morning, forgotten. No wonder that the prophetic artists of the age, the Blakes for example, were regarded as madmen; no wonder that the great German romantics turned their back on *schoene Kunst,* that Schiller, Schelling, and the rest poured forth notions of sentimental poetry, that they talked of and searched for something called the "characteristic," the sublime, the symbolic image of "ideas" behind and beyond the world of ordinary waking and conscious life. Particularly among the later romantics, the interest in art begins to shift to what lies behind the symbol or mask: the creator himself. Accordingly, as in the case of Beethoven and Goethe, the artist becomes a kind of hero or "fatality" to his audience, and the artist's life becomes a surrogate in the modern world for the life of the tragic hero. At once the artist is a fatality, a creature apart, the prime evidence of the possibility of personal freedom from the "laws" of an impersonal social order and from the routine duties imposed by a system of institutionalized activities that constrict and stifle the spirit. Still, at the same time, as in the case of Beethoven, the artist speaks not only for himself but for a liberated humanity toward which all of us yearn; his eccentricities, reflected in his art, above all his extraordinary personality, reflected in an art no less incomparable and strange, bears witness to a possibility in us all for individuality, for self-assertion, and self-transcendence.

Perhaps we lesser artists are capable only of acts of re-creation, owing to the stimulus of a great quartet or poem. Even so, we too participate in our own ways in the life of the spirit, and in ways that have no exact counterparts elsewhere. In short, everyone, the audience as well as the composer or the poet becomes or conceives himself as an artist in his own right. What romanticism represents, in a word, is not the autonomy of art, but of the artist, and the work of art becomes, in effect, an expression of that autonomy, interesting and moving as a gesture or assertion of independence. And if, by traditional standards, the work itself is formless, chaotic, or ugly, that very fact becomes something to prize.

III

But the autonomy of the artist is indeed one thing and the autonomy of art another. And in fact the movements toward the artist's autonomy, which were labelled "romanticism," are in a number of ways in deep, if implicit, conflict with the movement toward the autonomy of art, which at the same time came to be known as "aestheticism." The term "aesthetic" has in principle little intrinsically to do with the notion of art. Indeed, there is a certain natural opposition between them. For the "aesthetic" represents a mode of perception and a concern for appearances that applies as well to natural as to artistic phenomena, and that, as the preceding phrase itself ironically suggests, invites or requires us to view works of art, as we may view physical objects, precisely as meaningless (if also interesting and pleasurable) arrangements and manifolds of sensations. In fact, the very word "arrangement" and its near synonym "design" must be neutralized and dehumanized, deprived of their intentionality, if they are to serve the purpose of aesthetic experience and judgment. An aesthetic object is precisely not a work of *art*, not at all something meant, not in the least a human gesture, a word, or an utterance.

Aesthetics freed the arts from the rationalist's obsession with imitation, with instruction, and with knowledge. It also freed the arts from the moralist's preoccupation with homilies. But at a price. It freed the arts by depriving them of their artfulness, by systematically demanding of us that we denude them of their intentions, their expressiveness, their tendentiousness—what Kant called their "purposiveness." The ideology of the asthetic represents, at the heart of it, a revolt against the cognitive (or scientific), the moral (or practical), and the religious (or worshipful). It says, so far as the artist is concerned, that he need not be a scientist, a moralist, a servant of religion. It gives him the freedom of a new genre—the aesthetic—which had not been seen or heard before.

But from the point of view of the artist, as the romantics conceived him, as well as from the point of view of neoclassicists who continued to assert the right, or obligation, of the artist to instruct and give pleasure or beautify through representational forms, the autonomy of the arts was hardly won. Worse, it seemed to leave the work of the artist indistinguishable from a natural object; both, as aesthetic objects, exist only as appearances, or, rather, since appearances in the philosophical tradition in question meant simply sensuous presentations, they exist, as my old teacher David Prall used to put it, only as "sensuous surfaces" of reality. To the aestheticians, in fact, the slogan "art for art's sake" meant art for the sake of its sensuous immediacies, and sensuous immediacies for their own sake.

Of course no one who cares passionately about colors and sounds, not to mention smells and tastes and hot and cold, would deny his gratitude to any movement which insists upon the divine rights of sensation. Nor do I, certainly, wish to depreciate altogether a movement in philosophy, in criticism, and in the arts themselves that insisted upon the autonomy of the values of sensation. As Professor Mary Mothersill insists, it was, and still is, necessary to raise strenuous voices against the old condemnation, or fear, of the so-called lower pleasures of the bodily senses. And I myself used to dispute with Prall when he denied to the pleasures of the bodily senses the title "aesthetic" and hence of aesthetic art. And if Desessant, in Huysmans' *Against the Grain*, displayed a certain overripe ingenuity in his efforts to compose symphonies of smells, his heart at least was in the right place. Or if it wasn't, I fail to see what objections the aestheticians can properly make against him.

I shall go further: I too fancy that Desessant's smell symphonies were, in their own way, impure as objects of aesthetic art, for they were in fact subtly expressive of a decadent and, ultimately, despairing attitude toward existence which, to my mind, is more compelling than the blank arrangements of sense qualities which alone qualify for our admiration by true exponents of the aesthetic attitude. A purely aesthetic art, as Santayana, who himself repudiated his own earlier talk about aesthetics, put it, is a "penitent art," the unnatural philosophical child of the very cognitivism and moralism from which it seeks to escape. It has no independent will or life of its own, nor represents any positive creative artistic impulse on the part of poet, musician, or sculptor. In a word, the idea of aesthetic art is not that of imaginative free art; on the contrary it is the creature of a long history of rationalist philosophy and culture, of puritan self-distrust and moralism which can find its freedom only in the renunciation, not only of the concerns but even the memories, of ordinary life.

IV

But now to anti-art in earnest. As I conceive it, at its best, the movement of anti-art represents a repudiation of all the self-limiting "-isms" and "counter-isms" indelibly inscribed in traditional aesthetics and philosophies of criticism and of art. It values the assault of aesthetics upon doctrines of imitation that turn the art object into a vehicle for the realization of ends that are not its own. But it opposes the castration of the artist and his work which is the penalty paid by aesthetics and aesthetic art for its victory. It stands, however, not for the unaesthetic—that is, the merely utilitarian, economic, or political—interests of men, but for anti-aestheticism, which is quite another thing. Anti-aestheticism is opposed to such fashionable doctrines as "the intentional fallacy," which turns the work of art into an hermetically sealed aesthetic object whose deep secret, finally, is only that it is an illusion.

But it is not just the aesthetic object which anti-art opposes, but in one sense the work of art itself. It is opposed, first of all, to the reduction of poems and novels, not to mention films, dancing, and well-constructed buildings, to a single common denominator, toward which the interested person can properly stand in only one rigid relation: call it "contemplation" for short. It is opposed to a life of elegant, detached looking and over-looking, to rich and richly appointed houses for external objects which can be moved, but only at a price. It is opposed to the cult of the collector, the benefactor, the fetishism of the nearly priceless art object which only oil magnates and their progeny can afford. It opposes all the airless opulence, the goodish taste, the expensiveness, and the barely concealed commercialism symbolized by our national galleries and by what Harold Rosenberg calls the art establishment. And it opposes all the attendant gallimaufry of work-of-art-ism: the separation of literature, painting, sculpture, and the rest from other things, from the events and activities and decisions of common experience; the whole idea, in fact, of an intentionless artifact which, rid now of its embarrassing creator or producer, and at the same time demanding that its admirer remain a merely detached observer who keeps his distance, respects the immobile, self-enclosed and self-enclosing and now irrelevant *thing*, with no living being to keep it company. Anti-art and the anti-artist seek to restore the so-called work of art to its rightful place as a sublimated and sublimating focus of our whole unbearable humanity, not our senses or minds only, but our bodies, our very being. Or, if this seems a bit overdrawn and overwrought, the exponent of anti-art may be viewed more simply and truly as one who notices the curious way in which the notion of the art-lover, the lover of art, when we take it seriously, makes adulterers of us all, by forcing us to treat our "other" love for the work as something illicit, something we cannot acknowledge even to ourselves as a legitimate relation to the object. It is as though when we give the title "work of art" to a picture, a piece of music, or a coffee pot, we are forced by that act into a primarily ritual relation to it which deprives us at the same time of that intimate yet full and exuberant reality which we first found in Henry Moore, in Frank Lloyd Wright, or in Beckett. There is a sense in which I cannot bear even to discuss my relations to *Figaro* or to *Crazy Jane*. When I treat *Figaro* or *Crazy Jane* as works of art, however, when I try to view them merely as such, my relationship necessarily becomes a public relationship, and my act a public act. Now, perforce we begin to adopt poses toward one another. Our interlocking roles become stylized. And in short we become in effect the parties to a contract, with duties to one another, for which others may henceforth hold us accountable. But there remains, if you will, a more precious, a truly *Crazy Jane* which is merely mine, which permits me to do all sorts of unmentionable things to it, which ravishes me and, in turn, impatiently awaits my ravishment. This *Jane* is not an honest work of art but an incomparable mistress, impossibly demanding and intolerably ardent. Indeed, what has the work-of-art to do with all this sentimental, subjective, illicit affection that exists between poor *Jane* and me?

It is precisely this descent into subjective actuality over which the idea of anti-art presides. But there is another side of the matter which must now be mentioned. In our time the work of art has become, in its ritual way, a kind of surrogate god; as a work of art, a building, drama, or symphony invites, or requires, not mere admiration of its devotee, but a kind of worship. In fact it is precisely this tendency in the modern age to convert the artist into a surrogate priest and the work of art into a temple or shrine, or, worse, into a divinity in its own right, against which anti-art-ism is also a protest. Here, let me remind you, it was T. S. Eliot who, with his usual perceptiveness, pointed the way many years ago. There was a time when I, for one, felt that Eliot had simply become so preoccupied with Other Things that he neglected, or had forgotten, his muse. It seemed to me that, as in the case of Coleridge, his turning to religion, or theology, was merely a sign that his power as an artist was used up. I thought in fact that God for him was a kind of consolation prize. But Eliot of course was right and I simply uncomprehending, whatever may be the truth about the quality of his later work. Eliot was opposed, among other things, to idolatry and to the sentimentality of the idolater. God is not, cannot be, a work of art or an artist, though an analogy in this direction may perhaps help to give life to our fading love both of art and of God. The point, however, is that neither works of art nor artists are or should be treated as Gods. Their holiness is not definitive but at best exemplary, and this, for one thing, because works of art do not begin to exhaust the works of mind which are matters of intrinsic and enduring con-cern to us. They are a salient part of that significant being which makes life at once tolerable and incomparably precious. But they are a part only. And when we equate art with significant being we diminish both. Or worse, we all strangely begin to find the being of art appalling, something to escape from into something else we then misname Reality. There would be no life in works of art if life itself were meaningless; nor could tragic art help to redeem calamity or make meaningful our sense of mortality if death itself were nothing.

Work-of-art-ism, like its twin brother, aestheticism, is essenti-ally a frivolous attitude, as Bernard Berenson for one discovered in his own unexpectedly self-renewing old age. The pure work of art is indeed self-contained, just as, in the work of a well-known contemporary aesthetician, purely aesthetic perception is "intransitive." (I refer, of course, to Eliseo Vivas.) But for this reason also the anti-artist and the exponent of anti-art protest against a culture which treats the work of art as its essential holy work, and the artist, its creator, as a surrogate divinity. For divinity is never self-contained and holiness never intransitive. Eliot knew better when he pointed out, as early as "Tradition and the Individual Talent," that just as each genuine poem is a creature of the whole tradition of poetry, whether the poet realizes it or not, so each poem in turn subtly not indelibly alters our awareness of the tradition. In reading *The Four Quartets*, at the top of my own poor form, I find a constant alternation between my experience of the particular word, rhythm, or image and an expanding consciousness in which I find resonances of virtually most of the great poetry—and much great music—of which I am aware. Furthermore, these poems, as my living memory of them develops, become aspects of large organic wholes of which now the works of Eliot and Beethoven, among others, are aspects. Or, to vary the figure, they become links in a greater chain of being, each of which is indispensable to the others and therefore to the chain. And now, indeed, like Leibnizian monads, *The Four Quartets* become mirrors of all others, reflecting what is wonderful and alive in them. But this life in turn is reflected back in them, so that when one returns again to Beethoven's last quartets, a little forgetful or weary of what one fancied them to be, they again become marvelous as the birth of sound itself.

The point is that works of art and our experiences of them are and must be transitive. For their own sakes as well as ours, they must open out upon a larger life and take their places within that larger life. Nor, let it be emphatically added, is this merely a matter of artistic ties. Or, rather, genuinely literary or artistic works that *are* something, also belong to something more immense than they. Break the connection, as "the lemon-squeezer school of criticism," as Eliot once called it, tries to do, and what is left is a lifeless pulp, a mere subject matter for exegetes. It should be a platitude that art is a part of life; it should also be a platitude that because it is indispensably a part of life it cannot be a life in its own right, an absolute end in itself, a truly first cause of being.

V

And now for a penultimate maneuver which I must execute with some skill or else all is lost. For I must protect the anti-artist against the charge of philistinism, of failing, that is, to understand what literature, music, painting, and the rest really are. A sonata, painting, or poem must, as I say, belong to something more than itself, something also that is not purely musical, plastic, or literary. Fully felt and loved, it carries one on and out again into a larger world of mind. In this sense, the very experience of it, as I have suggested, is indeed transitive, open, full of expectation as well as fulfillment: as it could not possibly be if it were, as Hegel might say, wholly in and for and by itself. In analogous ways, all art whatever is dramatic, portentous, gravid, and every great moment in a work of art is like "the soul of the wide world," which so haunted Coleridge, "dreaming on things to come." On this the exponent of anti-art and anti-aesthetic rightly and interminably insists. Yet this happens, and must happen, without diminishing the presence, the actuality, of that which creates the longing, but on the contrary enhances it, gives it substance, power, and expressiveness. And the exponent of anti-art falls into a trap that will destroy him unless he realizes this. Again one must resort to analogies. As I, a complete outsider, understand it, essential being as conceived by the Thomistic tradition is always active, always an act. Mere being, as Plato knew, is nothing. Being itself really *is* only when it moves, or rather does something. But, conversely, significant action is itself a doing and not a mere means to an end, a negligible if curiously indispensable condition of something else. What we call an action has substance in its own right; indeed it is only, I sometimes think, actions that are fully real. A genuine poem is indeed, as Kenneth Burke insists, a symbolic action. But I would insist that its first and final mode of being is not symbolic but action. The symbol is merely its characteristic mode. And this quite literally is what in our time action painting, for example, makes us understand. The action painting means to be regarded as a *deed*.

Here we all owe a good deal to Mr. Harold Rosenberg, the great advocate of contemporary art. Rosenberg's use of the term "action" in recent visual art plays a critical role not unlike that played by the notion of "tactile values" which Bernard Berenson regarded as definitive of the greatest Florentine painting. If, like Rosenberg, Berenson sometimes made a fetish of his own insight, he has nonetheless enabled many of us to *see* values that are not in fact visible to the uninstructed eye in the frescos of Giotto and Masaccio. In so doing what Berenson did was to make us look at some old masters not only with our eyes but also with our imaginations. Or rather he made us realize that looking at a picture is more than a matter of tracing lines or distinguishing colors or pictorial forms. Rosenberg has done an analogous thing in the case of abstract art. But instead of invoking the tactile imagination he has invoked the whole range of our kinesthetic, motor, and even thermal associations, and in so doing has helped us to "see" *in* the abstract painting what less gifted observers would have been unable to perceive by themselves. And he has done more than this. It is, I believe, a great critical stroke to suggest that an abstract painting can and should be viewed, as it were, under the form not just of movement but of *action*. Here, the point is precisely not a series of accidental pulls and hauls, of jerks and dabs and drips; here, at its best, is something *done*, acted out and acted upon, and something, for that reason, which is not merely a manifestation of "behavior" (in the thin contemporary psychological sense of the word). Viewing the abstract painting under the form of action is therefore also to view it *not* merely as a neutral "aesthetic object" but as a human work, a great doing, as something, that is, which, although not directed to the fulfillment of some ulterior purpose is nonetheless, as Kant pointed out, essentially purposive.

Once one is set to view modern art in this way, a sense of communication and communion becomes possible as it would not were we to view such art as we regard the movements of a falling leaf or a rising wind. Here, that is to say, is an essentially, painfully, human *performance*. One doesn't have to like it, but one has to confront it, recognize it as something done by men not unlike oneself, living in and helping to form and fashion the moving world to which all of us belong. Feeling this is a necessary condition of entering into the world of modern art, and Rosenberg through his concept and imaginative applications of it is thereby our benefactor.

VI

But now, at last, I must bring these ruminations to a close. If I am right, the doctrine of anti-art really belongs to a very old tradition of which all great works of art and all great artists are instinctively representative. For the tradition of anti-art stands first of all for the freedom of the artisan, the worker, the doer to do and to be something in his own right and his own way, to start something going which is unclassifiable because it is an individual thing, which, for that very reason, cannot be dealt with, handled, approached in quite the same way as anything before it. If we contemplate Bellini, then we must not merely contemplate Giorgione; if we listen to Scarlatti, then we must do something a little different with Berlioz or Stravinski. If we enjoy Milton, then for that very reason we must do something else with Eliot, Robert Lowell, and W. D. Snodgrass. Aesthetic experience tells us nothing; it is a common denominator which, because it is and means to be nothing else, can never present the essential thing; it is the act which matters, to the audience as well as to the artist, not a manner of enactment which it shares with everything else. It is high time that the notion of re-creation, and not mere aesthetic re-creation, should be refurbished. Our engagements with acts and works of genius do indeed make of us men of second genius. They too are symbolic and imaginative purposive actions in their own right. Nor does it really matter much whether they match exactly that public action which we call the objective work of art. Of course we need the idea of the objective work of art, among other things, for academic and scholarly purposes, and the prudent man is always academic and scholarly, as I freely and happily allow. But the objective work of art is not what finally engages us, except as academicians and scholars. It is, as the anti-artist and his advocates insist, what happens to them, or rather what they do with the materials at hand that counts. And they are right. Anti-art represents the semi-divine prerogatives of subjectivity, of the irreducible individual, of that *being* which is finally worth bothering about. And the anti-artist, paradoxically, turns to art anything he brings into his work—

a tin can, a speck of dust, a cigarette butt. In a way the collage is the proof perfect that just as there is no boundary between art and reality, so there is none between reality and art. Mind is all.

But the tradition of anti-art represents, secondly, that freedom of the artist and his work, as well as their audiences, to affirm that they belong both ineluctably and freely to a reality, a true reality, which is and has always had its primary existence outside the museum, the concert hall, the reading room. And each artist, we must never tire of saying, is a man first and an artist second, who, if he will not assume the burden of his humanity, is thereby the weaker artist. The man who is an artist first is *ipso facto* a secondary, derivative mannerist, a cultivated stutterer of words that others have already spoken correctly. Make it new, said Pound, perhaps the most eloquent spokesman and practitioner of anti-art in our time. What Pound meant of course is: Break the stock response, the listener, the observer. Make it new. Don't do, or feel you ought to do, with a Motherwell or a Jasper Johns what you do with a Renoir or a Manet. Don't do, or feel you ought to do, with a thing of Cage what you do with the music of Stravinski. Don't above all try to contemplate it. It makes no sense to contemplate a Cage. Indeed, don't even try or hope to like it. Be content with your hate, your active revulsion, your rage. For that, at least, is a first step, a sign of involvement, the beginning—as it has become all too fashionable to say—of a dialogue.

I say this, now, and at last, both in the name of art and in praise of modern art. Just because our art belongs to life, is a part of life, it cannot simply be fondled, admired, enjoyed, appreciated. Caravaggio, I have found, always makes me slightly sick; therefore I am bound to look at him. *Finnegan's Wake* is a monster; therefore I should return to it. I adore *Figaro*; therefore I should beware of him—at least for the time being. Modern art is abrasive, ugly, ghastly, impossible. I can't stand it. But just for that reason I must go to it, not halfway, but all the way. For to go only halfway, so far as works of genius, so far as human beings are concerned, is to go nowhere. To make a far too quick and facile synthesis, anti-art becomes art and enters the great tradition of art through our involvement with it, through our insistence on bringing it, even against our wills, into our lives. The anti-hero is, after all, a hero in his own way, or becomes one when he forces us to identify with him. So with anti-art and the anti-artist. They command our attention because, as Susan Sontag rightly says, they are *there*. And it is in being there that they earn their own right—the only true right—to the precious titles of art and artist. Every artist worthy of the name must deny his paternity, must think of himself even as a kind of Caliban-Prospero, must marvel, before anyone else has a chance to, at the sea change which he has wrought. But it is, of course, the sea itself which has changed. And the sea is older, and more abiding than any of us.

Part IV

THE SITUATION OF THE YOUNG

15

The New Morals

WE HAVE HEARD MUCH LATELY ABOUT SOMETHING called "the new morality." The range of its application is unclear. To some new things on the scene, however, it plainly does not apply: for example, spokesmen of the New Right such as William Buckley (to mention the most fashionable of the lot), although their ungodly pastiche of Christian piety, sour-mash elitism, and holy-American nationalism and militarism, all packaged in a dandy box of old-hat conservatism, has a moral air all its own. The phrase is applied more characteristically to positions on the New Left. But this suggests an exclusively political orientation which is not the case. To some, no doubt, it suggests deviant sexual practices. But deviance, sexual or otherwise, is neither a new nor a moral phenomenon, and moralities obsessed with sex are of a much older vintage. More broadly, it is applied to various youth movements, and of course to the hippies and the new druggies. More deeply it applies to a whole spectrum of dropouts from the affluent society repelled by its prevailing culture and unmoved by its customary stations and duties. It has many representatives within the universities, particularly in the students' protest movements. In fact, because the university has become the indispensable feeder institution and hence a prime symbol of our whole national society, the forms of disquiet, disillusionment, and disaffection so widely manifest on the campuses of our great universities themselves provide salient clues to the moods from which the new morality has emerged.

[*293*

In all events, the new morality is no flash in the pan. It has touched many people in widely different peer- and age-groups: writers, artists, scientists, ministers, teachers, intellectuals employed at various jobs of work. And the predictably disdainful response which it receives from the "men of measured merriment" who form the cadres of our unofficial American Establishment has itself unwittingly served a purpose: to give exponents of the new morality a sense of common identity which they otherwise might lack. By their enemies shall ye know them.

But my use of Sinclair Lewis's mordant phrase may be misleading. For it calls up associations with an earlier generation of hell raisers very different from our own. The Jazz Age is celebrated as an era of splendid—but largely conventional—immoralities, a time of wild parties, hangovers, and well-heeled safaris into the exotic wilderness beyond Main Street: first New York, the jumping-off place, then Paris, Madrid, and points south. It was an age of facile disillusionment, but also of easy pleasures and hopes. Not very much like our own. The following decade was notably more earnest, though less inspired and less amusing. The shift from *The Great Gatsby* and *The Sun Also Rises* to *The Grapes of Wrath* and *For Whom the Bell Tolls* stood for an advance in manifest social consciousness but in little else. The thirties were in fact years of false loyalties, untried ideals, and of nearly universal *naïveté* and ignorance. How little did any of us understand then of what was in store either for ourselves or for our children. Not only did we have no premonition, we had literally no *conception* of the gas chambers of Belsen or the cloud over Hiroshima.

All the same, the Spanish Civil War marks the beginning of a great sea change in the attitudes of Western men toward their whole civilization which, as we shall see, bears directly upon the new morality. For this was the moment at which there set in a vague but sickening sense of general cultural disorder, of imponderable ideological conflicts and moral duplicities, of pervasive institutional incompetence and corruption. Nor was the malaise limited merely to "the others"; that is, to the Fascists, Nazis, Communists, and other "totalitarian" monsters unlike ourselves. On the contrary, it also afflicted the liberal democracies, the Christian churches, the universities: in short, all the presumptive traditional carriers of political and social progress, moral regeneration, and intellectual enlightenment. With the onset of the Second World War, there was momentarily a superficial clearing of the moral air; by their unprovoked total war against both the Western democracies and the Soviet Union, the Nazis localized problems which had been accumulating for over a decade. Soon, however, the whole world found itself involved in a new round of paradoxes whose very terms no one seemed able to comprehend. How, for example, does one cope with total war save by responding in kind? But then what moral difference finally remains between the two sides? And when it is all over, how and on what terms can something called "justice" be done the innocent dead and mutilated, the dispossessed and uprooted? If it comes to that, who is innocent or guilty? One can talk about crimes against humanity. What does "humanity" mean? Who shall decide and, having decided, serve as judge and witness? The victors? Then how shall one answer Thrasymachus' ancient jibe that justice is merely the interest of the stronger? What can be more monstrous than genocide? Nothing possibly—except nuclear war? But are such monstrosities moral acts at all or are they owing to diseases of the soul that can be dealt with only in clinical and therapeutic terms which have not yet even been formulated? Of such paradoxes—a meagre sample—the new morality is a function. There exists some doubt, however, whether it is to be regarded as merely a symptom of disorder or as evidence of a varied effort to create a new moral order—or moral orders—out of the encompassing spiritual chaos of our age. For my part (and this forms a premise of the remarks that follow), it seems possible that something immensely valuable is emerging, from a moral point of view, that could be the harbinger of a new day for many men.

At the moment, it must be admitted, such a belief is hard to sustain. For the word "revolution" is being heard—and not just at gatherings of the New Left but at chaste summer school symposia and meetings of well-groomed civic leaders in a hundred cities. Right and Left, hawk and dove, black and white, North and South, old and young, military and civilian, Jew and Arab; do we even possess any longer a common vocabulary of moral judgment? Let us see.

[*295*

The phrase "the new morality" suggests many things. For some, it undoubtedly conveys the idea that we are undergoing the "transvaluation of values" predicted by Nietzsche three-quarters of a century ago—possibly the first fundamental one since the onset of the Christian era. To others the phrase would have a more ironical, mocking ring, intimating that the Nietzschean prediction has been carried past the point where "superior men" are to find themselves beyond conventional ideas of good and evil and to the point where all men have divested themselves of that life which is at once represented and governed by judgments of moral right and wrong.

Can it, for instance, be that men are finally accepting it as a fact that remorse (as Spinoza long ago argued) and resentment (as Nietzsche contended) are really nothing more than signs of human "bondage" or weakness? And can it be that indignation (as Freud sometimes suggested) is merely the childish reaction of people who have no effective way of coping with people freer and more potent than themselves? If so, then it may not be far-fetched to suppose that we are simply outgrowing morality in the same way that we have outgrown magic, mythology, and superstition, and therefore (as some think) God. For remorse, resentment, and indignation are indeed moral sentiments *par excellence* without which it seems hard to imagine moral relations with other people.

The recent arguments about the Death of God, then, may have an analogy in the examination of the ethical life itself. Nor is the correspondence between those issues, the "death" of God and the "death" of morality, something that humanist philosophers can take lightly. For if, like the humanist's, one's only faith is in man, what happens to one's commitments to man when one has lost faith in *him?* In other words, can moral responsibilities any longer exist for men in despair of one another or of themselves; and can one go through the verbal ceremonies of promising, of contracting, of saying "I shall" and "I ought" where there is nothing to support the ceremony, to give it life and being? If man is to be the moral authority, then he must command respect. But since there is no morality without respect, a new morality must entail a new respect, a new loyalty—even, perhaps, a new faith.

And if morality, nowadays, must begin at home, then it is there also where respect begins.

Through a series of confrontations and arguments which cannot be rehearsed here, modern ethical theory has brought many "enlightened" people to a certain presumption about the nature of morality: unlike the objectively verifiable theories of science, moral judgments and principles are merely expressions and incitements of emotions. No doubt this presumption commonly harbors basic confusion about the difference between the psychological effects of words and their linguistic meanings or functions. For instance, it does not follow from the fact that the word "fire" may serve, in context, to empty a theater that this is any part of its meaning. On the contrary, it is because we understand what "fire" signifies that it can have such a devastating effect upon us. Nevertheless, this blurring of the difference between the logical functions of ethical terms such as "good" and "right" and their psychological effects upon us serves to reinforce a primary attitude of the new moralists: namely, that moral experience is something wholly real—but its reality is wholly personal.

The man who arrives at such an understanding of the nature of morality may experience a sense of loss that can be very keen. It may be only gradually that he picks himself up and says, "Well, it's up to me, then. My moral responsibilities are my own creations, but they are *mine* at least, and that hard fact no one can take away from me. What then ought *I* to do, and what shall *I* become?"

Such are the strains and stresses that provide a central part of the philosophical ambience for "the new morality." It must be said, of course, that there is no such thing as *the* new morality but only certain more or less newish moralities. They overlap undoubtedly in mood and in perspective, but they are not all one thing, and their representatives often radically disagree with one another. Further, although they all are critical of many aspects of contemporary American life, they do not all share a common "hatred" of everything American; nor are they part of an underground conspiracy to do America in. Just the contrary, most of their exponents are concerned to save the beloved country from itself, often in the name of ideals that derive from what is most generous and enlightened in our own American traditions. The phrase "the new morality," then, does not apply exclusively to the moral attitudes of people under thirty, but to people (many of whom do happen to be young in years) who are in one way or another peculiarly exposed to the predicaments of contemporary life. This vulnerability is usually a function of their thoughtfulness and sensitivity, their powers of imagination, and their readiness to assume personal responsibility for their choices and actions. Moreover, some of the men and women who have been most responsive to the moral challenges of our strange, distraught era are self-renewing ancients for whom today is the beginning, as well as conceivably the end, of time. In the matters that concern us here, neither age nor youth gives anyone an edge; we all start virtually from scratch, and the fastest and acutest among us will break no records.

For this, above all, is the age of extreme situations, preoccupation with which is a common factor inherent in all the new moralities. Accordingly there is something extreme, although not necessarily overwrought, about the styles as well as the positions of the new moralities. As we know, the mood of the Establishment in America is repelled by extremes—and by the necessity of confronting them. But the moralities of compromise and adjustment which prevail within the Establishment blind their exponents to the fact that in affairs of life or death, of what Paul Tillich used to call ultimate concern, no basis for compromise and no room for adjustment exist. Such precisely is the situation created by nuclear weapons.

It is still true, no matter how banal the reiteration may be, that the bomb has created the most extreme of all the predicaments that have ever confronted men: the ever-present possibility of the immediate extinction of mankind. The centrality of this possibility to the moral experience of the people I am writing about is incalculable. Somehow we "made it" through the Berlin crisis, the Cuban crisis; we may even make it in Vietnam. What matters is that the chance *has been taken again and again by "rational" men.* Doubtless it will be taken again and again. Until what?

The effect of this possibility on moral attitudes is, to begin with, that it makes it difficult to take seriously the traditional liberal commitment to the principle of the greatest happiness of the greatest number in the longest conceivable run. Happiness can hardly be a problem—whether for the greatest number or even only for ourselves—when what we must concern ourselves with first is simply to exist, to survive. Thus for so many new moralists *the* categorical imperative becomes the immediate and total dismantling of all nuclear weapons and all plants capable of producing them. Failing that, and it is a likely failure, the objective is to dispose one's own country to renounce the use of nuclear weapons and to shut down its own nuclear capacity. This second objective seems perhaps even more unlikely than the first. All the more reason, then, that it is so immensely difficult for new moralists to be patient with the complacencies of ordinary long-run-ist thinking about the general welfare and the greatest happiness of the greatest number. In short, the question of human survival qualifies the attitudes of the new moralists toward everything else.

For some of them the possibility of extinction leads directly to a refusal of all concern for the morrow; what exists, once for all, is a present with no real future built into it. It commits others to what may be called a morality of extreme personal chances or risks, a readiness to do *anything*, at whatever cost to oneself, to make others aware of the horror of nuclear war. Thus ordinary considerations of prudence, which are central in conventional moral deliberation, simply do not faze these new moralists. In this they have much in common with the company of European intellectuals among whom the doctrine of "the gratuitous act" has been prevalent throughout the twentieth century. But whereas the despairing exponents of *l'acte gratuite* deliberately performed acts of the grossest immorality in order to prove their freedom, or indeed their very existence, as moral beings, our new moralists, taking their moral freedom for granted, are often moved rather to extreme acts of selfless dedication to the causes in which they believe. And it is the extremism of such dedication which truly spooks the establishmentarian. From his point of view, the conduct of the new moralist is at best incomprehensible and at worst simply immoral. From the latter's point of view, conversely, it is the representatives of the Establishment, with their apparent capacity to play the game of nuclear poker, who are the extremists: they have risked annihilation not only for themselves but for the world.

It is not my task at this stage to try to settle the question; very likely there are touches of madness—as well as acts of faith—on both sides. But undoubtedly both *are* extremist. The point here, however, is that for the new moralists the pervasive, inescapable "normal madness" of the statesmen and their advisers is a function of the institution of which they are votaries. Patently, beyond reasonable doubt, ordinary "responsible" functionaries of the American nation-state, no less than their Communist counterparts, are systematically incapable of solving the problem of nuclear war. But the doubts engendered by this overwhelming incapacity of the national government and the institutions with which it is interlocked are not easily contained. And among the new moralists analogous doubts exist concerning virtually all of our most characteristic and central institutions: are they any more capable than the nation-states of handling, or indeed even taking seriously, the gigantic man-made problems of our time—the pollution of the air, the water, the land; the noisy, ugly, chaotic, increasingly dangerous, and ever-spreading mega-cities; the exponential overcrowding; "superfluous" millions of human beings incapable either of fending for themselves or of being fended for.

The most agonizing problem for the new moralists, however, does not so much concern the various issues currently racking our traditional system as it does the prior question, what is the real nature of that system? What, in other words, *has* the American liberal democracy itself come to—granted (which many Negroes, for example, understandably do not) that it ever really existed? Their argument is formidable: formally a democracy, they would say, the United States is in fact an oligarchy with a democratic front. In both political parties the "serious" candidates for our greatest office, the Presidency, appear term after term as so many interchangeable parts; regardless of who is elected, all goes on just as before. Who, in any effectual political sense, *uses* the liberties guaranteed in our Constitution? Not certainly the great masses, black or white. Economically there exists a greater span of relative inequality among men in America than anywhere else in the world. And, given the system, what can overcome it? Moreover, in practice, if not in theory, great economic inequality means gross political inequality. What about fraternity, or what is more commonly these days called community (to come to the third crucial term of the triad of revolutionary principles which our founding fathers, as well as the French, so passionately invoked)? As Professor Daniel Bell argues, we have become a national society every operative part of which is tied organically to every other. But an organic system by no means makes a community. In sum, it is as easy for dispossessed members to say of the American system as many have said of Christianity: the system has not failed for it has never been tried. Here, at bottom, is a crisis of faith. For many new moralists the question is whether one can any longer reasonably repose one's faith in bare forms of liberal democracy. The answer is not easy.

Less spectacular but more insidious are the collateral breakdowns in supporting institutions—schools, churches, families. Now, the possibility of tolerable popular government, as Jefferson foresaw, depends upon an enlightened electorate; and yet our great public secondary school system is, by general consent, a shambles. Nor is the problem here only one of segregation, whether of rich from poor, or of black from white. It is as much or more a matter of tenth-rate schooling where education is most desperately needed: in the great slums and ghettos, rural as well as urban, where *all* children so rarely get a second chance—and where for years now the blind have been leading the blind over cliffs of ignorance, boredom, and hatred of the whole life of the mind.

Far more shocking to the American people, of course, has been the discovery of failure in the most extensive, complex, and (it goes without saying) affluent system of higher education in the history of the race. One need not retell this dismal story in detail. In the present context what most needs emphasis are not so much anxieties about overcrowded classrooms, a frequently obsolescent curriculum, or the inadequacy of faculty, but the pervasive sense among many of the most alert students and the ablest junior faculty that the American multiversity, at the top of its own form, as in California, is an educational monster which devours its young, processing them into a kind of all-purpose compost for refertilizing the great briar patch of the national society. Such liberal, and liberalizing, education as our ablest young men and women get is either provided for them in high schools or else gleaned in a hit-or-miss fashion from a few "distribution" courses and such para-academic educational encounters as the university "communities" may provide. Yet it is these same bright, immensely skilled young people who will join the elite corps that sets the standards for the national society itself. The point cannot be overemphasized. Liberal education is neither a luxury nor a mere aesthetic prejudice of those inclined to it. As its very name implies, it is nothing less than the indispensable carrier of the formative ideals and restraints that constitute a large part of the formal ideology of traditional liberal culture. It is the universities themselves, by making that ideology irrelevant to the academic and professional aspirations of ordinary university students and teachers, that have helped to prepare the scripts for those new moralists who declare that our traditional ethics is an irrelevant subterfuge which not even its official professors sincerely believe.

The paradox of the multiversity is that, creating the very conditions that dispose the new moralists to scepticism about the value of the education it offers, it has also proven to be a breeding ground *par excellence* for some of the most vital impulses within the new morality itself. For it is impossible to bring together so many lively minds and varied talents in one concentrated environment as the multiversity does, without creating a myriad of unanticipated educational situations rich in meaning and interest.

When he turns to the churches, the new moralist, while certainly indifferent to their institutional demands, is rather surprisingly often moved to speak more kindly of them. Here, at least, there appears to be a deep internal reformation: Pope John XXIII and the ecumenical movement; the superb example set by churchmen of all sects, Christian and Jewish, as leaders in the civil rights and peace movements and other socially disreputable causes; the intellectual and moral vitality of some of the new theologians, with their willingness to abandon ancient shibboleths that distract men from forms of assent, trust, dedication, and love more central to the authentic religious consciousness.

It is, perhaps, the family, regarded by the whole Western tradition as *the* indispensable social institution, which has been most subject to the crises of our age. Indeed it is at the level of the family where the prevailing institutional malaise is evident even to the most conventional of minds. The decline of parental authority is scarcely worth remarking; even to talk in such terms is to speak out of a bygone era. More to the point, the family, which is critically affected by the ever-increasing mobility of human beings, has ceased to serve as a primary carrier of moral and religious ideals or to provide the fundamental psychological security for its members. No longer is it the enduring center of personal affections and loyalties. Many roles once performed by it are performed, however inadequately, by the welfare state. Once upon a time the breakup of a "home" was a calamity; now there hardly seems to be a home to break up.

And with the decline of the family, a whole series of attendant institutions has tended to disappear also. For one, the neighborhood, which once upon a time seemed an extension of the home and the family themselves. In megalopolis, including, in particular, suburbia, relationships with neighbors, though often amiable, *must* be casual, since quite literally today's neighbor is gone tomorrow. Indeed, the very amiability of suburban neighbors is itself typical and symbolic of the dispersed, casual, shallow amenities of modern life which have replaced the enduring affections and friendships of an earlier age. To be sure, such a way of life has its compensations. If one no longer deeply and abidingly loves other particular individuals, neither does one have the time to learn deeply to hate them. And so the whole schedule of human emotions and sentiments, signified by the words "friend" and "enemy," "love" and "hate," "loyalty" and "disloyalty," and the rest, tend to lose their meaning or, rather, acquire different sorts of focus, involving different sorts of commitment, affection, and disaffection. In one way we all live not only in a much less stable but in a much less concrete world. Processes replace substances; events, things; people, persons; movements, people. What does the personal identity symbolized by a proper name really come to when to the world one is a system of numbers and identity cards? And if the world does not care who *I* am, how indeed can I think of *myself* as an enduring person, a continuing center of loyalties, responsibilities, and human roles?

This fragmentation of the self, this replacement of the old casual-historical orders, this emulsification of the world is manifest in an art and a literature that have become abstract, nonpersonal, and "meaningless." How can there be, say, a serious art of portraiture, when a face is only a face; how can there be novels like

[*303*]

Jane Austen's or Leo Tolstoi's when there are no longer ties, identities, sentiments, and significant actions out of which one can form a history-story in the traditional sense? Our contemporary art is indeed an anti-art, inventive, ingenious, brilliant, extraordinary. But the emotions it expresses, the feelings it embodies, and the attitudes it engenders are an affront and a wound to conventional sensibilities. The new art, or anti-art, cuts off, or down, the "ordinary" expectations, identifications, emotional loyalties out of which older writers and artists formed their "worlds." And if it gives little "pleasure," it isn't meant to.

But, the reader asks, what is the point of this lugubrious recitation of failures and breakdowns? Not that, to be sure, it has all been lugubrious or wholly a record of breakdown. In the church and in the environment of the university are impressive signs of renewal, and in the art or anti-art of our time there is not only a profoundly interesting commentary on the "metaphysics" of contemporary social life, but an often exhilarating response to it. And in the realm of politics, the very intensity and range of the various protest movements may be construed as evidence of some kind of ideological reconstruction. Still, the picture is somber enough. My point in sketching it has been neither to create a sense of nostalgia nor to strike a just balance between the dark and the light on our institutional landscape. Rather is it to show that the assumptions inherent in the old conventional moralities are to a great extent functions of an institutionalized social and human world that does not exist for the new moralists. From an ethical point of view, the life of the ordinary person—that is, the conventional political man, educator, church-goer, family man, art lover, good citizen, and good man—is largely (if never entirely) a matter of what the philosopher F. H. Bradley called "my station and its duties." The code of such a person consists of obligations incurred by the institutional relationships and practices in which his life involves him. He does not elect to have a father and a mother, to be an American or the member of a particular race. Such ties are simply *there*, and in discovering them he also finds his ethical identity.

When this world breaks down, when its "stations" fail to stay put or involve him in conflicting responsibilities which he cannot resolve, his sense of objective right and wrong becomes insecure and, in extreme cases, disintegrates. To some extent, of course, this happens to every person. Alienation in some measure is part of the human lot. But conflict can be lived with only if the conflicting loyalties are genuine and the values they represent are themselves known to be stable and real. For "us," however, it is not a matter only of finding a way to resolve temporarily conflicting objective values, but of dealing with a world in perpetual crisis, full of shattering institutional changes, of unprecedented troubles created in large part by the very factors on which modern man has hitherto prided himself: the immense progress of exact science and the astounding inventiveness and productivity of technology.

Know the truth and the truth shall set you free, saith the sage. Is this any longer true? Most of us still believe it, but who knows it to be so? For the first time, the products of our knowledge have created an immense new ignorance about man and his society. Inadvertently, it seems science itself has presided over the birth of a new kind of man in a new kind of world, about which neither the ancient wisdom of the race nor the sciences themselves can tell us much.

Here, then, we have a significant factor in that special tension which is popularly known as the "generation gap." The older generation, if the preceding descriptions are right, still thinks mainly of "objective' ethical certitudes. Its members function within a "system" whose code forms a network of rules the authority of which they accept as a matter of course. This does not mean necessarily that they are uncritical or that they have no genuine moral problems. It means, rather, that their problems in the ordinary course have established boundaries. And even when they raise certain questions of boundary, as they do on occasion, there exist critical ground rules by which they justify proposed changes in some part of the system. They resemble the players of a game: they have a book, often quite informal, of rules governing proper forms of play, and umpires, agreed upon in advance, for adjudicating disputes that may arise in the course of the game. Should the issue arise, they themselves would finally have to decide whether to play the game at all; but normally the issue doesn't arise. Nor do they readily understand people who simply do not see the point of playing.

It should be emphasized that individuals who live simply as they like are *not* playing a new kind of moral game. Nor are they exponents of a new morality; for they do not live in moral terms at all. I do not know how many of them, old or young, exist in our society. Every age breeds its outlaws, just as every moral being has moments when the sense of responsibility fades out and moral agency seems a wholly external thing.

The new moralists, however, are not outlaws; they simply fail to see the point of the game as it is conventionally played. Given the overwhelming chaos of the age, the wonder is that they exist at all, that they display so much sensitivity, seriousness, and compassion, and that they should try so hard to find ways to cope responsibly with all the bafflements of contemporary life. For my own part, I am astonished not that there should be *new* moralities but that there should be new *moralities*.

Whatever the differences among new moralists, of which I shall say something presently, one thing they all have in common: a new sense of what morality is. For them any morality worth discussing begins at home, and judgment is directed above all to one's own problems and choices. Moral principles now become first-personal precepts for the guidance of one's own conduct through the maze of one's life. It is no longer possible to talk of something called "*the* moral point of view"; the question is not what "one" should do, but what "I" should do, not what are "the rights of man," but what, man or no man, "my" commitments and loyalties are to be. No doubt we are members of mankind, but before anything we are individual persons who must decide for ourselves not only whether we are to be men but what it is to be a man. The point is not that we are wiser or more precious than anyone else, but that this, our being, is not encompassed by definitions others have set for us. But whatever else we may be or become, we are not just things, not just values of a variable, not functions of a general run, social, institutional, or whatever. And if we should come together, form a community, it is, and can be, only for so long as "we" endure, and it is only we, by our common intent, who can make it endure, who can indeed make it real at all.

It is just here where one discerns a second distinctive feature of the new moralities. If morality begins in first-personal responsibility, only by mutual consent do "my" responsibilities and "yours" become "our" responsibilities. To be sure, we may assume responsibility for someone else as well, but he does not in virtue of that fact alone become "one of us." This does not mean that we intend to be exclusive; we may be ready to accept anyone who cares to join as our friend or comrade. There may be a rule between us that anybody at all can come in simply by opening the door. (That, in fact, is one of the most agreeable attitudes of the hippies, and in this respect the rest of us might very well go to school to them.) Still, community is not something any longer to be taken for granted; it has to be renewed each day, not just ceremonially, but by sacrificial acts of mutual trust and loyalty.

But the matter goes beyond this. Recently I heard an extremely serious and intelligent Negro explain what he took to be the root of the Black Power movement. For him it was not at bottom a matter of power but of community. The phrase, "We, the people of the United States, in order to form a more perfect union," meant, in his view, "We the white men of the United States." It did not include "them." As I understood him, he was saying that there are, at the very least, two Americas, one white and the other black. These ideally form two distinct communities with different fundamental loyalties and obligations. He did not condemn the whites; such condemnation was meaningless. Nor did he deny a certain sense of responsibility for the whites. The point was rather that his fundamental moral being belongs, first of all, to the black community or, better perhaps, to a community of blacks who have discovered at terrible cost a sense of common identity, mutual respect, and desire to be together, away from the alien whites with whom they are now entangled in a wholly abstract, unreal, and purely political society.

I have observed or felt the same sort of thing in other groups. Of course, such a position can be put to ugly use. But certainly in part the radically pluralist view of American society is a response to the sense of the unreality, the inauthentic canting thinness of much conventional liberal talk of "one world," "mankind," "the rational animal," "the community of men." And feelings of revulsion at the idea of an abstract "humanity"—as witness most of the best writing of the past decades—often presage the emergence of a sense of mutual concern and responsibility between people who, before, felt scarcely any sense even of personal identity and self-respect.

But one must speak more concretely of the new generation and the communities that are growing up within it. Plainly a great part of the brunt of every war must be borne by the very young. They must face, if anyone does, the dangers of physical combat, the psychological strains of military life, and the problems of rehabilitation when, if ever, peace returns. Yet, in formally democratic societies these same young people have no share in the so-called democratic process. They are peremptorily drafted by a government which is not theirs in "defence" of values they have not made their own. Who are "they?" Not the young only, but also, especially, the young poor who are systematically disadvantaged, educationally, psychologically, and physically. Out of school, it is they who find it difficult or impossible to find employment. And when they do, it is grubby, meaningless, degrading work. Their relationship to the national society is marginal, and their civil rights, for want of exercise or means of legal defense, remain vestigial and formal. The "social system," so far as they can form an idea of it, means one thing: exclusion. In the face of these and other deep cleavages between the young and the system—with which, naturally enough, they identify their elders—those belonging to the generation "under thirty," like the blacks, tend to form both a community and a subculture unto themselves. In lesser or greater degree, they become aware of a moral solidarity with one another, and of a responsibility to one another, sometimes against the system which, like the weather, they simply endure. And their odd costumes and manners, their beards and long hair, serve as identification cards which are at the same time badges of dissociation from the national society and its institutions.

To their elders, of course, all this too often means arrogance, selfishness, a diminished sense of public responsibility, immaturity. Reinforced by images of indiscriminate sex, drugs, wasted "opportunity," it also means, not a new morality, but a new immorality. And this conventional "moralism" of the elders who are all too ready to judge and to condemn does little more than reinforce in turn the solidarity of the young with one another and confirm them in their own sense of what is significant, decent, moral.

Their attitudes toward sex symbolize most strikingly the quality of this new morality. Whole books have been written about it, and every popular magazine exploits it for its own purposes. Here I offer no more than a few observations concerning immensely delicate and complex patterns of feelings which people of my generation have not always placed in perspective. Above all, it is essential to bear in mind the general breakdown, already alluded to, of the family as an institution and especially *the* basic social institution. Throughout our century sex has been increasingly dissociated from marriage and from the family. Contraceptives, however, have until recently been hard to come by, frequently illegal and expensive, and they all too often didn't work. Thus there were practical, if fewer and fewer moral, restraints in premarital sex. Now the dissociation is not only taken for granted by many, perhaps most, young people, but "the pill," cheap and safe, can be obtained by any high school or college girl without much difficulty.

With the ancient "dangers" of premarital sex apparently nonexistent, and the pleasures thereof obvious, to ask young people to abide by the sexual taboos by which their own mothers and fathers frequently did not and do not now abide is a little like asking executives of great corporations to abide by the medieval rules of the "fair market." It doesn't make sense to them, morally or any other way. This does not mean that in relation to sex and love young people have gone beyond good and evil. To be sure, the area within which they feel free in conscience to do as they please is much wider; taboos against homosexuality, for instance, are rapidly disappearing. Here, as elsewhere, new notions of loyalty and love are emerging, stripped of what are considered to be the hypocrisies of the traditional attitudes that go by these names.

The new moralists are more "cool" toward sex than their elders. But this does not mean that they have no sexual *morals*. It means that they are more careful or reticent about displays of moral feeling, rather in the way that the English are about displays of affection generally. It means also that they have fewer rules about sexual immorality. They deal with each situation in this sphere as they do in others, with a concern for its own integral worth, a question that can't be settled by mechanical application of a code book of sexual mores. Furthermore, the young are less disposed than their elders to confuse questions of manners with questions of morals, questions of conventional rudeness or incivility with questions of immorality. And since questions of etiquette interest them little or not at all, they tend to be less full of resentments, less disposed to take umbrage, less exposed to affronts, to conventional jealousy, to the whole emotional paraphernalia of conventional sexual relations. Given this different focus, the moral agent is accordingly faced with a new set of problems.

The younger new moralists, consciously or unconsciously taking a leaf out of the writings of certain radical Christian thinkers, including St. Augustine, Pascal, and Kierkegaard, are preoccupied with possibilities of self-discovery and self-transcendence, of being "twice-born," that may require a sharp break with the immanent personality with which one comes into the world. Their tendency to reject all "ideologies" may itself be taken, in part, as a token of their repudiation of the ideal—brought down to us from the Greeks—of a self whose norms are prefabricated, whether by society, by history, by human nature, whatever. And again, they decline to accept any form of activity, intellectual or otherwise, as self-evidently preeminent, or the exercise of the faculties required by it as constituting man's highest good. The crucial problem of freedom—of self-identification and self-determination—becomes for them the most intimate and most personal of problems, about which no one can speak for "all mankind."

The new moralists, less certain than their predecessors of a stable, predictable, not to say millennial, future for themselves and their offspring, are disposed, as Henry Adams once put it in describing the heroine of his novel *Democracy,* "to drive life into a corner" and to force it to bring forth its quotidian yield of authentic realities and intensities. In most of them there exists a deep fund of idealism; but it is the last-ditch idealism of young men and women who have had to discover their own resources of devotion and responsibility. To John F. Kennedy's overpublicized cry, "Ask not what your country can do for you: ask what you can do for your country," the reply is prompt: "*I* must first discover what is my own true country, and there alone shall I plant my flag." This reply belongs to a deep American tradition, inscribed in the Declaration of Independence, Whitman's *Leaves of Grass,* Emerson's "Self-Reliance," and above all Thoreau's "Civil Disobedience." The contemporary literature of dissent, too, is a literature whose central demand is for independence and self-respect—one which insists that morally speaking, "I" am the end of the line. In fact it is a literature of moral autodidacticism. And as such, no matter how admirable, it naturally runs the risk of breeding other attitudes that I, for one, find less admirable.

Not every liberty, for instance, is worth taking; not every act of rebellion is a stake for the good life. Some exponents of the new morality seem to me at once superficial and pretentious. Moreover, they too often exhibit a tendency toward out-group conformity which, sadly, seems little more than an inverted image of the official culture. Angry young men, too, can come dressed in uniform. And in the case of the new druggies, their rage for "experience" passes over into a form of hedonism—which is, of course, an abandonment of the life of self-determination.

Perhaps the most disturbing attitude among some of the new moralists is a pervasive failure of discrimination—what I call "the false democracy" and "the false equality." The fact that this failure is intentional, deriving from a principled opposition to discriminations of any sort, makes it seem no less idiotic to me. A free soul is more important than a free beer, and the inequality of human beings before the law is a profounder disgrace than the offensive status symbols of a culture that calls itself democratic but is really elitist from top to bottom. At present, there is also a tendency to confuse novelty with originality, oddity with independence. One is tempted nowadays to speak of the banality of the new. In a world where everything shocks, who needs the latest bit of clever perversity? And in a world of monstrous immorality, who is fetched by the latest immoralist?

These, however, are all matters of perspective and judgment. Important as they are, they are still more or less incidental. A more serious problem is the fickleness of many of the new intransigents. Nothing, I find, is so dead as last year's protest, no one so forgotten as the leader of last semester's sit-in. At the University of Michigan, where the teach-in originated, I recently asked a friend what had happened to the peace movement. It was there all right, but it was not very visible. Instead, that winter, Ann Arbor was all agog over the daring films—in particular *Flaming Creatures* and *Blow Job*—which the students' cinema guild was showing, or trying to show. And when the local police arrested the students in charge and confiscated the former movie, there was a tremendous uproar. Civil rights were being violated, academic freedom infringed by gross and arbitrary impositions from representatives of "the law." The university authorities declined to offer support or even legal counsel to its jugged students. "Questions of law," they said in effect, were not their affair. The university's behavior—not to say the police's—was nauseating. At the same time, I wondered (out loud in a talk that was the germ for this article) what had happened to the earlier passionate concern for rights that had been more profoundly infringed elsewhere in America. And while the students and junior faculty spent—I do not say wasted—their energies over the pornography bit, other and (as it seemed to me) deeper moral issues were temporarily forgotten. The students remained preoccupied with local campus affairs that were, in the winter and spring before "Detroit," minuscule. Where was the old insistent solidarity with other "disadvantaged" groups, with all the wretched of the land? No doubt "we" whites and academicians were not wanted (or trusted) by the successors to the old civil-rights movements. So what? Because "they" are black, must we then retreat into our whiteness? If the new moralists are to be taken as seriously as they deserve, they must learn to recognize the difference between matters of passing and local outrage and those of general, continuing concern. Too often the impression is conveyed, not of a new morality but of a new gadget, not of a new determination to discover one's own vocation through what Mill called "experiments in living," but of a new offbeat victory for current image-makers. The new moralists cannot expect others to take them seriously if they do not take themselves seriously. Sincerity like loyalty begins at home.

Nor am I at all impressed by the new amoralists who really mean to go beyond good and evil. For a life without responsibility to itself has abandoned altogether the Socratic search for self-understanding. And when Nietzsche and his successors praise, or seem to praise, a life that has passed altogether beyond morality, they are praising, perhaps unwittingly, a form of existence that is not Utopian but simply mindless. The moral life is ineluctably a part of the life of the mind, and it is for the sake of this life that I for my part am prepared to bear witness to and for the new moralities of my age, against the conventionalists, the establishmentarians, the realists, and the pragmatists who serve the national society, with its affluence and its bombs, its sleek suburbs and hideous cities, its fabulous scientific technology and its sick universities.

Finally I must express my own dismay about the abandonment by many new moralists on the political left of the noble tradition of *civil* liberty. If one wishes to make points, there are many scores to be made against the liberal tradition. I know this and have myself frequently pointed them out. But, like Irving Howe, I am astonished at the indifference of so many on the New Left to the liberal ideas of which their own are frequently bastard offspring. In my book, John Locke, John Stuart Mill, and Bertrand Russell are great, ever-to-be-revered names. I shall, on occasion, continue to attack their opinions, but I shall not forsake the great causes of liberal freedom because they sometimes faltered or were occasionally obtuse. I am prepared to admit (alas) that such liberals as Hubert Humphrey or Adlai Stevenson (you name them) "sold out." The neopragmatic liberals of the New Frontier are no allies of mine; not vaguely. No matter, we are talking here about principles and ideals, not about coteries, inside-men who have lost their way.

These admonitions, let me add, are addressed in the first instance to myself even more than to my younger friends, for I too am shallow, fickle, insincere, a victim of the image-makers. I too on occasion confuse a new resentment with moral insight. And I too have been misled by Ezra Pound's slogan "Make it new!" But all this is precautionary. I cast my lot irrevocably with all the young sons of Socrates who, in our time, insist that the only morality worthy of the name is one which, finally, one discovers for oneself. If an unreflective life is not worth living, an unreflective morality, whatever its sanctions or authority, is not worth having. Indeed, it is not a morality at all but a form of politics and ideology. And ideologies, indispensable as they are to an even tolerable social existence, must always be made to play second fiddle. This is what the exponents of the new moralities know. It is what they must try, by their sustained example, to make the appointed guardians of our own more fateful *polis* also understand. In the time of Socrates it was already too late, for Athens, which the Thucydidean

Pericles had so proudly called "the school of Greece," was doomed. Is it too late for our would-be free society, which was also once a light to the world, to save itself? I do not know. But I know this: the time is short, and the nights are growing longer.

16

Youth and Its Rights

I

WE LIVE IN A TIME OF MONUMENTAL PARADOXES. WHEN they occur in the mathematical and natural sciences, paradoxes represent a breakdown in thought. But when they occur in the social or political, the moral or religious spheres, where by definition thinking concerns our existence as human beings, they can become mortally dangerous. However, paradoxes wear two faces: one a face of puzzlement, confusion, defeat or despair, the other of fascination, challenge, opportunity. The most stunning breakthroughs, whether in the sciences, in philosophy, or in social and psychological thought, occur when someone discovers a new technique, invents a new tool, achieves a new perspective which, by enabling us to see through or around a paradox, enables us both to have our cake and eat it. Then we no longer need strive merely to shore up our ruins. Even tragedy is redeemed when we convert it into art. Now, for the time being, we are once more out in the blue, and so having given form to chaos, we can press on to new reaches of human possibility.

Some of the contemporary paradoxes I have called human or existential may be witnessed (the selection is virtually at random) in the so-called "death of God" movement in religion, in the new moralities which at first look seem merely new forms of immorality or amorality, in the cult of anti-art, in the resistance and civil disobedience movements, in various student revolt movements which appear to threaten the very conditions of student existence.

This last paradox, which might be called alternatively "the paradox of the student" or "the paradox of the university," is but one of a complex of "paradoxes of youth" or, again alternatively, "paradoxes of maturity." In this essay I shall suggest some ways of coping with those which confront us all in our thinking about rights and responsibilities of young people in an age in which many youths view themselves virtually as a race apart while at the same time demanding immediate entrance into the ranks of adult citizens. On this score, the young people's position is merely a counterimage of their elders'. We—and here I include many who still seek to preserve some identity with a tradition that calls itself liberal and democratic—subject our youth to a permanent Selective Service about whose existence, standards of selection, or uses youth has little or nothing to say. Our economic and educational systems undoubtedly offer extraordinary opportunities for rapid advancement at least to well-off or gifted young men and women. For example, youths who have not cut their wisdom teeth are offered full professorships or placed in charge of research projects demanding the most intricate skills and the subtlest forms of understanding. Yet our legal and political systems still treat them as minors or semi-majors who cannot vote or else are unable to hold public office. Beyond all this our affluent society has fathered an affluent youth, free to do and to possess many things of which a half century ago even the most extravagant members of the leisure class did not dream. Yet in matters of political judgment and social responsibility we treat them, especially in crucial situations, as children.

II

Now political, social and moral attitudes are always correlated, directly or indirectly, with conceptions of human nature. Before going on to develop a new theory about rights of youth, we must therefore ask whether certain traditional ideas about human development do not stand in need of revision. The classical view, inherited with little modification from the Greeks, is that man's nature is largely fixed, and that as in the case of all other natural kinds, there is a certain mature human character which every unthwarted human being seeks to actualize. About a half-century ago, a fascinating inversion of this theory, identified largely with the name of Freud, began to take its place. According to this view (vastly oversimplified), the fundamental psychological problems of adult life are set in infancy or early childhood. From the moment he is thrust into the world, each individual is subject to certain characteristic traumas, complexes, forms of repression and compulsory release or compensation, which largely govern his behavior for the rest of his life. Liberation comes, for a very few, through a lengthy and usually costly process of analysis, devoted to the uncovering of archetypal forms of maladjustment, based on the same infantile traumas and complexes.

Here, it is unnecessary to dwell upon the overwhelming preoccupation with the sexual drive and its misadventures in this psychology or its oversimplified conception of the mature human personality. Instead, let us look at some more recent ideas which provide bases for a more subtly differentiated account of the phases of human development, according to which the child is to be viewed neither as father to the man nor as the man in embryo, but on the contrary each child, like the aging individual that will one day replace it, is in certain respects a creature unto itself. In particular, I have in mind the work of psychologists such as Erik Erikson (who, significantly, came to his work as a psychoanalyst after a career as an artist) who now talk very compellingly about a number of distinct life-stages, each with its own qualities of being, its distinct forms of creativity and sterility, its corresponding fulfillments and failures, its characteristic crises and ways of coping with them. From this point of view, as it were, none of us is a single, developing person, but rather a sequence of related persons. In an important sense, two adolescents may in fact have a closer, more intimate identity with one another than either has with the strange oldster that will one day bear its name.

My own interest is in a conception of youth which overlaps but does not exactly coincide with Erikson's notion of the life stage of adolescence. Yet much that he has to say about adolescents as "transitory existentialists by nature because they become suddenly capable of realizing a separate identity," has direct bearing upon the ideas I have come to in developing a new theory about rights of youth. The conception of youth I have in mind also overlaps the next stage in Erikson's "epigenetic cycle," which he calls "young adulthood." At this stage, as he describes it, the individual youth, having made a start in dealing with his problems of personal identity, then moves on to issues created by interpersonal relationships, particularly such intensely personal ones as friendship, love, and sexual intimacy. But this is also a time when the crisis of identity, as Erikson calls it, partly resolves itself in the form of a special sense of "intimacy with oneself, one's inner resources, the range of one's excitements and commitments." And just as the adolescent, actively seeking his own identity, is subject to special problems concerning the social roles he is expected to play, which he often resolves through some sort of generalized religious or ideological conversion, through identification with some larger presence to which he can give his loyalty, so the young adult becomes involved in distinctive problems of isolation which he tries to resolve, for example, through marriage and, according to his talents and interests, through some form of dedicated work. The period of adolescence and young manhood is thus a time both of passionate searching for independence and of striving for ideal attachments and forms of unselfish achievement.

Much of this spells out what we already know intuitively. Who can fail to perceive the extraordinary precocity, the energy, and capacity for sympathetic involvement in great (as well as less great) "causes" which are so characteristic of human beings in this marvelous springtime of life? And who can be unaware of the special forms of vulnerability, the yearnings, restlessness, loneliness, and unspeakable unhappiness to which young people are liable?

Now it seems to me that if thinkers like Erikson are even half right, we must question all approaches to problems concerning rights and responsibilities of youths, inbred in us since the time of the Greek philosophers, which treat youth as merely a potential something else and the time of youth as merely a bridge between childhood and manhood. Every period of life, if it comes to that, is a time of transition, and this is no less true of the householder of fifty than of his youthful children. A youth is already something, with a form and an identity of his own. And if, from one point of view, he is not fully mature, the same can as well be said, from another, of the man supposedly "at the height of his powers" who has yet not attained to that distinctive ripeness and wisdom one finds in the works of such incomparable, self-rejuvenating old men as Dewey and Russell and Freud, as Verdi and Stravinski and Yeats, or as Tillich and Martin Buber. Indeed, the very word "rejuvenate" itself suggests that in restructuring our thinking about the problems of youth and the rights pertaining thereto, we may find clues to a reconstruction of our attitudes toward the problems of later phases of the human life cycle, and so discover good reasons to modify uninflected and uniformitarian doctrines about the rights of man which we have inherited, like pieces of old furniture, from another era when the pressing needs of men in societies created problems of equality and fraternity, as well as liberty, in many ways quite different from our own.

III

Our problems about rights of youth would remain formidable even with the help of the best available psychological theories about this extraordinary period of life. Unfortunately, the very terms in which the topic is discussed—youth, adulthood, maturity, and above all, rights—are subject to misconceptions that cause us to falter in the very act of thinking about them. Worse, they are not neutral terms. Through them, on the contrary, we contemplate roles, assign functions, and articulate decisions central to all political, social, and moral life. How can we answer one of the great and pressing questions of our age, whether youths should share the rights of adults, if because of misconceptions and preconceptions about what a right, a youth, or an adult is, we cannot clearly envision the possibilities which the question demands us to consider? I fear there is nothing for it, then, but to refurbish some parts of the conceptual apparatus with which we must work.

Our notions about the concept of a right are perhaps the most confused. By this time moral philosophers have done some part of the job of removing the accumulated dust that overlays our conceptions of good and evil and moral right and wrong. Legal and political philosophers are making progress with such terms as law, authority, revolution and, save us, ideology. But the elusive concept of a right, which has such important applications in every sphere of human action, is covered with a dozen coats of ideological varnish which are nearly impossible to remove.

For example, since the advent of utilitarianism and pragmatism in the ninteenth century, influential thinkers everywhere have tended to conflate the ideas of right and good. This error is egregious. Granted that many, though by no means all, rights are among our most precious political or human values, there are many goods, as matters stand, to which we can claim no right at all. The task of a doctrine of rights is to specify, and hence to restrict, those goods to which we can meaningfully regard ourselves as entitled. That is why a true bill of rights is of such immense importance to a society. For only after making sure that no relevant rights would be seriously infringed can we consider whether a good is justly to be pursued. The "pragmatic theory" of rights, as I shall call it, encourages its advocates, governmental officials as well as private citizens, to treat rights as merely one set of values among many which therefore may be thrown indiscriminately into the pot of deliberation where prospective policies are cooked. This is its overwhelming fault. For it returns us, in effect, to a Hobbesian state of nature where the liberties of each man, subject to no constraining bills of entitlement are unlimited.

I am not suggesting here that it is never proper to abridge or alter rights. But anyone who would do so has his work cut out for him, for it is the abridgment, not the right, that needs justification, and the good achieved by abridging or abandoning it must be at once overwhelming and at least as palpable as the right in question. This is why many young people, often conservative in their basic attitudes toward the American system, are moved to rebellion by pragmatic political and military policies which, in the name of an impalpable something called "the national interest," ride roughshod over their rights both as youths and as young citizens of a supposedly liberal democracy. It is also why black men, not ill-disposed to the principles of a free society, are maddened by pragmatic realists who calmly ask them to wait indefinitely for substantive enjoyment of their rights until, say, the Cold War has been won, until the city planners have cleared the slums, or the political parties have been made responsive to something other than their own interests.

Two other misconceptions are worth mentioning, for they also are prevailing sources of confused thinking and acting. One is the "gift theory" of rights. According to it, rights are happy benefits bestowed upon us by some beneficent person or institution: a relative, God, the state, the university. This will not do. All of us, I trust, are grateful for the gifts we receive from known or unknown donors. But unless we are mad we do not on that account claim them as rights. No right is violated when a gift is not forthcoming. Among the ancient Hebrews, men were held to enjoy certain rights, which God himself is bound to respect, in virtue of a Covenant made between Him and His people. That covenant in fact was taken as proof that God is a responsible person, not simply an all-powerful Santa Claus. The trouble with the gift theory, as we shall see more clearly presently, is that it ignores the correlative notion of responsibility, without which the concept of a right is meaningless. One of the things we perceive intuitively to be wrong with even the most benevolent of dictators is that the privileges they bestow are merely gifts. For what is given according to one's pleasure may be withheld for the same reason. Those radicals who profess to despise liberalism would do well to ponder that one of the immense strengths of the liberal tradition of John Locke and his followers among our own revolutionary founding fathers was their grasp of the confusions implicit in the gift theory of rights.

But now we have to consider, all too briefly, another theory which, while it contains much truth, still does not provide an adequate general conception of rights. This is the "juristic" or "legalist" theory, according to which, following the model of the law, a right is to be understood as a recognized social practice. From this point of view, for example, the right to be at liberty amounts in fact to a system of social or legal permissions which a society or its government recognizes and for violations of which it provides acknowledged remedies. Accordingly, this theory advances a great step beyond those previously considered. For by implication it clearly recognizes that when somebody has a right then some other person or persons have a responsibility to observe or protect it. Furthermore, legal rights are forms of practice determined by the rules of a legal-political system. In this connection it should be remarked that another merit of the classical liberal tradition is owing to its insistence that sound government, which includes an acceptable system of law, must have as its first objective the establishment of a set of such practices in the form of a constitutional bill of rights that limits the spheres of public as well as private action.

Two other merits of the juristic theory deserve mention; one concerning the concept of a law and hence, by implication, that of a legal right; the other, at least in its contemporary forms, concerning its view of the general relation of law to morality. As to the first point, because the juristic theory contends that a law as such cannot be fully understood as "a command of a sovereign," as realist utilitarians and pragmatists have contended, but only as a rule tied umbilically to a general rule of law, to which any rightful sovereign is also subject, it helps to protect us from discriminating forms of cynicism, to which young people in our times seem particularly prone, which treat legal rights as nothing more than *de facto* permissions of those who hold power.

I am not unmindful here that existing legal systems are very imperfect approximations to a true rule of law. Every black man, every migrant worker, and many, many youths (most recently in Chicago and on many of our university campuses) have learned to their sorrow that our own legal system is full of unpardonable lapses from the commonest principles of justice inherent in a rule of law. All the same, to vary a thesis of David Hume's, the first rational act of those driven to overthrow an existing legal-political system must be to establish another more equitable, surer, and closer to the principle of a true rule of law. Nor, important as it is, need we make a sacred cow of the idea of a rule of law; for no matter how excellent it may be it does not exhaust what we understand by justice. And justice is not the only good we require of a politically organized society. A rule of law, in short, is a necessary but by no means a sufficient condition of tolerable government or even of an acceptable legal system. For we must ask not only that justice be done, but that the justice done, however impeccable, is adequate in all the spheres of life which law and government affect.

But this leads directly to the other merit of the juristic theory; its recognition of the logical distinction between the law as it is and the law as it should or ought to be. This distinction, which provides the indispensable leverage for responsible demands for rightful changes in regard either to particular laws or to the legal system as a whole, is ignored both by sentimental exponents of "the law" as the embodiment of a system of ideals, and by legal realists and pragmatists whose distaste for moralism spills over into contempt for moral criticism itself. All systems of law fall short of what they ought to be, and sentimentalists do them no service by forever reminding us that "the spirit of the law" dwelling within them is something just and good. Law and morality are not the same thing, and the deliberations of a Solomon become confused when he runs them together.

My purpose, then, is not to raise questions about the need for qualification of the theory of law underlying modern versions of the juristic theory of rights. For the sake of argument, at least, I am prepared to accept it as a working hypothesis about the law itself in dealing with issues concerning rights of youth that are only in the second instance legal. I contest only the thesis that a legal right, viewed as an established practice within a system of law, affords a suitable model for a general conception of rights, especially those of the sort we call moral or ethical. On the contrary, it turns out in its own way to be prejudicial to a study of rights of youth which, although very real, are not yet embodied in any established social or legal practice.

In the following paragraphs it is possible to give only a bare outline of a general theory of rights for which I have argued elsewhere. First, let me say that in the widest sense a right is not definable as a kind of rule or practice, even though it may afford the basis for establishing a practice. It is entirely meaningful, for example, for one person to say to another, "I grant you the right to make a practice of walking over my land." The right in this case isn't a practice; rather does it provide the ground for a practice. Furthermore, it is meaningful to say, "I grant you the right, on this occasion, to walk across my land." This, note well, is no mere gift. For if I grant such a right then in so doing I hold myself responsible either to respect the freedom of him to whom it is granted or, conceivably, to guarantee that he will not be molested either by myself or others when he takes his walk. In short, in granting a right, I create a claim whose terms I thereby obligate myself to honor, even though, by the terms of the grant, it may lapse when a single action has been performed. Thus, whereas a legal right is not merely the basis of a practice or an action but a practice in its own right which, correspondingly, imposes a recurrent duty toward those who may claim the right in question, a moral right, on the other hand, exists whenever a claim may be made that some person or other obliges himself to respect, whether or not a practice of any sort as yet exists.

A second feature of significant ascriptions of rights, especially those of the moral sort, is that since they implicitly involve assignments of responsibility, they are never correctly understood simply as statements of fact. It is one thing to say that a young man possesses the abilities for entering college: but it is another to claim that those abilities entitle him to go to college. Statements of fact ask us merely to accept something as the case: ascriptions of rights impose responsibilities and therefore are always intended to dispose those to whom they are addressed to be ready to perform (or refrain from performing) an act or acts of a certain kind when the circumstances warrant. Ascriptions of rights, in short, belong to the domain, not of what philosophers (misleadingly) called theoretical, but of practical reason, and reason functions practically, only when it means, to vary a famous thesis of Karl Marx, not simply to describe reality but to change it.

But here we have reached a place where the liberal tradition must take its own licks. For, since the time of Locke, that tradition has been concerned largely with rights, whether moral or legal, that pertain only to so-called negative liberties. Such rights permit us to do as we please in certain circumstances—say, save our lives, enjoy and protect our property, or follow our own way to happiness—but permissions entail no primary obligation on the part of others save to refrain from interfering with the actions of those who possess them. If they elect to go to hell in a bucket, we pledge only not to stand in their way. The idealist and socialist traditions, which in this respect go back behind Locke to the Greeks, remind us that there is more to the rights of civilized life than entitlements to do as we like. Some rights lay claim to what are sometimes called "positive freedoms." These rights are not simply permissions, but on the contrary require all responsible persons actively to aid and support those who possess them. Rights of this sort are of particular importance in the case of young people who even when they already possess powers of judgment and discrimination, are commonly without the means of realizing their ends. And it is precisely with respect to rights of this sort that liberals, as John Stuart Mill for one came eventually to see, have had much to learn from the idealist and socialist tradition.

Now, as I have indicated, the concept of a right is inescapably correlated with that of responsibility. No one can truly claim a right unless there is someone who is obliged to honor the claim. Before ascribing rights, therefore, it is essential to inquire who, if anyone, may be held responsible for their observance. And in the case of rights of youth, this point is also of particular importance, since it is commonly, though by no means always, true that those who must assume the primary burden of responsibility no longer enjoy exactly similar rights. Efforts to enlarge or modify rights of youth thus impose great problems of understanding and sympathy, for most of us not unnaturally find it easier to acknowledge another's right when we ourselves also possess it. Those problems are further complicated in societies like our own where simplistic uniformitarian doctrines of justice prevail and where, especially in the economic sphere, people are still left so largely to their own inadequate devices. At the theoretical level, it is widely assumed that if all rights entail responsibilities, then all rights and responsibilities must be mutual. This is plainly false. For example, aged persons have rights which entail no mutual responsibilities. But this is not all. For in principle rights and responsibilities need not be reciprocal. Insane or senile persons (I should hope) have rights, though virtually by definition they can assume few or no responsibilities. But even when some form of reciprocity is just, it can by no means always be established by appeal to a principle of equality.

In sum, a tenable general theory of rights must make allowance in advance for many possibilities of differential treatment among human beings according to their various circumstances and powers. This does not mean that we should abandon entirely the principles inscribed in doctrines that speak of the rights of man. Nor does it mean that we renounce altogether libertarian doctrines about rights which are essentially permissive in character. It means, rather, that such principles and conceptions be amplified, amended, and supplemented by others in ways of which the generosity and good will of man's ethical consciousness, at its best, may be more discriminatingly inflected and extended.

IV

In preparing this essay, I already had a fairly clear idea of what I wanted to say about rights as such. The terms youth, adulthood, and maturity, which have been little studied by analytical philosophers, turned up some surprises: connotations I assumed to be straightforward turned out to have some curious angles, and both affinities and disaffinities I had taken for granted faded on closer scrutiny. As a preliminary exercise I have as usual consulted the *Oxford English Dictionary*, a book which, if not always profound, is useful when one wants to see in outline the lay of a conceptual land.

Youth, we are told, has three main connotations, which are somewhat more perplexing than they may seem at first glance: (a) the fact or state of being young and, more figuratively, newness and recentness; (b) that phase of life between childhood and adult age, and again more figuratively, any early stage of existence, and, (c) the qualities characteristic of the young, for example, freshness, vigor, vitality, creativity, and (more pejoratively) wantonness and rashness. What shall we say of all this? To take the last point first, I think we must say, rather firmly, that though many youths do appear rash or wanton in the eyes of their elders, and some of them doubtless are so by any standards, rashness is endemic to the human species, and that every stage of life presents its own forms of liability in this regard. The much discussed movie, *The Graduate*, whatever may be said of its artistic merits, certainly suggests that middle age is a time of immense hazards in both directions especially among the affluent. It also raises the question whether some of the rashness and most of the wantonness ascribed to youth may be functions of the examples set for it by people in the life-stage ahead. More interesting, however, is the likelihood that those forms of rashness and wantonness to which youths as such may be prone are merely deviant expressions of their other, more positive powers of freshness, vitality, vigor, imaginativeness and creativity. In any case, what the potentially rash and wanton of all ages need are not so much laws that restrict their liberties as knowledge to inform their vigor and vitality, and better opportunities for significant love and affection. More positive freedoms, not fewer negative ones, are the primary cures for these faults where they exist.

The second connotation, which distinguishes youth as that phase of life between childhood and adult age, raises many questions. Plainly it does not refer merely to a specific term of years. Many people retain the qualities and powers, as well perhaps as the vulnerabilities mentioned above, until well beyond their middle twenties; and some precocious youngsters enter upon the age of youth before their teens, just as others remain children, in effect, all their lives. Clearly the age of youth turns less upon questions of time than upon qualities of being, and for the most part I shall so treat it in what follows.

More puzzling are the relationships between youth and adulthood. If, for example, one understands by an adult one who is mature in a purely biological sense, then obviously many youths are as adult as they will ever be, and a great many fortunate adults are still youths. Evidently biological factors cannot be decisive here. On the other hand, if by an adult one refers to a person who is entitled to enjoy legal or other rights, not in potency only but also in act, then, from the perspective we have now reached, some youths are fully adult and others not—and *vice versa.*

Evidently it is time to take a closer look at the notion of an

[327

adult itself. The central entry in the *O.E.D.* tells us that a person is adult when he is "fully developed in mind and body" or else possessed of full powers of "thought, deliberation, and judgment." On the one side, an adult is somebody who is mature in a certain respect. On the other he is one who possesses certain psychological qualifications. Let us wave the notion of maturity aside for the moment. Certainly the powers of thought, deliberation, and judgment, as here understood, are not empirical concepts in the sense of the term currently employed in the so-called behavioral sciences. For while they do indeed have to do with questions of behavior, these are questions of intention and conduct, not of mere bodily movements or changes. And it is for just this reason that current behavioral psychology which attempts to correlate forms of bodily "inputs" and "outputs" (as the jargon goes) avoids like the plague all such intentional verbs as "deliberate" and "judge." Given their purposes they are right to do so. Unfortunately those concerned with problems about rights of youth cannot settle for input–output correlations, but must deal with psychological concepts of a wholly different sort. What are these?

We may get some leverage by observing that definitions of an adult make reference to a *person* who is developed in certain powers of mind (as well as body.) The concept of a person presents many problems. Still, enough is known about its use to make it clear that powers ascribed to persons are not the same sort of thing as the dispositions imputed to mere things or objects of a certain sort. Now as its etymological root (*persona*) suggests, the concept of a person is normally employed in speaking of someone or something to whom (or which) certain desirable roles or functions are ascribed.[1] Accordingly, a person is one who is assigned particular offices and duties, prerogatives and rights. And the psychological powers imputed to him are those required in order to perform the roles and fulfill the functions in question. Hence in speaking of an adult as a person who is fully developed in mind (and body) we are at the least of it ascribing to him mental powers pertaining, not to individuals of a certain age, but to those necessary to certain forms of achievement, in virtue of which he is entitled to perform relevant actions and, in some circumstances, may be held liable if he fails to perform them.

Adulthood is therefore not just any sort of maturity, and so far as youths and their rights are concerned, this is a matter of great importance. Thus, while we may speak of mature lions, elm trees, or parsnips, we would not, I believe, ever regard them as adults. The mature lion must meet certain specifications, but they do not suffice to make him an adult, and this for the reason that, as such, they give him no status as a person. What is required of adults, unlike merely mature creatures of a certain breed or species, are mental powers pertaining to the fulfillment of roles pertinent, or perhaps indispensable, to the aims of some institution, society, or way of life. And, in such matters, questions of age, in particular, seem entirely secondary.

v

But are they? Up to this point, I can well imagine that both young and old readers may feel, from their respective stations, that hitherto my remarks about the concepts of youth have been too abstractly functionalistic. What has been left out are the sheer unalterable facts of age and aging. The first entry on youth in the *O.E.D.* reminds us that youth is the fact or state of being young. Thus while Leonard Bernstein still may be the most youthful of middle-aged Americans, he is no longer a youth, whereas the teen-aged supporters of Eugene McCarthy were youths, whatever the quality of their political wisdom or moral rectitude. From the standpoint of the older generation, it may be argued further that although conceptions of adulthood are indeed tied to social practices or attitudes, there remain basic universal functions of adults in all historical societies, to which the thoroughly exoteric powers of judgment, deliberation, and thought have always been necessary. In short, adults are and must be people of mature age who must share the primary responsibilities of ordinary social life: the responsibilities of earning a living, parenthood, citizenship, performing the tasks essential to keeping of the basic institutions of society in working order. Thus older people, by and large, have and must continue to set the standards of adulthood, for their judgment, however fallible, is what we finally have to rely upon.

This sounds very concrete. Unhappily (or happily, depending upon your attitudes) other things are also concrete. I can imagine many intelligent, well-educated, and dedicated young people replying as follows: if youth connotes not only the fact or state of being young but, more figuratively, also newness and recentness, one thing is clear: we indeed live in a society whose institutions are not only run by old people, but which is itself old, and, like most old things, arthritic, incapable of making the freshly-conceived decisions and adjustments essential to the survival of the very society and its institutions which our putative adults cherish. For example, in our system, it is next to impossible for any but dodos to be elected President of the United States. And much the same holds with respect to the major managerial jobs of the great corporations, the great universities and foundations, and the military and police forces. Even our dictionaries are compiled by conventional scholars who reflect both the habits and speech and the attitudes of our *de facto* adults whose powers of judgment and thought are all too well suited to the "business" of a society which is no longer a light to the world.

In most important situations, our young people are indeed treated not as adults but as occupying ambiguous positions between childhood and adult age. In practice they are at best merely pre- or potential adults who may one day become adults *if* they behave themselves and submit to the forms of judgment and thought of those who effectively control the policies and activities of our major institutions. But what about those who resist or radically dissent; those who, as the phrase is, opt out? Will they be allowed to become adults? Business is indeed business, and the more unconventional the youth the more systematically is he excluded from its decisive transactions and operations.

But let us, as friends of youth, continue to play the game of connotations according to Hoyle, only demanding, like the graying eminences themselves, that all concrete realities be taken into account. Speaking thus as presumptive youths, therefore, we will accept, subject only to qualifications that "our" experience shows to be realistic, the conditions of adulthood that existing adults regard as *sine qua non:* judgment, deliberation, and thought. In passing we may observe that most existing institutions, political, legal, educational, and religious, are systematically calculated to delay our acquisition of the powers of judgment necessary to established ways of adult life. And if, from our elders' point of view, we are often rash and wanton, is it not their fault as much as ours? Or rather, is it not owing to a prevailing social order that compels us, even from our own point of view, to take long shots, to take our fun where we can find it, and to make up our own games as we go along? But, speaking as soberly and concretely as we know how, we already possess powers that entitle us to the sort of adulthood which a decent contemporary society would accept as a matter of course. Take the matter of thought, essential to sensible deliberations and judgments in affairs of government. We know more about the world, human and otherwise, possess more finely honed conceptual and intellectual skills, than all but a handful of our elders. However, let us not only concede, but insist that knowledge of matters of fact is not the only thing essential to sound deliberations and judgments. What is wanted also is the capacity for emotional development, powers of imagination, sympathy and affection, the capacity for idealism and of identification with great causes, such as are inscribed, for example, in our own *Declaration of Independence* and our *Bill of Rights*. These surely should be the auxiliary powers of adult persons capable of making the great decisions upon which not only our well-being but our very lives depend.

Yet (speaking once more in my own person) if the freshest, most imaginative of our contemporary psychologists are to be believed, it is in the age of youth that men possess these powers more abundantly than at any other time of life. And surely our own experience during this troubled and immensely troubling period in our history confirms this. I am not forgetting the contributions of some young people to the disorders that have made repression the great theme of both political parties in the recent presidential campaign. But surely if adult Americans have learned anything from history it is that repression—call it "law and order" if you prefer—is the last response which creative minds would make to the general disorders to which our youths have contributed their own destructive bit. Repression is the response

[33]

not of wise adults but of men who have lost the powers of reflection that can enliven the judgments, political and otherwise,
our people so desperately need. Our great trouble is not lawlessness but something far worse: the loss among our law-abiding
leaders of that saving "sweetness" of spirit (the word of course
is Matthew Arnold's) which, in calling men to order, conveys at
the same time a sense not of hardness but of care, not of a desire
to hang on to one's own but to share it, not of a demand for
"justice," which here becomes another word for retribution, but
of need for rehabilitation and reunion. But what is true of our
leaders is true of ourselves who have chosen, or permitted, them
to represent us. In the end, the only response to anarchy, as Arnold knew, must be from that cultivation and elevation of the
spirit which adds the sweetness of the heart to the light of the
mind. And we "adults" seem incapable of making that response
in any sustained and moving way worthy of emulation among
our own offspring.

I am not unaware that, so far as our contemporary youth are
concerned, Matthew Arnold can hardly be regarded as our man
in the nineteenth century. That is partly why I have mentioned
him rather than, say, Nietzsche or Kierkegaard. But he is also
worth remembering here, not only because he himself tried to
find a way toward understanding and meeting the responsibilities
of adulthood in a time which was after all a prelude to our own,
but because he himself, as he all too well knew, was afflicted in
his own phrase with "this strange disease of modern life," an ill-
ness from which another writer, closer in style to ourselves, William James, also suffered throughout his life. What is the disease?
It has many names, but skepticism will do.

What does skepticism mean in the sphere that here concerns
us: the sphere of judgment and deliberation and hence not of
purely theoretical but also of practical reason whose aim is choice
and action? Here where James like Arnold knew whereof he
spoke, skepticism means on the one side loss of faith, of concern
for loyalty and trust, and on the other, a failure of will. Judgment is listless, spectatorial, and therefore pointless, unless it
moves the will. And it is sporadic, desperate, merely compulsive,
unless it is infused with faith and the vital urgency which is the

offspring of faith. Yet if Erikson is even half right, it is in the age of youth that these qualities of being still exist as actualities, not as something to be recovered for a dying moment through someone else's rhetoric. As every teacher knows, he needs his students more than they need him. For they enable him first of all to perceive that *his* skepticism is not the result of uncynical wariness and experience, but all too often of a disabling, self-protective loss of heart. It is our students and our children who bring us back to life by revealing to us the preciousness and precariousness of all significant human being, without which ordinary adulthood, with all its flimflam of "judgment" and "deliberation" and indeed the whole business of practical reason, becomes a dreary farce which we run through each day for want of something better to do. It is the young, by forcing us to reconsider our "principles," which for the most part are merely the routine responses of party men, professional men, members of a social class, that help us to recover a significant, functional skepticism out of which—who knows?—even we might come up with a new idea or a fresh hope for our kind.

How little do we know ourselves, we adult Americans, managers of the world's greatest novelty shop? What do we sell there that could make us new men? We are masters of gadgetry. But we have let our institutions, once examples to all mankind, become rigid and lethargic, unresponsive to serious demands for rapid social change. In our fear of the outside world we outdo the Russians themselves. Who are our statesmen and preceptors? They are, quite literally, creations of cosmeticians, ghostwriters, image-makers, pollsters. Thought, deliberation, judgment: what an incredibly sad joke it is that at the circuses where major parties pretend to conduct the deliberations that are supposed to enable a great democracy to make reasonable judgments, by whom and how it shall be ruled, these balding eagles can find no way of visibly demonstrating their manhood except to surround themselves with flag-waving children, pinup girls, rosy-cheeked daughters and handsome sons, and (slightly less obviously) cadres of sleek, well-groomed young bodyguards. Youth: only its circumambient image seems able to prove, either to themselves or to their audiences, that they even exist. But all they want is the image; the presence, the actuality scares them stiff. And real youths, serious youths who have proven their adulthood, are held at bay by Mace, teargas, and nightsticks. Now how can this tragedy be stopped, and how can a democratic people renew its strength? Only, I am convinced, by enabling all youths to participate fully in forming the judgments of our common social and institutional life. Only, that is to say, by enabling them to view themselves as adults. If some of them are not yet mature—as I realize—then we ourselves can match them two for one. But, young or old, one learns to walk by walking, and until our youth walks, our society will remain in a wheelchair.

VI

Thus, by pondering the meanings and applications of the terms of our discourse in some of the concrete circumstances of their contemporary use we are brought directly around to the immense problem of this essay: rights of youth. Notice, however, that I have spoken only of "rights" not of "the rights" of youth. For I am concerned in the first instance with moral rights and only in consequence with the political, legal, educational, and other institutional rights which reflective men may consider to be ascribable to youths in the modern age. And because, as we have seen, rights do not exist apart from responsibilities, and the sense of moral responsibility, as exponents of the new morals have taught us, must begin at home where alone free and sober men can find what their own moral commitments are, I propose to begin by asking, in the form of an imaginative experiment, not what rights young people may claim of some abstract entity called "mankind," but what sorts of rights enlightened young people may ascribe to, and claim of, one another, when viewed as members of a distinct moral community.

Let us suppose them to be reflective, tolerably informed, and generously inclined, yet disposed also to give a certain primacy to the claims of their own community: call it, for convenience, "the league of youth." This sense of priority, as they themselves recognize, stems partly from a sense of exclusion and hence of alienation from the prevailing institutional and social life of the American system. More positively it stems also from a sense of their identity with one another as youths, as well as from an awareness both of stress and of opportunity which distinguish them not merely from their elders but in some measure from previous generations of young people. Owing to the existence of the various media and forms of transportation which make possible virtually immediate communication with other youths, both at home and abroad, they realize that community, for them (as well as for others) is no longer a function of geographical closeness, of superficial cultural similarities, of ties owing to accidents of birth and nurture in a particular town or country or social class. For this and other reasons, they feel themselves to be the bearers of a new culture which, were it allowed to spread, could help toward the rejuvenation of the whole race of men. Perhaps it is not too fanciful to say that they see themselves as filling an historic role in our time somewhat analogous to the roles which other reformist and revolutionary classes believed themselves to be filling during the great revolutionary ages between the eighteenth and early twentieth centuries in America and Europe. And if this imposes upon them special responsibilities it also disposes them to regard one another as possessing certain correlative rights. Analogously they feel a kinship with contemporary revolutionary movements in Latin America, in Africa, and in Asia, and consider all disenfranchised and disadvantaged people as having trans-national and trans-cultural rights which it is their right, as members of the league of youth, to defend as advocates.

Some have called them "anarchists" because they talk of "participatory democracy," because they engage in seemingly unorganized, isolated, and gratuitous acts "against the system." This, I think, is a shallow view. For, though militant, they abhor all military and paramilitary forms of organization and unity. Actually they are trying out forms of organization, inspired in part by men like Gandhi, that require both extraordinary selflessness and self-discipline. Perhaps they will fail in this but what a pity if they do. For, if I understand them, their view is that the alternative is not gradual piecemeal progress through "legitimate" institutional channels, but very conceivably a dead planet. And, more generally, in a time of unique danger not for themselves alone but for *their* successors—their children and their students—it is not their task only but a right which they bestow upon one another, to serve as agents of a general spiritual and social reformation. And it is by this right that they justify their continuing resistance to "the system" and their exemplary acts of extreme refusal and defiance. What appear from a conventional moral or legal point of view to be acts of immorality or rebellion are consequences of collateral obligations which their rights as active members of the league of youth entail.

Some foolish spokesmen for the league of youth profess to be contemptuous of the liberal tradition. Yet in many ways our youths strike me as reaffirming a fundamental contention of that tradition, which views rights primarily as permissions or liberties to do as one pleases without interference, particularly in the sphere of personal life. In fact, I should argue that one of the salient characteristics of their community is their insistence on extending the range of such permissions, in matters not only of taste, including such things as dress, manners, and modes of speech, but also, more importantly, of sex. However they do not equate personal freedom with privacy. And, whereas the Victorian liberals and their Bloomsbury successors were often very free indeed in sexual as well as in other matters of personal life, they performed their rites behind closed doors in thick-walled houses well back from the road. Here I think we must see that in the classical liberal tradition there was a deep connection between the rights or permissions associated with personal liberty, and the rights pertaining to private property. I have a right to do as I please in my house or in houses where I am invited, in such affairs as sex, because that is the proper sphere of personal life. I have no such right—just the contrary—in public places where, presumably, my roles are no longer purely or primarily personal. On this score, the league of youth, less concerned with private property and possessions, are at once more permissive about what may be done in public and less observant of rights of privacy. What shouldn't be done in public simply shouldn't be done at all, and what is permissible in private is in effect permissible anywhere. In this respect, in short, their sense of community, like that of the socialists, is so strong that they can scarcely understand why anyone should claim rights to privacy, where, in the name of liberty, the individual for the time being cuts himself off from his kind.

This of course creates an impression of vulgarity, of callousness, of plain indecency among solid citizens who, in their carefully-guarded penthouses and suburban homes feel free to do just as they please, however debased or debasing. And I have no doubt that there is here a profound generation gap. But it is closely tied to different primary attitudes, regarding both the sense of community and something entirely different: the institutions belonging to a social system. Accordingly, that generation gap is accompanied by radical differences in regard to the moral claims which people may lay upon one another in the names both of negative and of positive freedom. Solid citizens, quite properly from their point of view, began their deliberations concerning their own moral responsibilities toward other members of society by reflecting upon their various institutional rights which they assume at the same time to have a *prima facie* moral claim upon themselves and others. The members of the league of youth, enjoying only a modicum of such rights, and thinking of themselves in the first instance as members of a community which the society does not even know exists, attach no such moral significance to the institutional rights in question. And so, what are virtually indefeasible rights to their elders are for them functions of social policies whose worth appears to them entirely problematic.

The implication is plain: if youths are to think as solid citizens, attaching an inherent moral significance to the institutional rights of the social system, they must be transformed into solid citizens. This can only be done by treating them as full-fledged, adult members of the system who can therefore make some identification with its institutions. They must possess these rights, moreover, not merely potentially, but also actually and in full.

But now we have to consider briefly another dimension of the moral outlook of the league of youth which is, as I have observed, profoundly at variance with a deep stratum in our cultural tradition and which has been reinforced in recent years by the advent of the graduate university and the commanding position of the university among the primary institutions of our emerging national society. Once again, I shall call this aspect of our tradition "rationalism," and indeed it does derive, as an ideology, largely from the writings of the great classical philosophers, beginning with Plato and Aristotle.[2] From this point of view, human normality and maturity are derived from a conception of man as "the rational animal" whose highest good is knowledge, and whose highest knowledge is of the sort we nowadays call "scientific." Further, possession of the intellectual powers and skills necessary to the achievement of such knowledge is itself an evidence of wisdom and hence of a *prima facie* right to leadership, if not to rule, within the society. A democratic society, like our own, professedly denies this intellectual elite the right to rule, but increasingly it bestows upon it an informal but nonetheless powerful right to be heard, to advisory positions of immense prestige and power, and of course to leadership and governance within the university. Let me quote a recent candid formulation of this point of view by Professor George Kateb in an essay, "Utopia and the Good Life." In his defense of the life of the mind, Kateb acknowledges the importance of "educated feelings" and the significance of play in that life. He speaks of the values of "playing at life," and of its virtue in the "enrichment of character" and in enabling people to "experience the higher pleasures" which, however, must be kept under control by the higher faculties. What are these faculties? Kateb's answer is revealing:

> . . . play is play: there must be some steadiness, some seriousness in the midst of this release and fluidity. Once again, the cultivation of higher faculties provides the answer. Greater in seriousness than even the making of beautiful objects and the doing of glorious deeds is the life of knowing. . . . We would compound the intellectualist heresy and say that man possessed of the higher faculties in their perfection is the model for utopia and already exists outside it. . . .[3]

Kateb, a very up-to-date Plato, makes it clear that no "metaphysical theory of the world" underlies this contention. He is talking as a plain scholar in behalf of the plain factual knowledge to which the contemporary university professor and researcher aspires, which decidedly does *not* include such *outré* things as, say, the knowledge of God, the playful knowledge of the lover of Mozart, or the presumptive wisdom of sages and prophets.

It must suffice to say that Mr. Kateb, no doubt happily, does not belong to what I have called the league of youth. For one thing they conceive the life of the mind in a way very different from the tradition which he represents. They do not despise scholarship, certainly. But they are more skeptical of the undisputedly supreme worth of investigations of which the sciences provide a paradigm, and of the tendency, from the Greek philosophers on, to view the arts either as inferior vehicles of knowledge or else as expressions of emotion and feeling which are therefore of secondary value. The new youth tends to view man's higher faculties and indeed the whole life of the mind itself in less abstractly intellectualistic and hierarchical terms. Accordingly, they regard the prerogatives of science in the educational sphere and the rights of scientifically-oriented youths as in no sense primary or preemptive. The love of truth, particularly as the scholar-scientist views it, is only one of the major passions of the mind. In a certain way, indeed, the deep vein of equalitarianism, which is elsewhere such a persistent theme among members of the new youth, also shows itself here in the equal respect it pays scientists, poets, painters, dancers, and philosophers.

Beyond this, however, they find distasteful the whole mentality which so delights in ranking "glorious deeds" below (or above) other forms of action. Imaginative works of love and affection are as wonderful and often as difficult as any others. Why should we not accept them with the same regard as we accord other manifestations of human genius? But this brings us finally to corresponding differences between their religious attitudes and those of many exponents of the Judeo-Christian tradition for whom the supreme, not to say the only authentic, religious act, is comprehended exclusively in such phrases as "the love of God." Most of them are unorthodox. But I am impressed both by their sustained religious seriousness and by their tolerance for all genuine expressions of the sense of the holy and the wonderful. And in fact, among no group in our time is the sense of the *profane* in our common social life a source of greater sorrow. Indeed, it is the absence of any authentic religious spirit in the routines of conventional institutional activity which makes them despair of their human worth.

VII

In bringing this discussion of youth and its rights toward a conclusion, I now propose to shift perspectives, moving outside the league of youth to a conceivably wider community of human beings of which the members of that league may well (and I think rightly) regard themselves as members. In the first instance, however, I shall continue the discussion in essentially moral terms. It is for this reason that I have stressed the term "community" here rather than "society" or "social system." As here understood a community is not itself an institution or network of institutions, though it may establish institutions that serve in various ways as its agencies.[4] An individual can be the member of a society against his will; he may also unwittingly and in some measure fulfill the functions of a class or perform the functions assigned to him by a social system while feeling little or no sense of moral obligation in doing so. Or, like many of us, he may be self-divided in this respect. And so he may proceed by stages from dissent, to resistance, and from thence to rebellion and revolution, according to the quality and direction of that self-division. But one cannot revolt against a community; one can only leave it, cease to acknowledge oneself as one of its members. This is because a community is by definition like a "congregation" of religious worshippers: it has no reality or meaning save insofar as its members conceive themselves as belonging to one another in continuing relations of mutual trust and respect. In short, one cannot be a member of a community without feeling a basic moral responsibility to it and to its members.

But while it is impossible to conceive anyone as being a member of a community, in the sense I have in mind, without enjoying certain rights which are among the conditions of membership, there seems to be no reason in logic to suppose that every member of a community should have exactly the same rights and responsibilities.[5] Accordingly, I shall make a distinction between two sorts of communal rights, one generic, the other more special. Thus, for example, while, as one may well imagine, every member of a community might properly claim a right to life and to as much negative freedom as is compatible with the survival and the pursuance of other primary ends of the community, it might also be agreed that certain rights are to be enjoyed, or enjoyed in full, only by certain members of classes thereof. Thus, for example, elderly persons, no longer capable of fending for themselves, might properly claim rights to certain forms of protection or to comforts to which other members of a community have no rightful claim.

Now let me emphatically assert that if youths are to be regarded as members of the wider community of men of which I have spoken, their youth does not exempt them from responsibilities pertaining to the generic rights of all its members. Thus they must (let us assume) respect or even be obliged to protect, in many situations, the lives of their fellows. And they must at the same time respect the negative freedoms of other members.[6] But in this essay our concern is primarily with rights of youth. And it is their special rights within the community of men that now concern me, and in particular those rights that derive not from their common powers of judgment and deliberation, nor even from their capacities to acquire or develop such powers— their potentialities, that is, as "adults"—but rather from the qualities of their youth itself. Here our earlier psychological and conceptual analyses, provide useful clues. Thus, specifically, I have in mind among the special rights of youth in the wider community of men those necessary for them to fulfill themselves as youths: their enormous capacities for learning, invention, and creation. But also, quite unsentimentally, I believe it all the more necessary to stress, in these days when pundits talk endlessly of "law and order," their extraordinary problems of love and companionship, of identity and self-discovery, in virtue of which they should have rights to a special tolerance, patience, and quiet assistance that are more extensive than older members of the wider community may decently claim for themselves. And if this tolerance and patience are not forthcoming, and they are not accordingly protected against the thuggery of police and the retributive justice of benighted administrators of the draft, the price in alienation and disassociation from the wider community will be a calamity, not for themselves alone, but for us all.

But the preceding sentence places the accent in the wrong place. For the proper emphasis here should be on the positive endowment of young people, not potentialities from which other, presumably more mature, powers may come if they are to be accorded liberties "we" would not claim for ourselves. This endowment, in the age of youth, is already a flood tide, in some respects as strong and mature as it will ever be. Save for unconscionable accident, a Keats or a Schubert, a Pascal or a Frank Ramsey might have gone on in later years to fulfill a genius at which the rest of us could only marvel. This in no way blunts my point. At eighteen or twenty or twenty-five, many men are more "mature" than they will ever be again and have already done things—performed "glorious deeds," created "beautiful objects," discovered theorems—and paradoxes—which are as splendid, as lovely, as true as the human spirit and mind can ever achieve.

From this I conclude that in certain directions rights of youth are not in the least like the rights of "minors": the rights, that is, of potential adults or the potential rights of adults. They are rights in full being that belong to youth itself. And if these rights carry with them subsidiary rights to forgiveness and excuse, this only proves the greatness and the wisdom—the adulthood—of the great community of men which I have in mind and to which I aspire to belong. This is not to suggest that every youth is a genius, or every young person, just because he is young, is a great benefactor of the human race. It is to say rather that there exist dimensions and possibilities of experience as fully realized in youth as they are likely ever to be again, and hence that the great community of men owes them special consideration in the form of rights of youth which by nature of the case can involve no corresponding obligations on the part of youths to other members of that community. I have argued that generically rights are not practices. But now I can powerfully use the point in saying that such rights ought, as far as possible, to be translated into social practices in the form both of economic supports and of continuing educational support, fellowships, grants-in-aid, and the like, which will afford them the leisure necessary to fulfill themselves as youths. Too often in our society youth is treated either as a period of rapid preparation for adult life or else as a time in which, if they have no special intellectual or artistic talents, youths should be put to work at jobs that are menial, less interesting, and less rewarding than those of their elders. Older people, we sometimes think, have thereby earned the right to an increasingly early retirement, a time of leisure, in which to do as they please. But an affluent society, were it wise, should, as it could, extend to the young comparable periods, or intervals, of prolonged leisure in which they too could follow their bent as youths. In short, an inconceivably wealthy society like ours might well turn its immense economic and technological resources to the liberation of all young people from the full necessities comprehended under the phrase "earning a living." One can even look forward to an age in which it will be time enough to start earning a living after one has lost the bloom of youth. Nor is there any need to view such a period of leisure as a period either of idleness or of more extended preparation for the rigors of later life. Just the contrary. It is possible, moreover, to envisage forms of education, artistic, intellectual, or cultural activity in which, instead of being taught by elders who seek to pass on skills, forms of knowledge, technical or otherwise, which they as elders greatly prize, young people would do better to teach one another in ways that are appropriate to their own perspectives and interests and that develop powers which youths as such find worthy of cultivation. Institutions of higher learning of and not merely for the young need not be separated entirely from existing institutions. And multiversities which contain schools of dentistry and departments of home economics, not to mention the burgeoning cross-departmental area studies that enlist the energies of teachers trained in widely different disciplines, might very well establish "colleges" in which, at the same time, the young could engage in forms of study whose content, modes of instruction, and personnel they themselves largely determine. Well, why not?

Finally a word must be said about those more generic human rights which, at present, youths possess to a large degree only in potency. The odd thing about the present situation is that although we like to pretend that owing to their immaturity they are also exempt from many of the responsibilities of adult persons, many harsh and dangerous responsibilities are now borne mainly by young people that require of them skills, understanding, and judgment at least as complex as those possessed by their elders. Further, when we consider the subtle problems of conscience which must be confronted, for example, by youthful dissenters and conscientious objectors, it is evident that we expect of them forms of moral development and powers of religious and ethical discrimination at least as advanced as those which we old-sters fancy ourselves as possessing. However, the age of youth, especially in our time, has proved itself to be an age of moral idealism and dedication which fully entitles our youths to enjoy in act most, or all, of the generic rights we claim for ourselves. As I have elsewhere remarked, a young person mature enough to understand what it may mean to die for his country is also old enough to decide, or to help decide, whether the cause is worth dying for.

It is a fact that, despite various breakdowns in our school systems, including our institutions of higher learning, many young people, in virtue of their extraordinarily extensive informal as well as formal educations, are vastly more developed as persons than either the youths of twenty or thirty years ago, when I myself was young, or the middle-agers the youths of that time have now become. Like many of my academic colleagues, I find, to my acute embarrassment that many of my students are not only more sensitive and imaginative than I am—that I take for granted—they are also more cultivated and, in some respects, by my own standards, wiser. For, among other things, they know in the fullest sense, how near to death is all mankind. I am astonished both by the gentleness of their manners and by the simplicity of their lives. And if drugs are a problem for them, they, or their analogues, are problems for us all. It goes without remark that in the face of all the forms of suffering, mental as well as physical, with which our society and its institutions have threatened them or else inflicted upon them over and over again, their courage shames us all. Neither dismissal from college, social harassment and ostracism, jail, injury, or murder deflect them from their determination to see not only that justice is done themselves, but also that our whole society commit itself to that reawakening of the community spirit which begins with justice but ends with greatheartedness and love. By any standards that we, as their elders, may in reason apply to ourselves, they have attained adulthood.

This being true, the problem of their political and legal rights in principle pretty well takes care of itself. The state and the legal system, so far as they strive to be just and to serve the common good, deserve respect from members of the party of humanity. But the state and the legal systems are not ends in themselves, but serviceable agencies of human communities, or if they may sometimes be more, then this is so only insofar as they become primary carriers and symbols of man's communal life. Hence no political and legal order that deserves our loyalty can be repressive or deny to any member of the human community which it serves and symbolizes any right relevant to the maintenance and progress of that order. There can be no quarrel with the thesis that the state, as an agency of that community, may properly be viewed as a guardian that in effect holds in trust the rights of children, of the senile, or the insane. But, despite Plato, it cannot be a guardian to adult citizens. Thus, if as I claim our youth is adult and already belongs to the human community in the most active sense of the term, then it is entitled to every legal and political right required for participation in the political process.

Such rights, we must remember, cannot include merely negative liberties, permissions to vote, run for office, and the rest. For important as they may be they do not remotely suffice for effective citizenship. Hence such negative liberties must be implemented by rights that enable their full and proper exercise. In the case of youth, particularly, this means above all, more and better education. For in the modern age education is virtually the condition of all the other positive freedoms, economic and political, as well as intellectual and spiritual. But education, decidedly, is not enough, even if our education system were, as it so tragically is not, up to its own responsibilities. Youths must therefore be entitled to all the forms of social security, as we call it, required for realization of their powers, not now simply as youths, but as citizens.

These, I have been told, are utopian dreams. Are they? Well then, as the poet has said, responsibilities begin in dreams, and unless someone holds himself responsible, as we have seen, rights do not exist. With all possible emphasis I say it: they had better not remain dreams forever. For youth is not only restless; it is also knowledgeable and determined. As never before it has reached an understanding of its own identity, its strength, its indispensability to any advanced social system like our own. But this is no reason to be afraid. Rather is it a reason for us, not their guardians, but their advocates and friends, to make certain that the league of youth remains part of the good society of which the word "America" was once a symbol. For only we ourselves can finally drive them out.

Part V

CONCLUSION

17

Rationalism, Education, and the Good Society

THE AIM OF THIS CONCLUDING ESSAY IS FRANKLY PO-
lemical. I mean, now systematically, to attack views of education and the good society widely prevalent in our culture, particularly in our institutions of higher learning, i.e., the colleges
and universities, and, more recently, the institutes for advanced
study. But the point of view I shall call in question goes deeper
and extends more widely. It involves a conception of higher
learning, accepted by virtually the whole society in which we
live and the civilization of which we are a part, and this in turn
reflects conceptions of knowledge, of human nature, and of human values and attainments to be found in the writings of formative thinkers of our entire western tradition. In some considerable
part, the breakdown of our civilization is evidence of the errors—
I should call them philosophical—inherent in that point of view
which I have called "rationalism." Unlike some others, however,
I do not believe that the whole aim of educators, concerned with
liberal education, is to try to shore up the ruins of the rationalist
tradition. Here, in my judgment, we would do well to let the
dead bury their dead. What is worthy of survival—and of course
much is—has developed in spite of and against the grain of the
rationalist tradition. What should be saved must be set free from
the bonds by which it has hitherto been tied. In fact, what is
most worthy of survival belongs to an unofficial, almost an underground culture, that has grown up despite attempts of rationalists
to destroy or else to conceal it.

As these last sentences suggest, I shall not be merely polemical, however. In later sections I shall offer some more positive suggestions about education and the good society, but the bases for them will emerge gradually through my dialectical opposition to rationalism.

1. The Ideology of Rationalism

In speaking of the "ideology" of rationalism, I do not use the word "ideology" itself pejoratively. Accordingly, I do not mean that rationalism is wicked or a form of "false consciousness" simply because it is an ideology; some ideologies, kept within bounds, may be quite benign. Nor does it seem to me possible for a society with continuous traditions or a people with a sense of its own identity to persist without some form of ideology. Ideologies, which are in part the products of philosophical ideas and points of view, are semi-systems of ideals, principles, standards, aspirations, along with their supporting overbeliefs about the world, the nature of man, his history and his destiny, his capacities and limitations, his institutions and forms of life. Such overbeliefs, moreover, may be either scientific or wildly speculative, explicit or implicit, literal or figurative. What makes them ideological, as I use the term, are (a) their active social roles, and (b) the fact that their roles are social. The social roles of ideological attitudes and beliefs are active and practical in the sense that they serve as determinants and conditions of action, as mental sets, attitudes, presuppositions, assumptions that guide not only action but thought conceived as symbolic action and as a preparation for actions that are overt and explicit. As ideological, however, such roles are not selected by individuals at their own pleasure; rather are they ingrained in the whole institutional life of a society or people or social class. And for a society, they form a large part of its lore, its official intellectual and social history, what it conceives to be its traditions. Inevitably they are also ingrained in its basic educational practices and institutions; its teachers tend to follow it; its administrators expound it, its students assimilate it; and students and teachers who oppose "the system" are usually in one way or another opposed to its ideology. I am convinced that many of the "dropouts" from our own contemporary institutions of higher learning are in fact people disaffected with the ideology of rationalism. Hence, even if one wants merely to understand the sources of disquiet, of disaffection and revolt in our contemporary universities, one must look to the rationalist ideology that animates much of our established culture.

Just because rationalism as an ideology is a pervasive set of social attitudes and beliefs, it cannot be ascribed *in toto* to any particular philosopher or even to a certain philosophical succession. Plato, undoubtedly, is preeminent among the philosophical progenitors of the rationalist ideology, but I do not, save for purposes of reference and illustration, identify rationalism with Plato's philosophy. Likewise, the great succession of Continental rationalists, from Descartes to Leibniz, have also had considerable formative influence upon the ideology of rationalism. But they did not, so to say, write its constitution. And no doubt rationalism betrays, or caricatures, the thought of these great thinkers at one point or another. Sometimes, indeed, it betrays some of their deeper intentions. Furthermore, one can find, as one would expect if my view of the matter is right, evidences of rationalism in the thought of many philosophers, historians, and men of letters, who are, or think they are, opposed to major aspects of Plato's or Descartes' thought, or who are, or think they are, simply preoccupied with different questions. Although in textbooks the theory of knowledge called "empiricism" is commonly set in opposition to rationalist theories of knowledge, many empiricists hold views about knowledge and its place in human affairs that are virtually paradigms of what I here understand by rationalism.

The following outline of rationalism as an ideology is intended merely as a rough, though I hope serviceable, sketch. Let us begin by noticing a fact or two about the term rationalism itself. As an "*ism*" word, rationalism in its ordinary use refers primarily to a cluster of attitudes, points of view, ways of taking things. It stands to reason and rationality as evolutionism stands to evolution or historicism to history. In short, it is not only a theory about reason and rationality, though it indeed involves such a theory, but also it is a perspective upon human experience and conduct which ascribes to reason and rationality a central and controlling place in our scheme of things. The rationalist, it is plain, not merely defends reason against its detractors: plenty of people, myself included, would wish to do this against irrationalists, mystagogues, and obscurantists. The rationalist also asserts the supremacy of reason as a human faculty, the fundamentality of its norms, and its sufficiency as an organ for thought and action. In Santayana's phrase, the rationalist is committed, symptomatically and above all else, to something he envisages as "the life of reason."

But there is a second aspect of the use of the term "rationalism" in most quarters. Some "ism" words are mainly pejorative, or are conceived by people who employ them pejoratively. Thus "historicism" is, for most people, Karl Popper for instance, a bugaboo, a scapegoat, a kind of original sin philosophically and ideologically. In a primarily rationalist tradition and culture, rationalism is not unnaturally a word with a halo around it, as one discovers when one attacks the point of view associated with it. And when one avows oneself to be an antirationalist, one automatically declares oneself to be a deviant, a kind of dropout from the prevailing culture.

As here conceived, the principle doctrines or contentions of rationalism and rationalists are as follows: [1]

1. First of all, rationalism is a doctrine about man and his culture. Man, for the rationalist, is par excellence the rational animal. It is rationality which distinguishes him from other creatures. And it is rationality which is his salient gift, his most precious faculty. The classical rationalists of course conceived the exercise of reason teleologically as man's own distinctive and proper end. But they also conceived it quasi-administratively, as the faculty which properly coordinates and controls all other human faculties, activities, and affairs. It is, or ought to be, the master of the passions and emotions. If certain other ends are also inherent in human nature, reason not only discovers the means to their realization, but, where they conflict, it is empowered and entitled to reorient and harmonize them in various appropriate ways. Finally, not only is human rationality thus conceived immanent in human nature so that all men, unless perverted or deprived in some way, strive, at first unconsciously and then more and more consciously, to become rational animals, but also

the principles of rationality are, both in thought and in action, to be regarded eternalistically as unamenable to change.[2] Its norms, whose paradigms of course are the norms of logic and exact science, are not only universalistic but universal rules of order to which every man is at all times beholden. Questions of genesis, history, social or pyschological context, have nothing to do with and are always strictly irrelevant to questions of rationality. Nor is it merely that rational standards and claims are formulated ahistorically; it is also and more saliently that no metadescriptive account of them, which suggests that they are subject to fundamental change, is acceptable. Such an account is not an account of rationality in history but only of fallible human metabeliefs about it or else of vagaries in the practices of historical individuals and societies.

Certain important consequences concerning human nature follow at once. The rationalist sees, or tends to see, man's faculties as forming a kind of hierarchy, and, so to say, the internal political economy of a human life as properly a sort of aristocracy. Here, however, there is considerable room for variation within the rationalist tradition. In the view of some rationalists, rationality, though exhibited most saliently in the work of the logician and scientist, may also be somehow implicitly present in art and poetry or in religious thought. In short, some rationalists are, as we may call them, "inclusivists" and informalists who seek to find in every sphere of activity redemptive and entitling evidences of rationality. From their point of view, although poets may be less perfect examples of the rational animal than logicians, a rational poet is superior to a nonrational or irrational one. Others are "exclusivists" or rigorists who limit rationality strictly to logical and scientific thought. From their point of view, any activity, such as painting or sculpture, perhaps even morality and religion, which is found to be (from the preferred point of view) essentially nonrational, is *ipso facto* below the salt of essentially *human* aspiration. And to this extent, poets, musicians, ministers, et al., are not in their characteristic work acting as human beings.

2. Taking classical rationalism again as a preliminary point of reference, we are to view man's good as complex. His complete good consists in the fulfillment of his whole nature, including his basic appetitive and emotional drives. Usually the rationalists

have envisaged man's complete good as a harmony, each propensity or power being fulfilled only to the extent that it does not impair fulfillment of the rest. Such a harmony, however, is minimal, for it envisages nothing more than a mutual compatibility or consistency. Maximally, the fulfilled propensities would be a form of a kind of consortium, each of which provided a positive reinforcement or support for the rest. Thus a man whose hunger and whose sexual impulses are adequately satisfied is so far enabled to devote his energies more fully to his proper work as a rational being than one who is continually hungry or sexually deprived. Man's highest good, however, consists alone in the exercise of his rational faculty.

On this point, again, rationalists have not always taken precisely the same view of what this good involves. In part this is owing to variant theories of human cognition; in part also it is owing to different views about the degrees of worth to be ascribed to the several objects or levels of knowledge; and finally, it is owing to different views about the diversity of intellectual capacity among men.

The following broad tendencies may be noted here. Among classical rationalists, who conceive at least of the higher forms of knowledge as a direct intellectual intuition of the object known, the exercise of reason, in its higher, theoretical reaches, is essentially contemplative. However, among modern rationalist theories of knowledge, for which scientific knowledge serves as a paradigm, the cognitive role assigned to intuition has continually declined. Knowledge is now conceived largely in verificationist terms and one who knows is one who is able to, or knows how to, verify the propositions and theories that he is said to know. In another way, scientific knowledge, which is now understood as controlled inquiry and explanation, does not consist in intuitive perceptions of the thing known, but rather in an ability to offer satisfactory explanations of it. Thus knowing that certain propositions are true or probable depends essentially upon skills necessary to knowing how to explain that which one knows. This in particular involves both powers of logico-mathematical formulation and manipulation for the statement and organization of theories and skills required for the performance of controlled experiments and observations required for their verification.[3]

Now it is no accident that all forms of rationalism which view theoretical science as the paradigm of human knowledge also tend to assign to the most exact and certain of the sciences the place of highest intrinsic value in the hierarchy of cognitive disciplines. Correspondingly, the scientists who possess this knowledge and the skills pertaining thereto are regarded as individuals of the highest dignity and authority among those who know. Such persons, moreover, tend to be esteemed by rationalists as paradigms of human excellence generally, to be emulated wherever possible, to be deferred to where not. In classical times this meant that philosophers were the most exemplary of men, not just because they loved wisdom but because the knowledge they aspired to possess was the highest, most perfect of all. Such a view with some variations prevailed down through the time of Descartes and Spinoza. It is notable, however, that John Locke regarded his own philosophical activity in less exalted terms, and since Locke, rationalists have tended to demote philosophy, at best, to a subordinate place in the hierarchy of cognitive disciplines. Nowadays, as we know, few professional philosophers love wisdom and those who do love it occupy an even lower place in the hierarchy than do their colleagues.

In passing it is also worth remarking that so-called rational theology, which during the middle ages surpassed even philosophy as an intellectual discipline, has fallen to a position even lower than philosophy in the modern rationalist hierarchy. Indeed the general view among rationalists nowadays appears to be that rational theology is a contradiction in terms, and that among theologians, semantical atheists who repudiate "god-talk" altogether are by all odds the most reputable. In mentioning the theologians here, let me add, my aim is merely to remove a possible objection to this part of my synopsis of rationalism. Remembering Plato and Aristotle, as well as the Medieval philosophers and theologians, it is arguable that some thinkers who belong to the rationalist tradition have assigned priority to philosophy or theology, not only because it was considered to be the most exact and perfect of all forms of knowledge, but also because the object of philosophical or theological study is the highest of all forms of being. And certainly many rationalists have taken such a view. But this does not require a serious qualification of my account of rationalism as an ideology. On the contrary, it serves indirectly to reinforce that account. For upon discovering that knowledge of God or of the good is neither clear nor exact, at least from a scientific point of view, rationalists do not conclude that there are forms of knowledge that surpass the sciences in value and authority, or knowers who possess a higher dignity than the scientists; on the contrary, they conclude that such forms of knowledge are of much lower value, and those who profess it of much less distinction as knowers.

In our universities, at the present time, such is precisely the prevailing view. In general, the sciences most highly esteemed are mathematics and the exact physical sciences; and theologians who at least try to be rational in their investigations occupy places of far less intellectual prestige than their colleagues. And if, in some academic circles, philosophy has to some extent recouped its losses, this is largely, or entirely, because of the rise of mathematical logic and its widespread use among analytical philosophers and in particular among philosophers of science.[4]

But now a word must be said about the attitudes of rationalists regarding the abilities of men to achieve man's highest good. It is, of course, not enough simply to say that man's highest good consists in the possession of exact, scientific knowledge. For if there are men who have little scientific ability, and if therefore they are highly imperfect and inadequate rational animals (and indeed to that extent imperfect and inadequate human beings), then the conclusion likely to be drawn is that man's highest good is simply beyond their grasp, or else is available to them only in a diminished or diluted form. And if it is believed, as Plato and Aristotle for example plainly did believe, that such ability is relatively rare, or restricted to particular races or classes of men, then the basis for certain forms of elitism is already prepared.

But here again we must proceed with caution. And though, as I am convinced, rationalism is inherently elitist, just to the extent that its view of the highest good is not accessible or else accessible only in a diminished form to many, or most, men, it does not follow that rationalism is thereby committed, for example, to elitist political ideologies in the ordinary sense. There are many elites and accordingly many kinds of elitism, just as there are many views of the diversity of human abilities. Moreover, there are, within rationalist theories of knowledge, countervailing tendencies which to some extent offset its proneness to elitism.

Let me speak of the latter. In the first place, modern rationalists have increasingly stressed the public, objective, impersonal, and impartial character of scientific inquiry and knowledge. Such knowledge therefore is accessible in some degree to anyone who can master the skills required for scientific analysis, experimentation, and observation. Hence, questions of race, color, wealth, social class, or political power are wholly irrelevant to an individual's ability to share in the scientific enterprise or to enjoy the benefits of a scientific education. Indeed, it is commonly argued that the scientific community is a perfect democracy, a society of equals, each of whom is free to confute his fellow, if he can, and everyone is pledged to subordinate his judgment to the immanent consensus of qualified scientific observers or judges. But of course a scientific consensus is at best an ideal one, since no member of the scientific community at any given time has the time, energy, or relevant knowledge necessary to test the theories of his peers. And in truth, the amount of faith actually required to keep the enterprise of empirical science going has become, in our time, exponential.

In brief, the equalitarian and democratic tendencies implied by modern rationalist doctrines of knowledge are both in principle and in practice restrictive. Perhaps the least misleading analogy here is the institution of science and the restrictive democracy of ancient Athens. In principle, anyone who possesses the necessary aptitudes and can acquire the requisite skills for performing the appropriate intellectual operations is free to enter the scientific establishment. Even so, such a principle is by definition restrictive.[5] Here we shall discount restrictions that arise from historical social factors, which are generally regarded by rationalists as accidental rather than essential. Even so it is impossible to ignore the great native differences in scientific aptitude. Bertrand Russell, himself a great liberal as well as rationalist, has said somewhere that the difference in intellectual capacity between an Einstein and an ordinary man is hardly less great than the difference in this regard between an ordinary man and a chimpanzee. Russell has often been given to hyperboles, but I think we all get the point: a great number of human beings, even under optimum conditions, cannot be expected to understand clearly, not to say make contributions to, the most advanced forms of exact science. And if intellectual power, not to say rationality itself, is measured primarily as the ability to do exact science, then it may be taken for granted that scientific institutions, and especially those concerned with the so-called higher learning, provide little basis or support for principles of extensive human equality and general social or political democracy. And from the standpoint of society as a whole, any rationalist ideology preoccupied with the greatest possible realization of man's highest good, itself conceived essentially in terms of scientific understanding, is bound to that extent to be elitist and hence undemocratic.

No doubt such a conception of rationalism as a general ideology is too simplistic, though I think that it is well to have it in the record before its lines are softened. With this understanding, several important qualifications of it may now be introduced. From Plato on down, rationalists have generally emphasized that there should be an equal opportunity among the members of society to receive as much intellectual training as possible, and so to fulfill whatever powers they may have for realizing man's distinctive or highest good. Secondly, many rationalists, including Plato, have argued that *high* intellectual capacity (again measured by rationalistic assumptions) may not be required for the creditable performance of other jobs of work essential to any tolerable, not to say good, society. Moreover, such jobs of work themselves both presuppose and realize some measure of intellectual power. In the performance of such jobs, imaginatively conceived and understood, men of relatively low intelligence (once more conceived in rationalist terms) thus realize their own limits of man's highest good. More important, however, rationalism need not ignore the common requirements for citizenship and, still more important, for moral respect. On these scores, rationalists often argue that the essential thing is not high intelligence but simply intelligence, not perfect rationality but essential rationality. Citizenship may be intellectually less demanding than set theory or nuclear physics, but every chump above the level of a chimp can qualify for the citizen's bit. So the basic forms of social and political life in a rationalist utopia (which as a utopia aspires only to the not-impossible) might still be conceived as quite broadly equalitarian and democratic. As for moral respect, which the rationalist is disposed to conceive, at least by analogy, in law-like terms, it is the respect owed any individual in so far as he is "human." And all that being human requires, from this point of view, is a modicum of the power to perform the operations essential to scientific understanding. What I must respect in the case of every son of man who can qualify as human is his essential rationality, not the degree of his brilliance as a potential mathematician or physicist or logician.

3. We have now to consider, also only schematically, the rationalist approach to the ideal of the good society. Broadly speaking, it follows from the rationalist conceptions of man, his nature and good.

Already I have remarked upon rationalism's fundamental view concerning the moral relations among men. Something more must now be said about rationalist approaches to morality. This is a sticky wicket. To begin with, as I have said, the ground of *moral* rights and responsibilities for most rationalists is human rationality itself. But now this thesis must itself be qualified. Here we may distinguish a strong or exclusivist rationalism *in ethics* from a weaker inclusivist rationalism. Here strong or exclusivist rationalism maintains that the sole basis of moral regard or concern should be man's nature as a rational being. This may be taken to imply that the fundamental human right is a right to respect for the rationality of the individual: his capacity, that is to say, for scientific understanding and judgment. All other human rights are derived from or justified by this right. Thus, if the fundamental right is a right to respect for the rational faculty of every individual who possesses it, it follows, since every faculty exists not simply to be possessed as a latent power but to be exercised in practice and in act, that each individual has a right (a) to respect for those opinions which are rationally arrived at and which therefore fall within the range of his intellectual competence and (b) to as much education as his natural powers permit. Other rights, accordingly, could be justified as conditions of these primary rights of rational beings as such. Thus, for example, the rights to life, security, the satisfaction of natural appetites or drives, liberty, and so on, might be justified through their utility in relation to the life of reason, which is the life of knowledge. But it must be added at once, exclusivist rationalism does not acknowledge any independent human right to any of these other putative goods or satisfactions.

It is not clear that any great moral philosopher has been an exponent of exclusivist rationalism, though some Kantians appear to have come very close to such a view. However, Kant himself (as I understand him) contended that although each rational being has a right to be regarded as an end unto himself, he is, to himself, not merely a rational being but also one who desires happiness. And for present purposes this may be taken to include the satisfaction of his natural desires. Hence, it could be argued that Kant's own view implies that although the right to exercise and develop one's rational faculty is the absolutely unconditional and primary human right, there is another right, that is, the right to regard and respect as a rational being and conditional upon one's being a rational being (nonrational beings, that is, cannot claim a right to pursue happiness) which is *not* dependent merely upon its utility as a means to the life of reason as such.

The Greeks generally talked less of rights and duties than of goods and virtues. However, a weak or inclusivist rationalism may be easily derived from the classical rationalist conception of man's complete good. From this inclusivist point of view, one could readily argue that although man's primary, or in cases of conflict, prior rights pertain to his essential rationality, his other fundamental propensities provide the basis of rights which, as such, need not be defended on utilitarian grounds as causal conditions of the exercise and enjoyment of the rights of rational beings. These rights pertain only to *rational* beings, but, on this condition, though secondary or lower, they deserve respect. The rights pertaining to rationality always take precedence. But where no problem of conflict exists, they provide the basis of moral claims by individuals both upon society and it own members.

There remains another position open to rationalists which is of considerable interest both on its own account and in the light of certain developments in the institutional life of modern science. The rationalist may begin by returning to the basic premise of his notion of the good life, namely, that man's highest good consists in the pursuit and enjoyment of knowledge, and that the exemplary form of human knowledge is exact positive science. He then may argue that the rights of men as functioning *rational* beings are not owing exclusively to their native endowment of judgment and understanding. Man is through and through a social being, and his rationality, both in potency and in act, is a social achievement. And the more exact and systematic human knowledge becomes, the more evident is this fact. Both the advancement of learning and its transmission through the educational process are increasingly products of corporate institutional activities. To be sure, the collective fund of human knowledge is acquired, saved, and transmitted through the work of men. Nevertheless, the individual scholar, scientist, and teacher of science, remains, so to say, the legatee and trustee of a corporate fund of knowledge. His rights and his dignity as a rational animal derive entirely from his ability to fill these roles. In short, the scientist as such is a truly anonymous public servant whose goals, standards, and works belong entirely to the social institutions which he serves.

In times past, to be sure, the advancement of learning was, or appeared to be, largely the work of independent scholars and inquirers and the transmission of the skills and powers essential to this advancement was a far more loosely organized social enterprise than it has become in our own time. Accordingly, the progress of human knowledge was intermittent, spotty, and uncertain. Now the reverse is true. The exponential enlargement of human learning is itself a direct function of the development of modern institutions for controlled experimental inquiry. These corporate bodies, with their own indispensable divisions of labor, involve sharply differentiated and stratified intellectual responsibilities and prerogatives. In the great scientific laboratories, for example, section heads, laboratory technicians, secretarial aides, and the rest are in practice organized in a quasi-platonic manner, under the direction of administrative "guardians" who at once set the goals for inquiry and determine the rights of various classes of scientific workers. And even in universities, where the organization is looser than in industrial research corporations, stratifications remain and individual freedom of inquiry, except among tenured professors, is severely limited. And the freedom of teachers to teach what they please, as they please, is perhaps still more restricted by departmental and university needs and by corporate standards of objectivity and truth.

If, then, the highest of human goods is the advancement of knowledge, then in the modern world that good must be regarded, progressively and ideally, as the collective achievement of a highly organized and stratified institution or hierarchy of institutions. And if the society of scientific inquirers and scholars is still considered, as it commonly is by rationalists, as a paradigm of the rational and hence good society itself, then rationalism is to that extent increasingly committed to a corporatist rather than an individualist or contractualist conception of the ideal social system. This suggests also that old-fashioned libertarian notions of free thought and inquiry should be radically qualified, if indeed not replaced altogether, in ways that take account of the real social conditions of scientific research. Indeed, one can readily imagine that, to a rationalist, the free-lance inquirer who investigates whatever he pleases in accordance with whatever procedures and standards of truth and meaning he may consider appropriate, must seem intellectually irresponsible and hence socially undesirable.

To a certain extent, in fact, such a view already prevails in practice within the universities and scientific institutes, if not yet in the society at large. This is evidenced by the observation that, as a number of leading sociologists, including Daniel Bell and Lewis Coser, have suggested, the old individualist ideal of the intellectual, along with those of his progenitors, the *philosoph* and the general man of letters, have now been replaced by those of the academician and the scholar. And though the free-floating intellectual still exists, he tends to be regarded by professional scholars as, at best, a "journalist," and, at worst, as an incompetent meddler in affairs that are not his concern.

In sum, then, corporatist or institutionalist rationalism, as it may be called, tends increasingly to regard the rights of men as rational beings as entirely a function of their potentialities as participants in the collective work of scientific research and education. The *fundamental* right, however, belongs to the enterprise of science itself and to the research and academic institutions to which that enterprise is entrusted. Freedom of inquiry, as far as the individual is concerned, is a derivative freedom, at once justified by his institutional roles and limited by the appropriate rules that govern them. The fundamental respect that is due man as the rational being is thus a respect for the self-determining and the self-correcting corporate enterprise of science as a whole. Accordingly, the correlative rights of individual men, as rational beings, are essentially social rights which it is for that enterprise, through its appropriate qualified representatives, to determine.

Modern rationalist ideologies, I believe, are increasingly a cross between what I have called inclusive rationalism and corporatist rationalism. Undoubtedly this is responsible for some of the profound tensions which now exist within the primary institution concerned with the advancement and transmission of human knowledge in modern societies: the university itself. On the one side, there remains an ideal of a society of human individuals in whom, as such, are invested certain inalienable rights to respect and nurture. According to this ideal each individual is to be entirely free to inquire, to think, and to express himself as he sees fit, subject only to the inner checks within his conscience of right reason. Indeed because the multiversity is not only a "science factory," but also a kind of republic in its own right, complete with facilities that minister not only to the student's scientific development but also (if incidentally) to his artistic, religious, and moral nurture, as well as to his basic bodily needs for shelter, food, and sexual gratification. As suggested above, it can indeed be viewed to a certain extent, microcosmically, as an inclusive rationalist's modern paradigm of the good society itself.[6]

At the same time, there can be no doubt that the multiversity, however diversified its activities, however pluralistic its internal organization, remains a corporate institution which (with a qualification presently to be observed) not only seeks to advance and transmit knowledge but which, through its own governing bodies, its various departments and schools, its area studies and research projects, establishes the rules and principles by which the advancement and transmission of knowledge are in practice to be understood. Here of course it is impossible to describe what all this means from the standpoint of the several groups which constitute the multiversity: the administration, the faculty, the student body, and the great miscellany of workers that operate the physical plant, the housekeeping and dining facilities, the stores, and the extracurricular activities essential to the life of the institution and its communities. In his book *Bureaucracy in Higher Education*, Dean Herbert Stroup, has illuminatingly described the organization of offices in the modern American university as a cross between two systems or types of hierarchy: (a) the scalar and (b) the functional.[7] From his account, it is clear that the hierarchical organization of the university itself cannot be understood through simplistic analogies provided by the pyramidal hierarchies to be found in some military or business organizations (though even there, one suspects, the hierarchies are not as simplistic as they may appear to the casual observer). Nonetheless, the importance of the integral hierarchies of the university, which also pervade its structures of formal instruction and research, cannot be minimized. One simple way of testing this estimate is to compare the modern university with Paul Goodman's quasi-medieval ideal of a university as an anarchist community of more or less independent scholars and students who gather together, for the time being, for whatever intellectual and personal companionship and mutual illumination their friendly company may afford. Goodman's ideal, relatively to what exists, is admittedly utopian. Nor is it a utopia to which modern academicians generally aspire. Only the so-called "free universities" that have sprung up in the shadows of the multiversity bear any resemblance to the Goodmanian ideal. From any modern rationalist's point of view, they are accordingly subversive.

Before closing this resume of the drift of rationalism as an ideology, two further points remain to be made. Both concern the institutions of education, and in particular the institutions of higher learning. In the first place, as Plato, the archetypal rationalist, long ago foresaw, the educational system is for the rationalist ideology the indispensable human conveyor belt to the good society or *polis*. In an era of advanced scientific technology such as our own, in which every other institution from industry to government—from business to the so-called media, from Madison Avenue image makers and advertisers to city planners—depends continually upon the achievements and products of modern science, there is scarcely a human activity that is not directly dependent upon or vitally affected by the educational system.

Indeed, what is called "self-defense" is itself now largely dependent upon the establishments of scientific education. In this regard, modern national societies, such as our own, have out platonized Plato himself.

But the Platonic analogy goes still deeper. For just as in the *Republic*, the state and the educational system are, in effect, one and the same, the educators serving as guardians and the guardians as educators, so in our own national society the government and the educational system are similarly intertwined. Hence, as it now becomes impossible within the university to separate James Perkins's "missions" of research and teaching from those of public service—which in practice means primarily service in and to the federal government—so it becomes increasingly difficult, even in a formal congressional system like our own, to separate the "leaders" of the academy from those who at once implement and determine the working policies of the state. Without a cooperative educational system, including in particular the universities, the state quite simply could neither sustain nor defend itself. And without the interlocking ties to the state and its government, the educational system itself would disintegrate. To be sure, this need not mean that the proximate aims of the state are indistinguishable from those of the educational system, though in practice they increasingly overlap. Nor does it mean that the educational system, including again in particular the universities, are simply pawns of the nation-state or its government. Rather does it mean that the destinies of the state and the educational system, and in particular the university conceived as the primary institution for the propagation and advancement of scientific learning, are mutually interdependent.

The second main point concerns the role of the educational system generally and the university in particular in relation not simply to the concerns of the nation-state but to the society as a whole. Here I shall adopt for the sake of discussion the point of view of the inclusive rationalist who, while envisaging the corporate advancement of scientific knowledge as man's highest good, also accepts the notion of a common social good which includes satisfaction of the noncognitive propensities of men. In the *Republic* Plato does not always keep steadily in view the complete good of the community, and so he sometimes overstresses, or appears to overstress, the role of education in the *polis*. In a way Plato, its founder, fell in love with the Academy. However, the enlightened rationalist acknowledges that the educational system is a necessary but not sufficient institution for a tolerable, not to say a good society. Furthermore, the inclusive rationalist insists on not only the necessity of ministering to the needs of all members of society (and not merely those who show promise of intellectual distinction and hence usefulness to the state) but of serving them all in depth as whole men who have needs that cannot be the immediate concern of education, including of educational institutions as far-flung in their activities and roles as the multiversity. Education, no matter how encompassing its own activities, has ends in view different from those of government and the economy. There are also many lower-order cultural activities that have different proximate goals from those of the educational system, no matter how broadly gauged. For example, art, literature, music, and the dance, as well as the newer media, are as such, intended less as contributions to learning than as forms of consummatory satisfaction or pleasure. Their aim, as Bernard Berenson used to say, is immediately "life-enhancing." And just because of this, they must not be tied too closely to activities concerned primarily with learning and teaching. The proper complaint against academic art is simply that it is a bore. And rationalists, no more than other people, are obliged to approve of boredom. Thus, while the university should cultivate (in moderation) all of the arts, it should distinguish between the work of the teacher and the apprentice on the one side, and the mature, creative artist and his audience on the other, even though in practice both, or all, of these groups may in fact overlap.

The rationalist himself may be the first to insist that an educational system whose concern is with the advancement and propagation of knowledge cannot in the nature of the case be all things to all men, however much the universities may tend to become microcosmic societies and social systems in their own right. Education cannot be all, because learning cannot be all. Man is indeed, as Ralph Barton Perry used to put it, the "docile" animal, by which he meant the animal that learns from his experience. However, docility is not manhood, only its condition. And when we become "men"—as, one may hope, we are always becoming from the moment of birth—we seek, rightly and rightfully, to use our acquired skills and abilities to make and form and act and do things which, as such, are not the learner's immediate business—nor yet, therefore, the teacher's. A society dominated by its teachers and learners is a society committed to the ideal that learning is man's only, or primary, good. And this is not true. Such a society, ironically, makes a fetish of immaturity.

II

It is evident from the preceding remarks that we have been passing implicitly from the description of rationalism as an ideology, including its sense in its more inclusive forms of the role of education, toward its critique. Let us now bring that critique into the open.

I shall begin by saying something about the fundamental weaknesses of rationalism as an ideology, even at its best, and hence the radical errors to which, at that best, its view of man, society, and education are prone. This is also a critique of an ever more deeply ingrained tradition in our whole Western culture with which, in my judgment, it is necessary to make a final and radical break. Of necessity, I shall have to deal with these difficult matters in a very summary fashion which may make it appear that I am more dogmatic, as well as surer of my ground, than I am. The following remarks are thus to be taken as challenges and as explorations, rather than as finished positions.

Bluntly: although rationality is one dimension of a tolerable human nature, it is by no means the only propensity that distinguishes man from other creatures; nor does it form *the* basis of his highest good.

Consider how much is either left out or misconceived when man's rational faculty is viewed as his unique, controlling, and highest human endowment. For example, man is also uniquely the religous animal, the being capable of grasping his own mortality and of making something beyond his own individual existence a matter of ultimate concern. This is something that escapes the rational animal as such. Secondly (and here I am not interested in questions of priority or rank), man is the communal animal,

capable of friendship, comradeship, and the forms of love sometimes grouped under the heading of *agape*. Man, if you will, is
the animal that loves; he is therefore the animal that reciprocates
and needs reciprocity. At the same time, man is also the self-
perfecting, self-overcoming, and self-transcending being. And
this, not only in the religious or social or intellectual dimension
but, in the widest sense, in the ethical dimension. Now, however, another ideal comes more distinctly into view: the ideal of
self-determination, of self-control, of what Kant called "giving
oneself the law." The very notion of morality is impossible apart
from the ideal of the individual as an autonomous agent, who
assumes responsibility for his own conduct, his own principles,
his own comportment. In fact, apart from such a view of man,
free personal relations among men, including above all the relations of contract and personal loyalty and love, can scarcely
exist.

But the moment the word "person" is introduced a whole dimension of human character comes into view which cannot be
adequately comprehended by the notion of rationality. In fact
rationality itself is but one of the forms which this dimension of
character normally takes. Man is, inventively, the role-playing,
the acting, and not merely the active animal. His cultural and
spiritual life, indeed his mental life itself, is largely a matter of
role-playing and of acting. Clearly role-playing involves the
ability to follow rules, and the attitudes attendant thereto. The
role-player requires the ability to subordinate his interests, feelings, indeed his whole "subjective" personality, as it is sometimes
called, to the role itself. But it requires much more; in most cases
it requires also the capacity for identification which is sometimes
called empathy. And since the mode of identification is in this case
freely imaginative, it is not something that can be fully understood by means of rule-governed activities and practices. In fact
it is to the latter what the actual, open-ended, dialogical, and
speculative use of language is to rules of grammar and of usages.

Summarily we may say that man is or should be distinctively
the animal capable of living the life of the mind. This, among
other things, means the power to turn or to transform every
motion, every bodily change, every purely behavioral process into
an action, a passion, an event, an occasion. If this sounds insuffer-

ably loose and romantic, we may say more exactly that man is the creature whose own bodily processes, changes, and motions have no *being* for him save in so far as he can relate them to mental events, developments, actions.

But such a conception of man is not adequately conveyed by the notion of the rational animal. I should be prepared to argue that the rationalist misconceives the life of the mind and that his reductivist view of knowledge is itself symptomatic of that misconception. His own fault, curiously, is itself a failure of understanding and of knowledge. In consequence he at once misconceives and misrepresents man's good, high as well as complete, and as a result the forms of social life and of education required for both endurable and well being. Worse, he has an inadequate understanding of rationality itself. Rationality in fact must be saved from the ideology of rationalism.

In saying this let me add that I do not object to the view, which Professor William Frankena (in conversation) considers very rationalistic indeed, that the task of education as such being with learning, is therefore with knowledge. For I conceive the proximate aim of all learning to be some form of knowledge, and knowledge to be the achievement which learning, and hence education itself, can bestow. My objections to rationalism are (a) that it woefully narrows both the proper range of human knowledge and hence the proper forms of learning and education, and (b) that even when that range is extended as far as it legitimately may be, there is still much more to the life of the mind than the idea of knowledge adequately comprehends.

To take the last point first, we want to do and ought to do more with our minds than seek knowledge. We want and ought, for one thing, simply to exercise them. Physical exercise is a pleasure, but so is mental exercise. Study, inquiry, analysis can be intrinsic goods even for those who do not succeed very far in advancing learning. But the point is more extensive. I am not proposing a bill of rights, educational or otherwise, for intellectual failures. The great romantics, however much they may have overstated or misrepresented their own aspirations, recognized above all the incomparable values and virtues of what they called the imagination. Every form of cultural and mental life yields satisfactions as well as achievements which are more and less than cognitive. And the value of these achievements is often mixed: it is intrinsic to the satisfaction or to the act as well as instrumental to other ends.

Now many inclusive rationalists doubtless mean to do justice to the "lower" pleasures and to the satisfactions afforded by the body. I am not talking of them here, though the rationalist's hierarchies strike me as absurd. I am not, in short, talking about the plainly *mental* values inherent in sensory experience, or in the affective gratifications which sensation may yield, important as they may be. What I have here in view is the entire, incomparable life of the constructive imagination, whose aim at least in part, is not to inform us about what is or ought to be but to offer envisagements of what might be and to fashion symbolic forms to which questions of literal fact are not determining. Nothing is more indispensable to the domains of literature and indeed of all art than the tropes, in which the mind finds a great part of its own inner life and happiness. Their loss, or worse their repudiation among literal-minded "cognitivists," concerned exclusively to describe or explain what is the case, entails not only for themselves but for societies and educational systems which view them as exemplary, a terrible constriction of the whole life of the human spirit and a ghastly depletion of man's capacity for refreshment and self-renewal.

But if the rationalist misunderstands the mind he so greatly prizes, no less does he foolishly disenfranchise familiar ranges of human cognition. This is all the more perverse since, from his point of view, knowledge itself is the proper end and achievement of the human mind. Here, let me emphasize, I do not mean to dwell simply upon the nonempirical elements in scientific understanding itself: its essential dependence, that is, upon mathematics and logic, its involvement in contrafactual or subjunctive modes of understanding, and the sophisticated perceptual and motor drills and skills required for experimental inquiries and confirmations. The issue now concerns forms of knowledge that are *not* merely dimensions or vehicles of scientific inquiry or conditions of the cognitive achievements which it affords.

In such a paper as this it is perhaps most useful to proceed by reference to domains of activity that the modern rationalist, at least, generally concedes to lie outside of the scope of positive science. Of most importance is the understanding of ordinary language and symbolic forms themselves. The rationalist often appears to take linguistic understanding for granted. And in fact the great rationalists have often treated language as little more than an auxiliary device for communicating ideas and beliefs, perceptions and understandings, already acquired and possessed in some other way. Here I can do no more than remind you of a truth, tersely stated by one of the great modern rationalists, C. S. Peirce, namely, that "thought and expression are one," and that without the intelligent use of language as well as other modes of expression there could be no thought and no knowledge of any sort. Language is essential not to communication only, but also to the very formation of scientific propositions, theories, and doctrines. It is indispensable to that dialogue of the soul with itself in terms of which Socrates conceived self-knowledge. Without it, in fact, the life of the mind would shrivel virtually to nothing. But the knowledge achieved by anyone who knows how to use any natural language (together with its attendant symbolisms) properly and hence discriminately is a knowledge of an enormously varied range of forms of expression (and thought) that serve to articulate and to guide corresponding forms of life. To know how to read and to speak a natural language is automatically to know what it is to participate in all such correlative ways of life.

Of course such understandings may be jammed, confused, impoverished by a prevailing rationalist ideology of culture. But they cannot be entirely destroyed by it. Men who know what it means to love God may be hobbled by a misguided semantics, a mistaken theory of knowledge, or an ontology beset by preconceptions about "what there is." But the language they learn and the knowledge thereby acquired permit a hobbling no more. Likewise, those who know what is done when the moralist, or the poet, or the politician says his bit, know and learn more than any rationalist ideology can undo. If an atheist learns the King's English he automatically learns in spite of himself what it means and is to pray. And if a platonist learns the marvelous language of his forebears, he learns more than any tendentious Plato can try to make him unlearn.

I need go no further. Knowledge of a natural language constitutes a basic human culture in its own right, an ability to achieve many things that the rationalist always misunderstands or falsifies. Let me be more specific. The person who learns how to read the Bible knows also what it can be to know or love God. The person who knows how to read Hamlet knows what it is to understand and appreciate a work of art. The individual who knows what a "person" is knows at the same time what it means to assume or to be assigned a role, along with the responsibilities and rights that pertain thereto. And the person who knows how to address another as a "you" and a "Thou," knows what communication and fraternity, what contract and community are. To emphasize the point: language is all. Or if it is not (and it is not), a statement of what the knower of a language really knows suffices both to confute and to enlarge the understanding of anyone who fancies himself to be a rationalist.

But of course the knowledge of a language makes possible many forms of achievement that are *not* intrinsically cognitive. Thus, giving an order, though it indeed presupposes and involves a considerable range of cognitive skills, including knowing how to give an order, is not itself a cognitive achievement. Not everything we do with words, by a very long shot, is to articulate or communicate something we know—even in the very widest sense of the term. Nor is every successful verbal expression or communication intended to convey a cognition. Yet one of the major ranges (or system of ranges) of human utterance is indeed cognitive. And cognition, in one form or another, is the proximate goal of a very great part of human expression and thought. In fact, my main intention in mentioning the centrality of the knowledge required for the use of a natural language is, not only to show what other things are presupposed by linguistic skills, but first of all to set the stage for a review of the gamut of essentially cognitive activities for which the knowledge of a natural language prepares us:

1. Understanding of a (natural) language makes possible, and is essential to, all the forms of theoretical knowledge which the rationalist himself most saliently emphasizes: that is to say, general knowledge of matters of fact, and, no less important, those systematic bodies of such knowledge which comprise a theory or, more broadly, a science.

2. It makes possible, furthermore, the basic modes of the formal knowledge which comprise logic and mathematics. And because the conditions of this sort of knowledge are not exactly the same as those required for general factual knowledge, or of the sorts embodied in the empirical sciences, the adequate understanding of a language at least introduces the user to the differential conditions required for formal logical understanding and for empirical knowledge.

3. Understanding of the roles and functions of a natural knowledge also enables us to grasp the forms of knowledge concerned with the life of conduct and of action. In so doing it introduces us to the principles and ranges of practical reason. Here I must simply state what I believe to be true, that although these forms of knowledge do indeed involve and presuppose empirical factual knowledge, practical understanding is not reducible to the latter. In fact one of the ways of bringing out the differences between the latter and the knowledge involved in matters of action is through the sorts of desultory logico-linguistic study to which the so-called ordinary language philosophers have so usefully devoted themselves in recent decades.

3a. Among the forms of knowledge essential to the life of action are first of all those comprised under the headings of want, desire, and interest. Rational action would be impossible if individuals could not know, or come to know, *what* they desire. And I consider it a very grave error on the part of philosophers in the tradition of Hume to set human knowledge generally in contrast or opposition to those forms of deliberation and action that determine, inform, and issue from desire. Knowing what one wants is a distinctive and often difficult human achievement, rendered all the more difficult by philosophies which systematically deny it cognitive status as such. But knowing what one wants also presupposes another preliminary form of knowledge to which Stuart Hampshire, among others, has called attention in his recent book, *The Freedom of the Individual*.[8] This is the knowledge of the kinds of possibility which I shall here call "human" in order to distinguish them from merely logical or physical possibilities. I have space only to mention the knowledge of possible objectives as well as possible lines of action which one could pursue, or institute, if one chose to do so. This sort of knowledge, let me add, is an indispensable phase of that range of human understanding we call self-knowledge.

3b. But of course knowing what one wants, or could do if one wanted to, is only a part of what one needs to know in order to understand oneself or in order to engage in rational action. Here we may simply follow Kant in making a general but necessary distinction between the knowledge of what is wanted or desired and the knowledge of what is good or right, of what ought to be and to be done (including what *ought* to be affirmed and said). All the same, I believe Kant to be mistaken in certain fundamental particulars as to the nature of the latter forms of knowledge. Again there is space only for the barest mention of what I take to be the correct view. First is the knowledge derived from and dependent upon the employment of public standards and grading systems. Participation in such routine collective enterprises as various as going to market, getting an academic degree, passing an examination, or returning a bad egg to the waiter, all essentially involve both the knowledge of standards and the ability to apply them. Knowing what is good and bad is in very large part knowledge of just this sort. But one has not learned all that is involved and required in distinguishing between the good and the bad unless one also knows what it is to be involved in a grading situation, to perform grading operations, and not least to establish and *to modify* the standards by which things may be graded. By analogical extension, we move by stages from the simple knowledge of grades and of things as graded to the knowledge, also essentially public and impersonal, involved in the understanding of institutions and the forms of activity essential or proper to them. Here in particular I have in mind the knowledge of what particular institutions and forms of activity are for, the ends they serve, by which alone they are distinguished from one another as institutions. Here indeed, at a distance, there is something to be learned from the classical rationalists, and especially Plato himself. Among such forms of activity are the various arts and crafts, and indeed all the various disciplines whose principles must be known if one is to engage in or to obtain a competence in them. In many instances, it may be added, such knowledge would be difficult or impossible to acquire without formal instruction of some sort. For involved also in full knowledge of a discipline is understanding of its various offices, and of distinctive responsibilities and rights pertaining thereto. All this knowledge is also entirely public and impersonal, although it has aspects which again radically distinguish it from the sorts of knowledge that are usually called scientific. Where Plato and Aristotle went wrong is in supposing that institutions and hence their constitutions are unalterable. Full knowledge of an institution entails a grasp of its history and its possibilities and directions of change.

3c. But no man is merely a bundle of stations and duties, and only the mythological organization man has solved the problems about what he should do with himself when he knows the institutions, the activities, and the responsibilities and rights pertaning thereto, in which his life is entangled. And if we use the term "ethics" in referring to the codes of right action which such institutional activities involve, then let us reserve the term "moral," here, for responsibilities and problems of conduct not covered by such codes. This way of putting the matter, however, may be misleading, for I do not mean to suggest that morality is simply what is left over after, so to say, we have done our various ethical sums and received the grades we accordingly deserve. In particular there are problems of "personal relations," which I conceive of as distinctively and crucially *moral* problems, that cannot be settled by appeal to any institutional or disciplinary principles whatever. Nonetheless, for each individual there *is* such a thing as moral knowledge, the knowledge that is to say of what "I" ought to aim at and to do. And, correlatively, there is an irreducible first-personal knowledge of moral responsibilities or obligations. This knowledge, as I have argued elsewhere, may itself be (and be called) objective. But this precisely does not entail that such knowledge is of the sorts acquired by following either the public routines of the positive sciences or the lines of activity which our public stations and duties impose upon us. Objectivity is *not* the special or exclusive prerogative of public or of institutional life, not to mention the form of institutional life of which "science" is the inadequate summary name.

3d. But it is essential now to say something about philosophical knowledge. As I conceive it, morality is concerned with problems of personal relations and hence with problems of conduct concerned essentially with what we, as human beings, ought to do in our dealings with persons—including ourselves as persons. But if all of us, *as moral beings*, are more and less than systems of stations and duties, so also are we as individual human beings more than persons. Our selves encompass and are not encompassed by our various personae; we also encompass and are not encompassed by our personalities as moral agents. I agree with Professor Frankena, although for different reasons, that what he calls the good life includes more than the moral life. But from my point of view the moral life and the moral problems which it involves are an inalienable part of the good, or at least the tolerable life. Nor, on the other hand, do I believe the good or tolerable life to consist either of ends set by our interests or desires or even of their harmonious or inclusive satisfaction. For a tolerable life would involve, among other things, living or trying to live up to one's moral responsibilities, being able, as we say suggestively, to live with oneself. But a good life encompasses more than a life both of satisfied desires and of good conscience in the moral sense. For a good life must, in principle, provide some fulfillment or satisfaction of every range and dimension of the self. And this includes fulfillment of those responsibilities which one sets oneself, simply as such, but which go beyond the range of personal relations. Here, for purposes of discussion, let me invoke the useful protestant notion of the vocation or calling. Thus conceived, an individual self becomes involved, by stages in a *life* and in a destiny that is peculiarly and poignantly his own. And the knowledge or understanding of that life, and of the vocation it commits him to is reached only by many stages, not all of them moral. No one, I should argue, can finally know my vocation but me (and God, if God there be). Others may offer advice, which may and doubtless should be gratefully listened to on occasion. But the knowledge their advice is based on or may embody is not, as such, the knowledge of what I am finally to be and to become. For it remains general and impersonal, a knowledge of human character and human nature, which, again, is at once both more and much less than a knowledge of myself.

What has this to do with philosophy? In the end quite simply everything. For if morality concerns the problems of first-personal relations among self-determining persons, philosophy concerns the problems faced by the would-be self-governing self in its great confrontations with its total environment and in its developing and cumulative efforts to discover for itself those modes of self-identification out of which it can make a life. The philosopher, who by definition seeks not just the wisdom of life in general but the wisdom of and for his own life, is driven precisely to raise all the limiting questions which the establishmentarian, the bureaucrat, and the functionary do not answer because they have neither a need nor a duty to ask them. For the latter, in fact, such questions are precisely meaningless, without point, silly. For the philosopher (and of course in some fashion everyone of us is a philosopher), however, they and his efforts to answer them are in a way his very life. And, conversely, his life is a series of *agones:* struggles, or arguments with himself whose ever-unfinished and unfinishable end is precisely that positive freedom to which (among others) Socrates and Spinoza, the great idealists, and in our time the existentialists, have all, in one way or another, aspired. This is why the dialogical form adopted by Plato, and recurrently employed and readapted by many philosophers since his time, seems so naturally to be the classical literary genre for the presentation of philosophical problems. It is also why, at a certain stage, it becomes necessary for the philosopher to move, as Kant, for one, so conspicuously did, from analysis to dialectic. For analysis offers only the elucidation of a distinctive form of words or symbols and its corresponding form of activity and life. Dialectic, however, is required when one moves beyond the principles that govern it to their ever unstable places in one's own scheme of things and hence to the claims they may rightly make upon one's own encompassing being.

Thus conceived, there can be strictly no such thing as *the* philosophy of science, *the* philosophy of art, or *the* philosophy of education, but only philosophies of science, art, and education. And these themselves become philosophies, or rather partial philosophies, only when they are brought eventually into dialectical relation to the other "philosophies of x" which concern one's life.

Now the analytic stages of philosophical inquiry do, or can, yield *bona fide* public knowledge, though properly conceived this can never be a purely "empirical" knowledge, precisely because the "object" to be known is not a pattern of physical change but a form of thought and action, a system not of phenomena, but of principles, rules, methods. But the philosopher, again, can never content himself with analysis; for having discovered, as he thinks, what the principles governing a form of activity are, he then must go on to ask normative questions about them which in the final instance are essentially first-personal. And if the answers he comes to are illuminating to others, this is only because they have asked analogous questions for themselves and find themselves involved in corresponding predicaments of their own. But each of us must finally discover the "essential facts" for himself.

Much more would have to be said of course to turn this rude sketch into a convincing portrait. If I am right, however, philosophical knowledge or understanding, like moral knowledge, can never aspire to become part of the cumulative public knowledge which the rationalist so exclusively prizes and indeed regards as the paradigmatic form of human knowledge itself. But this means that philosophy, like morality (let me now add), like religion, literature and the arts, and indeed like all the humanities, when they go to fundamentals, presents educational problems, and particularly for formal educational institutions such as the school, the college, and the university, which are essentially different from those presented by the sciences.[9]

But before saying anything about these problems by way of a conclusion, let me express my own commitment to the humanities, not just as indispensable parts of a liberal education and of a decent or free life, but also therefore, as inalienable activities of a decent and properly free society. Or, rather, it is just because they are, as I view them, inalienable functions of a free life and a free society, that any tolerable system of public education must make them central features of its curriculum. And indeed, it is only when the sciences themselves are taught and learned in a liberal and philosophical spirit that they themselves become proper parts of that liberal education required by free men in a free society. I will go further: until the humanities, properly conceived, are again regarded as the very heartland of such an education, and a humanistic spirit is made to prevail throughout the whole educational system, but especially and increasingly throughout its institutions of higher learning, that system and those institutions will remain inadequate to their occasions. Worse, when, as now, they are regarded as incidental studies, cultural adornments to be satisfied mainly in the form of a meagre and haphazard distribution requirement, or else are viewed like the sciences themselves as specialties, fit for a few unchosen spirits who haven't the wits to do proper science, the educational system so far becomes a positive impediment to personal and social freedom.

Nothing could be educationally more subversive from the standpoint of a free society than a system of higher learning dominated exclusively by the aspirations—wholly legitimate of course in their own way—of positive science and scientific technology, that is to say, the spirit of rationalism. And in fact it is precisely in the closed and totalitarian society that the institutions of higher learning become nothing but institutes of science and technology. Make no mistake, in the Soviet Union, for example, the exact physical sciences and the forms of education that serve them flourish as well or better than they do in so-called free societies. It is the humanities, and in particular philosophy, which must go underground if they are to exist at all in the totalitarian state. I have no doubt that there are true philosophers in the Soviet Union, just as I have no doubt that there are true philosophers wherever individual men ask limiting questions, however secretly, about "the system." And just to the extent that philosophers exist, the system is already broken, whether its masters know it or not. In a tolerable society, however, the system is broken in public.

But now I must say a word about the problems which philosophy in particular and the humanities in general present to the educator and especially to the formal educational institution. One may ask whether philosophy, as I conceive it, can be taught at all. And if in some sense it can be taught the question remains whether it can be properly taught within the university. Let me say at once that no problems of special difficulty arise—up to a point at least—so long as one confines oneself to the history of philosophy and to analytical philosophical preliminaries and prologomenas. Intellectual history generally requires skills which are no doubt beyond the reach of the ordinary political or social historian. Still, formal courses in intellectual history and in the history of philosophy conceived as a branch of intellectual history, are taught, and well taught, in many contemporary universities. Similarly, excellent courses in so-called analytical and linguistic philosophy are given in many universities and colleges. And the same is true of other preliminary forms of humanistic study.

It is also arguable that the only way in which philosophy can be taught is through its history. And the same may be said of other humanistic studies, including literature, the arts, and religion. I should argue, however, that the historian as such can never finally penetrate the heart of a philosophical work, any more than he can penetrate the heart of a work of literature, a musical composition, or a bible. And the reason is simply this: the matters to which such a work addresses itself are philosophical problems, and if one has no philosophical impulses of one's own, one cannot understand finally what it is all about, any more than a musicologist with a tin ear can understand what a string quartet is all about. Understanding here presupposes the possibility of first-personal appreciation, which requires a direct individual engagement and involvement with the object. In the case of philosophy, however, there is in a sense no "object" at all, but only a series of meditations which the reader or listener is permitted, for his own edification and use, to overhear. Or, to vary the figure, it is only the internal dialogue which the reader carries on with the philosophical work which is the true philosophical object. Until the historian is ready and able to conduct such a dialogue with Spinoza or Hume or Hegel or Wittgenstein, he is inadequate to the work he seeks to study and to understand as a work of *philosophy*.

In philosophy, as such, the following stages can be regarded in principle as forms of learning. First of all is the task of learning how to read a philosophical work. This requires a grasp of its intention as a search for clarification and self-control on the part of its author. And this means that one must come to know what such searches are and what results are to be expected from them. Here one learns and comes to know only by doing, that is by entering directly and freely into the philosophical enterprise itself. This involves, for the reader, impersonating the philosopher one reads or listens to by asking or coming to ask his questions and struggling toward the answers he seeks and sometimes finds. But if one reads philosophically this requires not only impersonation but, as I have already suggested, a continuing dialogical relationship on the reader's part to the work, to its questions and answers: that is to say, a questioning of the point and significance of the questions themselves, a demand for their further clarification, and a continuing struggle to make the question one's own or else, as is sometimes the case, to see why one must repudiate the questions along with their answers. As Moore once said, a large part of learning philosophy is learning what questions to ask. Another large part consists in learning what questions not to ask, what are merely pseudoquestions or show-questions that have no significance for one's life. Said Peirce in one of his profoundest *dicta:* "Dismiss make-believe!" But dismissing make-believe often takes a bit of doing. Moreover, one sometimes finds, as I have done, that one begins by making believe and ends by asking in dead earnest. Each person must finally dismiss his own make-believe. There is a sense in which the playfulness of Socrates is an essential part of his ultimate seriousness. Just because philosophy is, in part, a search for significant questions, it requires a touch of the child's play at raising questions. The question "Why?" begins as a game, and ends, sometimes, as the puzzle of a lifetime.

No doubt philosophy can, by various forms of indirection, imitation, and emulation, be learned. And no doubt the philosopher is, and must be, a supreme example of the autodidact. The question rather is whether anyone can teach a man philosophy but the man himself. Here the answers are of great difficulty and my suggestions are made diffidently.

Confining myself now to the ultimate aspirations of philosophers, rather than to the analytical preliminaries, I think one must say, first of all: that all philosophical learning and hence teaching must be at once informal and dialogical. And if, on occasion, the philosophical teacher "lectures," as I am doing here, he must try to impersonate his pupils by trying to anticipate their questions, by raising their difficulties, and by conveying the sense of struggle

—the agony, if you will—involved in all genuine philosophical reflection. Socrates remains, in my view, the archetypal philosophical teacher, that is, one who teaches by asking leading questions, and then by forcing his "pupils" to question and re-question their own successive answers. All philosophical teaching is indeed a kind of spiritual midwivery. The philosopher does not and cannot teach by telling or even, finally, by explaining. Or rather, all his tellings and explainings are at best leading and exemplary. But even these will misfire without a plentiful and continual dose of the irony, including the self-mockery, of which Socrates was so great a master.

Now I must bring these remarks to a head and close. I do not mean to suggest that Socrates is the ideal teacher; in many spheres of learning his way of teaching is either impossible or immensely inefficient. There is a place for the pedagogue who teaches by telling and explaining, by formal demonstrations, and the rest. What I do contend is that philosophical education and the forms of learning and teaching possible and proper to it, is an indispensable part of any education that pretends to be liberal and that aims at the cultivation of free men and free minds for a free society.

What does all this really come to? It means, I think, that there are not and can never be "objective" paradigm cases of the philosopher, of a philosophical problem, or even, indeed, of a philosophical activity. Philosophy is not a science, but neither is it an art. Philosophers want discipline, but not entrance into a discipline. There are, and can be, no principles of philosophy, in the way that there are, say, principles of logic or of physics, Philosophical principles, like moral ones, are at best or worst first-personal precepts, even when, on occasion, the first person happens to be not singular but plural. Philosophy in short is the indispensable free activity of the liberal mind and the free man. Its possibility is also a condition and a token of the free or tolerable society. And philosophical education, accordingly, must be an ingredient in any system of higher education proper to a free society.

One may go a step further. The informality of philosophical study, and hence of philosophical learning and teaching, its playfulness and seriousness, its imitativeness and its refusal to put up with imitation, its exemplars and undercutting of all exemplars and leaders, and finally, its aspiration to go beyond study to mature acts of self-commitment and self-creation offers, not a model for the good society or the good life, but a necessary dimension or aspect of a tolerable society and an endurable human life. Accordingly, it is because rationalism so totally perverts the philosophical spirit and aspiration that it must be exorcised not only from academic philosophy itself, but also, and for deeper, more fundamental reasons, from the implicit ideologies both of the university and of our contemporary *polis* in America. Or it must be exorcised if the American university is to be a truly liberal institution of higher education and if the American *polis* is to be, or to aspire to be, a society fit for free men.

As it is, I am bound to say it, it is entirely problematic whether American universities, deeply interpenetrated as they are by the spirit of rationalism, and the American social system, overwhelmed as it is by the cant and by all the status symbols of a rationalist ideology, are very much better fitted than their "totalitarian" counterparts to be the objects of a philosopher's piety and love.

Notes

Introduction

1. Professor Robert Wolff's recent book, *The Ideal of the University*, which came to my hands as this preface was being written, proves to be no exception. Among other things, Wolff does propose, as I would, that the Ph.D. be abolished. But his proposals to sever the institutional connections between professional schools and their home universities would have the effect of reconverting the university into a somewhat modernized *Gymnasium*. He would put in place of the Ph.D. a three-year professional degree designed to certify candidates to teach their subjects at the college or graduate level. But if Wolff's proposal were adopted, even such vestigial connections as now exist between the College and the University would disappear. Accordingly the whole idea of the university as a place where teachers and their students may cooperate in recreative as well as original activities of the mind would be foreclosed. What active thinker would wish to spend his life in Wolff's university? What creative student would care to linger there in order to enlarge his understanding of the human condition? More deeply, what "pro," whether young or old, would be continually challenged to relate his own advanced studies to the problems of men in the modern world? Wolff's "practical proposals" leave the whole problem of liberalizing the professional school untouched, just as they also leave untouched the educational problem of converting professional men into fuller human beings.

2. On Leaving Harvard

1. This is not to deny that there were other consequences of the tutorial system of great benefit to many students. Those fortunate enough to get a "great" tutor, interested in the fullest ramifications of his subject, acquired a more liberal conception of their major itself. Not everyone, unfortunately, was so fortunate.

2. Let me add, however, that my withdrawal did not mean the end of "Hum. 5." Fortunately, both for the department and for the cause of general education itself, a younger colleague, Rogers Albritton, agreed to take over my part of the course, and I am glad to say that he proved to be a great success.

3. Seymor M. Lipset and Sheldon S. Wolin, "Introduction," *The Berkeley Student Revolt* (Garden City, New York: Anchor Books, 1965).

3. On Going to Brandeis: The Promise

1. Perhaps it is well to add here that, aside from some revisions made principally in the first and third sections, this essay was conceived and written months before the appearance in *Commentary* of Irving Howe's long essay, "The New York Intellectuals," October 1968. My use of the term is looser than his since he has in view mainly "the intellectuals of New York who began to appear in the thirties, most of whom were Jewish," and he focuses largely upon people who have been connected with certain literary journals, including in particular *Partisan Review*. Only one philosopher, Sidney Hook, figures prominently in Howe's discussion, and, not unnaturally, the interests of other people to whom he refers are mainly literary and political. I have in mind here many philosophers who owe little or nothing to Hook, as well as social scientists, historians, and artists, many of whose political and social attitudes have not turned essentially on the fortunes of the Russian Revolution and its aftermath. Moreover, although most of the people here in view have lived in New York for considerable periods of time, not all of them regard that city as home. Indeed, because of the continuing wide-spread influence of the New York intellectuals, many people, outside as well as inside the universities, are affiliated with the group in spirit who have never lived in the

city and know its members mainly through their writings and the journals they edit.

2. The confusions implicit in such a quadrivium were serious (as if literature itself were not a creative art!) though scarcely more so than those already inherent in the conventional trivium that prevails elsewhere. In this instance they were unlikely to prove fatal, since in practice the educational value of active literary criticism and creation was largely taken for granted.

5. Coda: Outward Bound

1. Christopher Jencks and David Riesman, *The Academic Revolution.* New York City: Doubleday, 1968. A detailed discussion of their ideas is presented in chapter seven.

2. Quoted from "Wordsworth, a Preliminary Survey," by James Smith, in *A Selection from Scrutiny*, Vol. 2, compiled by F. R. Leavis, p. 139. Cambridge, England: Cambridge University Press, 1968.

3. Ibid., p. 142.

6. Enter the Multiversity

1. Clark Kerr, *The Uses of the University*. New York City: Harper and Row, 1964.

2. Alexander Bickel, "The Tolerance of Violence on the Campus," *The New Republic*, June 13, 1970.

7. The American University: Part I—Defenders of the Status Quo

1. Daniel Bell, *The Reforming of General Education*. New York City: Columbia Press, 1966.

2. Bell, p. 69.

3. It is no accident that the chairman (Professor Paul M. Doty) of the Doty Committee (the full title of its report is "Report of the Special Committee to Review the Present Status and Problems of the General Education Program") and most of its leading members were scientists and that its report accurately reflected attitudes prevalent at Harvard's scientific center. Only very eloquent opposition, in part by certain humanistically-oriented scientists, prevented a radical

revision of the general education program which would have broken down the uneasy three-fold distinction between the natural sciences, the social sciences, and the humanities, into a new two-fold distinction between "the sciences" and "the humanities," with the "true social sciences," now properly oriented in the direction of exact "behavioral science," grouped with the natural sciences, and the humanities themselves ranged with history and with those historically-oriented parts of social science that cannot quite cut the "behavioral" mustard. The defeat of the Doty Committee's proposal, I may add, astonished us all. It also showed, implicitly, how anxious are many professors about the take-over of university policy and the idea of liberal education by exponents of a culture whose mind belongs wholly to the purposes and uses of positive science. Nor is it entirely an accident that it should be a leading social scientist who was invited by the Dean of the College to make a corresponding report to the faculty concerning the general education at Columbia. Professor Bell is more of a traditionalist regarding the formal groupings of academic disciplines than his Harvard counterparts. But this does not, I think, reflect fundamental differences of orientation between the points of view that prevail, respectively, at the "centers" of Harvard and Columbia.

4. James A. Perkins, *The University in Transition*. Princeton, New Jersey, 1966.

5. This sense of drabness, drift, confusion, and above all of pervasive hypocrisy is reinforced and deepened by Nicholas van Hoffman's book, *The Multiversity: A Personal Report on What Happens to Today's Students in American Universities* (New York City: Holt, Rinehart and Winston, 1966). The book, which is cast mainly in (presumably factual) dialogue form, necessarily misses a good deal of those sides of university life which students cannot directly observe and which—one sometimes thinks—they would misconstrue if they did; particularly is this true of the serious, independent intellectual life of the faculty. There is an inwardness, an intellectual passion, and a sweetness which can pervade the study of a dedicated professor *or* student which Mr. van Hoffman does not fully appreciate. But his indictment, impressionistic though it is, remains overwhelming.

6. In this connection it is amusing to recall a revealing tiff a few years ago between Clark Kerr and two Berkeley professors, Sheldon S. Wolin and John H. Shaar, in the pages of *The New York Review*, March 11, 1965. In the course of a devastating but not intemperate review of the student revolt at Berkeley entitled "The Abuses of the Multiversity," Wolin and Shaar had something to say about Kerr's deep, if largely unconscious, acquiescence in the idea of the university

as a business. Along with a number of genuine quotations from Kerr's writings which illustrated the point, the phrase "knowledge factory" was ascribed to him. In a heavily ironical reply, which here and there did score off Wolin and Sharr, Kerr pointed out that "knowledge factory" was not his phrase but Mario Savio's and that the phrase *he* had used in his book—"knowledge industry"—was itself quoted from Professor Fritz Machlup—"a concept" (save us) which, as Kerr said, "he used in quite a different sense than 'factory.' " But, so far as education is concerned, what a difference! In the passage at issue, Kerr, following Machlup, talks with a face even straighter than Perkins's about "the production, distribution, and consumption" of knowledge which now accounts for "29 per cent of gross national product" [sic] and which "is growing at about twice the rate of the rest of the economy." And the "center" of the industry which has accomplished this prodigious feat, says Kerr, is the university. *Of course*, Machlup's concept of the "knowledge industry" is not the same as Savio's bitter "knowledge factory." But what Kerr sees no more than Perkins is that if one treats the production of knowledge as an industry and the university as its center, one has defined the university's institutional function in industrial terms. And if, as Kerr also says, the university is, in what are plainly metaphorical terms, "the city of the intellect," then that city, like, say, Dearborn, is an industrial city. Nor is that overwhelming fact mitigated by the presence within the "university" of an art gallery, a campanile, a daily newspaper, a resident string quartet, and some other "departments" which supply remedial reading to hoi polloi. And if the president of the university likes to think of himself as a mayor, or rather, since he is not elected but appointed by a board of regents, as a kind of town manager, it must be understood that his job is not vaguely that of leader and coordinator of a company of his peers, whose scholar-teacher vocation remains his own and to which, hopefully, he will soon return. His town is, in quite a different sense, a company town, and he, its manager, is a company man. When a strike or riot occurs, his role is to protect the company's interests. Never, never is it to join his fellow citizens in their strike against the established order.

7. *Bureaucracy in Higher Education* by Herbert Stroup (New York City: The Free Press, 1966).

8. The American University: Part II—What Is Liberal Education?

1. It should be noted, as Bell acknowledges, that he has been much influenced in the formulation of these proposals not only by Ernest Nagel's *The Structure of Science*, which sets out a "logic of explanation in dealing with the nature of scientific inquiry," but also by Joseph J. Schwab's *The Teaching of Sciences as Enquiry*, which, as Bell puts it, "discusses in a wonderfully lucid way the dependence of science upon conceptual innovation, and applies these ideas to problems of teaching."

9. The Revolting Academy

1. Christopher Jencks and David Riesman, *The Academic Revolution*. Garden City, New York: Doubleday, 1968.
2. Brzezinski, Zbigniew, "Revolution and Counter-Revolution," *The New Republic*, June 1 and July 6, 1968.
3. Kenneth Keniston, *Young Radicals: Notes on Committed Youth*. New York City: Harcourt, Brace and World, 1968.

10. Guardians of Law and Order

1. See the Vice-President's speech of November 20, 1969, as reported in *The New York Times*: "Today, Dr. Sidney Hook writes of 'storm troopers' on the campus: that 'fanaticism seems to be in the saddle.'" Mr. Agnew comments, referring to Hook, Arnold Beichman, Irving Kristol, and others whose statements he quotes: "Now those are not names drawn at random from the letter head of an Agnew-for-Vice President committee. Those are men more eloquent and erudite than I, and they raise questions that I've tried to raise."
2. In passing it is worth calling attention to Hook's view about the basis for allocating resources among the various fields of academic study. According to him, all such allocations should be made entirely by "the citizens or their representatives on the advice of scholars and not by the scholars themselves." As it stands, such a thesis seems to me abominable. What if state legislatures or boards of trustees or alumni associations were free, say, to cut off funds from an unpopular

philosophy or sociology department or to allocate three-quarters of the academic budget to scientific departments that play ball with the military establishment? All the same I do agree that in such matters citizens and their representatives should have a voice, including in particular students and dispossessed or disadvantaged groups whose "non-negotiable" demands so outrage Hook. The fact is, as we shall see, that when it comes to the rights of students in matters of educational policy—and certainly the allocation of funds is a vital part of that policy—Hook takes precisely the opposite line: "Advice yes! decision no!"

3. Note here the gradual diminution of the verb "to demand"!

4. Even in matters concerning the rights of students to regulate their own "social life," the faculty, in Hook's view, must retain ultimate veto when basic issues of educational policy or even human rights are involved. Hook drags out the hackneyed example of the pregnant daughter whose irate parents sued the college on the ground that it had failed to exercise proper supervisory care of its dormitories. Of course he gives no evidence that matters were better in the old days when faculty proctors and fraternity housemothers did the policing.

11. How Late is It?

1. It may be helpful to describe briefly some of the salient features of the Danforth Workshop. First of all, the Danforth Foundation is one of the most thoughtful as well as liberal of the larger foundations. Its deep but nonsectarian religious orientation lends a particular seriousness to the various projects and activities which it supports.

The lay membership of the Danforth Workshop changes from year to year, since no individual college or university is represented two years running. However, the workshop mix, with minor variations, changes only slowly. Included are representatives of great state and private universities as well as of four-year colleges whose very accreditation is marginal; representatives of new urban community universities and of colleges in rural backwaters; representatives both of aggressively secular academics and poor denominational schools. There are deans and department heads, lively and often dissident junior professors and instructors. There are research scholars with connections in industry and government, and overworked teachers whose duties preclude the luxury of sustained independent study. There are men whose reputations extend no farther than their campuses and others whose reputations are national.

The workshop seminar leaders are selected not only for the variety of their academic interests but also for the diversity of their educational perspectives and philosophies. Some are scientists, others psychologists and social scientists, still others, humanists, and professional educationists. One or two seminar leaders hold administrative posts, but most are professors whose energies are committed mainly to teaching and research in their respective fields of inquiry. And, like the lay members of the workshop, the seminar leaders come from universities and colleges in different parts of the country.

The varied activities of the workshop include seminars, lectures, panel discussions, and many extracurricular activities, formal and informal, including many continuing discussions that go on sometimes into the later hours with the "shadow workshop," as I call it, which bears such a striking resemblance to the "shadow university."

In sum, the workshop becomes a microcosmic semi-academy. And just because our time is so short, the various points of view represented, the resultant tensions, the hopes and fears expressed, achieve an unusual compression and clarity of definition which serves the purposes of this paper extremely well.

2. One noteworthy feature of the present hardening of attitudes within the university is a noticeable self-division within the ranks of the administrators themselves.

3. Of course, there is nearly always an escape clause built into such demands. At Brandeis, for example, the demands of revolting black students were nonnegotiable, but their "meaning" was not.

4. One distinguished ex-colleague of mine at Harvard, never pausing to consider the rationale of his own God-given values, simply disposes of such people as mere "attitudinizers" who perhaps may be tolerated in times of tranquility, but simply put down when they refuse to keep their place.

5. Quoted from an unpublished typescript entitled "Impressions on the Danforth Workshop on the Liberal Arts," by Charles Long.

12. *Analytical Philosophy and Educational Development*

1. *Prima facie* these theories, I should emphasize, are presented as opposing theories of the meaning of the idea or concept of teaching. Whether they really are so, remains to be seen.

2. In this paper I do no justice to the problems of learning what and why, but no account of education and educational development can afford to neglect them. Discussion of these problems appears in the following chapters.

13. Learning and Teaching in the Arts

1. This fact was graphically and amusingly revealed some years ago during a debate within the Harvard faculty over certain proposals to regroup courses offered in the General Education program in such a way that courses in the harder social sciences would thereafter be listed simply as "sciences" and those in the softer ones would be listed under the humanities. Historians and social scientists whose offerings would thenceforth fall within the humanities at once perceived a mortal blow to their academic prestige, despite the Committee's disclaimer that the only purpose of the reclassification was one of convenience. As it turned out, they managed to defeat the proposals, thus retaining their formal status as social *scientists,* though the actual content of their courses and the methods employed in teaching them remained precisely the same as they had been before.

2. Here I am concerned only with one main sense of the phrase "work of art." I do not claim that this is its only meaning. Indeed this term, like other recurrent terms and phrases of critical humanistic discourse, such as "art," fine arts," and "aesthetic," has acquired a whole range of meanings during the history of its use. In another essay ("Art and Anti-Art" which forms chapter fourteen of this volume), I briefly consider some of the circumstances in which these terms were first introduced and subsequently modified. From the point of view of a philosophy of humanistic education, the extraordinary history of these ideas is of the greatest interest, for it shows not only the conceptual muddles we can get into when these accumulations of meaning are ignored, but the educational chaos that results from shifting unwittingly back and forth between the various frames of reference which such clusters of meaning supply. In fact, the term "aesthetic" has by this time been so badly mangled that I habitually treat it simply as a throw-away word when I employ it in discussions of the philosophy of art and art education. In this essay, it will be noted, I rarely use it.

3. My reasons for choosing this work are several. First, I myself am greatly enamoured of it. Secondly, it is well known, and its artistic distinction is not in dispute. Thirdly, its interest and many of its levels of significance, though complex, are fairly stable; hence my reading of it will probably be accepted as typical. Fourthly, it contains margins of ambiguity so that what it means and is are probably not accessible immediately even to persons of considerable sensibility. And

fifthly, it is a transitional work whose meanings and values are, for most of us, somewhat unstable: one knows it to be a distinguished work of art; one realizes very quickly its wide range and complexities of interest; but even after much study it remains in certain ways problematic, so that some important questions of meaning and value remain, even for sophisticated observers. It will be unnecessary to add that I approach this wonderful picture with fear and trembling, as a "lay reader" and not as a learned art historian.

4. The work "see" here is, of course, employed in an extended sense which includes but is not confined to narrowly visual apprehensions.

5. Here, as throughout this discussion, I am much indebted to the acute comments of my wife, Helen R. Aiken, who, as always, is so much better a teacher than I am a learner.

6. Fundamentally I am convinced that these categorial distinctions of intention are acquired in the very process of learning how to use a developed "natural language." I am prepared to accept Professor Noam Chomsky's theory that this learning is a form of maturation which depends upon powers of expression and understanding inherent in the human mind. Even so, maturations of this sort need to be elicited and prompted. The maturations of the sexual impulse are inevitable and, as it sometimes seems, incorrigible. Those involved in learning a language are not. Furthermore, they may be confused and corrupted by metalinguistic theories, or ideologies, which overlay and overcast them with principles of interpretation and misinterpretation. Thus we not only learn in some sense how to use a word and how to construe its intention in particular cases; we also acquire by processes of contextual imitation ideas about their uses and intentions, which can block or frustrate our more natural ways of construing them. Interpretation in short is an inescapable adjunct of thought and discourse. And habits of interpretation frequently have to be unlearned if we are truly to perceive what is actually meant and said.

7. The analogues of metaphor in the other arts are the subject of an entire book which cannot be gone into here. One instance must suffice. In a piece of music, the introduction of a theme in a new key and instrumentation presents us not simply with a mere likeness or simulation of the theme, but a transmutation of it into something quite new and strange. It *reveals* the theme in a new way which at the same time is and is not the theme, but something in itself, wholly fresh and unprecedented.

8. Here my remarks about play, imitation, and metaphor provide cases in point.

[*393*

9. This statement is qualified below. For Giorgione, when it suits his purpose, is also a superb draftsman.

10. See "Aesthetic Concepts," by Frank Sibley, republished in *Philosophy Looks at the Arts,* edited by Joseph Margolis (New York City: Scribner, 1962), pp. 63–87. I have my doubts about some of the details of Professor Sibley's account of these expressions. Nor am I impressed as he is by their importance in critical discourse. Moreover, his interest, unlike mine, is not directed primarily to the use of language in describing works of art but to the whole range of what he calls "aesthetic discrimination and appreciation," a domain whose boundaries seem to be exceedingly tenuous indeed. Nevertheless, Sibley's essay is an interesting application of Wittgenstein's important contributions to our understanding of ordinary language, and it contains many remarks which corroborate things said here and elsewhere in this paper.

11. Quoted in *Three Historical Philosophies of Education,* by William Frankena (Glenview, Illinois: Scott Foresman, 1965), pp. 89 ff.

16. Youth and Its Rights

1. This point becomes obvious enough when we recall what is involved, for example, in the concepts of legal, moral, or religious persons.

2. The idea or ideology of rationalism is developed in Part Five in "Rationalism, Education, and the Good Society."

3. Page 257, "Utopia and the Good Life," by George Kateb in *Utopias and Utopian Thought,* edited by Frank E. Manuel (Boston: Houghton Mifflin, 1965).

4. By an institution here I have in mind such things as banks, courts of law, electoral colleges, and universities.

5. As we have already seen, all rights impose responsibilities somewhere. But we have also seen that those who enjoy the rights in question must be supposed to assume reciprocal responsibilities; indeed, it is possible to have rights and yet be incapable of assuming responsibilities of any sort. But an individual incapable of assuming responsibilities of any sort would, in effect, merely be a dependency of a community, not one of its members. On the other hand, there seems to me to be no reason to suppose that every member of a community should have exactly the same responsibilities and rights.

6. Here as elsewhere we may also reasonably assume that rights, like

responsibilities, are rarely, if ever, absolutely unconditional; they hold, as we say, *ceteris paribus*, so that it may on occasion be necessary to perform acts that radically limit or override a particular right.

17. Rationalism, Education, and the Good Society

1. Later I will mention several variant forms of rationalism. My purpose in so doing is in part to make it clear that rationalism, like all living ideologies, is not a static but an historically developing point of view.

2. It is on this point of course that Hegel differs from ordinary rationalists, as it is also a main reason for their disdain for his philosophy.

3. Henceforth it is these latter conceptions of the powers essential to scientific thought and understanding which will be emphasized.

4. Let me add that in my opinion it is largely owing to the pervasive influence of rationalism as an ideology both within the universities generally and also within academic departments of philosophy, despite the great interest of students in it. For a similar reason, the so-called informalist linguistic and analytical philosophy that stems from the work of the later Wittgenstein may now be seen for what is always has been: a mere episode in the history of academic philosophy in the twentieth century.

5. In practice, of course, there are *de facto* limitations which always make such a principle still more restrictive. For apart from the question of native ability, there is the problem of utilizable ability, of what, in view of their early nurture or "background," economic, social, educational, and psychological, individuals can manage to accomplish. In any actual, historical society, the working abilities of men, so far as potential scientific understanding is concerned, vary and doubtless will continue to vary enormously. Many, perhaps most, men in actual societies, and certainly in our own, would be unable to make use of the sort of training Plato envisaged for the philosophers-guardians in the Republic. And it is for this reason that scientifically-oriented educators, such as James Conant, have argued that the ideal of a university education for everyone is impractical, even in a society which could afford it.

6. Let me emphasize that I am aware that important qualifications of such a conception would have to be made in any full account, since a multiversity is precisely not a complete *polis,* and doubtless should not be permitted to become one. Even for the rationalist it remains

merely *one* highly complex and indispensable institution within a still more inclusive and complex system. I am also aware that most rationalists themselves would insist that there are corporate responsibilities which the multiversity cannot, and doubtless should not, assume in relation either to its individual faculty members or to its students.

7. The former, exemplified in certain military and business organizations, is pyramidal, involving chains and levels of authority and responsibility that begin with the trustees and run down through the various offices of the president, the deans, department heads, professors, assistants, and so on. The latter, or functional type, is a class structure whose rights and duties are established by various specific functions of roles essential to the activities and the work of the university as a whole. It is in terms of this structure that the familiar distinctions between students, faculty, and administration are conceived, as well as the divisions of the faculties themselves into schools and departments, and the so-called liberal arts departments are arranged in the well-known trivium of natural sciences, social sciences, and humanities.

8. *The Freedom of the Individual*, by Stuart Hampshire (New York City: Harper and Row, 1965).

9. Of course, this as it stands won't do either.

Predicament of the University

BY HENRY DAVID AIKEN

This volume brings together Mr. Aiken's challenging essays dealing with many aspects of the question, "What's wrong with the American university?" Mr. Aiken, an acute and unorthodox critic, cuts through various current proposals for patching up and extending the present system and confronts the basic unresolved contradictions in American higher learning today.

The central problem of the universities, Mr. Aiken believes, is to reconcile the demands of graduate programs of narrow, professional training with the traditional values of general humane education. In the opening chapters, he tells of his search for new approaches to higher learning as he left a secure post at Harvard to go to newly created Brandeis. He criticizes some influential commentaries on the modern university (like those of Clark Kerr) and urges that the university be reconceived to create a continuous interaction between professional and liberal education so that consideration of humane values and quality of life may permeate the academy—from freshman to trustee.

In other essays he attacks the "ideology of rationalism," which reveres reason and neglects imagination, creativity, ethics, religion, and other qualities that, like reason, are unique to man. He outlines what a liberated analytical philosophy might contribute to a reform of educational practice, especially on the higher levels, and offers cogent comments on the anti-art movement that has scandalized many orthodox academicians. He attacks departmental parochialism, the government-industry-university complex, the multiversity, and the core-of-traditional-wisdom programs, and he defends free universities, modern art, and the religious impulse.

(continued on back flap)